D1559577

CONSTITUTIONAL INTERPRETATION

CONSTITUTIONAL INTERPRETATION

*Textual Meaning,
Original Intent, and
Judicial Review*

Keith E. Whittington

UNIVERSITY PRESS OF KANSAS

Published by the University Press of Kansas (Lawrence, Kansas 66049), which was organized by the Kansas Board of Regents and is operated and funded by Emporia State University, Fort Hays University, Kansas State University, Pittsburg State University, the University of Kansas, and Wichita State University

Library of Congress Cataloging-in-Publication Data

Whittington, Keith E.

    Constitutional interpretation : textual meaning, original intent, and judicial review / Keith E. Whittington.

      p.   cm.

    Includes index.

    ISBN 0-7006-0969-5 (cloth : alk. paper)

    1. Constitutional law—United States—Interpretation and construction.   I. Title.

KF4550.W475   1999

342.73'02—dc21   98-55213

British Library Cataloguing in Publication Data is available.

Printed in the United States of America

10 9 8 7 6 5 4 3 2 1

The paper used in this publication meets the minimum requirements of the American National Standard for Permanence of Paper for Printed Library Materials Z39.48-1984.

For my parents

And once a thing is put in writing, the composition, whatever it may be, drifts all over the place, getting into the hands not only of those who understand it, but equally of those who have no business with it; it doesn't know how to address the right people, and not address the wrong. And when it is ill-treated and unfairly abused it always needs its parent to come to its help, being unable to defend or help itself.

—Plato, *Phaedrus*

Contents

Preface

This book is concerned with the production of constitutional law. In it I develop an explanation and defense of a theory of constitutional interpretation by the judiciary. As a written, legal text, the Constitution is designed to limit government actions, and the judiciary is primarily charged with enforcing those constraints. The problem that has plagued constitutional law is in determining what interpretive method is appropriate to the Constitution. In exploring this problem, I conclude that the Constitution is most appropriately interpreted in accord with a jurisprudence of original intent, which seeks to recover the textual intentions of the ratifiers in order to bring them to bear in settling current constitutional disputes.

Establishing the appropriate interpretive method for judicial review requires the development of a theory of the Constitution and of the judiciary's relationship to it. It is important to note that these are distinct tasks. I contend that the essential aspect of the judiciary's relationship to the Constitution is the courts' role as interpreters of the text. The judiciary is neither an aristocratic element within a democracy nor a set of philosopher-kings leading the polity. Rather, it is a legal institution, though one charged with special functions in the context of a liberal constitutional republic. The courts' authority is grounded in the accuracy of their interpretation of the supreme law. Thus, it is essential that we understand what is necessary to the process of interpreting the Constitution and what about the Constitution is open to interpretation. We also need to know why we should interpret. We must ask the last question not only because we still need to justify the practice of judicial review but also because we need to understand the basis for it in order to understand its continuing practice. An adequate account of constitutional interpretation necessarily leads us beyond that process in order to understand the Constitution as a whole. This step opens up additional facets of the Constitution that are not legal at all but that are primarily political. Constitutional interpretation makes sense. But it makes sense only as a part of the constitutional design, not its entirety.

Scholars concerned with theories of constitutional interpretation have been too quick to dismiss originalism. It is time to take another look. Even for non-originalists, the academic rout of originalism has not been beneficial. By discounting it so quickly, we have failed to engage the real problems and insights that it has to offer. I have no illusions about the difficulty of the task of recovering originalism, however. I have couched the argument in defensive terms because I think originalists are in a defensive position. They have not always held up their side of the scholarly argument, and the task now is to convince critics to take originalism seriously again. In part, this attempt requires addressing more sophisticated theories of language and interpretation, which originalists have often eschewed. I have also chosen to avoid detailed discussions of cases. It is an integral part of my approach that interpretive results are separate from interpretive methods. The justification for an interpretive method is a task for political and constitutional theory. The application of that method is a matter for legal practice and detailed historical work. There is a tendency to push originalists to meet some judicial litmus test and to evaluate interpretive approaches by their ability to reach desired results in designated cases. This is a tendency that I think should be resisted. Cases are discussed in this book for the sake of illustration only. Efforts to answer specific questions of constitutional law can be made later. Once we agree on the practice of constitutional interpretation, then we can argue about the correct product of that practice.

I have been fortunate in being able to subject a large number and variety of scholars to the ideas contained in this book over the past few years. My debts are too numerous to catalog and too burdensome ever to repay in full. Nonetheless, several individuals must be singled out for particular thanks. In particular, I wish to thank J. Budziszewski, Robert Clinton, Robby George, Mark Graber, Don Green, Ronald Kahn, Sandy Levinson, Joe Mink, Walter Murphy, David O'Brien, Jeff Paul, Corey Robin, Jim Scott, Steven Smith, Tracey Storey, Alex Tabarrok, and Jeff Tulis.

I also owe a special debt to Rogers Smith, Stephen Skowronek, and David Mayhew. Each offered unique insights into the nature of American politics, political theory, and constitutional meaning and development that I have incorporated shamelessly. David Mayhew and Stephen Skowronek have been much appreciated teachers and critics, willing to follow me into a field that I thought relevant but to which they had no deep attraction.

Rogers Smith has been an enthusiastic mentor, colleague, and friend. He generously dedicated more time and effort to me and to this effort than any student could expect or deserve. His knowledge of American politics, constitutional law, and political theory is reflected throughout this work in points large and small. Both his agreements and disagreements with my arguments have uniformly improved their development.

Completion of this book was made possible by the financial and administrative support of the Social Philosophy and Policy Center, Bowling Green State University. Delay in its completion was engineered by my wife, who continually persuaded me that there is more to life than constitutional theory.

CONSTITUTIONAL INTERPRETATION

1. Constitutional Interpretation

The Supreme Court holds a special place in constitutional theory. The Court has largely set the scholarly agenda for the study of the Constitution. Its activities have determined which aspects of the Constitution are deemed worthy of study and elaboration, and which are not. The Court's example has helped define what we think the Constitution means and how we go about the task of illuminating that meaning. Even if the Constitution is not what the Court says it is, the judiciary remains our primary point of access to it.

This focus on the judiciary is not entirely misplaced. The practice of judicial review has given the Court a particularly important role in determining effective constitutional meaning. The institutional features of the Court ensure that the legal logic employed by the justices remains the center of our attention. The judiciary has come to symbolize the American commitment to constitutionalism and limited government, beyond whatever effect the courts might have in securing those goals. The high esteem in which we hold the Court reflects our political aspirations: for a government that justifies its actions, for the virtues of the rule of law, and for the protection of the rights of individuals and minorities. The Court reminds us of political fundamentals.

The Supreme Court represents an important requirement of American government, the need to interpret the Constitution. It is not alone in this task. Other courts interpret. More important, other government officials, and ultimately engaged citizens, share the responsibility for interpreting the text. Nonetheless, the work of the judiciary can be taken as representative of this task. For the unelected judiciary, the putative American commitment to constitutional interpretation serves as a foundation for political authority. That the judiciary exercises neither force nor will but merely interprets our own previously established commitments alleviates the tensions inherent in giving such a prominent place to an unelected body within a democratic political system. Judicial review is justified because the courts are understood to be correctly interpreting the Constitution, at least most of the time.

If the authority of the judiciary is rooted in the practice of constitutional interpretation, then it becomes particularly important that we understand what interpretation requires. That is my task in this book. I seek to understand how we should go about interpreting our Constitution, what the limitations of interpretation are, and how constitutional interpretation can fit into a larger theory of constitutional practice and authority. In order to do so, I am not interested primarily in how the Court has approached its work in the past. The judiciary and the historical practice of judicial review frame the problem, but they cannot provide the solution. The Court justifies itself, and has been justified to us by others, with the claim that it engages in interpretation. Judicial practice may or may not conform to that prescription. Before historical practice can be evaluated, however, or future practice recommended, the requirements of interpretation must be clarified. This is the work of constitutional theory, not of constitutional law.

Originalism and Interpretation

My goal in this book is to explore the requirements of our commitment to constitutional interpretation. I assume the reality of that commitment. My concern is with demonstrating its implications. What are the goals of interpretation? What does it mean for a judiciary to interpret a constitutional text? What interpretive methods are most appropriate to the task, and under what conditions? After thinking about these issues, we may well decide that our commitment to interpretation was misguided. Constitutional interpretation is not our only political goal, and there are other grounds for political authority besides fidelity to the written Constitution.[1] I offer some reasons for thinking that the interpretation of this Constitution is valuable and worth retaining, but the possibility that we would rather not be governed in this way should be faced squarely.

Constitutional interpretation has been central to contemporary theorizing about the Constitution and about judicial review. The need to interpret is taken as the starting point for theory, whether the goal is to elaborate some particular point of constitutional meaning or to justify the practice of judicial review. This is my starting point as well. I take it as a given that the purpose of judicial review is to interpret the Constitution. I do not ask what other purposes an institution like judicial review could serve in a system of representative government. I assume that other purposes are available and therefore that other justifications for judicial review could be offered. But contemporary scholars have been at great pains to emphasize that they are not offering any such alternative justifications, and the Court has refused to describe its practice in noninterpretive terms.[2] Interpretation is the touchstone of judicial authority. My goal here is a modest one in that I take constitutional theorists at their word and seek to justify an interpretive method.

This exploration of constitutional interpretation is presented as a defense of a jurisprudence of original intent. Originalism best fulfills the requirements of constitutional interpretation. It is not the only method available for interpreting the Constitution; there are other ways to interpret. But the adoption of a method should presumably be guided by the purposes of interpretation. Some methods are better than others at producing faithful interpretations of the constitutional text. It makes little sense to evince a commitment to constitutional interpretation but then to adopt an interpretive method that undermines that project or that does not advance us toward the goals of interpretation. If the practice of judicial review is to be maintained in order to achieve goals other than faithful adherence to the requirements of the Constitution, then those alternative purposes should be admitted, clarified, and justified. The Constitution need not serve as law. Some interpretive methods may produce "better" outcomes in particular cases than an originalist method would. If we favor those approaches for their ability to generate preferred outcomes, however, then they are serving as political ideologies, not as methods of legal interpretation.

Methods of interpretation require justification, and those justifications are distinct from the method itself. The interpretation of the Constitution is a matter of constitutional law and, primarily, of judicial practice. An interpretive method provides guidance for that practice. The justification for adopting any particular interpretive method depends on external reasons of normative political theory. As a consequence, originalism cannot be justified by reference to the intent of the founders or by a purely historical argument. Originalism, like other methods of interpretation, must be justified by reference to our best understanding of the constitutional project. There is nothing anomalous, therefore, in grounding an originalist method on pragmatic arguments about judicial restraint or on normative arguments about democratic theory. My argument employs history, but it does so in order to illuminate the task that we have set for ourselves and that we claim has value. The argument is consistent with our historical experience, but its persuasiveness depends on its derivation from axiomatic principles.

I intend to demonstrate that originalism is the method most consistent with the judicial effort to interpret the written constitutional text and that an originalist jurisprudence facilitates the realization of a political system grounded on popular sovereignty. Other methods are consistent with efforts to interpret the written Constitution, but they are flawed. Ultimately, adherence to originalist guidelines provides the most direct and consistent route to a correct interpretive practice. Moreover, the commitment to judicial interpretation need not be left as a mere assumption. Judicial interpretation of the Constitution serves important interests in liberty and democracy. By requiring government officials to demonstrate the constitutional authority for their actions, the judiciary can reemphasize the constraints of limited government while reinvigorating political debate over first principles.

It is worth emphasizing that I do not rely on traditional originalist arguments in favor of judicial restraint. Judicial restraint is an inadequate basis for justifying an originalist jurisprudence. The incidence of judicial review is highly contingent on political circumstances. An originalist Court may well find itself quite active in striking down legislation at odds with the clear requirements of the inherited text. Originalism requires deference only to the Constitution and to the limits of human knowledge, not to contemporary politicians. The Constitution makes substantive commitments to counter-majoritarian principles. If the Court is to enforce the requirements of the Constitution, it must be willing to act in a countermajoritarian fashion. Such actions can be justified, but American constitutionalism cannot be adequately described through a reliance on majoritarianism and judicial deference to elected officials.

Originalism is also unlikely to provide the type of restraints on judicial decision making favored by some of its advocates. There is nothing mechanical about an originalist interpretive method. An originalist practice raises difficult questions of interpretive judgment, given uncertain and fragmentary evidence, complicated constitutional commitments, and difficult contemporary application of discoverable principles. To this extent, an originalist judge is faced with many of the same difficulties and temptations that are faced by non-originalist judges. Originalism can be defended because it points to the goals and evidence most appropriate to judicial interpretation of the Constitution, but it cannot be expected to free judges from the exercise of contestable interpretive judgment. Our expectations for an originalist jurisprudence must be lowered so that it can be evaluated more realistically and advocated more persuasively.

Thus, my goal in this book is to take interpretation seriously. Doing so requires that we adopt an originalist approach to interpretation. A more elaborate consideration of the aims of interpretation and of the possible justifications for originalism indicates that it should at least be readmitted to the ranks of viable contenders to guide the practice of judicial review. Moreover, not only does originalism have much to offer on its own terms, but further examination of originalist arguments can also help illuminate continuing problems in constitutional theory and can contribute to a more general reconsideration of what constitutional interpretation is supposed to accomplish and how it might fit into a larger constitutional theory.

Interpretation and Construction

In examining constitutional interpretation generally, and an originalist method specifically, it will be useful to bear in mind a general categorization between two ways of understanding constitutional meaning. Drawing a distinction between constitutional interpretation and constitutional construction can ultimately help clarify both the role of judicial review in constitutional government and the specific function of originalism within constitutional theory.[3] Although not fully elaborated here, the distinction does serve to highlight the limitations of originalism (and, I think, any theory of constitutional interpretation) as a general theory of constitutionalism. Interpretation has an important role to play in the elaboration of constitutional meaning, but it is a limited one. Constitutional practice ultimately requires that we be able to address questions to which interpretation by itself has no determinate answer.

The distinction between interpretation and construction is analytical, in that it builds on two different ways of elaborating constitutional meaning that have been and could be used.[4] Further, each category is capable of accommodating a variety of specific interpretive methods. As the name suggests, constitutional interpretation is a fairly familiar process of discovering the meaning of the constitutional text. The results of this process are recognizable as constitutional law, capable of being expounded and applied by the courts. Though still concerned with the meaning of the text, constitutional construction cannot claim merely to discover a preexisting, if deeply hidden, meaning within the founding document. It employs the "imaginative vision" of politics rather than the "discerning wit" of judicial judgment. Construction is essentially creative, though the foundations for the ultimate structure are taken as given. The text is not discarded but brought into being. Such constructions are essentially political and cannot be captured by purely legal forms, and thus they remain irreducible to constitutional law and the jurisdiction of the courts. These two mechanisms of constitutional elaboration, taken together, provide a device for "conjoining" the constitution as binding law with the "constitution as a political order."[5]

Constitutional interpretation is characteristically the legalistic interpretation of the constitutional text familiar from the records of the courts. The judiciary takes up the Constitution in order to discover standards to dispose of the case at hand.[6] As Chief Justice John Marshall long ago claimed, "Those who apply the rule to particular cases, must of necessity expound and interpret that rule." Marshall then claimed the Constitution as a "rule" and a "law," and as such, open to judicial investigation, applicable to particular cases, and supreme in a hierarchy of potentially conflicting rules that the Court must consider.[7] As this phrasing makes clear, such interpretation is concerned with formalizing constitutional meaning in the interest of settling relatively narrow disputes. Meaning cannot simply be discovered but must be discovered in a particular way. Interpretation is the translation of the constitutional text into the specifically useful formulas within which a given fact situation can be fit. In order to interpret the founding document, it must be taken not simply as constituting a nation but as establishing rules for its future governance. Its history within this context is a history of specification, of replacing a relatively sparse collection of general terms with a vast corpus of constitutional law.

This substitution of the law for the text is not simply accidental but is essential to the process of governing. In order for the text to serve as law, it must be rulelike. In order to be a governing rule, it must possess a certain specificity in order to connect it to a given situation. Further, it must indicate a decision with a fair degree of certainty. Such certainty and specificity need not be absolute, but the law does need to provide determinate and dichotomous answers to questions of legal authority. In order for the Constitution to be legally binding, judges must be able to determine that a given action either is or is not allowed by its terms. Similarly, the Constitution is binding only to the extent that judges do not have discretion in its application. Although the application of the law may require controversial judgments, the law nonetheless imposes obligations on the judge that are reflected in the vindication of the legal entitlements of one party or another. For the Constitution to serve this purpose, it must be elaborated as a series of doctrines, formulas, or tests. Thus, constitutional interpretation necessarily is the unfolding of constitutional law. Debates over constitutional meaning become debates over the proper formulation of relatively narrow rules.

Another inescapable feature of interpretation is that it represents a search for meaning already in the text. Interpretation is discovery. Although the process of discovery may be complex and require good judgment by the interpreter, it nonetheless results in something that has plausibly been found in the original text. Interpretation is not essentially creative, for though new formulas are developed and promulgated, these new texts are sustained only by their direct link to the original. If that connection becomes too tenuous, they can no longer be maintained as interpretations of the original.[8] Within the context of debates over constitutional meaning, the short-lived distinction between "interpretivists" and "noninterpretivists" reflected this basic fact.[9] As the labels recognized, interpretation finds meaning already existent in the constitutional text. The noninterpretivists go beyond mere interpretation by going beyond the text, importing values from current politics and incorporating them into judicial decisions. The terms were soon abandoned, not because this definition of interpretation was challenged but because the location of the text was called into question. If textual literalism or originalism failed to consider the "whole Constitution" by ignoring such things as the natural law tradition or current social norms, then other schools of constitutional meaning could still be regarded as interpreting the Constitution, discovering meaning within its, now broadened, text. The question was no longer "whether" to interpret but "what" to interpret. Constitutional meaning may remain deeply contested, but it had to be discovered, not invented, if the text were to be interpreted.

The case of constitutional construction is quite different. Constitutional interpretation is essentially legalistic, but constitutional construction is essentially political. Its precondition is that parts of the constitutional text have no discoverable meaning. Although the clauses and structures that make up the text cannot be simply empty of meaning, for they are clearly recognizable as language, the meaning that they do convey may be so broad and underdetermined as to be incapable of faithful reduction to legal rules. This is not so much a problem of a given clause possessing absolutely no judicially formalizable meaning as it is the inability of the judiciary to define exhaustively the meaning of the text. Regardless of the extent of judicial interpretation of certain aspects of the Constitution, there will remain an impenetrable sphere of meaning that cannot be simply discovered. The judiciary may be able to delimit textual meaning, hedging in the possibilities, but after all judgments have been rendered specifying discoverable meaning, major indeterminacies may remain. The specification of a single governing meaning from these possibilities requires an act of creativity beyond interpretation. For example, if given the text, "buy a dog," the interpreter can draw the boundaries of meaning embodied in the text. You must buy a dog; you may not buy a cat, horse, or elephant. But the choice of what dog to buy is a noninterpretive choice. Though there may be reasons supporting the choice, and though the text may be suggestive as to those reasons, a pure interpreter could have no decisive justification for purchasing any particular dog. While all texts may not do so, this one necessarily calls for something beyond interpretation in order to develop fully its meaning.[10] This additional step is the construction of meaning.[11]

Such legal gaps in the Constitution may have a number of sources. It is possible that the textual meaning is clear in that it specifies an identifiable principle but that the principle becomes indeterminate in the application to a particular situation. Either the facts at issue or the principle in the particular context may be vague and incapable of adequate legal specification. Thus, a prohibition against "vehicles" in a park may have clear meaning, but there may be no determinate answer as to whether a child's sled is a "vehicle." Similarly, a statute against taking a "human life" sets a legal rule, but it may be unclear whether a fetus is a "human life."[12] Moreover, the principle established by a text may itself be unclear. In prohibiting "unreasonable" restraints on trade a legislature may have had a rather determinate understanding of what types of restraint were unreasonable, but it may instead be the case that the legislature could reach no agreement as to what constituted unreasonable restraint. The codified phrase actually covers over legislative disagreement rather than conveying agreed-upon meaning. Such problems could be either actual or evidentiary. There may be contradictory indications as to meaning or no substantive indications at all. It is possible that the text employs internally complex phrases and that insufficient information is provided to an interpreter to arbitrate among contested meanings.[13] For example, the founders at least thought that a "Republican Form of Government" required the electoral accountability of government officials, but a "republican" government includes other aspects with indeterminate weight in the founders' thinking.[14]

A law may appear on its face to have gaps, but there are mechanisms available for avoiding or closing them. In order for construction to operate to the exclusion of interpretation, the gaps must remain open.[15] Although many legal systems have closure rules—for example, everything not prohibited is permitted—it is not an essential feature of the law that this be the case. It is possible that the Constitution does not include such closure rules or that any such supplementary interpretive rules that it does include are not complete. Perhaps more important, in the constitutional context, closure rules may not be enough to eliminate the space for construction.[16] A constitution, unlike a law, does not simply express legal rights and duties but also expresses normative sensibilities. The mere fact that something is constitutionally permitted may not make it constitutionally appropriate or right.[17] Statements of principle such as preambles and proto-bills of rights that employ a normatively prescriptive "ought not" rather than a legally binding "shall not" have provided guidance for governmental action without necessarily imposing legal constraints on political officials.[18] The fact that the regulation of obscene material is legally permissible does not necessarily determine whether it is constitutionally appropriate, nor does it indicate what kind of regulation is most consistent with constitutional principles. Closing the legal question may well leave the larger question of constitutional authority open for political determination. To this degree, the legal constitution frames the issue, but its ultimate determination depends on the construction of the political constitution.[19] The Constitution not only serves as a judicially applicable rule but also guides and permeates political debate.

Cases addressing individual rights against the government can illustrate this process. In each case, the Court interpreted the requirements of the Bill of Rights "narrowly," allowing a contested government action. In each case, there was a political response that rejected such actions as inconsistent with constitutional principles and political interests. As a consequence, the government has created additional protections for individual rights through ordinary statute and executive action beyond those required by the Constitution itself. For immediate purposes, we can bracket the issue of whether the Court was correct in its initial interpretation of the constitutional requirements. Even if the Court was wrong in these particular cases, and drew the boundary between permissible and impermissible government action in the wrong place, the constitutional process at issue is clear, and these individual examples could be readily multiplied. Political actors have responded to "gaps" in textually provided constitutional protections by enforcing broader constitutional principles.[20] The first examples derive from the Fourth Amendment's bar against unreasonable police searches. In 1978 the Court upheld a search warrant that allowed the police to search the offices of the *Stanford Daily* in pursuit of photographs that might identify student protesters who had attacked police during a campus demonstration. Employing fairly standard rhetoric, Justice Byron White argued for the Court that the "Fourth Amendment has itself struck the balance between privacy and public need, and there is no occasion or justification for a court to revise the Amendment and strike a new balance" so as to disallow "third party" searches of the property of individuals uninvolved in any crime in pursuit of evidence that might be useful to a criminal prosecution.[21] White concluded, however, with an invitation to Congress, noting that "the Fourth Amendment does not prevent or advise against legislative or executive efforts to establish nonconstitutional protections against possible abuses of the search warrant procedure."[22] Congress accepted the invitation, using its own legislative powers to strike a new balance between privacy and the public need in the context of newsroom searches, finding that constitutional principles required extending additional protections against searches beyond those required by the Fourth Amendment and constitutional law.[23]

Similarly, the Court declined to include police wiretaps under the constitutional definition of a "search" requiring a warrant, but Chief Justice William

Howard Taft noted that Congress could "depart from the common law of evidence" and "protect the secrecy of telephone messages . . . by direct legislation."[24] In the case of wiretaps, Congress and the executive branch worked through a variety of ways of balancing the interests of personal privacy and public security over the next several decades, extending and modifying protections by both statute and executive decision.[25] The free exercise clause of the First Amendment has provided similar examples of this process, notably in relation to the governmental accommodation of religious practices. In 1986 the Court upheld an Air Force regulation prohibiting the wearing of headgear indoors, despite the fact that it made no accommodations for religious attire such as yarmulkes. In such cases, the appropriate balance between particular religious practices and military discipline could be guided by constitutional principles but could not be clearly derived from the Constitution itself.[26] Constitutional issues may be at stake in such disputes, but the Constitution cannot be said to draw fixed lines determining whether and when the military must accommodate the wearing of yarmulkes (or turbans or dreadlocks). Again, Congress filled the gap by constructing its own, admittedly contingent, balance between the competing constitutional principles.[27] Regardless of which institution undertook to strike those particular balances—whether Congress, the executive, or the Court—constitutional interpretation alone could not have provided determinate outcomes. Government officials were forced to construct effective constitutional meaning to guide their particular actions in these situations from an amalgam of textual principle, political interest, and pragmatic judgment. The products were consistent with the inherited Constitution but could not be said to be required by it.

To paraphrase the imagery of Edward Corwin, the relationship between the text, interpretation, and construction can be portrayed diagrammatically.[28] The constitutional text itself serves as a nucleus of a set of constitutional requirements. Surrounding this and overlapping it to a greater or lesser extent, is constitutional law, which translates the text into formal rules for decision. Outside this, finally, but interpenetrating it and underlying it is constitutional construction, which serves to extend the application of the text further by mediating between the text itself and an external environment of policy ideas and political principles. Neither interpretation nor construction changes the core nucleus of the text, but they do provide its extensions and points of contact with political practice. Interpretation flows immediately from the text and thus has a limited reach. Construction bears a more tenuous and alloyed connection with the text but as a result can extend constitutional meaning even further before it too exhausts the possibilities of the existing text.

The boundaries between these categories are inexact. Distinguishing between an interpretation and a construction in any given instance is by no means certain. The issue is further complicated by the fact that multiple and overlapping institutions may engage in both tasks and that constructions may result in legislation that is enforceable by the courts as is other legislation.[29] By throwing off new legislative and administrative actions, constructions will influence the direction of judicial interpretation of the Constitution by shaping the Court's agenda and the types of issues likely to come before it. The judiciary should seek to enforce the correct interpretation of the Constitution, but it should also avoid enforcing even venerable constructions. This caution does not require that the judiciary identify constructions per se, only that it keep its eye on interpreting the Constitution while simultaneously bearing in mind the possibility of constitutional indeterminacy.[30] The judiciary should not prop up old constructions that are no longer politically authoritative, and it should avoid stifling the development of new constructions by placing the judicial imprimatur on the old and contributing to its hegemonic status. Constructions claim the fidelity of political actors through their continuing political authority, not through judicial enforcement.

The modes of constitutional elaboration also include the possibility of constitutional creation (see diagram). Constitutional interpretation discovers meaning, and constitutional construction develops it in relation to the existing text, but constitutional creation invents wholly new meaning. The Constitution has formalized constitutional creation in its provisions for its own ratification and amendment.[31] The creation amends the text, provides new authoritative meaning. Hidden creations, or *un*constitutional constructions, may develop as political leaders go far beyond the existing document while refusing to seek a formal adjustment in the constitutional text.[32] Such actions may be difficult to identify, and even harder to enforce, such as in the instance of the division of the state of Virginia during the Civil War.[33] Constructions are marked by the very success of political actors in persuading others to accept their constructed meaning as a legitimate articulation of constitutional principles, yet some boundaries to the possibilities of legitimate construction within the confines of the existing text must be recognized in principle.

Despite these difficulties, constitutional meaning must not be perceived to be unlimited in its malleability. The Constitution as a constraining force on political action would be seriously undermined if political participants could cynically offer up as "constructions" meanings that are recognizably at variance with the text simply in order to avoid the more arduous process of formal amendment. Certainly the perception of the document as fixed and meaningful is at risk if such unconstitutional constructions are accepted

	Old Text	New Text	
Discoverable	Interpretation	Creation	Proper
Creative	Construction		
	Unconstitutional Construction	Unconstitutional Creation	Improper

Forms of Constitutional Elaboration

insincerely. Perhaps the greater danger of such implicit creations is the risk of a complete collapse of all distinctions and the Court's acceptance of them as sources of constitutional interpretation.[34] Until constructions are ratified by the sovereign people and formally embedded in the supreme law, the Court cannot regard them as interpretable constitutional meaning. Political action may well be constitutionally permissible and legally binding without being constitutionally authoritative—that is, without being part of the constitutional text and thus judicially enforceable as such. The Court's premature acceptance of a construction as an interpretation or a legitimate creation not only undermines the people's capacity to bind their agents with a fundamental law but also subverts the proper role of the other branches of government. The Court's refusal to distinguish between interpretation and other forms of constitutional elaboration is a subtle grasp at judicial supremacy, for it draws all claims of constitutional meaning into the judiciary's purview and subjects them to its standards and judgment. Both the limiting capacity of a fundamental law and a genuine separation of powers in a constitutional government require that the judiciary recognize the different forms of constitutional meaning and respect its own limited role in the process of specifying that meaning. Recognition of an initial distinction between interpretation and construction can help in clarifying those limits.

The distinction between interpretation and construction is universal to all methods of constitutional elaboration.[35] The particular breakpoint between these two forms of elaboration, however, varies depending on the particular interpretive method adopted. The opportunity for construction exists whenever interpreted textual meaning is indeterminate as a guide for action. Nearly all interpretive methods will find some textual phrases to have an uncertain meaning.[36] Originalists, textualists, natural lawyers, and libertarians may disagree as to which phrases are unclear and to what known meaning the text does have, but they will each find their own "hard cases" in which interpretation does not provide a determinate answer to a contemporary problem. Two familiar examples can illustrate this point. The first officials elected under the Constitution were quickly faced with various uncertainties about the new constitutional framework. Despite these uncertainties, however, the need for government action demanded that appropriate constitutional practice be clarified. Thus, George Washington determined that the "advice and consent" of the Senate on treaties could be obtained after the treaties had already been negotiated. Faced with the evident impracticality of contemporaneous Senate involvement in treaty making, Washington shifted the Senate from being a potential executive council to being a "ratifier" of presidential action. Similarly, in creating the executive departments, the first Congress was faced with the still-open constitutional question of how executive officers were to be removed. The Constitution specified only one method of removal: impeachment. Congress specified another that was neither required nor prohibited by the text: unilateral presidential removal. In both cases, looking beyond the text in order to establish a practical meaning for an indeterminate constitutional framework filled constitutional gaps.[37] Moreover, for all methods of interpretation, the appropriateness of government action, as opposed to its permissibility, remains an open question.[38] Thus, considerations of federalism may carry normative weight in evaluating national policy, even if comprehensive legal rules to fix barriers between layers of government cannot be formulated. The necessity and propriety of congressional action, or the requirements of republican government, or the substance of interbranch comity may impose constraints on government officials beyond those articulated or enforced by the courts.[39]

In this book, I am concerned with supplying a normative argument for specifying a particular interpretive method from among this range of possibilities as most appropriate. The need for a categorization of interpretation and construction emerges almost naturally from that discussion. Examination of the goals and limitations of interpretation emphasizes the fact that other modes of constitutional elaboration are both possible and necessary. Moreover, the particular method of originalist interpretation highlights the existence of gaps in the discoverable meaning of the Constitution and the need to fill those gaps by noninterpretive means. The possibility of multiple modes of constitutional elaboration is implicit in many traditional elements of constitutional scholarship, from the existence of "hard cases" to discussion of "elastic" and "general" clauses to the scope of the "political questions" doctrine. In the context here, constructions result when originalist interpretation breaks down. As such, it plays a supporting role in our exploration of interpretation, suggesting a complementary constitutional backdrop against which judicial interpretation takes place.[40]

Defining Interpretive Standards

A vast literature has developed attempting to define the appropriate method of constitutional interpretation, an effort proper for at least two reasons. First, interpretations of any text are not self-evident but require a method in order to develop them and an argument in order to defend them. The substance of a particular interpretation is often crucially affected by the prior choice of an interpretive method, and thus arguments over constitutional meaning have been forced onto the prior ground of interpretive standards. Such a proliferation of theories of interpretation has been a common occurrence in many fields that revolve around an interpretive practice. Second, the debate over interpretive method has been built on a debate over the legitimacy of judicial review. Since the beginning of the practice of review in the United States, it has been defended on the basis of the peculiar interpretive role constitutionally assigned to the courts. If judicial legitimacy hinges on its interpretive practice, then the practice must be properly grounded. Thus, the defense of judicial review as an institution has been intertwined with the defense of particular interpretive standards.

The definition of a single appropriate interpretive method serves several useful purposes in addition to and as part of establishing the legitimacy of judicial review and guiding the practice of interpretation.[41] The judiciary of course is not the only branch that can engage in constitutional interpretation, though it may be preeminent. The recognition of a single method not only allows the various participants in the dialogue to speak intelligibly to one another but also provides the framework for judicial accountability. Recognized interpretive standards allow criticism of the Court. A debate over genuine questions of constitutional interpretation tends to be displaced in a debate over institutional power or interpretive methods. The elaboration of a single standard provides the basis for holding the Court to the same constitutional rule that it is supposed to be expounding and contrasting with the law under review. The adopted standard specifies the points of evaluation, indicating where the Court has erred and how it may be corrected.

The introduction of a distinction between interpretation and construction provides a language for emphasizing the fact that the choice of an interpretive method cannot itself be determined through an act of interpretation. The specification of an interpretive method is an important constitutional issue, but it is not a matter of constitutional law. Constitutional law does not specify the terms of its own existence. A recurrent criticism of originalist theory is that it cannot rely upon original intentions to justify the use of those same intentions, and the point is correct. The choice of interpretive standards cannot be justified on interpretive grounds but is an aspect of constitutional construction. This issue of construction, like all others, must proceed in accord with other standards. Like all constructions, however, the answer to this question is not arbitrary. There are better and worse answers. Moreover, though many issues of constitutional construction are relatively temporary, in that the conditions and arguments that justified the constitutional settlement may in the course of the republic change and require a new construction, I contend that the conditions that govern this construction are embedded in the existence of the republic itself and thus will hold true as long as this Constitution lasts. I argue that not only is there a right answer to the construction of an interpretive standard but also that that answer is fixed in the essential forms of the Constitution and does not change. Though this construction, like all constructions, must be contended for in the political sphere in order to be made good, the arguments presented here indicate the results to which the outcome of that political debate should conform.

In chapter 2 I briefly review the recent academic literature on constitutional interpretive methods. This discussion clears the ground of the current tangle of conflicting theories in order to demonstrate the need for a persuasive theory of interpretation. I then outline such a theory in the form of originalism. The general contours of this theory are (in)famous enough to require only a brief outline of its main components. My focus is on describing what I regard as the essential features of a correct theory of originalism and arguments as to what should, and should not, be included within originalism.

In chapters 3 and 4 I examine in detail one of the most important arguments for the unique authority of originalist interpretation. I take up the claim that originalism is required by the nature of a written constitution. Though this claim has not been developed beyond the point of mere assertion in the current literature, I develop three possible supports for this contention in chapter 3, indicating how an interpretive method derives from the form of our written Constitution. Moreover, I develop three alternative readings of the nature of constitutional textuality, which not only do not require originalism but specifically contradict it. In chapter 4 I subject these three alternatives to extended criticism. In the process of developing this critique, I also expand and revise the theory of originalism in order to develop more thoroughly the philosophical supports necessary to sustain it as an interpretive method. The arguments in these chapters draw heavily on recent theories of language and interpretation, not because the Constitution is like literature but because there are common concerns in all interpretive enterprises.

In chapter 5 I consider a second type of foundational argument, that of popular sovereignty. Unlike the argument from the textuality of the Constitution, this justification does not depend on the prior acceptance of the current constitutional system but instead argues that the present system is positively desirable and deserves our respect and continued support. Current originalist suggestions of the authority of popular sovereignty must be reconsidered and critically evaluated, however.

In chapter 6 I build upon these twin justifications in order to return to a variety of standard criticisms of originalist theory. Armed with these expanded arguments, I demonstrate how originalism can answer these charges and indicate why it is a coherent interpretive position. I conclude with a consideration of the limitations on any interpretive project and how originalism can take advantage of them. Although constitutional interpretation is an important part of constitutional theory, it cannot be regarded as the entirety of American constitutionalism. This defense of one method of interpretation suggests the limitations of any such approach and the continuing need to examine how the Constitution serves as more than just a law.

2. The Dilemmas of Contemporary Constitutional Theory

Since the early stages of the professionalization of law and political science as academic disciplines, constitutional theory has been an active cottage industry. Although the primary concerns and language of this pursuit have evolved over time, the fundamental commitment to articulating an understanding of the Constitution and the Supreme Court's role under it has been constant. Whether urging, defending, or criticizing the judicial activism of the *Lochner* era, guarding or ravaging the Court during the New Deal, or justifying or bemoaning the activism of the Warren Court, constitutional theorists have attempted to define the principles that should guide the judiciary when exercising judicial review and thereby hoped to provide a justification for that practice.[1] The results of the current debate have not been wholly satisfactory to any of its participants. Though there have been a number of plausible entrants, none has yet proven sufficient to indicate how the Constitution should be interpreted and how the imposition of judicial decisions on political actors is to be justified.

The extended history of the federal Constitution has now allowed for different cycles of judicial activism. The practice of judicial review has been separated from its most prominent practitioners of the late nineteenth and early twentieth centuries. Before the late nineteenth century, judicial activism moved in more subtle patterns and was less complicit in the practice of judicial review. In the last years of the century, however, the federal courts markedly increased their activities both in striking down state and federal laws and in interpreting laws to support the socioeconomic vision of the justices. By the New Deal, judicial activism was firmly linked with the political program of economic libertarianism, and rejection of that policy stance required undermining the Court's authority as well. The rise of Warren Court activism connected the power of the courts with a rather different political coalition. For liberal scholars, judicial activism became politically useful and thus defensible. For a much smaller contingent of conservative scholars, the lingering memory of the *Lochner* years suggested the possibility that the newly activist Court could be turned in more favorable directions. The authority for the Court's activities, therefore, became deeply entangled with efforts to guide them, to construct a theory of constitutional interpretation.[2]

We shall thus examine the rise of contemporary constitutional theory and the primary alternatives that have emerged within it. The interpretive approaches that various commentators urge the courts to take are summarized and then criticized to demonstrate the deficiencies in the available alternatives and the need for further consideration. This critique does not seek to be exhaustive or wholly new. It merely seeks to illustrate the continuing uncertainty of constitutional theory and the challenges to be addressed. We can then examine the alternative ultimately favored in this book: originalism. The theory of original intent is first summarized, and as necessary modified, to indicate the principles by which an originalist court should be guided. The various justifications for originalism are then considered in turn for their own persuasiveness, indicating how it should be reconceived and justified in order for it to underwrite the practice of constitutional interpretation.

Contemporary Constitutional Theory

Modern constitutional theory emerged to fill the vacuum left by the Sociological Jurisprudence and Legal Realist movements of the early twentieth century. These movements in the law schools, eventually matched by the behaviorist turn in political science, abandoned the quest for normative principles to guide constitutional interpretation or to ground the institution of judicial review. Both dissatisfaction with the theoretical commitments of the Sociologists and Realists and the unavoidable presence of an active, idealistic Court sparked a revival in constitutional theory. The theorists of the late 1950s and early 1960s largely structured the debate as it has developed over the last three decades. The present alternatives in this debate can be categorized as emphasizing democracy, rights, natural law, or pragmatism.

THE RETURN OF THEORY: NEUTRAL PRINCIPLES AND THE COUNTERMAJORITARIAN DIFFICULTY

The early twentieth century witnessed a sharp reaction in legal scholarship to the formalism, strict constructionism, and laissez-faire commitments of the late nineteenth-century judiciary. New movements such as the Sociologists and then the Realists challenged old assumptions of the stability and objectivity of law, contending that judges not only made policy from the bench but also did so in accord with internal preferences instead of with objective principles. These movements were given special impetus by the constitutional opinions emerging from the judiciary striking down a variety of

Progressive and New Deal reforms and relying on the types of arguments criticized by proponents of the new movements.[3] In their view, the frequent exercise of judicial review in the *Lochner* years was simply the final expression of misguided conceptions that were pervasive in law.

Although differing in important respects, Sociological Jurisprudence and Legal Realism shared a common contempt for abstract theorizing. Both the substantive theory of natural individual rights and its procedural adjunct, that the judiciary should mechanically apply a general rule to a particular situation in order to vindicate those rights, were seen as wrong. Judges were themselves part of the social context from which private disputes emerged and could not be regarded as neutral arbiters imposing external rules on those conflicts. The reformers recommended that judges recognize their own social position and their responsibilities as policymakers. The Constitution was only intended for "the *practical* securing" of individual welfare, and the rules that bind government could not be expected to remain stable as "facts and opinions" changed.[4]

The Sociologists rejected abstract theorizing on constitutional principles in favor of the scientific analysis of how law could be used to better society; the Realists, however, rejected the Sociologists' faith in even scientifically modified legal rules and moral progress, though retaining their instrumental conception of law. Realism emphasized the subjective nature of judicial decision making. Self-aware judges would give up the study of "the Text" and prior judicial decisions and instead "study the structure and functioning of going government" in order to make constitutional law. The starting point for Realism was the awareness that law and society are both in "flux" and that judges engage in the "creation of law . . . as a means to social ends."[5] Ultimately, for the Realists as for their predecessors, the Constitution was not an inherited set of rules to be understood and applied by judges but an instrument to be used by judges pragmatically to advance desired political goals on a case-by-case basis.[6] Constitutional law was moral, but not principled. Concerns for interpretation could be replaced with concerns for good policy.

Just as the horrors of World War I undermined the sense of scientific progress upon which Sociology was built, World War II undermined the American acceptance of the moral relativism and legal instrumentalism that grounded Realism.[7] In the postwar world, America stood for certain principles, and the judiciary could not stand apart from that by retaining a belief in the power of judges willfully to use the power of the state to impose their sensibilities on society. Moreover, the turnover of the Court's personnel with the New Deal elevated a new set of judicial policy views that required legitimation as rational principles, to be contrasted to the mere subjective will of the

Four Horsemen of the *Lochner* Court. As America changed enemies in its fight against totalitarianism, ideas mattered. If the Constitution was about ideas, then interpretive methods once again mattered, too.

Given the acceptance of correct political principle as the basic justification for judicial review, concern for interpretation could no longer be regarded as an expendable distraction. Against the cynicism of the older generation, postwar scholars such as Erwin Griswold insisted on the reality of the influence of reasoned deliberation, noting that "many times clearly held views of mine have been radically changed by discussions with associates or colleagues" and extrapolating his own experience as a law professor to those of judges who could also practice "intellectual detachment and disinterestedness."[8] The reality of judicial argument suggested a new standard for evaluating interpretive efforts: "It must be genuinely principled, resting with respect to every step that is involved in reaching judgment on analysis and reasons quite transcending the immediate result that is achieved." Only by articulating neutral principles to justify and constrain judicial interpretation of the Constitution could the courts "function otherwise than as a naked power organ" and thereby justify reversing the actions of more representative institutions of government.[9] Engaging in the correct method of interpreting the Constitution that authorized all government action legitimated the institution of judicial review.

The new generation of constitutional theorizing perhaps reached its culmination with the publication of Alexander Bickel's *The Least Dangerous Branch* in 1962. Bickel presented both an elaborate interpretive method and an extensive justification for judicial review linked to that method. He accepted the insight of the prewar scholars that the Constitution did not have a clear meaning in all cases and therefore that its interpretation was often "an issue of policy." Given that fact, however, the question remained as to who would decide the issue. For Bickel, the judiciary did not have an immediate advantage, nor could it simply pose as just one more governmental institution. "The root difficulty," Bickel observed, "is that judicial review is a countermajoritarian force in our system."[10] He added that in the American system, deviations from majoritarianism required special explanation. Postulating an interpretive method that could overcome the countermajoritarian difficulty became the chief task of constitutional theory.

Principled adjudication became not only the necessary condition for judicial activism but also the sufficient condition. The one thing the Court "injects into representative government . . . that is not already there . . . is principle." It was not enough that judicial decisions conform to standards of justifiability, neutrality, and generality. Court opinions must express principles, or values, to its audience of the American citizenry. Judicial review was not primarily about dispute resolution, nor did judges possess the authority to substitute their policy judgment as to what would better society for those of elected representatives. The function of judicial review was "to define values and proclaim principles," ensuring that the elected branches of government did not slip into pure expediency.[11]

The Bickelian interpretive method was itself rejected almost as soon as it was offered. The increasing activism of the Warren Court, and its apparent ability to impose its will on the other branches successfully, fed desires to loosen the constraints on the judiciary that Bickel had imposed and to provide an interpretive method that was more substantive than Bickel's rather vague call for principles. Bickel himself emphasized the qualifications of his earlier work with a more conservative critique of the Warren Court for not adhering to rigorous standards of principled decision making, even as it acted to impose its own moral vision on the nation.[12] Ironically, Bickel's critics moved toward even more abstract theorizing in order to embrace the judicial policy making favored by the Realists. While Bickel cautioned against judicial activism for fear of the political and institutional weaknesses of the courts, other constitutional theorists focused on the idealism displayed by the Court and began to construct interpretive methods rooted in abstract principles.[13] Thus one commentator concluded, "Both judges and critics best serve their common cause when their focus is on the Constitution rather than on processes and problems of judicial review."[14] The more empirical aspect of the countermajoritarian problem—that the Court had a limited capacity to counter the other branches of government—was rejected as constitutional theorists increasingly dismissed the lessons of Roosevelt's attack on the *Lochner* Court and focused on the possibilities of the Warren Court. The reality of constitutional principle justified judicial action against current majorities, if the correct principles could be discovered.

The post-Bickelian task of constitutional theory has been to articulate the interpretive method that would provide the Court with those principles, and thus with its answer to the countermajoritarian difficulty. There have been several responses to that project. Some commentators have tried to dissolve the difficulty by demonstrating that the courts actually enhance democracy. Others have taken a different approach, seeking to trump the majoritarian assumption by emphasizing the judiciary's role in defending the rights of individuals against current majorities. Similarly, the natural law tradition provides a framework for legal action that overrides majority will. Finally, by various paths, other scholars have sought to avoid Bickel's challenge entirely by returning to a neo-Realist pragmatic approach that emphasizes the judiciary's role as a policymaker supplementing the actions of the other branches of government.

A commitment to democracy has given two competing answers to the Bickelian question. One simply favors majoritarianism at the expense of judicial review; the other embraces judicial review as actually consistent with democracy, correctly understood.[15] Of course, given the continuing practice of judicial review in the United States, few commentators have maintained the first response—that is, admitted their inability to overcome the counter-majoritarian difficulty.[16] Nonetheless, democratic concerns have led a number of theorists to curtail sharply the space available for the exercise of judicial review, which must ultimately be justified on some other grounds.[17] The foremost proponent of the view that democracy actually legitimates an active exercise of the power of judicial review is John Hart Ely.

According to Ely, Bickel had both the question and the answer wrong. Bickel's answer, "that the proper role of the Court is the definition and imposition of values," was an unqualified failure for Ely. His question, however, was somewhat more subtly wrong. The judicial veto of legislative action could only be considered countermajoritarian, or undemocratic, if the legislature were assumed to represent faithfully the will of the majority of the populace. In detailing his theory of judicial review, Ely shifts Bickel's dilemma, not by a detailed showing of the undemocratic nature of American political institutions in practice but by developing a theory of judicial activism in which the Court is charged with increasing the representativeness of those political institutions.[18]

Ely construes the Constitution as being, fundamentally and exhaustively, about securing procedural democracy, and he recommends that the Court adopt an interpretive method appropriate to drawing this meaning out and applying it to current political practice. Contrary to common perception, he argues, the activism of the Warren Court was not in opposition to democratic principles—that is, concerned with vindicating "particular substantive values it had determined were important or fundamental." Rather, the Court was motivated by "a desire to ensure that the political process—which is where such values *are* properly identified, weighed, and accommodated—was open to those of all viewpoints on something approaching an equal basis."[19] Not only the Court but the Constitution itself was value neutral. The only concern of the Constitution is to provide a forum for all competing value systems to be debated until a majority eventually settles on one to elevate above the rest. The role of the judiciary is not to strike down that chosen value but to ensure that all values have an equal opportunity for consideration and selection.

Ely's defense of judicial activism in favor of maintaining a procedural democracy rests on a number of points. First, he is committed to a form of value skepticism that excludes the rational basis for any substantive values. Values derive not from reason but from subjective preference and thus can be imposed on others only by force of will. Worse yet, the values imposed by the Court are likely to be "flagrantly elitist and undemocratic."[20] Second, Ely's skepticism feeds into a form of value neutrality, in which all values are entitled to "equal concern and respect." Procedural democracy has the advantage of establishing pluralist institutions that ensure that no single value system retains its dominance for any length of time, helping to sustain the equality of all values. Further, by fostering a sense of "virtual representation" the Court can impose a requirement of neutrality and ensure that even a persistent majority treat minority values as being of equal worth to the majority's own.[21] Third, the Constitution is "preeminently" and "most successfully" concerned with fostering procedural democracy. Thus, by fostering democracy, the Court is merely enforcing the Constitution as it has developed on its historical trajectory toward maximizing democracy.[22] Finally, the judiciary has a functional advantage in enforcing and improving the procedures of democracy since the former is external to the latter's operation.[23]

There are multiple insuperable difficulties with Ely's work. Despite an extended effort, Ely is not convincing in demonstrating that the Constitution is uniquely concerned with procedural values to the exclusion of various substantive commitments. Although he admits that the Constitution's procedural devices are designed to advance the cause of liberty, he neglects the specific ways in which the Constitution conceives of liberty and safeguards it. Constitutional prohibitions on ex post facto laws, cruel and unusual punishments, impairments of contracts, or export taxes are difficult to reconcile with a purely procedural document.[24] Similarly, the enumeration of various positive grants of power, such as the federal power to collect imposts or raise armies, suggested substantive values that have shaped American political development since the founding.[25] Reliance upon such a process-based theory provides no guidance for the Court as to how to interpret these substantive provisions of the Constitution, either leaving them underenforced relative to the clear requirements of the text or arbitrarily enforced in accord with some unspecified interpretive method.[26] This tendency is manifested in Ely's reliance not only on a procedural interpretation of existing constitutional clauses but also on the presumed historical trajectory of the Constitution to ever greater democratic inclusion.[27] Such an extrapolation of some patterns within the constitutional text to the exclusion of others necessarily withers the importance of additional commitments. The choice of limits is as important as the choice of positive grants in the creation and maintenance of a balance among competing political goals. Ely's positing of a democratic trajectory operates in contravention to those limitations and thus replaces the weighting of values contained in the text with one of his own choosing.

Ely's de-emphasis of textually indicated substantive values is matched by the concealment of his own substantive values behind procedural cloaks. In part, his value skepticism cannot carry the burden he imposes on it. He rejects substantive judicial activism on the grounds that it would impose "elitist" values, yet he cannot consistently justify condemning elitist values in favor of more populist ones. Ultimately, Ely cannot even rationally explain his preference for democratic decision making over an aristocratic method, given his commitment to value skepticism. At another level, his insistence that all groups be treated as if they were represented in the majority coalition begs a host of questions that cannot be answered in either a value skeptical or value neutral manner. Both the definition of the relevant "groups" and the determination of their relevantly protected interests cannot be specified within the context of pure proceduralism. Although there are defensible reasons for regarding women, for example, as an identifiable political grouping for some purposes, or for regarding their access to abortion services as a protected interest, none is available without the articulation of some substantive conception of politics that singles gender out as a relevant category or abortion as an important interest. The same logic also indicates that the definition of political structures that unacceptably restrict democratic choices is also driven by substantive concerns. Whether bicameral state legislatures or a particular gerrymandering of legislative districts fosters better democratic outcomes or unduly biases the results in favor of privileged groups or interests depends on the particular substantive vision of democracy and the ends of politics adopted by the Court. The judiciary's functional advantage of being outside politics is vitiated if judges must employ undefended political judgments to intervene in existing political procedures.[28]

Some of these problems are avoided in the latest wave of democratic justifications for judicial review known as the republican revival. Like Ely, the republicans ground judicial review in its capacity to foster the decision-making processes of popular government. Moreover, the ultimate goal of republican theorizing is not to limit majoritarian political action but to include more groups in the deliberative process and to improve the character of those deliberations in order to reach better, but substantively unspecified, decisions. Like Ely's, the republican Court would serve as a guardian of the procedures of deliberation.

Although there are several prominent advocates of a republican judiciary,[29] consideration of Cass Sunstein's relatively well-articulated version should clarify both the unique contributions of this line of theorizing and its limitations.[30] For Sunstein, the essential aspect of republicanism is the requirement that reasons be given for political action. The judiciary can aid in the development and maintenance of this discourse by opening paths of public participation in the political dialogue and by directing it along particularly reasonable lines. One primary means for ensuring an elevation of public discussion is by increasing the scrutiny that the courts give to government actions, in order to determine that public-regarding reasons are given to support them.[31]

While continuing to recommend a largely proceduralist mission for the Court, republicanism purports to solve several of the problems found in Ely's work. The republicans are explicit about the substantive commitments of their work. Public participation in politics is a positive good, in the republican vision, and should be encouraged. Moreover, rationality in public discourse is good, and thus participation in politics and the outcome of political discussion must reflect genuine deliberation and not simple power politics. The recognition of these substantive ends both provides a justification for adopting republicanism over other interpretive methods and suggests a framework for understanding the constitutional text as a whole. Constraints on democratic decision making and guarantees of individual rights, for example, can be understood and interpreted as means to the advancement of popular politics itself.[32] Given a thicker understanding of democratic politics, the preconditions of republican government are more extensive, and thus more of the constitutional constraints on majoritarianism are explainable than in Ely's pure proceduralist, pluralist model. Moreover, the emphasis on the deliberative character of democracy, and not just on its character as a decision device, suggests the fluidity of individual preferences. If preferences can be changed through discussion, and not simply registered and aggregated through voting, then the Court need not be immediately deferential to democratic outcomes but must also investigate whether those outcomes were fully considered and representative of the citizenry's reflective judgment.[33]

Despite these advances, there remain difficulties with the republican alternative.[34] Among these problems is that the legal republicans do not take history seriously. This is true in their understanding of both republican theory and the nature of politics.[35] It can simply be noted briefly that republicanism shares with Ely a willingness to reduce the Constitution to a single theoretical

spirit, despite the conflicting political philosophies that were behind its drafting and that were reflected in its text.[36] More directly, compared to traditional
republican theory, the legal republicans' conception of substantive values is
both thin and wavering. In emphasizing political participation, rather than the
historical political community within which such participation was to occur,
Sunstein is cut off from the traditional explanation as to why politics was valuable in the first place, its capacity to express and advance the ends of the community. As a method for individual self-realization, politics has an uncertain
appeal compared to a vast number of other pursuits, and its elevation to legal
priority poses unclear risks in that regard. Yet modern republicans also want
to elevate certain substantive norms beyond the inherent value of participation in governance, such as the "opposition to caste" and equality of citizenship, which again beg many of the same questions as Ely in terms of identifying
what will qualify as a caste, what is necessary to oppose it, and what is necessary for equal citizenship.[37]

The thinning of the historical basis of republicanism creates two additional problems, both related to the artificiality of the modern republican conception of politics. The legal republicans seek to disassociate themselves from
the hierarchical and exclusionary aspects of historical republicanism, yet this
selectivity calls into question not only the purpose (politics without the historical polity) but also the dynamics of their republican politics. Within republicanism, popular politics has been essentially concerned with defining
and maintaining community. In order to do so, it has historically struggled
over boundaries, marginalizing and excluding various groups in order to sustain the central core, whether the excluded are defined by ideology, race, geography, occupation, or wealth.[38] Current events are not reassuring that the
elevation of popular politics can be successfully separated from such efforts;
yet this is a tension within a liberal-republican synthesis that is not fully
acknowledged, let alone successfully dealt with, by modern republicans.

Moreover, modern republicanism is of two minds as to the nature of popular politics. On the one hand, deliberative democracy is celebrated, but no
real effort is made to discover whether this image of popular politics is
matched by any historical reality. On the other hand, interest-group pluralism is derided, but again with little effort to discover how common it is or
why and how it emerges. Traditional republicanism, with its emphasis on
extraordinary founding moments followed by cycles of corruption and decay,
could at least explain the emergence of privatistic politics.[39] In doing so, it also
recognized the limited capacity of the populace for constant engagement in
politics and the need for mechanisms periodically to renew public virtue. In
seeking to eliminate pluralism from political life, especially without an inves-

tigation of the nature of public deliberation, modern republicanism has divorced itself from the realities of politics.[40]

JUDICIAL PROTECTION OF FUNDAMENTAL RIGHTS

Perhaps the primary alternative to such majoritarian theories is the explicit defense of favored substantive values. Such theories respond to Bickel's challenge by trumping the presumed priority of democracy. If democratic decision making is primarily a means to reach other substantive ends, then the ability of the judiciary to reach those ends directly and more effectively than more representative institutions would authorize judicial activism in contravention of legislative outcomes. The range of favored fundamental values is broad, but such theories can be illustrated by brief consideration of approaches from the left and the right.[41]

Ronald Dworkin is among the most thoughtful of the fundamental rights theorists. For him, judicial review does not present any serious countermajoritarian "difficulty" at all, for constitutionalism is intended to control majorities. "The Constitution, and particularly the Bill of Rights, is designed to protect individual citizens and groups against certain decisions that a majority of citizens might want to make, even when that majority acts in what it takes to be the general or common interest." Such protection is rooted in the "moral rights which individuals possess against the majority."[42] In contrast to Ely's value skepticism, Dworkin argues forthrightly that "judicial activism presupposes a certain objectivity of moral principle." However, the very reality of moral principles frees Dworkin from reliance on the constitutional text, for such a reliance would replace firm moral rights with mere "*legal* rights as the Constitution grants" to individuals.[43] Moreover, the existence of moral rights authorizes judicial activism in particular because judges are separated from the pressures of policy interests that can obscure prior rights claims.[44]

Dworkin finds a foundation for his conception of individual rights in two considerations: the intrinsic human dignity of each individual and the ideal of political equality. These twin foundations indicate that rights are essential to the very recognition of the humanity of the citizenry, and therefore rights cannot be balanced against policy concerns but must trump them as prior constraints on any government action. In Dworkin's version of neo-Kantianism, the preservation of moral values requires treating each individual with "equal concern and respect." Regardless of the desires of the political majority, the government cannot impose burdens on some individuals simply because their value system is disfavored. Thus, for example, blacks cannot be treated differently by the state simply because of the discriminating preference of the white majority, nor can homosexuals be punished because their activities contradict values of a religious majority as to how all individuals should live.[45]

Dworkin disparages property rights as nonfundamental and unworthy of judicial protection, but theorists from the political right have elaborated alternative approaches that emphasize the fundamental status of property rights. In constructing his theory, Richard Epstein likewise challenges the assumptions of Bickel's dilemma. In the former's judgment, "The Constitution clearly does not endorse any version of popular democracy," and thus presumptions favoring majoritarian action should not be imposed on the text or used to confine the judiciary. Instead, Epstein urges the construction of a constitutional theory endorsing activism based on the "necessary implications derived from the constitutional text and the underlying theory of the state that it embodies."[46] In practice, his theory depends a great deal more on the "underlying theory of the state" than on the constitutional text.

The social contract theory that forms Epstein's starting point provides that the state has no rights against individual citizens that have not been delegated to it. Moreover, individuals are assumed to have delegated power to the state only in exchange for benefits of equal or greater value. The combination of these features results in the state possessing the power to coerce individuals but only in order to benefit their own individual position. The constitutional role of the judiciary is to ensure that exertions of governmental force actually benefit the affected individuals. In contrast to Dworkin, Epstein has no interest in the motivations of government actors but only in the concrete effects of their actions. Furthermore, whereas Dworkin dismisses property rights as irrelevant to the true core of human dignity, Epstein begins with the assumption that humans can be regarded as little more than a collection of interests and entitlements to be exercised and exchanged. In either case, constitutionalism is primarily concerned with limiting government action through rule making, and the judiciary's task is to enforce those constraints.[47]

Such works are indicative of the general tendency of the rights theories, although each differs somewhat in the specific rights favored and their justifications. Overall, the constitutional text is taken as a mere indication of a larger moral universe standing behind it that judges should access directly to enforce fundamental values against the state. Moreover, the value of democratic decision making is regarded as largely instrumental and thus expendable if the judiciary can adequately conceptualize and enforce rights. A full critique of rights theorists would have to examine each in turn, pointing out the specific difficulties with individual foundations and applications. Without such an exhaustive inventory of theories and criticisms, however, a number of general problems with the rights approach can still be noted.

The general difficulty with rights theories is less in the reality of the values they advocate than in the overall imbalance in constitutional theory that the approach encourages.[48] In both theory and practice, the rights approach has been highly selective in its choice of values to elevate to a fundamental position worthy of judicial protection. The absolutism of rights language, combined with the rigidity of legal doctrines, makes the judicial protection of all identifiable rights unrealistic. Certainly, this exclusive focus on the rights elements of constitutionalism subverts the other obvious aspect of the Constitution, the creation and empowerment of the state to act on behalf of the polity. Yet the separation of some rights among others for "fundamental" status, the specification of the relevant level of abstraction at which those rights should be framed, and the balancing among competing rights and governmental interests rely as much or more on moral intuition, buried assumptions, and subjective preferences as on a reasoned defense of the objective moral universe from which they are allegedly derived. One need not adhere to value skepticism to question the underdetermined nature of rights theorizing in a legal context.[49]

This balance problem is exacerbated by the disassociation of rights theories from the constitutional text. Rights theorists are almost exclusively concerned with a handful of textual clauses, to the extent that their theories are largely incapable of establishing the relationship between the judiciary and the majority of the Constitution. Moreover, even within the context of rights-oriented clauses, some aspects of the Constitution are disregarded even as others are celebrated. Such selective judicial activism within the context of a constitutional system focused on a written text creates severe difficulties in establishing the authority of the judiciary within the confines of the Constitution. Although such efforts at political philosophy have a value of their own, they cannot be so easily transferred to an arena of judicial enforcement while maintaining the pretext of operating under a preexisting constitutional system.

Finally, rights theories are particularly prone to abstractions that do not give adequate weight to actual political settlements. By developing a rights template in relative isolation from political practice and then applying it to an actual political context, rights theorists are predisposing their theory to judicial intervention. As one such theorist asserted, legislatures "are not ideologically committed or institutionally suited to search for the meaning of constitutional values, but instead see their primary function in terms of registering the actual, occurrent preference of the people—what they want and what they believe should be done."[50] On the one hand, rights theorists are unwilling to recognize the compromises and enumerations that are captured in the constitutional text itself. On the other, they exclude by assumption the significance of the compromises and deliberations of current political actors. In simultaneously assuming the empirical reality of the judicial adherence to rational principle to the exclusion of policy preference and excluding the political branches from their normative theorizing, rights theorists have created an imbalanced framework that urges judicial activism in the name of abstract ideals in disregard of any values that may be internally represented within the larger constitutional system. Such a blinkered vision of constitutional discourse is particularly troubling, given the deeply contested nature of the rights theories themselves and the political philosophies they rely upon.

CONSTITUTIONAL MORALITY AND NATURAL LAW

The proceduralist and rights strands of constitutional theory remain dominant, but other theories have struggled persistently at the margins of the contemporary discourse and occasionally made forays into momentary prominence. One such approach, with the risk of some misunderstanding, can be loosely labeled "natural law."[51] Like the rights theorists, these moralists conceive of the Constitution as the expression of a larger political theory that can be accessed directly, and they similarly urge the courts to take an active role in defending that moral vision. The natural law theorists differ, however, in largely rejecting the conventionalist, neo-Kantian conceptual backdrop of the rights theorists in favor of a classical, theological, or moral realist foundation. Such different philosophical roots not only lead to a distinct form of theorizing and substantive outcomes but also tend to de-emphasize individual rights in order to elevate other political ends, such as human welfare or the moral worth of the community.

For the natural lawyer, the written Constitution is a reflection of larger moral truths. This reflective character has a number of implications. Notably, it means that the Constitution cannot be properly understood without reference to those moral truths. The moral universe from which the text is derived both defines appropriate judicial reasoning and the substantive meaning of the text. Shifting perspective from the natural law to some other basis has the effect of replacing an "independent ground of right and wrong" with "cultural relativism" and "anthropology." Rather than being embedded in firm and durable truths, legal meaning would on occasion embrace demonstrable moral wrongs, as it did for example in the nineteenth century when the courts enforced the laws of slavery.[52] Without the backdrop of moral theory, aspects of the Constitution simply would not make sense, and judges would be left haphazardly grasping at textual hooks to rationalize decisions without any principled and reasoned guidance. Reference to the "reasoning spirit" of the

Constitution both provides coherence in decision making and constrains judges from rendering idiosyncratic decisions.[53]

The same moral principles that provide guidance for the judge also provide authority for his decisions. The judge, like all other citizens, is bound by the moral obligations of the natural law. A particular decision "claimed its authority because it could be deduced from a deeper principle of law, which did not need to be set down within the text of the Constitution."[54] Judicial opinions are binding for the same reason that the Constitution itself is, that both are just. In contrast to the rights theorist, the natural lawyer has no difficulty extending his logic to the whole of the constitutional text. To the extent that the Constitution is meaningful, it is rooted in the natural law. Expansive interpretations do not rest upon the vagueness or generality of particular textual clauses but upon the motivating force of the whole document. A relatively clear clause such as the prohibition of ex post facto laws gains its meaning from the same source as relatively broad guarantees of due process.[55] Nonetheless, "That is not to say that anything that we can plausibly describe as a 'wrong' ought to come within the reach of the law. Prudence may rightly make us pause before we bring every dispute, or every villainy, within the jurisdiction of the state." The judge and the state itself are equally constrained not by the absence of power but by the limitations of the prudent use of that power.[56]

One constitutional moralist aptly brings out the difficulty with this approach himself. Moral realism says

> in effect, that a constitution should be a windowpane, letting in on the public life as much of the pure light of moral principle as prudence determines feasible. Prudence may find that conditions require slow going sometimes, but the goal is to arrive at the point where the glass is no longer even noticed because of the brilliance of the sunlight. This scheme of things seems to evacuate the very notion of a constitution; it reduces a constitution to a fiction of prudence. If, in the final analysis, this is what constitutions are, why then bother with them at all?[57]

Such criticism goes to the heart of the difficulty with moral constitutionalism as enforced by the judiciary. Ultimately, it cannot fit with the experience of possessing a constitution at all. To point to the natural law foundations held by those who drafted the Constitution, and then seek to access them directly, is to miss the point of the drafting, which was to provide political reminders of and legal force for those moral requirements. The text can only serve as a reminder, however, if it has reality as a text—that is, if it is observed and understood as the primary object of analysis. Otherwise, the text cannot bring political actors back to first principles, because they remain convinced of their own prior knowledge of those standards.

One need not call into question the reality of moral principles, as moral theorists often assume, in order to doubt whether judges have adequate access to them to employ the tools of the state to enforce their judgment as to the requirements of those principles. Disagreements over interpretation are not adequate to dismiss the reality of the object of interpretation, but they may be sufficient to require reconsideration of goals and methods. The commitment to moralist interpretation directs judges to continue to peer through the glass, even if they can only "see darkly." Yet, this recommendation merely collapses into the kind of prudential effort at perfectionism already criticized.[58] The existence of a written text provides a mediating point between the judge and the natural law, allowing an epistemologically confident interpretation of a potentially flawed but publicly cognizable and correctable instrument. The recommendation to pursue a dimly perceived truth with prudential caution erases the distinction between the legal and the political realm and once again calls into question the authority of the jurist when opposed to the judgments of more representative political agents.[59]

POLICY MAKING AND NEO-PRAGMATISM

The final category of contemporary constitutional theory is actually a collection of diverse approaches to the Constitution. The common trait among them is that they ultimately conclude that the judiciary should act as a pragmatic policymaker and that constitutional theorizing and its concerns for the legitimacy of judicial review are irrelevant to the continuing practice of judicial lawmaking. Thus, contemporary political science is dominated by an empirical, behaviorist approach to public law that seeks to explain judicial behavior in terms of individual political preferences and the interaction of political interests without reference to legal norms or the normative legitimacy of such conduct.[60] The Critical Legal Studies movement dismisses theorizing as hopelessly contradictory and indeterminate and grounds judicial behavior instead in the sociological and political background and commitments of individual judges.[61] Others have rooted good judicial decision making in the rejection of narrow and abstract constraints in favor of a flexible use of available legal tools to reach substantively desirable ends.[62] Despite these differences, their collective challenge is to the enterprise of constitutional theory itself.

Neo-pragmatist jurisprudence differs within itself as to the appropriate direction that judges should take constitutional law. Federal judge and law-and-economics scholar Richard Posner has suggested a useful catalog of three "essential" characteristics of pragmatism.

The first is a distrust of metaphysical entities ("reality," "truth," "nature," etc.) viewed as warrants for certitude whether in epistemology, ethics, or politics. The second is an insistence that propositions be tested by their consequences, by the difference they make. . . . The third is an insistence on judging our projects, whether scientific, ethical, political, or legal, by their conformity to social or other human needs rather than to "objective," "impersonal" criteria.[63]

Although phrased in largely positive terms, the list is mostly negative in its rejection of truth, objectivity, and formalism. Writing in 1982, Martin Shapiro was perhaps prophetic in predicting that by "the 1990s we will discover that moral philosophers aren't equipped to do moral philosophy either and the jurisprudence of values will subside," to be once again replaced with an understanding that the Court acts as an "independent policymaker."[64] From this neo-Realist perspective, efforts at constitutional theory amount to little more than a "mixture of doctrinal manipulation, literary criticism, selective history and seat-of-the-pants policy analysis." Jurisprudence is still just looking for "good public policy."[65]

This rejection of abstractions, whether in the form of theorizing about values or about objective textual interpretation, leads to increasingly narrow decision making. Although always working within the context of broader politics, a pragmatic judiciary should embrace a form of "situated" reasoning in which a judge builds up a decision from the context of the controversy itself. Instead of seeking to impose previously developed categories and rules on a case, pragmatists are required "to immerse ourselves in the particulars of historical situations."[66] The creative and beneficent power of the judgment itself serves as justification for the Court's actions, and adherence to the forms of legal reasoning provides legitimacy for the judiciary's exercise of the power of review.[67]

One difficulty with this mode of argument, of course, is that it is highly dependent on the success of its critical case. I argue that in fact constitutional interpretation is possible, that the case against formalism and objectivity largely depends on the prior creation of straw men (see chapter 4). If such arguments are correct, and interpretive theory is possible, then the normative difficulty with the neo-pragmatist position quickly becomes apparent. Although, as a descriptive matter, there can be little doubt that the Court is occasionally influenced by external political concerns and that there is an internal politics to the judicial system, just as there is an internal politics to academia, it was long ago argued that it is "unrealistic" to reduce judicial deliberations to political horse-trading.[68] The common experience of legal debate indicates that minds can be and have been changed through discussion. It is not sufficient to respond by questioning whether the "Court is a group of legal scholars or a group of politicians."[69] Even politicians are open to advocacy and can be persuaded, as well as motivated, to change their position. In any case, the behavior of the justices indicates they at least sometimes act on jurisprudential judgments and are constrained by theoretical conclusions.[70] Further, it does not follow that such moments of political negotiation are the defining feature of the judiciary. As even the pragmatists realize, the judicial enterprise is sustained by its use of legal forms. Advocacy of the "pragmatic" (i.e., hypocritical) use of those forms to provide cover for the "true" political calculus that actually determines a judicial decision does worse than remove the distinction between courts and other political actors. The explicit use of policy-making tools by the courts may even be appropriate in some contexts, as when the legislature effectively makes the judiciary part of the administrative arm of the state for certain purposes.[71] But there are well-known institutional limitations to the courts' adopting such a position as general policy.[72] The reduction of the constitutional exercise of judicial review to a form of policy making, however, effectively supplants the decisions of politically accountable policymakers with those of judges. That move at least requires some effort at justification in terms of its systematic effects and philosophical basis as compared to nonjudicial policy making.[73]

Such problems are heightened when the prescriptive side of the pragmatist's case is considered. Proponents of the pragmatist movement are themselves torn with disagreements over the substantive effects of their philosophical commitments. In response, judges appear to be thrown back on the same interpretive tools that presumably have been discredited. In the alternative, judges could heed the exhortation that they "just do it" and impose the results of their own political commitments and moral choices.[74] In response, it is worth recalling that when it is suggested that pragmatism "frees us . . . to explore more space," the "us" consists only of the judiciary and its attorney-advocates, and the "space" with which judges experiment is constitutional principle.[75]

The Nature and Purpose of Originalism

Contemporary constitutional theory remains mired in the dilemma originally proposed by Bickel nearly forty years ago. Notably, existing theories suffer from their lack of a principled reason for supporting judicial review. Moreover, existing interpretive theories are often myopic in that they can elaborate some parts of the constitutional text but have little to say about others, are radically underdetermined in that they cannot faithfully translate their moti-

vating political theories into applied judicial results, and are decentered from
the text. In short, interpretive constitutional theory has not yet provided an
approach that can guide the judiciary in interpreting the constitutional text
and provide principled authority for the exercise of judicial review against
other government officials.

I think that the best opportunity for escaping this dilemma may be offered
by what is often regarded as the traditional alternative. Like much of modern
constitutional theory, a jurisprudence of original intent is rooted in an interpretive method that promises to establish its own authority for judicial review.
It offers to overcome the countermajoritarian difficulty not by favoring one
side of the conflict over the other but by dissolving the problem by setting it
in a larger constitutional context.[76] In order to do so, however, originalism
must be clarified and in part reconceived. Thus my concern here is with out-
lining a defensible originalist program and considering some aspects of its
justification.

THE NATURE OF ORIGINALISM

The basic originalist program is relatively easy to describe, with the bulk
of the literature being dedicated to criticizing alternative schools of interpretation or developing specific historical-legal interpretations of given constitutional clauses.[77] The critical originalist directive is that the Constitution
should be interpreted according to the understandings made public at the
time of the drafting and ratification. The primary source of those understandings is the text of the Constitution itself, including both its wording and
structure. The text is supplemented by a variety of secondary sources of information, however. Historical sources are to be used to elucidate the understanding of the terms involved and to indicate the principles that were
supposed to be embodied in them. The guiding principle is that the judge
should be seeking to make plain the "meaning understood at the time of the
law's enactment."[78]

Several clarifying points can be made about this basic maxim. The relevant "founders" providing meaning for an ambiguous text are always those
who authored the specific text in question. Thus, the intentions supporting
later amendments are independent of the intentions of those who drafted the
original Constitution.[79] Although the convention device gave a democratic
imprimatur to the Constitution and thereby legitimated it, the conventions
cannot be taken simply as one source of public opinion. They were the specifically designated device for gathering public sentiment on the Constitution,
and that device was chosen in part to mediate public opinion and to provide

a more deliberative result than the raw data of popular sentiment.[80] Granting the priority of such direct evidence of the intent of the ratifiers, then additional information from the drafting convention, the popular debates surrounding ratification, and contemporary commentary are allowable as indicators of ratifying intent. The ultimate value of such additional sources, however, is merely evidentiary in the effort to elucidate the intent of the ratifiers. Another implication of the use of the convention device is that the Constitution did reflect genuinely public understandings of the document. Thus, although some individuals can be expected to have expressed and understood that meaning better than others did, the document cannot be taken to mean by definition whatever the "best" minds of the period thought or hoped. As a democratic document, the Constitution reflects the results of the best mechanism available and trusted for deliberating on public affairs, not the results of post hoc judgments as to who would have written the best text. The public nature of the document and its ratification also exclude the authoritativeness of any hidden agenda intended by any particular drafter or contender in the constitutional debates in contradiction to their public expressions.[81]

The second critical aspect of originalism is that it gives the presumption to the current majority's legislative action. As equal branches of government themselves charged with obeying the Constitution, the nonjudicial branches cannot be presumed to violate the Constitution as a regular practice. Moreover, as representative institutions, the other branches carry a certain presumptive authority over the unelected judiciary. Nonetheless, that presumption cannot be carried to the point of judicial passivism. The judiciary does have a particular role to play in interpreting the Constitution, and in the context of interpretation it is likely to have greater expertise than the other branches. Therefore, though originalism cannot accept the assumption of some commentators that the legislatures are unconcerned with, if not hostile to, constitutional principles, neither can it embrace James Bradley Thayer's strong form of judicial deference as a necessary component.[82] It remains true that "from the premise of an unknowable or irrelevant Constitution, the conclusion should follow that judges have no basis or justification for declaring laws unconstitutional."[83] However, when the Constitution is knowable, the Court must act vigorously to enforce the limits it places on governmental action.

The presumption of constitutionality also provides a basis for defining the level of generality at which constitutional provisions should be elaborated. The originalist's expectation is that the Constitution provides a general principle that can be applied to a specific fact situation. The difficulty comes not only in discovering the principle or in determining how best to apply it to the facts, but also in deciding how broadly to draw the principles that the constitutional text demonstrably embodies.[84] Thus, for example, there is general originalist agreement that the broad right to privacy developed by Justice William Douglas in *Griswold* to allow the purchase of contraceptives is unjustified by the discoverable Constitution.[85] This level of generality is excluded by a focus on the meaning of specific clauses rather than on the animating principle that resulted in those more specific clauses being drafted and ratified. The Constitution details a number of rights that shield the privacy of individuals from government intervention, including rights to speech, religion, association, security from martial occupation, and security from warrantless searches. None of these specific rights, however, reasonably applies to either sexual autonomy or commercial transactions, even though the belief that citizens should be free from excessive government involvement in the conduct of their lives could have motivated the inclusion of such additional rights. Since only the detailed clauses, and intentions about their meaning, and not a general statement of principle were ratified, judges are constrained from extending those clauses to reduce the legislative sphere of free action.[86]

Other constitutional provisions do express general principles within a single clause, and the Court must determine how broadly it will draw this protection in carrying out its own duties relative to the other branches of government. The same approach can be applied in either case. The equal protection clause of the Fourteenth Amendment is relatively broad in both text and intent, for example. In order to determine the outer boundaries of its scope, the originalist premise would lead to a stepwise progression from a narrow to a broader reading. Once a layer of protection is posited that can no longer be supported by the weight of historical evidence, judicial interpretation and application of that principle must stop, leaving any further protection to political construction.[87]

These considerations clarify the basic originalist framework. Even at this level some distinctions have been made among originalists, and some versions of originalism have been implicitly rejected. For example, "originalist" readings relying simply on the understanding of the populace at the time of the founding or on the philosophical roots of American constitutional thought[88] were rejected in favor of a reliance on the specific intent of the ratifiers. The more specific shape of originalist jurisprudence, including the response to common criticisms of its method, turns critically on the ultimate justifications offered for adopting an originalist strategy for constitutional interpretation. Therefore, further evaluation of the nature and practice of originalism can be held in suspense until the foundations for it have been laid.

JUSTIFICATIONS

Originalists have proposed a variety and number of justifications for their interpretive method. Some are grounded primarily in pragmatic, policy-making considerations. Others are rooted in more theoretical considerations of constitutional authority. Although these justifications contain certain valuable insights, they are not equally successful. Moreover, final acceptance of a number of the proffered justifications has had the effect of pushing originalism in the wrong direction, leading to misconceptions as to its methodological nature and to the role of the judiciary within the constitutional system. Therefore, the available originalist justifications need to be considered and either adapted or abandoned. The most common justifications for an originalist method will be examined and found insufficient as currently developed.

At a relatively pragmatic level, originalists have denied the early Bickelian claim that the judiciary is well suited to discovering and establishing the principles that should guide the nation in the future. Although most strongly formulated by Bickel, the conception of judges as arbiters of contemporary moral values underlies a number of post-Bickelian theories.[89] According to originalists, institutions that are close to society and have broad information-gathering capacity are better able to engage in institutional and policy innovation than the judiciary, which values independence and insulation from popular passion and activity. Further, representative institutions in the American system are designed to encourage compromise and relatively slow change. The judiciary, alternatively, though operating under its own constraints, has little guidance in balancing multiple interests given real conflicts in society among different interests and ideals. At the most basic level, interests not directly represented in the litigation before the courts are likely to be underrepresented in the eventual decision. Similarly, since the judiciary only episodically intervenes in the political process, it is not capable of fully accounting for the effect on limited resources across the policy sphere of judicially imposed solutions in particular disputes.

Moreover, there is little reason to believe that isolation from popular pressure in and of itself would be conducive to the unique articulation of public values. Judges ultimately share many of the same traits and values as other political actors, having been drawn from the ranks of politically affiliated professional attorneys and promoted through complex political procedures. At the same time, the features that have led to elevation to the bench include no particular talents or skills that suggest greater capacity for moral reasoning than that which is common to other public agents. At best, the claim for judicial prophecy depends on the assumption that judges will be more likely to articulate the values shared by government officials but held in check by the latters' continuing contact with the public.[90]

This line of argument is more insufficient than simply wrong as a justification for an originalist method. This form of critique neither fully undermines the case for fundamental values activism nor establishes a positive case for originalism.[91] Even if other officials are better suited for articulating social values and policy directions than are judges, the remaining space for judicial action may go beyond originalism to include the proceduralist activism advocated by democrats such as Ely, for example.[92] More broadly, the possibility of the political development of constitutional principles suggests the need to examine how and if elected officials actually engage in such discussion, which originalists have not done. The possibility that the political sphere does in fact constitute the "Madisonian nightmare" of interest-group pluralism that Sunstein fears[93] would at least weaken the originalist claim that judges should not take the lead in defining public values.

A second pragmatic justification for originalism is that it would prevent judges from engaging in willful or arbitrary behavior. Robert Bork, for example, has argued that "the only way in which the Constitution can constrain judges is if the judges interpret the document's words according to the intentions of those who drafted, proposed, and ratified its provisions and various amendments."[94] This argument for originalism has in part been advanced in response to earlier Realist insights into the inconsistency and occasional arbitrariness of American jurisprudence. Originalism is said to offer at least a comparative advantage in being able to constrain judges by providing fairly objective and specific criteria by which to evaluate judicial performance. Even in the case of genuine judicial bad faith, originalism would force the judge to conform to known standards and "to that extent, curb his freedom."[95] The mistrust of government power underlying constitutionalism generally dictates that a proper interpretive theory incorporate a concern with controlling the judiciary as well as other governmental institutions.[96]

Originalists have been particularly concerned about the discretion available to judges and therefore have been careful to clarify and emphasize the limits placed on them by the adoption of their interpretive method. Such limits, however, are not unique to originalism. Advocates of alternative approaches have been motivated by an interest in expanding the realm of judicial activism and thus in de-emphasizing the need or reality of constraints on judges by the adoption of their methodologies. Nonetheless, the adoption of any interpretive method constrains judges from engaging in arbitrary or willful behavior. Current criticisms by originalists of judicial activism hinge more on disagreements with the interpretive methods adopted by activist judges than with the failure of such methods to provide guidance for their users.[97] The activism of the judiciary in striking down laws in the interest of various sweeping principles must be distinguished from judicial arbitrariness. In the former case, judges may be constrained in the sense that their actions may be empirically predictable and normatively criticizable, even if their sphere of operation is quite broad. All interpretive approaches are not equal, however, even on the narrow issue of providing judicial guidance and standards for the evaluation of judicial opinions. The neo-pragmatic approach, for example, by its very nature disavows the possibility of general rules for judges. Somewhat differently, some value-oriented approaches to interpretation may offer little guidance to judges as a result of the vagueness of the values they recommend. Nonetheless, most interpretive approaches can at least constrain judges within bounds and in all likelihood could provide greater constraints over time as techniques of application are worked out in practice.

When isolated, it soon becomes apparent that such pragmatic justifications for originalism are really dependent on more theoretical concerns about the judiciary's authority. Concerns with the institutional efficacy of the judiciary to provide political norms and to arrange compromises and with the relative discretion of judges to create legally binding principles reflect more fundamental commitments to a vision of separation of powers that gives priority in lawmaking to representative institutions. The originalist effort to "depoliticize the law" by ensuring "fidelity to the Constitution" depends on a limited conception of the constitutional authorization of the judiciary to incorporate extraconstitutional and political considerations into constitutional law.[98]

The first of these interconnected arguments for the authority of originalism depends on the distinction between the judicial and the legislative function. According to the originalists, the legislature is charged with making law, but the judiciary is supposed to be limited to applying preexisting law. Grounded in the textual separation of the "judicial power" from the "legislative powers," this originalist argument would exclude the more explicit modern use of extraconstitutional sources to create principles to guide the nation. It would also exclude any interpretive strategy that does not seek to understand the purpose and intent of the actual lawmakers. Deviating from the intent of the Constitution would be tantamount to creating a new fundamental law from the bench, thereby exceeding the judicial role by creating constitutional law instead of merely elaborating and applying it. Without being constrained to the interpretation and application of previously created law, the judiciary would subvert the place of the elected and accountable representatives in favor of the forceful imposition of the will of a legal aristocracy.[99]

Full consideration of this argument would exceed the scope of this book, but it should be noted that originalists have not been particularly clear on the nature of lawmaking and legal interpretation. In part, their arguments for a strong separation between the lawmaking and the judicial functions suggest a pre-Realist conception of the judiciary that would be difficult to sustain in its entirety. Nonetheless, for the normative purposes of constitutional theory, such strictures are often laid aside or at least moderated in order to develop the abstractly correct judicial position, even if actual courts are likely to deviate from that established standard. More important, such a separation of the lawmaking and the interpretive functions is sustainable, if the complications of interpretation are recognized.

It is generally accepted, if not frequently emphasized, that there is a substantial core of discoverable legal meaning within which the judiciary can interpret the law without raising questions of its own lawmaking. Nearly all federal appellate court cases, for example, are decided without filed dissents, suggesting that there does in fact exist a consensus of informed opinion on the application of the law in most instances.[100] The more problematic case is at the (thin) margins of this accepted core, the so-called "hard cases." H. L. A. Hart characterized this as the "problem of the penumbra" and advocated that we admit that "laws are incurably incomplete." In order to resolve disputes that occur in these legal gaps, Hart thought that judges must simply legislate, that is, "decide the penumbral cases rationally by reference to social aims" but without reference to preexisting, discoverable law. The judge is left with "discretion" in such cases; his "conclusion, even though it may not be arbitrary or irrational, is in effect a choice."[101] Dworkin has argued that there are interpretive answers in such hard cases, yet he provides them not only by introducing the device of a superhuman Hercules, who is capable of discovering them, but also by integrating a form of natural law into the positive law. At the margins of the positive law, the Dworkinian judge draws upon moral principles in order to put the law in its "best light" and render it complete. Hercules avoids "legislating" because the moral principles he draws upon are concerned with rights rather than with the utilitarian social welfare concerns of legislative "policy" and because his decisions are not "chosen" at his "discretion" but are drawn from an external moral reality.[102] Neither response to hard cases is satisfactory to the originalist. The first explicitly involves judicial lawmaking, which is precisely what the originalist is hoping to avoid. The second circumvents judicial legislation by invoking unlegislated natural law, which has already been rejected. If the distinction of separate functions is to be maintained, some third option must be identified.

Several options are available to the originalist to deal with these hard cases.

One option is simply to constrain judicial review to the settled core of legal meaning, thus largely excluding judges from any risk of extending the law in an illegitimate fashion. This is, in essence, the response of those individuals who advocate judicial restraint in the absence of obvious violations of constitutional requirements. The risk of this approach is that it will serve to shrink the core of constitutional meaning, as the clear-mistake rule of the deferential judge exchanges false positives for false negatives. More cases are regarded as "hard" if a clear-mistake rule is adopted, to the extent that any reasonable disagreement is regarded as seriously unsettling legal meaning.

Another option, however, is to recognize that within the context of interpretation there are mechanisms for expanding the boundaries of the core legal meaning. Legal interpretation includes not only the explication of the core meaning of the law but also subsidiary rules for extending that meaning. Such interpretive guidelines are not the product of judicial additions to the law or internally included in the law itself but are constitutive of the judicial function.[103] Thus, while avoiding reliance on moral theories of the "best" meaning of the existing law, interpreters can nonetheless decide hard cases through developing the logical implications of the settled law. This approach can be called one of seeking the "best fit" with existing law.[104] In attempting to analyze various elements in Dworkin's approach, one critic contended that "one important aspect of the soundest theory is simply that the theory fits best with the settled law. But this aspect of the soundest theory is not normative, for the judge has to construct the theory from the settled law, whether or not he himself finds the theory morally acceptable."[105] The aspect of seeking the best fit of a decision with the law does not invoke a critical morality on the part of the judge but seeks the best interpretive resolution of apparent indeterminacy.[106] Although such hard cases may require the integration of several existing strands of the law in order to reach a determinate result, and therefore cannot strictly rely upon deduction from clear premises, they do not require the judge to abandon positive law. "Any judicial decision takes place against the background of an entire legal system containing a wide variety of interrelated and interdependent decisions, rules, principles, policies, etc. In any case, it may be argued, the obligation of the judge is to reach that decision which coheres best with the total body of authoritative legal standards which he is bound to apply."[107] Further, supplementary closure rules may well be built into the legal code in order to provide guidance to interpreters faced with prima facie gaps in the law.[108] Recognition of such interpretive devices to extend the bounds of settled law leads to a mitigation, if not the elimination, of the "problem of the penumbra." The set of hard cases is reduced to "really hard cases" that continue to be "inherently unconventional, inherently controversial, and inherently incapable of producing 'interpersonal checks' as respects the substantive correctness of the result."[109]

Whether such mechanisms effectively eliminate the existence of legal gaps or merely reduce the number of hard cases to a small subset of the total cases, they do suggest that the originalist faith in a separation of functions between legislators and judges rests on a firm theoretical basis. Far from relying on a naive conception of the nature of the law and the judicial function, originalists can actually employ relatively sophisticated understandings that cohere well with both a normative theory of separated powers and the experience of judicial interpretation.[110] If the judicial function cannot be reduced to a constant process of legislating from the bench, however, originalists are still faced with the problem of addressing the handful of remaining hard cases. In fact, the existence of such gaps in constitutional meaning that cannot be filled through interpretation is not a problem at all for a properly developed theory of originalism. Indeed, the recognition of the possibility of such gaps can be one of the virtues of originalism.[111]

Closely related to this separation of powers argument is the contention that judges should accept the right of popular majorities to have their political way through their elected representatives in most instances, given that the American system is primarily republican in nature. As currently developed by advocates of originalism, this argument divides into two forms. First, originalism supports democratic values in the form of present majoritarianism by fostering judicial restraint. The American system of government is premised on the right of democratic majorities to determine public policy. Since the political restrictions contained in the originalist text are relatively few and clear, judges would rarely be called upon to exercise the power of review and strike down laws. Thus, government decisions would primarily be made in the political branches with little interference from the unelected judiciary, expanding the realm for democratic action.

The second aspect of the argument from democratic values is that to the extent that judges do strike down government acts, they do so in the name of prior, popularly approved law. Reliance on an originalist interpretive method not only results in the "neutral" application of constitutional principles—in that judges apply the same rules consistently to all parties—but also in the neutral derivation of those principles as the founders' intentions serve as an objective source of law independent of the judicial will. By relying on "neutral" criteria of deciding constitutional cases, the judiciary avoids placing its own substantive spin on current political outcomes. Originalism thus does not seek to bind the nation to the ideals and understandings of the dead past but to ensure that any new values are developed and articulated by current, living majorities. By not defining the judiciary's function as that of serving one side of the Bickelian dilemma to the exclusion of the other, originalism maintains the tension inherent in the constitutional design.[112]

By respecting the balances of the constitutional text, originalism does promise to retain the choices and compromises written into the Constitution by the people. Unlike the democratic visionaries, the rights theorists, or the natural lawyers, originalists do not look past the Constitution to a larger and prior moral commitment. To the extent that both rights and democratic values are embodied in the document, each is protected by originalism. Nonetheless, the virtues of this approach should not be overstated. In part, the very point that originalism protects both the rights and democratic values embodied in the text indicates the contradiction between the two forms of the argument from democracy. As is clear from both the text and history, the founders were not pure majoritarians but were also interested in limiting government. To this degree, the neutral enforcement of embodied values will necessarily go against current majoritarianism.[113] Although a philosophy of restraint may be justifiable, it may not be consistent with advocacy of originalism per se. The majoritarian impact of originalism cannot be assumed. In addition, the "neutrality" of the decision to rely upon original intentions should not be overstated. Like the adoption of other interpretive methods, the selection of originalism requires a nonneutral defense. Moreover, to the extent that other approaches provide a relatively determinate method, then judges pursuing them can also claim to make rulings based on principles neutrally derived, whether drawn from the natural law or from democratic theory.[114]

Such justifications of originalism can hide the fact that the courts do have a special role within the constitutional system. In being partially separated from normal political pressures, in embodying the institutional norms of the legal profession, and in serving a specialized function, the judiciary is suited to interpreting the Constitution and enforcing its legal requirements on other governmental actors. This same limited perspective, however, prevents the courts from articulating the full meaning of the Constitution. If originalism provides a more balanced interpretive method than other theories do, it nonetheless cannot provide a complete picture of the operative Constitution since there remain gaps in the information its methodology can provide. A broader constitutional theory must be concerned with those gaps as well, or else our constitutional perspective will remain imbalanced by a focus on constitutional law. Similarly, a more nuanced constitutional theory should note that not all government action is equal. An exclusive emphasis on simple deference to current majorities conceals the manner and extent to which current political actors sometimes supplement the value choices of the founders.

Originalism has also been advocated on the grounds of a moral skepticism that denies the possibility that judges and legal scholars can discover or create an objective moral philosophy to support their judicial rulings. Without an objective and rationally defensible moral vision to lead the political community, judges must resort to the sheer force of their institutional position to impose their will. As a matter of personal preference, "There is no reason for the rest of us, who have our own moral visions, to be governed by the judge's moral predilections." If all political philosophies are grounded in subjective personal preference, then indeed judges cannot objectively derive constitutional principles from an external moral realm that does not exist. In following the historical intentions of the founders, the judge can appeal to an objective and external standard that can be the subject of reasoned argument and thus restore principled judgment to politics while isolating himself from lawmaking.[115]

The argument for originalism from moral skepticism must be rejected in its entirety. As noted in the case of Ely, skepticism by itself cannot create any presumption in favor of majoritarian politics. Reducing political values to personal preferences, such an originalism undermines the basis of constitutional theory more generally, including the authority of the Constitution and the putative moral value of republican government. Robert Bork's own skepticism is in fact reflected in his refrain that those who reject originalism may as well make their appeals to the Joint Chiefs of Staff as to the justices of the Supreme Court since the former are more likely to be able to enforce their subjective decisions.[116] For Bork, there is no alternative to force in politics. His pragmatic judgment that the community would reject non-originalist decisions leads to his assessment that greater force would be needed to enforce those judgments. The originalist judge is no more "right" than any other; he is just more likely to be obeyed. Such a (questionable) empirical judgment offers no support for the assertions of democratic values but in fact lends credence to the argument that judges should simply use the tools at their disposal to achieve most effectively their own policy preferences. Originalism would be reduced to a dispensable tactic by strategic judges.

More generally, such skepticism is antagonistic to the principles of constitutionalism itself. The Constitution is grounded on a belief in the value and possibility of rational discourse about political values. The effort to draft and ratify the Constitution was characterized as an experiment to determine "whether societies of men are really capable or not of establishing good government from reflection and choice, or whether they are forever destined to depend for their political constitutions on accident and force."[117] Reliance on the force of political majority to determine effective political values abandons that constitutional project and eliminates the possibility of establishing a rationale for judicial review of any kind. Rather than struggle to sustain the complicated procedures and limitations of constitutionalism, a consistent skeptic could only abandon it to its continuing practice or subvert it in the interest of his own personal preferences. Bork's dilemma is that there would be no principled reason for the skeptical observer to obey the Court, regardless of the interpretive method employed by the justices.

A final justification for originalism is that the practice of judicial review derives from the Court's claim to be enforcing the supreme law of the sovereign people, which in turn requires an originalist approach. Judges gain their authority by their institutional obligation to enforce the law established by the people against the representatives of the people, not by possessing special insight into the nature of the moral universe or by being situated so as to expand democratic values at the expense of existing representative institutions. In pursuing the will of the sovereign people, the judiciary does not act contrary to democratic values at all but upholds them by recognizing the distinction between the government and the populace that it claims to represent. In order to do so, however, judges must themselves be enforcing the demonstrable will of the people. The embodiment of that will, of course, is the written Constitution.[118]

In order to establish the persuasiveness of this justificatory argument, however, its advocates must be able to demonstrate that the enforcement of the Constitution as supreme law of the sovereign people requires an originalist interpretive method. In emphasizing that the enforcement of the Constitution as written requires the enforcement of the original intentions of those who wrote it, the originalists have largely begged the question of whether the two are in fact linked. The authority of originalism depends on the contention that the textual nature of the evidence of popular sovereignty points back to the origins of the Constitution (see chapters 4 and 5). Although such arguments may be persuasive if a theory of popular sovereignty is accepted, and the Constitution itself is accepted as authoritative law, such points cannot be left as purely axiomatic. Not only have these assumptions been challenged as supports of judicial review, but they have also been questioned in their specific character as supportive of originalist jurisprudence. Thus, originalists must go beyond asserting the identity of the text and the founders' intentions. And they must offer a plausible theory as to why we should accept the continuing practice of textual constitutionalism and not seek to replace it, either covertly or overtly, with some other governing system.

3. The Authority of Originalism and the Nature of the Written Constitution

Proponents of an originalist interpretive strategy have produced a number of loosely related justifications for their program (see chapter 2). These arguments range from pragmatic judgments as to how government policy is best formulated and implemented and how liberties can best be safeguarded from unscrupulous officials to more absolutist claims for the special authority and legitimacy of originalism in a constitutional system. At several points, these claims had to be scaled back, if not abandoned. Two of the strongest claims warrant further analysis, however. We shall focus first on the claim that an originalist interpretive approach is somehow required by the very fact that the United States has a written constitution. The rejection of originalism in favor of some other approach would represent a fundamental usurpation by the judiciary of powers not granted to it under the Constitution and a perversion of the constitutional enterprise.

Though obviously a strong claim, this justification has not been thoroughly developed by originalists. They seem content simply to assert the point without fully explaining its basis, let alone attempting to make a plausible case for it. Several possible implications of the textuality of the Constitution are developed here, leading ultimately to the conclusion that although some of them do indeed lend support to the originalist position, certain concessions must be made to non-originalist arguments. These accommodations help set the stage for a more complete picture of the continuing process of elaborating the federal Constitution. At the same time, this analysis forces a confrontation between originalism and its most radical critiques, which hold that the original intent of the Constitution's framers is not simply practically difficult to reconstruct but is in principle closed to us. In the process of this confrontation, it will be shown how the intent of the framers is inescapably involved in the act of interpretation, and what this relationship implies.

This justification for an originalism grounded in the nature of a written constitution is most often raised in a question-begging form. Thus, for example, originalists tend to use "original intent" and "written constitution" or the "text of the Constitution" as if they were interchangeable terms, gaining the rhetorical advantage of identifying their interpretive strategy with the foundation for judicial review but without facing the analytical difficulties.[1] Non-originalists are well aware of both the significance that originalists place on the written nature of the Constitution and the lack of analysis offered to make sense of that significance: "The questions about which methodology and which interpretations are proper cannot be determined by simply asserting that it is somehow 'definitional' or 'intrinsic' to a constitution that it be interpreted in a particular way. The only people likely to accept such an answer are those who already believe it."[2] Yet this is precisely the argument originalists have thus far produced. Having failed in their discursive duty, they have allowed the point to be passed over as nonsensical. Without an elaborated version of the originalist argument available to consider, non-originalists have moved on, carrying the argument onto different ground: contemporary moral standards. Larry Simon contends, "At a heuristic level, the basic criterion for evaluating the arguments supporting the various methodologies or interpretations is the extent to which those methodologies and interpretations promote a good and just society. . . . The evaluative standards must come from the external perspectives of political and moral theory."[3] Originalists must wrest the debate back onto their grounds, not because their methodology does not provide for a "good and just society" but because on their view the framework for such a society has already been provided for in the Constitution. If judicial review is to exist, it must do so through the authority of that document.

Despite doubts that some interpretive methodology may be "intrinsic" to a constitution, it is nonetheless true that form can elucidate content. Attention to the form of a text or practice may well contribute to an understanding of its content and may further dictate the approach most appropriate for grasping that content. As many scholars are concluding, some formal structures are better suited for conveying given substantive information than others are.[4] Moreover, rearranging the form of a text can be sufficient to alter substantially its meaning and the interpretive strategy appropriate to it.[5]

In the case of the Constitution, I suggest that it is of some significance that America's is a written one. While it now seems natural that a constitution be written, there is no necessary relationship between the two. Setting the constituting principles of the government into writing was one of the revolutionary aspects of the American founding. By shaping the Constitution into a written text, certain interpretive approaches were implicated.[6] A written constitution is appropriate for some purposes and rather ill suited for others. The practices that can reasonably revolve around such a document are limited, and the nature of the text authorizes certain approaches to it. Any theory of constitutional interpretation should be able to account for the major institutional fact of American constitutionalism, the presence of a written constitution.

In order to make this argument for the interrelationship between the legitimacy of judicial review and the particular interpretive method of originalism, I do not wish to hide the political choice that must be made in adopting that method. The argument that the constitutional text entails originalism is not the same as the naive assertion that the Constitution simply is an originalist one. It is true, however, that an argument from the form of the text takes the authority of the written constitution as axiomatic. Although such an assumption may be problematic from the perspective of broader political theory, it is not exceptional within the context of constitutional theory. As Cass Sunstein has observed, with only slight overstatement, "Everyone agrees that the Constitution is law. If the Constitution is law, then it stands above politics. All public officials . . . must obey."[7] Given this starting point, a jurisprudence of original intent follows. Whether we as a nation should accept this starting point—that is, whether we should continue to be governed by a written constitution—is another question.

Before extrapolating several possible implications of the written nature of the Constitution, I should also make clear that this analysis does not hinge upon the intentions of the founders in creating a written constitution. Bootstrapping ourselves into originalism by turning to the founders to authorize such a methodology has been justly criticized. The "interpretive intention" of the founders, or the founders' ideas on theories of interpretation as opposed to substantive constitutional meaning, cannot itself either require or dismiss originalism as an interpretive strategy but can only provide arguments about our present constitutional enterprise.[8] Originalism is a strategy for interpreting the constitutional text, a strategy that recommends recurring to the framers in order to define its meaning. The justification for originalism is a separate step requiring a different form of argumentation. To this extent, choosing an originalist interpretive strategy is not a "neutral" or nonpolitical activity. The choice of an interpretive method does indeed require justification external to the practice itself. In developing possible implications of a written constitution, we would be well advised to go back to the founders, not in search of authorities but in search of other people who have thought about this particular issue. Unlike us, the founders were immediately faced with the question of whether or not to have a written constitution and thus may be expected to have considered the matter in depth. Thus, if we recur to the founders for arguments on this issue, we must bear in mind that those arguments have weight because of their content, not their source.[9] The authority gleaned from the nature of a written text derives from the inherent judicial duty of interpreting law, not from the specific commands of the Constitution as law. The nature of that duty is context-dependent, however, and my goal is to clarify the nature of the constitutional system within which the American judiciary operates.[10]

Originalism and the Written Constitution

The founders "not only took it for granted that they should have a written basis for their government, but that this instrument should be explicitly denominated as their fundamental law and should not be altered save by a very special process."[11] This widespread assumption has been incorporated into the modern scholarly literature, such that relatively little has been made explicit about why this should be the case and what it really means. In constructing an account of the significance and nature of a written constitution, it is necessary to draw freely from a number of sources, both modern and historical, in an attempt to piece together and make explicit what has only been suggested in the debates. The result is that three broad and interrelated arguments can be reconstructed that support the claim that a written constitution requires an originalist interpretation. The first of these arguments draws upon the revolutionary break from Great Britain and the perceived need to fix the inherited fundamental principles of government in a clear and permanent text. The second contends that a stable textual reference is necessary in order to make the Constitution law in the sense of being judicially enforceable. The third argument draws more generally from the nature of writing and law, claiming that all writing and especially legal writing carries the intent of the author.

THE TEXT AS FIXED PRINCIPLE

The first argument can be made most clearly by considering the context within which written constitutions were drafted, notably in contrast to the British constitutional system. Being unwritten, the British constitution consisted of a tradition of practice, general understandings, and occasional declarations. Theoretically, Parliament was constrained by the need for a connection with these ancient customs, but it was also engaged in a constant creation of custom since every political and legal act became a part of the tradition of practice. The English constitution, though a guiding thread connecting and informing the historical stream of legal acts, could not be distinguished from the acts of government. The power of the British legislature increasingly came to be seen as absolute, by both itself and its observers, until no checks on its authority could be distinguished in the latter half of the eighteenth century. The British philosopher William Paley could write, "The con-

stitution is one principle division, head, section, or title of the code of pub-
lick laws. . . . Therefore the terms *constitutional* and *unconstitutional,* mean
legal and *illegal.*"[12] No distinction between the actual behavior of government
and the higher power that authorized government was meaningful.[13]

Nonetheless, the American patriots appealed to the principles that they
understood to stand behind government action. On the political level, appeal
to the ancient constitution was still acceptable, and claims to the moral
authority of those customs could be persuasive. Against the increasingly obvious reality of absolute parliamentary power, Americans reasserted the political principles of the prior century, which held that Parliament may be
absolute but it could not be arbitrary.[14] If its deviations from accepted principles could be adequately demonstrated, it was believed, Parliament and the
British courts would act accordingly and correct their errors. Failure to do so
would be proof of Parliament's usurpation of the rights of all Englishmen and
justification for resistance.

The difficulty for both sides in this debate was that the same ambiguity
that allowed the British government to justify its actions also allowed the
American patriots to ground their claims in recognized principles. Custom
and practice changed over time, adapting to circumstances; yet it was all part
of a single tradition, which itself was supposed to be unchanging, existing
from "time immemorial" and thus having the authority of the ages.[15] The
ambiguity of the very concept of custom carries over into an ambiguity in
practice, for the constant attempt to update custom while denying any change
requires substantial flexibility in the interpretation and editing of earlier custom. In order to make such an ideal workable, the system relies not only on
practice but on reasoning by analogy, including reference to historical and
current events whether from within or without the British government, opening the constitution to all of world history and present practice.[16]

Such a mode of political and legal reasoning is, of course, rife with uncertainty, so much so that one could question the assumption that Parliament was
restrained at all under such a system. By the end of the Revolution, the belief
that principles could not be fixed under an unwritten constitution was com-
monplace.[17] A written text was necessary to eliminate ambiguity and the possibility of deceit, manipulation, and passionate lapses in fidelity. The example
of the Magna Carta, which Samuel Adams noted was "very explicit," demonstrated that government must be limited by "certain terms of agreement,"
freeing the people from "an indefinite dependence upon an undetermined
power," for "vague and uncertain laws, and more especially constitutions, are
the very instruments of slavery."[18] As the strains of not having a written constitution became evident, Benjamin Franklin wrote to a British correspondent,

"I wish most sincerely with you that a Constitution was formed and settled for America, that we might know what we are and what we have, what our Rights and what our Duties, in the Judgment of this Country as well as in our own." Until such a fixed and clear instrument was designed, "Misunderstandings" on all sides were inevitable.[19]

The Americans' own experience with colonial charters indicated a mechanism for eradicating the ambiguity and the instability of the larger British system.[20] The example of the contract recommended itself, as the Americans had long relied on their own colonial charters as equivalents to written constitutions.[21] Once reduced to writing, constitutional terms and guarantees seemed to demand universal recognition, replacing the need for arguments employing complex analogies and referring to an undefined set of multiplying and changing principles. Instead of the interminable equivocation characteristic of British governors, a written constitution appeared to force all sides to admit to, confirm, and guarantee a known set of principles. The constitutional text was to provide clear evidence of promises exchanged and accepted, a contract following the Whig-interpreted tradition of the colonial charters in restraining the actions of the governors and upon which the citizenry could place reliance.[22] Although the British constitution and common law may have in part provided the founders with "the *idea* of limited government . . . in the American constitutional tradition, what *replaced* the common law was a new political technique, the written constitution."[23]

Unlike the ambiguity and uncertainty of both the English common law tradition and the chaos of the American Revolution and Confederation, a written constitution promised to create precision, balancing and reconciling conflicting traditions and interests and constraining future debate within a limited framework.[24] As Justice William Paterson wrote, "It is difficult to say, what the constitution of England is; because, not being reduced to written certainty and precision, it lies entirely at the mercy of parliament: it bends to every governmental exigency; it varies and is blown about by every breeze of legislative humor or political caprice." In contrast to England, where "there is no written constitution," and therefore "nothing visible, nothing real, nothing certain," America "has its constitution reduced to written exactitude and precision."[25] The written nature of the Constitution, instituted in order to reduce uncertainty, should not change with the passage of time, as the common law necessarily does. Thus, the passions of the moment would not change the fundamental law.

> Temporary delusions, prejudices, excitements, and objects have irresistible influence in mere questions of policy. And the policy of one age may ill suit the wishes or the policy of another. The constitution is not subject to such fluctuations. It is

to have a fixed, uniform, permanent construction. It should be, so far at least as human infirmity will allow, not dependent upon the passions or parties of particular times, but the same yesterday, to-day, and for ever.[26]

Fixing constitutional principles in a written text against the transient shifts in the public mood or social condition becomes tantamount to an originalist jurisprudence. As storms of popular passion sweep across the political landscape, it is to be expected that rapid and extreme shifts in public attitudes will guide political action. Further, such shifts may lead political actors some distance from the founding principles of the republic, as short-term considerations temporarily obscure principles that would otherwise be revered and followed. In order to prevent government actions, which may have significant and lasting consequences, from being taken in pursuit of momentary interests, a written constitution, properly construed, serves as a reminder and a barrier, constraining politics within a relatively narrow range of deliberately chosen rights, powers, and institutions. The demanding and solemn process of amending the written Constitution ensures that current moods are relatively stable and widespread, or so advocates of a written constitution hoped.[27]

In contrast, the unwritten constitution, exemplified by the British, necessarily called forth an interpretive strategy combining moral reasoning, historical analogy, and appeals to contemporary practice and judgment, intertwining momentary "policy" with constitutional principle.[28] The abandonment of this tradition with the adoption of a written text, for better or worse, demanded the discarding of such an interpretive methodology. The choice of interpretive methodology was bound up with the choice of constitutional form. The Court must "*declare the law as written*," for the "meaning of the constitution is fixed when it is adopted," and the judge must offer no interpretation for "a written constitution not warranted by the intention of the founders."[29] If American constitutional experience has not borne out the hopes that the document would ensure stability against political tides and moral speculation, it nonetheless offers a corrective.[30] As numerous commentators have indicated, the value of the constitutional form depended upon the appropriate action by constitutional interpreters. Although the form alone cannot control the interpretation, it does suggest its path and constitutes an impediment to those who wish to return to the British custom.

THE TEXT AS LAW

The second line of argument interpreting the nature of a written text so as to require originalism focuses on the Constitution's status as fundamental law. The British constitution, though unwritten, was to serve as the fundamental law of Britain but did so largely in a political, rather than a judicial, sense. In order to realize the fundamental law as a judicially enforceable instrument to restrain the legislature, the unwritten principles behind government had to be fixed in writing. As a fixed and written text, the supreme law of the Constitution can be self-consciously considered and properly ratified and can have the specificity to provide judicial instruction.

The first contention needed to build this argument is that only a fixed text can provide judicial instruction and therefore be judicially enforceable against legislative encroachment.[31] The judicial requirement of a fixed text not only authorizes judicial review but also limits it within the context of determinate meaning. The purposeful exploitation or construction of textual indeterminacy in order to foster greater judicial activism, as advocated by such commentators as Ronald Dworkin and Michael Perry, undercuts the very base on which judicial review rests.[32] At the time of the Revolution Americans discovered that the traditional understandings of the British constitution that they had come to rely upon had changed. By the eighteenth century, the increasing separation of powers had revoked from the British courts the powers of review that judges such as Sir Edward Coke had once successfully claimed.[33] Americans, used to their written colonial charters and a regular process of review of legislation, reasserted a belief that judges should be able to take cognizance of the natural and long-respected rights of British citizens.[34] Since an independent judiciary requires law to act, then in order to defend constitutional rights in the future they had to be embodied in a legal, written document. The value of a written constitution was evident through the example of the negative case of Britain.[35]

A written rule is relatively determinate. It is not "an imaginary thing," as was the British constitution, "about which ten thousand opinions may be formed." The written law is available for all to see, and thus, James Iredell argued in 1787, "The judges cannot willfully blind themselves" to it but "must take notice of it."[36] Alexander Hamilton relied on similar reasoning in contending that where meaning is uncertain and subject to continued dispute, the judiciary cannot reasonably act, for a court's only claim to authority is the force of its reason and the clear accuracy of its decision. If the court were "to have neither FORCE nor WILL but merely judgment," the judges must appear to have no will of their own but must merely make explicit what is already known.[37] This was also Chief Justice John Marshall's ploy in asserting the power of judicial review as he asked, employing the same metaphor as Iredell, whether the "courts must close their eyes on the constitution, and see only the law."[38] Clearly Marshall is being somewhat disingenuous in his suggestion that the language of the Constitution is so clear that judges need merely open their eyes to it and see what is "expressly forbidden," or else close their eyes and "disregard the constitution." Nonetheless, given the context, to which Marshall calls attention with repeated emphasis on the writtenness of the American constitution, the Court was also expressing an important truth.[39] In the United States, the Constitution is as clear and available as statutory law, for both are equally defined in single documents. In sharp contrast to the British case in which a statute stands clear against a fuzzy constitutional background, in America all can easily lay their eyes on the written Constitution, and thus it requires willful blindness either to circumvent its terms or avoid its obligations. If the application of the fundamental law is not exactly mechanical, the premises are at least indisputably common to all.[40] As long as the fundamental law is fixed, "Congress and the president must follow the Court because the same syllogism which drives the Court's action drives everyone else's."[41]

The judiciary is capable of taking an active role in articulating the Constitution, if provided a fixed text. As Virginia's Judge St. George Tucker pointed out, in Britain "the judiciary, having no *written constitution* to refer to, were obliged to *receive* whatever *exposition* of it the legislature may think proper to make."[42] This constraint on the judiciary holds true even if the constitution is thought to be an objective, if ideal, entity; the charge of subjectivism is not the only problem the judiciary faces. In order to activate the courts, constitutional principles must be "produced in written form," so that they "can be ascertained from the living letter, not from obscure reasoning or deduction only."[43] It was in this sense, as a fixed and relatively clear text, that the Constitution can refer to itself as "Law of the Land," and presumably be judicially recognizable as are other laws.[44]

The second aspect of accepting a written constitution as law is that only a fixed text can be adequately ratified, that is, legislated into fundamental law.[45] In order to create law, the legislating body must be able to demonstrate its will and have an instrument that its members can examine and to which they can eventually give their assent.[46] The public display of an authoritative text is essential to the lawmaking process, though not necessarily to the governing process.[47] By drafting a written constitution, the framers could simultaneously fix its terms and give it the authority of ratification. The process of ratification, the appeal to the sovereign people in convention, makes sense only in the context of a written document. Having gathered the representatives of the people, their will could be expressed and rendered lasting beyond the convention itself through the creation of written instruments.[48] "The promulgation that takes place now extends to future time by reason of the durability of written characters, by which means it is continually promulgated."[49]

In the case of the Constitution, the legislating bodies are the ratification conventions of the people, though other forms can be imagined. Having received a written document from the drafters in Philadelphia, these conventions were able to examine a real document and legislate that instrument into the supreme law.[50] The agency of convention was necessary to elevate the Constitution to the status of law; yet such an agency could not have acted except through a written constitution.[51] A written text not only makes it possible for the lawmaker to make his will known but also for the people to identify the lawmaker. Unlike custom, which is ubiquitous, and without a particular, let alone an authoritative, author, law is essentially connected to its author, embodying the will of an institution that is clothed with the recognized authority to govern the community.[52]

The third part of the argument for the text as law derives from the two premises thus established and posits that the written Constitution, ratified by the sovereign people in convention, is the fundamental law, authorizing and limiting governmental action and thereby establishing judicial review of legislative behavior. The people can constrain their governmental agents only by fixing their will in an unchanging text. Under a written constitution, the actions of the legislature are derivative of the sovereign will and therefore are void if they violate the authoritative expression of that will. As the Constitution is legislated by the most authoritative body within the political system, all other legislation is inferior to that law and void if contradictory.[53] Moreover, the very establishment of textual limits to government action implicates the judiciary in interpreting that document and enforcing those limits.[54]

The constitutional constraint on the people's agents can emerge from the text as intended, however, only if the text has the fixed meaning it is uniquely capable of carrying. "The concept of a written constitution is that it defines the authority of government and its limits, that government is the creature of the constitution and cannot do what it does not authorize and must not do what it forbids. *A priori,* such a constitution could have only a fixed and unchanging meaning, if it were to fulfill its function."[55] The institutions of government have no independent authority or legitimate existence but are the mere creatures of the words of the Constitution. These government bodies are not simply created by the document but are established as servants to that document, executing the will of the people contained therein.[56]

An immediate objection arises to this argument as expressed in the preceding quote, for surely the "government" can be forbidden from doing what the "written constitution" prohibits without the latter having unchanging meaning. Indeed, we can easily imagine judges constraining government officials in accord with our best contemporary moral principles or some other changing standard. But the judiciary is just as much a creature of the Constitution as any other governmental office. Thus, it would be itself undermining constitutional constraints even as it stepped outside the text's fixed meaning to constrain others. It would not be the Constitution that would be constraining, but the courts operating outside its bounds. Yet it was the grounding of the judiciary in the same source, and system of constraints, as the institutions of government action that legitimated judicial review.[57] If the legislative and executive branches cannot expand their powers by altering the meaning of the constitutional text, neither can the judiciary expand, or contract, its own or the other branches' power through interpretation. It is the fixity of the written Constitution that empowers the judiciary to determine that a statutory law may be repugnant to it.[58]

The separation of powers that excludes the judiciary from the legislative sphere authorizes judges only to apply the will of the legislature to particular circumstances. In interpreting the written law, the judiciary may not strike out on its own and articulate new principles[59] but must act in good faith to carry out the will of those who created the law, whether for good or ill. Emerging from the "real" social compact of the constitutional conventions and the revolutionary break from the common law of Britain, the Constitution represents the compromises that the people made in contracting with one another to form a new nation, just as statutory law represents the compromises of conflicting interests. Although the common law could change to embrace new values and evolve to improve tradition, the written law is unchanging until replaced, marked by sharp breaks rather than the smooth paradox of the unchanging evolution of common law.[60]

Of course, the separation of powers is not complete. The continuing development of the common law in the United States indicates the legislative role of the courts. Nonetheless, such activity is now clearly subordinate to legislative action, as statutory law supersedes the common law. The claim here is not about the capacity of the courts to elaborate the common law but about their role in interpreting the written law received from a legislature, in this case the fundamental law received from popular convention. In this system, the judiciary can have little legitimate role in constructing the Constitution, unlike the British case in which the legislative and judicial roles are not so distinct and the constitution is created by the same entities that operate under it. The British practice of having one house of Parliament sit as the court of final appeal, or the present Canadian override provision to allow the legislature to set aside some judicial interpretations of the constitution, provided some leeway not only for judge-made law, but also for judicial participation in the formulation of the fundamental law. The American rejection of this system signals both a greater separation of powers and a greater distinction between law and constitution. Moreover, the Realist demystification of the common law claim to be simply the discovery and elaboration of an implicit law indicates that even the common law cannot easily survive in such a critical environment. In a system of separated powers, adjudicators require a plausible deniability relative to any legislative function.[61] Proposals such as Dworkin's for judges to take on an explicitly creative role in interpreting the constitutional language in its "best light" run afoul of this requirement. This difficulty calls into question whether Dworkin's Herculean judge could politically sustain his interpretive principles, if he were to make explicit that his "best light" readings were an exercise in judicial lawmaking in accord with the judge's own aesthetic sensibilities.[62] The inability of the more representative branches to overrule judicial legislation sets a sharp limit on the extent to which common law practice can be imported into the American constitutional context.[63]

The choice of avoiding the ambiguity of the uncertain tradition of the British constitution by drafting a single constitutional text balances the imperfections inherent in the circumstances against the danger of corruption and usurpation. To give the words of the Constitution new meanings over time would deny both the value and risk of a system of written constitutions. The founders themselves were well aware that the attempt to frame constitutional principles in writing was fraught with difficulties, not only in the task of focusing rational deliberation in order to gain assent for the document but also in limiting the imperfections certain to appear within any such text. Hamilton began the *Federalist* expressing doubts on whether men were capable of "establishing good government from reflection and choice," and Madison admitted that any constitutional convention would be fallible and produce an imperfect document.[64] The risk of error is intrinsic to written constitutions, and they must be borne along with the evident value of fixing fundamental principles in writing.

Despite the difficulties contained in the text as understood by the ratifiers, Madison recognized that "in that sense alone it is the legitimate Constitution." Though the "meaning of the words composing it" may change with time, the meaning of the text of a law, especially the supreme law that establishes all government, cannot change.[65] The Constitution is composed of the underlying conceptions to which the words refer, not the textual language itself. At this point, the founders were relying on a Lockean conception of language in which words express stable ideas, which are then related to an external reality. The meaning of the words used could not be separated from the ideas that they represented, and thus they were stable over time.[66] Careful attention to textual detail would help clarify the concepts being expressed but could not

alter the fact that it was a prior and fixed idea that was contained in the textual language.[67] Consequently, it was not merely a set of words but a set of distinct ideas that was ratified by the people. The new meanings that words may
acquire over time could not have been foreseen and intended by anyone, and
the meaning they may appear to give the law is not a meaning that has been
authorized by any legitimate body. Judicial interpretation must "by fair reason reach the mind of the Constitution of the United States."[68] The text is not
simply a list of words but is the embodied will of the people. If the Constitution is to be the law that its text and history indicate that it is, then it must be
construed in the manner of law, according to original intent.

THE TEXT AS SYMBOL OF INTENT

The final argument for the claim that a written constitution requires an
originalist interpretation is that writing, especially legal writing, is a means of
transmitting intent. Thus "interpretation" of writing means conveying that
intent. Writing, as a subset of language, is a means for communicating with
others. Communication requires that both writer and reader share certain
characteristics in common, but communication assumes both commonality
and intentionality by those attempting to communicate. Those who attempt
communication are trying to convey a particular message; the content of the
message as well as the process is important. These basic points are particularly true of legal writing, which is concerned not merely with action but with
particular action.

Wittgenstein's analysis of the impossibility of a private language elucidates,
among other things, the fact that language is essentially communicative. The
very idea of a language that attempts to avoid communication, that is, a private language that has no known or stable intersubjective referent, is nonsensical.[69] If language is to communicate a meaning, that meaning must not
only be available to others but must also be available to others by means of
the language used.[70] Such meaning is available to others not because of some
natural relationship between objects and words but because the meaning of
words is defined through their intersubjective use. Language is not private,
because meanings are not private. The goal of interpreting meaning is not to
penetrate into some alien mind, for a shared language is indicative of the fact
that our separate minds are not alien to each other. Noting this common
ground of language also brings out the fact that meaning is not something
that exists behind language. To search for intent is not an attempt to avoid
language in search of something hidden by it. Rather, meaning, or intention,
is embedded in the language itself, is realized with the utterance.[71]

It can be certain that the founders did intend to convey meaning in writing the Constitution. The written document was intended to reduce uncertainty and create stability, something tangible to which the judiciary could refer in recalling the legislature to basic principles. Legal writing is purposeful not only in that it intends to achieve certain results, but also in that it will achieve some kind of result. Moreover, the communication is directed to an interested political community. Thus the writer has strong incentives to try to convey intent in a way that can be understood. The Constitution had to be drafted so as to be comprehensible to the public that must give effect and authority to it. In ratifying the document, the people appropriated it, giving its text the meaning that was publicly understood.

All writing and communication occurs within a context, which may help clarify the meaning of the words used in the text. In addition to such linguistic conventions as vocabulary and grammar, legal writing in particular occurs in a context of problem solving, whether those problems are immediate or expected. Both contexts provide information for interpreting a legal document.[72] No reader is likely to be in perfect harmony with the relevant contexts, but perfect commonality between the writer and reader is unnecessary for communication.[73] As contexts and conventions change, greater effort may be necessary to recover the original contexts in order fully to discover the intended meaning, but meaning ultimately remains as long as the text qua text survives. "If, in the course of time, as is often the case with language, the meaning of words or terms is changed, the meaning of the constitution is not therefore changed."[74]

The particular interpretive activity of the judiciary further limits the indeterminacy of language. Judicial interpretation operates through individual cases, which do not require settling all possible meanings, reference to all available terms, or the resolution of all uncertainty, but which require only a fairly limited degree of determinacy. The courts are not asked to provide a general rendering of the text as a whole, as a historian might offer of a historical epoch or a critic of an entire novel. Rather, the court can be content to develop the text piecemeal and to the degree necessary to settle the particular case before it. Further, in the context of constitutional interpretation, settling a particular case primarily involves determining whether a given state action is constitutionally acceptable. Instead of attempting to fill out a positive conception of the text, again as is characteristically the case in other interpretive activities, judges must only answer a negative question of whether a given action is disallowed. The court may approach the question at issue from the outside, as it were, determining what is excluded by given constitutional language rather than what is included, often the more difficult and less conclusive task.

The court is interested in delimiting a sphere of acceptable governmental action and can accept a degree of indeterminacy within that sphere, for it is within that sphere that the legislature acts to construct meaning.[75] The court need not, and perhaps should not, pursue the remaining indeterminacies that may exist in any language, a pursuit that is unnecessary and that could render the foundations of government uncertain.[76] This is not to deny that there remain indeterminacies that judges must necessarily face. There will always be hard cases. Nonetheless, constitutional interpretation generally and originalist interpretation specifically should not be held to an excessive standard of certainty.[77] The existence of some indeterminacy does not justify an assumption of radical indeterminacy or the abandonment of the search for intent. Judicial judgment may be exercised without implying that the interpreter is free from all constraints, or even free from a rather narrow conception of the intent of the author.[78]

Thus, the originalist claim that the nature of a written constitution requires an originalist interpretive stance need not be accepted as an unjustifiable first principle. Moreover, the arguments that support this understanding of the legal text readily connect with many of the traditional, external justifications for originalism, such as its support for the rule of law and the division of powers in a liberal constitutional system. The adoption of a written constitution can be understood as establishing a fixed rule that does not change over time except through written amendment and a fundamental law capable of providing judicial instruction. Originalists can also stand on theoretical arguments that hold that all texts, and especially legal texts, carry a knowable, authoritative meaning corresponding to the original intent of the writer. Unlike other approaches, an originalist interpretive method accounts for significant features of our particular constitutional tradition: the existence of a written constitution and a judiciary committed to interpreting that text. Only an originalist judiciary is consistent with the constitutional project that we claim to be pursuing.

The Non-originalist Text

The originalist approach is not the only possible conception of the significance of a written text. In part the early originalist assertion on this point was not universally accepted because alternative conceptions could be imagined, though few critics actually laid out such an alternative. I shall sketch out these alternatives, suggesting the degree to which they require accommodation by originalist theory. In addition to the originalist understanding, the nature of the constitutional text can be conceived of as a fixed referent for political debate, a promissory note, or as essentially indeterminate. Understanding these alternatives will allow us to gain a better perspective on the link between the written constitution and an originalist interpretive method.

THE TEXT AS POLITICAL REFERENT

The U.S. Constitution is not simply a supreme legal guidebook addressed to judges. The document is essentially political, arising from political discourses and establishing the framework for future political action. Like the British constitution before it, the U.S. Constitution defines the moral boundaries within which political debate should take place. Claims of unconstitutionality are powerful trump cards in policy discussions, and revolutionary politics modifying traditional constitutional conceptions make up some of the most significant moments in American political history. Thus, political actors cannot be expected to refrain from using the constitutional text for their own momentary purposes, and they do not. If the document is removed from the rarefied environment of the Supreme Court and its coterie of informal advisers and placed within the more public and rhetorically charged arena of electoral politics, then the significance of a written constitution to its interpretation may well be changed to suit its new environment. The Constitution not only emerges from the people but also appeals directly to them. The citizenry necessarily formulate their own interpretations of the document and apply those understandings in their own political activities.

America's colonial experience not only taught it that the judiciary could not be trusted to act on an uncertain text but also that the persistent ambiguity of the legitimating traditions for political action in Britain could ensnare any political protest. The colonial charters provided tangible evidence of American rights under the British regime, but not in order to invoke judicial review. Instead, as Madison reminded Jefferson, these charters served most spectacularly "as a standard for trying the validity of public acts, and a signal for rousing & uniting the superior force of the community."[79] The superior force here is the majority of the political community, and a written constitution serves as the platform for its mobilization. In an imperial monarchy, such mobilization took the form of revolution, but in a republic it could take a more moderate form of changing the legislature.

This understanding of the constitutional text does not stress any reference to the original intent of the framers or recourse to the judges whom the originalists charge with discovering and applying that intent. As a political referent, the primary value of the written Constitution is not that its terms are fixed for judicial inquiry but that they are universally known, readily available to the average citizen. The document itself is short, its terms relatively clear and understandable to a literate person. Constitutional principles are contained within a single text, not spread throughout a vast and amorphous corpus of legal precedents.[80] The U.S. Constitution does not resort to a distinct elite language and need not be the exclusive possession of a caste of legal professionals. Every citizen has the authority and the right to find the meaning of the public text.[81] In a very protestant sense, the written Constitution can serve as "the political bible of the State. Scarcely a family is without it."[82] Franklin Roosevelt was addressing the people when he urged that "like the Bible," the Constitution "should be read again and again."[83] The Constitution is not only a fundamental source of guidance but also one that can speak directly to the people, unmitigated by complex interpretations. Having been put into writing, the Constitution became essentially public, being available for popular discussion and thus subject to popular definition.[84]

Having committed constitutional principles to writing, the founders have provided a fixed referent for future political debate. These principles always stand above normal politics, calling political actors back to first principles. When public officials themselves depart from the constitutional guides, the standards laid out in a written constitution provide the basis for mobilizing opposition. In reassuring Madison of the efficacy of a bill of rights in the federal Constitution, Jefferson emphasized the states' role as sentinels against centralized encroachment against individual liberty. "The jealousy of the subordinate governments is a precious reliance. But observe that those governments are only agents. They must have principles furnished them whereon to found their opposition. The declaration of rights will be the text whereby they will try all the acts of the federal government."[85] The text provided the federal government with a similar ability to check the states from violating their constitutional promises.[86] This argument is similar to the one previously analyzed that regards the text as fundamental law authorizing judicial action, but the two arguments look to different constraints on government and, as a result, different interpretive strategies. Unlike the argument from fundamental law, which reacted to the failure of judicial review in England, Jefferson is here looking back on the example of his own declaration of American independence and its success as a rallying point for the Revolution. By taking the Constitution as a banner around which to rally political opposition, Jefferson removes the document from the realm of law as such and into the realm of political symbols.[87] Jefferson does not direct Madison to the legalistic judiciary but addresses his argument to the political actors in the constitutional system, the state and federal governments. They can pick up a statement of principles and call the people to their defense. Madison was doubtful as to whether there could be some "other force in the community" to which to appeal besides the popular majority that passed the questionable law in the first place. He nonetheless adopted Jefferson's reasoning to the degree to which evils may spring from the "usurped acts of the Government," when "a bill of rights will be a good ground for an appeal to the sense of the community."[88] Being available to the electorate itself, the written Constitution establishes a direct connection with the individual citizen and thus can provide a source of political authority and power within the community but independent of the government.

The constitutional text acts as a basic political referent long before the extreme case of opposition massing against tyrannical acts, however. Having reduced political principles to writing, the founders provided relatively clear guidelines for normal political practice. Since the written Constitution need not be delegated to a specialized organ, such as the Supreme Court, for its articulation and promulgation, its terms enter into political argument from the very beginning. The constitutional document is placed in the hands of all political contenders. Not only did Thomas Paine marvel at the fact that every citizen had a copy of the Constitution but also that "every member of the Government had a copy; and nothing was more common when any debate arose on the principle of a bill, or an extent of any species of authority, than for the members to take the printed Constitution out of their pocket, and read the chapter with which such matter in debate was connected."[89]

The letters of the document became living through their constant use in normal political discourse, in which the text could be read directly to provide guiding principles, preventing the passage of unconstitutional legislation at the first instance.[90] In time, the text of the constitutional document ceases to be separate from the community, standing above its actors as a kind of guardian, but becomes "incorporated with the national sentiment," forming the national political culture and the ideological framework within which politics is conceived.[91] In a system of government that strives to enact the will of the people, a written constitution can be used to shape the long-term "public opinion," as its principles become "familiar to the mass of the people."[92] Becoming so ingrained in the political community, however, the text also loses its particular meaning. It can be appropriated for divergent and alien purposes, for the functioning of a political symbol rests on its utility in gaining support and inspiring action, not on its accuracy to historical detail. As the text is carried forth by many hands and into many debates, competence and inclination to elucidate original intentions decline.[93] The Constitution ceases to be a means of communicating between the founders and the government and becomes a means by which the current citizenry communicate among themselves.

Once individual citizens are allowed an unmediated relation to the foundational document, a possibility that exists only by virtue of there being an actual document, the prevalence of an originalist interpretation cannot be guaranteed. In reading the Constitution "again and again," the citizenry may indeed be reminded of the first principles of the republic, but not as an originalist judge may formulate them. Moreover, the principles of the text are only the leaping-off point for public discourse. Where judges are concerned with correcting the particular unconstitutional abuse represented in the case before them, the people may well be sparked by a specific incident to expand and develop their claims to address broader institutional and principled concerns. Though the text may serve to rally the people to action, the people, once aroused, may not feel constrained by the intentions of the text.

THE TEXT AS PROMISSORY NOTE

Admitting the text into political debate subjects it to interpretive attempts that are not necessarily in keeping with strong originalist constructions. Nonetheless, the underlying assumption of the prior argument is that the text is useful in recalling wayward public officials or passionate majorities back to original principles. The argument that the text is a promissory note makes no such presumption, for the polity is explicitly not called back but is constantly challenged by the text to meet new principles. Aspirationalist goals need not be contrary to original intent, for the founders may have embedded within the text their own aspirations that they relied on future generations to achieve; but these new principles need not have been held by the founders.[94] The distinctive aspect of this position is that it is enough for the current political community to be able to locate its own aspirations in the symbol of a constitutional document.

The written Constitution is not to be understood merely as a fundamental law structuring and limiting political powers but also as the sacred text of a community of moral and rational individuals.[95] Such a sacred text is concerned with ideals as well as structures. The Preamble's claim to be forming a "more perfect union" should be taken as an invitation for national moral improvement, setting the country on a path to earthly perfection, which would ensure advancement toward such a state if not its actual attainment.[96] If the Constitution is to be a "text worth reading," it must be "the lodestar of our aspirations." To that end it is felicitously provided with "majestic generalities and ennobling pronouncements" that are "both luminous and obscure," freeing readers from any "crystalline" interpretation and inviting them to find within its terms their own "faith in progress." The founding document, in this reading, "embodies the aspiration to social justice, brotherhood, and human dignity" and "solemnly committed" the nation to realizing these goals. Previous generations of Americans were incapable of fully realizing these aspirations in fact, but the "pretension" to these values remains until a more capable community can emerge to execute them into reality.[97]

The aspirational quality of the text can also be derived from sources other than the specific provisions of the U.S. Constitution. The more significant basis for this understanding emerges from a consideration of the nature of a written constitution generally, laying aside any consideration of a document's particular terms. First, the process of writing down principles and subsequently creating material practices as a result of that idealistic enterprise uncovers meanings and aspirations that were previously hidden in the imagined state.[98] The text and the institutions it creates acquire an existence independent of the original principles from which they emerged and thus confront the community with a system of meaningful practices that are not entirely familiar and yet are recognizably dependent creations. In realizing itself in practice the constitutional text "deconstructs" itself, laying bare its latent meaning as it unfolds over time and space. Moreover, the people "deconstruct themselves in the construction of the text," for the principles and practices that were previously unarticulated have to be made formal and relatively clear, leading to greater self-understanding and internal debate.[99]

The British, under an unwritten constitution, were capable of leaving much of their heritage and ideological tradition unquestioned and undeveloped. A written constitution, on the other hand, requires a conscious grappling with previously assumed fundamentals. Madison feared exactly this struggle and thus preferred to leave a federal bill of rights unwritten and the nation's liberal principles unstated, "because there is reason to fear that a positive declaration of some of the most essential rights could not be obtained in the requisite latitude. . . . The rights of conscience in particular, if submitted to public definition would be narrowed much more than they are likely ever to be by an assumed power."[100] Once written, however, the constitutional text becomes a "promise," a promise by the people to their represented, and necessarily ideal, "collective character." Having committed itself to writing, the nation begins a quest to overcome itself, to become the perfect state represented in the text.[101] The foundational text brings forth a new nation and thus serves a "transformative purpose." The Constitution necessarily constitutes a political community, destroying the preexisting society and making a new one, establishing new principles that the old community failed to recognize.[102] The public recognition of these new principles not only remakes the governmental structure but also transforms the people of the nation. Once the vestiges of the old society are destroyed, this generation of citizenry, fully accustomed to the new paradigm, is fundamentally different from the previous generation. It therefore understands the aspirations of the text somewhat differently and is prepared to take a further step to making the nation into "a shining city upon the hill."[103]

The second major argument for understanding the text as a promissory note is that the Constitution can be the supreme law of the political community only if the people constantly reaffirm it. "Because the Constitution's ways must constitute our best conception of the good society for us to make sense of the Constitution as supreme law, a practice of continuing reaffirmation is essential to a constitutional state of affairs."[104] If the Constitution is to act as supreme law, requiring the deference of all political actors to its privileged commitments, then its status must be rationally justified. The legalistic process of drafting and popular ratification is insufficient to provide such authority, however, for "we did not adopt the Constitution, and those who did are dead and gone." Since the present generation of Americans did not give explicit consent to the document, the Constitution has "questionable authority" and can be taken as law only through "a history of continuing assent or acquiescence."[105] Moreover, an actual process of gathering the explicit consent of every individual living under the document is simply impossible. Thus the text must gain the consent of the people by another method. For example, by means of a process of imaginary discourse individuals can conceptualize a vision of a just society, which would then carry normative weight and demand a moral individual's obedience to this ideal.[106] A society that does not meet this ideal, or that at least is not working toward it, is morally suspect and has little claim on its citizenry. Therefore, if the Constitution is to be fundamental law, demanding fidelity to its text and principles, it must conform to the individual's understanding of a good society, even if this requires destabilizing those textual principles.

"Having abandoned both consent and fidelity to the text and original understanding as the touchstones of constitutional decisionmaking, let me propose a designedly vague criterion. . . . The practice of constitutional adjudication should enforce those, but only those, values which are fundamental to our society."[107] The text can demand political obligation only if it is consistent with current political principles. Given that only a vision of the good society is supreme in politics, the community is engaged in a constant process of "testing the Constitution's supremacy." If the document as written is found wanting, then it can be safely ignored, and indeed must be ignored. Thus, we must "improve our conceptions of constitutional provisions accordingly," if the latter are to remain authoritative.[108] An unwritten constitution would not require this constant reaffirmation, since it would naturally embody the community's current moral vision. Only a written constitution faces the possibility of becoming obsolete. That possibility uniquely necessitates that a written constitution be aspirational, marking a promise by the community to itself that it will eventually be better and meet its ideals of a perfect society.[109]

THE TEXT AS INDETERMINATE

A final alternative understanding of a written constitution turns on the broader question of the nature of writing and the interpretation of writing generally. Recent theory has challenged the idea that the reader is a passive participant in the process of written communication. Instead of assuming that the writer's intentions are clearly displayed in the text, we must face the possibility that writing may be essentially indeterminate. In terms of the preceding argument, the radical indeterminacy kicks out from under originalism the suppositions that principles can be fixed by writing, that texts can provide relatively clear instructions upon which to base judicial action, and that texts communicate the intent of their writers. If these legs are removed, the originalist case necessarily collapses. Further, the radicalness of this claim is not simply that an original intent is practically difficult to discover and apply but that it is in principle inaccessible to the modern judge. There can be no space left for originalism, for the text is never determinate, the intent never clear.

Unsurprisingly, this case has not been fully developed in the legal literature, for it would undermine a great deal of accepted legal theory and practice. Nonetheless, these and similar theories are influential within academic legal thought and require an originalist response. Not only are the prime proponents of these arguments cited with some frequency in legal contexts,[110] but some of these theorists have been directly involved in the debate over legal interpretation.[111] Perhaps even more significantly, these types of arguments draw upon and underlie a great deal of postmodernist and antifoundationalist thought that is pervasive across the intellectual landscape.[112] As such, these arguments and theorists often do not rise to the level of conscious citation but nevertheless ground an attitude highly dismissive of originalist thought throughout academia. Moreover, these theories are directly relevant to evaluating the textuality of the Constitution, which is central to the originalist project. As such, originalism should look closely at the arguments most responsive to their own concerns, regardless of their current influence within the legal literature.

Upon examination, the argument for textual indeterminacy is actually a bundle of related arguments, irreducible to a single school of thought. The common core of these various schools is that the readers of texts necessarily create the meaning of those texts and that this meaning bears no necessary connection to the authorially intended meaning. Although I divide the argument for textual indeterminacy into four distinct contentions, this categorization should not obscure the similarities between schools or the differences within them.

Structuralism and the Death of the Author. Structuralism is a multifaceted collection of approaches grounded in the linguistic theory of Ferdinand de Saussure and has had substantial influence, especially in linguistics, literary criticism, and anthropology.[113] The core of structuralism is the idea that meaning is defined through a structure of differentiation. Thus, for example, phonetic sounds are heard as phonemes by differentiating innumerable vocalizations into a limited number of meaningful categories,[114] linguistic concepts are defined by opposing them to other concepts,[115] and mythic symbols can be reduced to key oppositional structures and thus meaningfully related to one another. Meaning is conveyed, understood, and defined by these linguistic structures. Thought is, at bottom, the capacity to categorize. We can begin to mean something only after we have differentiated a seamless stream of experiences into manipulable forms. Indeed, since any given speaker can do no more than manipulate the available forms in order to produce a given statement, comprehension of the forms available to the speaker is not only essential to understanding the speaker's meaning but can give the examiner a superior knowledge of the speaker's meaning. The examiner may well be more conscious of the relevant structures than the speaker.[116]

Two distinctions are essential for structuralism. The first differentiates between *langue* and *parole*. The former identifies the overall system of structures; thus, in linguistics, *langue* refers to a given language, the universe of possible utterances, some number of which may in fact never actually be spoken. *Parole,* on the other hand, refers to the particular expressions within that *langue,* such as a given utterance or a particular dream symbol. The second distinction is between diachronic and synchronic analysis. The former focuses on the historic evolution of parts of a given subject; thus, linguistics prior to Saussure was primarily etymological. Synchronic analysis, in contrast, ignores the past in favor of a study of contemporary systems. Structuralism focuses on the synchronic *langue,* for structures exist within a given moment and can exist only in the context of a system of differentiation, a comprehensive whole.[117] Since structuralism defines concepts purely negatively, isolated elements are meaningless and pointless for analysis. The presuppositions of structuralism drive it toward systematic analysis. Given sufficient information about the *langue,* for example, it should be possible to predict any given *parole,* whether the subject of study is economics or linguistics. Regardless of the empirical capacity for such "scientific" prediction, the logic of structuralism is embodied in this goal. Any given *parole* is wholly subsumed under the relevant *langue,* and thus the structures themselves are the generative "agents" of history, producing and transforming particular meanings that are merely epiphenominal.[118]

The consequences of these foundations are several. First, the author largely drops from consideration, being a mere site for the play of structures. Though there must be an "author-function" to focus the structural *langue* into a *parole,* the author himself is of little or no importance for interpreting meaning. The name of the author is more important for the reader's classificatory purposes and ability to access the relevant discourse than for defining meaning. The very process of writing works an effacement of the author, as the individual enters the encompassing body of linguistic structures and is lost to future readers except through those structures.[119] To pursue the meaning of a work in its author is to focus on an intermediary and thus to attempt to close off the text's meaning prematurely.[120]

A related result of structuralist analysis is that we, authors and readers, are trapped by language, for our vocabulary defines our thoughts.[121] As one of the key presuppositions of structuralism is that language and thought only come into existence, the world only gains meaning, once the stream of experience is divided into forms, it follows that the nature of those forms defines the conceptual universe within which a given individual must operate.[122] Not only are written texts defined by these overarching structures, but the author's very thoughts themselves are so defined, again calling into question the existence of a significant agent behind the text. The interpretive focus is necessarily on interpersonal conventions, not individual intentions.[123]

Structuralism's emphasis on synchronic over diachronic analysis removes history from the text. A search for the historical origins of the text, regardless of when the text itself was produced, is misguided, for the interpretive structures that provide meaning must be part of a contemporaneous system. Since structures must exist within totalizing systems, they are incapable of assimilating disparate aspects of a distinct *langue.* The text that physically transverses the conceptual divide between the two systems enters into the structural field of the reader and invokes the meanings that the reader's conventions give to those marks, or the reader's conventions may fail to recognize the alien marks as meaningful signs at all. In either case, the reader is cut off from the author and his intended meaning. Given that structures operate in an all-or-nothing fashion, the reader cannot hope to replicate all the experiences of historic actors, nor can he forget the fundamental conceptions that constitute his own thinking.[124] History, in this conception, is a series of transformative breaks or ruptures between discursive universes, with each individual trapped within the confines of his own linguistic "world." We can elucidate the text only in terms of current structures, recognizing that in time these too will be replaced and new interpretations will be necessary to correspond to the new system.[125]

Poststructuralism, Deconstruction, and Intertextual Traces. Poststructuralist thought is a direct derivative of structuralism, building on the latter's key insights and general approach to language.[126] Structuralism is essentially binary in its analysis, and meaning is defined purely in terms of systems of negative differences.[127] Poststructuralist thought reacts to this tradition, calling into question the stability of rigid oppositions and thus the determinacy of systems grounded upon them. If meaning is dependent on the ability to define terms negatively, through the exclusion of other terms, and no terms can be fully excluded as external to a given term, then the determinate meaning of structuralism breaks down into a mere "play of differences." The oppositions necessary for meaning to emerge continually undermine themselves, evoking new meanings.[128] Moreover, poststructuralism calls into question the assumption that only a single, overarching structure is in operation at any given time. The synchronic analysis of structuralism is designed to limit the number of operative conventions, allowing determinate meaning to emerge within a definable system. If multiple structures crowd the site of discourse, however, any one cannot define the text. Textual meaning alternates, as a series of conventions is overlaid upon the marks on the page. Textual meaning not only appears through the system of synchronic differences composing a linguistic structure, but it is also deferred as it oscillates through an infinite, diachronic series of possible structures. Thus, Jacques Derrida melds two French terms to capture both difference and deferment, *différance.*[129] Meaning is constantly held in suspension as the nonsystem endlessly plays itself out.[130]

Not only does deconstruction dissolve the stability of structuralism by positing an infinite number of conventions, but it also emphasizes structuralism's concern with systems of difference. If meaning is defined by systems and by differences, then there is no positive term at the core of meaning. The structural system is an enclosed universe of negative terms, constantly playing off one another; within such a system, there can be no center, origin, or agent from which the rest are derived. The *langue* exists in every part while every *parole* invokes the whole; thus, every part is indeterminate, waiting to be filled in by the larger whole. The further difficulty, added by poststructuralism, is that the true whole that can fill any given part transcends any single *langue* or synchronous system, for each part, or word, can necessarily be grafted into new contexts that effect the meaning of that term.

The written text is by its very nature iterable, and thus decontextualized. Written words are essentially distanced from the original author and context within which they emerged, for as soon as the text is written it is necessarily lifted into new contexts by the reader, where it can generate meaning as easily and as validly as it could in the original context.[131] Moreover, this iterability within the context of a multitude of structures of meaning suggests that a word carries implicit within it the traces of the meanings imposed by all of these structures. A word that only has meaning within a convention necessarily bears within it potential meanings of those past and future conventions; in fact, a text is little more than the shadow of that multitude. A given text is indissolubly bound up with every other text, the ever-expanding profusion of structures that provide textual meaning, all of which refer only to one another. "This interweaving, this textile, is the *text* produced only in the transformation of another text. . . . There are only, everywhere, differences and traces of traces."[132] To turn to the author is to attempt to limit this play of intertextual references, to define an origin that cannot exist. The fallacy of "logocentrism" is the attempt to find something behind the text to fix its meaning. The example of the written text brings out this error most clearly, for the author is obviously absent and the words on the page separated from the thoughts in our head, but the problem is general to language.[133] Ultimately, the "space of writing is to be ranged over, not pierced," and it is the reader "who holds together in a single field all the traces by which the written text is constituted."[134] But even the reader cannot delimit meaning and must surrender to "the Nietzschean *affirmation,* that is the joyous affirmation of the play of the world and of the innocence of becoming, the affirmation of a world of signs without fault, without truth, and without origin which is offered to an active interpretation."[135]

Reader-Response and Fish Stories. An independent movement in literary criticism known as reader-response theory does not rest on the theoretical scaffolding of structuralism but nonetheless comes to the conclusion that the author cannot determine meaning.[136] For reader-response theory, as for the theories just examined, the author is essentially absent from the text. When confronted with a text, the reader has nowhere else to turn but to his own understandings to provide meaning for the marks on the page. Those physical marks cannot speak for themselves and compel a given understanding, for only agents can create meaning; in the absence of the author, the only available agent to create meaning is the reader. Moreover, the reader has no resources but those he himself brings to the text, and thus the meaning he supplies for the text is necessarily his own.[137] "This being so, it follows that a poem really means whatever any reader seriously believes it to mean. Just as the number of mental contexts into which [a given text] can be translated is infinite, so is the number of possible meanings of the poem itself infinite."[138]

Reader-response criticism has developed in several directions, with different strands focusing on different "readers," whether actual historical audiences, psychologically subjective readers, a posited ideal reader of a given text or genre, or interpretive communities that share given literary conventions.[139] Each form of the theory downplays the significance of the actual author or his possible intentions, though the author may play a role by triggering through the text certain interpretive conventions. Even here, however, the reader knows the author only through those conventions and only assumes that an imagined author once placed those triggers into the reader's text. Depending on the version of the theory, the reader may well be highly constrained in his interpretations. There is no necessary assumption of interpretive freedom, for individual psychological drives or pervasive interpretive conventions can provide a subjective experience for the reader of having "no choice" but to interpret the text in the "obvious way," or in accord with its "plain meaning." From the perspective of the theorist, however, these allegedly plain meanings only become obvious as a result of the interpretive conventions the reader brings to bear on the text, conventions that may well be so ingrained in the reader as to seem perfectly natural. This lack of reader discretion does not bring the reader any closer to the author's intentions, however, nor does it prevent several readers operating within different interpretive assumptions from disagreeing among themselves about the "correct" meaning of the text.[140] Textual meaning may be determinate, but it is not fixed.

The author's intentions constitute a text like any other and thus are just another locus for further reader-dominated interpretation.[141] Likewise, appeals to the Constitution or other forms of evidence cannot bring the dispute any closer to consensus, for there is no evidence not subject to the same interpretive impasse as before.[142] If interpretive conventions are loose enough, many readings may be consistent with the "language-meaning" of the constitutional text, and the reader must adopt "external" standards of evaluation to determine which interpretation is to be preferred.[143] The interpreter must strive to put the text in the "best light," as understood by the reader.[144] In a modulated version of this thesis, the "best" reading may well be that made by the "strong" reader, who most fully recognizes his position as reader and creatively acts to impose his will upon the text.[145] In any case, the reader's goal should be to become self-aware of his position relative to the text and author and recognize that authorial intention is ultimately irrelevant to the practice of interpretation.

Hermeneutics, History, and Lost Worlds. This set of arguments focuses somewhat more than the previous ones on the nature of specifically historical texts. Though hermeneutics also accepts the idea that written texts are inherently indeterminate, it tends to be more historically grounded, focusing on the difficulty of recovering texts written in distant cultures and on the particular cultural foundation from which each reader approaches a text.[146] Hermeneutics accepts the conventional notion that texts have meaning imparted to them by authorial intention, and thus textual interpretation should be grounded on the dialogical model of spoken discourse.[147] Intentional agents are necessary to create meaning; and although historical context forms the necessary precondition for intentional behavior, it is the individual agent as author who creates a work that bears an indelible imprint of his activity. Hermeneutics comes to doubt the determinacy of textual meaning, however, in its insistence that the reader cannot, in principle, adequately grasp that authorial meaning. The absence of the author, and his historical context, still works a radical separation, or "distanciation," which requires the reader to reconstruct the author's meaning, a reconstruction that must necessarily take place on the reader's own terms.[148]

In reconstructing the meaning of the text, the reader can approach the text only from his own historically situated perspective. The reader comes to the text with a preunderstanding or, in Hans-Georg Gadamer's terms, a "prejudice" informing its possible meanings.[149] This prejudgment is grounded in the reader's own historical experience, which notably includes an interpretive tradition that informs the reader's approach to the text.[150] Thus, the reader never approaches a text "fresh" but is always burdened, or empowered, by a tradition that fills the text with meaning and directs how it may be construed in the future. Though the authorial intention constitutes the first link in that tradition, it is nothing more than a link. Given the complete absorption of the text by this mediating tradition, the "real meaning" of the text can exist only within the context of a living tradition and thus hinges not just on original intentions but also on the productive audience that acts upon the text in constituting the tradition.[151] The reader cannot hope to re-imagine the mind of the author. The best that the reader can do is to remain open to the author and thus open the possibility for a "fusion of horizons" between the two, as the reader comes to terms with the author's work but in the context of the former's own time and expectations.[152]

Although the author and reader are embedded in a specific historical context, written texts are capable of transcending that context, carrying meaning across time and space.[153] Being autonomous of any individual, the text can enter into new contexts and constitute new meanings unintended by the author.[154] The reader must supply a context within which a text may have meaning, and in recontextualizing a text, the reader brings out new meanings that existed unrealized in the words on the page. This process of recontextualization, variously described as "appropriation" or "application," does not provide freedom to transform the text into whatever the reader may want, for the reader is bound by interpretive traditions and the good faith effort to reach for the buried intent.[155] Nonetheless, since history is composed of constantly changing contexts, and context defines determinate meaning, no two readings of a single text will ever be the same. The interpreter of a text is always reading the text for some purpose, and that purpose, that historical situation, will determine how the text is provided with concrete meaning. Since history is constantly unfolding, textual meaning must also continually develop, playing out in new situations in previously unforeseen ways. Moreover, this unfolding of a text in history cannot be imagined as the further specification of a single, consistent general meaning, for history as a whole is composed of qualitatively different parts that do not add up to a unified whole.[156] Once again, the interpretive convention may provide determinacy at any given moment, but it does not create a fixed meaning through time.

A related movement in historiography builds on similar ideas in order to develop the thesis that history is necessarily subjective, and thus historical knowledge is never a perfect representation of past intentions but always a reconstruction for present purposes.[157] If true, this contention would undermine the originalist claim that the intentions of historic actors can provide a textual meaning independent of the interpreter, fixed across time and between readers. As noted by reader-response theorists, the historical evidence marshaled to support originalist interpretations of the Constitution requires just as much interpretation as the original text itself. The constitutional text is surrounded only by other texts, each of which requires interpretation and thus the reader's active participation in order to make it meaningful.[158] This difficulty with approaching a "foundational" text on which to base all further interpretations is compounded by the incompleteness of any historical record.[159] Not only are critical pieces of information missing or corrupted, a difficult practical problem but one that does not itself bar the possibility of objective history or originalism, but no historical record can fully capture the richness of the original context or convey the infinite expanse of the original experience. History necessarily singles out a limited number of events with which to infuse historical experience with meaning.[160] Further, an agent is required to impose significance on the world, to transform mere occurrences into events, to enliven dead texts with intentionality.[161] Without consideration of the particular content of any given history, it becomes clear that "historical discourse is in its essence a form of ideological elaboration, or to put it more precisely, an *imaginary* elaboration."[162]

This understanding of historical representation does not merely question the accuracy of any particular history but calls into question the potential for accuracy in any history. Historical knowledge, in this model, does not change simply through an incremental process of gradually discovering and correcting the errors of earlier histories, nor through the expansion of historical knowledge by widening the historical investigation to include new subjects. The attribution of meaning to historical events requires the active involvement of the historian, and different historians will appropriately fashion different meanings from the raw material of historical data. Historical knowledge is not simply unreliable as a representation of the past, for it is perhaps primarily self-presentation by the interpreter and thus is not fundamentally about the recovery of a world now lost.[163] The very process of trying to represent history distorts it, removes it from its own terms, and reformulates it in ours.[164]

Despite their differences in theory, orientation, and subject matter, each of these movements represents a fundamental threat to the originalist project by calling into question its most basic assumptions about the nature of writing and its ability to communicate intent. For a variety of reasons, these theorists question the prominence of the writer, replacing him with the constitutive force of the reader who is now empowered to imbue the lifeless text with meaning. Having written the Constitution, the founders have sent it into the world on its own. Its text necessarily transcends the context within which it was created and enters into a flux of new contexts, which equally determine the meaning of the document. In attempting to fix their will in writing, the founders in fact lost control over their product, and if this alienated text is to have any meaning at all, it must be supplied by its consumers.

We have examined the case for understanding the written Constitution as specifically requiring the use of an originalist interpretive method by the judiciary and have explored three alternative conceptions of the nature of the written text that do not suggest, and are often hostile to, originalist methods. In order for originalism to claim unique authority from the Constitution, it must either reach an accommodation with these alternative conceptions or refute them.

4. A Defense of Originalism and the Written Constitution

The alternative understandings of the nature of a written constitution indicate that the originalist claim to unique constitutional authority can be both defended and challenged (see chapter 3). These challenges strike at the root of originalist jurisprudence. If they are correct, they undermine not just originalism's strongest claim to authority but its very possibility for existence. Serious consideration of these issues is lacking in modern originalist literature, yet arguments are available to indicate how these alternatives can be deflated. If originalism is to answer the first two charges—that the nature of the constitutional text can be conceived of as a fixed referent for political debate or as a promissory note—then constitutional theory will have to be expanded beyond its current narrow emphasis on judicially centered models of interpretation. The idea of a political and an aspirational constitution can complement originalist interpretive theory. Although suggestive, the arguments for the indeterminacy of texts are fully persuasive only in a highly moderated form. Again, these more plausible contentions can be accommodated by a thoroughly developed theory of constitutional meaning. Moreover, consideration of these arguments can help clarify why the effort at interpretation necessarily involves the search for authorial intentions and how intentions and texts are connected.

Accommodation, Politics, and Aspirations

The textual Constitution may be regarded as indeterminate as a consequence of the effects that it has on its readers. Such arguments are quite distinct from the indeterminacy that may be inherent in the process of reading itself. The problem of effects is, in some ways, distinguishable from the text and the task of judicial interpretation. As a result, those effects may be addressed by making room for them within an expanded vision of constitutional practice. The legalized Constitution that emerges from judicial interpretation need not be regarded as exclusive. Recognizing the ability of the Constitution to enter political life, as well as legal practice, can enrich our overall understanding of constitutionalism, without necessarily undermining our ability to delimit the boundaries of judicial interpretation.

ACCOMMODATING THE POLITICAL TEXT

The idea of the constitutional text as a fixed referent in the general political discourse is the most easily assimilated into originalism, although there is no guarantee that the Constitution will be consistently interpreted in an originalist manner. As the historical context of the document's framing and ratification recedes from national memory, careful scholarly investigation may be necessary to give full weight to the original intent. Although such an investigation may be possible within the context of judicial deliberations, it seems less likely that elected officials, political agitators, and ordinary citizens can and will undertake such a task and defend its results in public discourse. Consequently, in order to sustain the originalist case, the effort to provide an authoritative interpretation of the written Constitution must either be removed from political debate or the originalist position must be modified to legitimate potentially non-originalist interpretations.

Many of the arguments that support the concept of a political document dovetail with arguments supporting originalism, suggesting room for accommodation. Both originalist and political referent arguments derive from colonial experience under British rule and the apparent danger of covert revisions and the relative uncertainty of fundamental principles under an unwritten constitution. Appeals to scripture, historical analogies, or moral reasoning were hardly removed from political discourse, but they were relegated to a secondary role, at least in terms of constitutional argument. Moreover, the democratic assumptions underlying much originalist thought, especially those that advocate a form of judicial restraint that accepts the authoritative judgment of the elected branches, call forth a political conception of the Constitution. The fact that all parties face the same text results in relatively few obvious constitutional violations; the two interpretive approaches should lead to the same outcomes in most cases.[1] Originalist doctrines place special restraints on the courts, however, for the judiciary is not authorized to act unless clear, historical intentions can be gathered. When the originalist interpretation of the document fails for lack of information, the legislative construction is presumed true. At least in some circumstances, therefore, originalism already implicitly assumes that the legislature operates with a different interpretive standard from the judiciary's, a result of its different role in a constitutional system.

But this conclusion is somewhat optimistic, and the assumptions upon which it rests need to be made explicit and properly grounded. Some originalists do not seem to assume different standards of interpretation so much as they assume a limited sphere of constitutionalism. They urge judges to defer to political majorities because they are skeptical that the Constitution holds any meaning on certain issues. Originalist judges defend constitutionalism as far as they are able; majoritarianism holds sway beyond that point, where originalism provides no determinate answers. Nevertheless, arguments for judicial restraint need not rest on various forms of skepticism and, as judicial activists have pointed out, such arguments are insufficient to justify restraint.[2] Judicial deference, instead, must hinge on the different interpretive strategies appropriate to different constitutional interpreters. Government officials may not be operating in the dark but may simply be relying on a different light. The judiciary must sometimes yield to political constitutional construction not because the judges are less certain or less capable in their reasoning, but because as judges they must reason differently.[3] The Constitution that emerges from judicial interpretation is not the same as the one constructed by political actors. This difference does not lead to simple judicial restraint, however, for a judicial interpretation firmly grounded in originalist reasoning must trump inconsistent political constructions of the document, authorizing instances of judicial activism.

The overall results of this approach are neither consistent restraint nor consistent activism but a pattern of constitutional interpretation that complements that of political actors and occasionally requires judicial intervention. The constitutional text authorizes judicial review but also inspires political action. The known terms of the text provide the basis for public appeals for the authority to take political action as well as the basis for rallying opposition to actions that do not conform to the generally accepted understanding of the document. The amended Constitution may not provide the clear historical guidance for an originalist judge to strike down legislative restrictions on abortion or the ages of workers. Nonetheless, the document's terms may well inspire political action accomplishing the same results as activists latch on to constitutional terms for their rhetorical utility and as citizens are mobilized to give new meanings to inherited language. Ultimately, it may seem to political actors that fundamental concerns of privacy or equality or the general welfare do require protection for abortions or older workers. The political understanding of what the text requires is not dependent on judicial interpretation or upon historical investigation of the document's drafting and ratification, but it is dependent on a fixed text that can carry only a limited range of meanings.[4]

ASPIRATION AND TRANSFORMATION

The second non-originalist implication of written constitutionalism, that of the promissory note, can also be accommodated by originalism but with somewhat greater difficulty. On the one hand, an aspirational understanding of the Constitution may provide the substantive content to guide the political branches in their efforts to continue the republic founded in the document. As such, aspirationalism is subject to the same considerations that apply to the text as political referent, for political actors may draw from the constitutional text what they can, always subject to a judiciary guided by a different interpretive strategy.[5] On the other hand, these aspirationalist arguments do not simply offer a vision of constitutional substance to instruct political actors but contend instead for an exclusive vision of the text as such. To this extent, any form of originalism must reject aspirationalism as inappropriate for the judiciary.

As the case for taking the text as a promissory note rests on two arguments, its refutation must consider each separately. The first contends that the constitutional text is necessarily transformative. This contention fails for several reasons. Perhaps most notably, the argument suffers from an unacceptable circularity, for the constitutional text is transformative only if given a particular aspirationalist interpretation. The Constitution may be used in a transformative manner, but it need not be interpreted in this way. The aspirational reading has by no means monopolized, or even dominated, historical constitutional discourse. The mere existence of a written constitution has not served to transform the nation's ideological stance. Some constitutional phrases have certainly been elaborated by institutional practice, such as the vesting of "executive power" in the president,[6] but this does not constitute a "deconstruction" of either the constitutional text or the American citizenry. Moreover, although the conscious articulation of fundamental principles may lead to greater self-awareness and a process of national self-improvement, the process could just as easily go the other way and lead to a reduction of liberties.[7] Written principles may be substantially less than aspirational, perhaps even encouraging political backsliding as the expanse of accepted rights is reduced to the minimum guaranteed by the text.[8] At best, such an aspirational quality of the text seems to take effect only sporadically and only in relation to particular constitutional clauses that political actors advocate reading in an aspirational manner.[9]

The second response supplies the complement to the first: a written constitution may be preservative rather than transformative. The transformative reading lays particular stress on the root of the word "constitution," pointing out that to constitute something is to create something new.[10] Constitutions, contracts, and promises need not be so sweeping, however, nor do they need to establish an ideal world outside of the present reality. Although the focus of the contract is on the future, it is not necessarily a future substantially different from the past. Promises are necessary not only to force an individual to strive in the future to meet an ideal but also to force an individual to continue to meet current standards in an uncertain future.

For the aspirationalist, the collective nature of the people authorizing the Constitution creates a particular difficulty in securing the promise keeping, for the many individuals entering the contract will suffer from various disagreements and personal failings that prevent them from keeping their faith with the original contract. Thus, the contracting people must imagine a more perfect citizenry, an ideal citizenry capable of keeping promises. The ideal transforms the actual citizenry, leading them to progress toward the realization of the ideal. The reality of the contract does not require such a "transubstantiation," however. The constitutional contract does not presume so much the bad faith of the contracting citizens as the bad faith of alien, corrupt elements that might be introduced into the community. The written Constitution primarily serves as a bulwark against usurpers, individuals, and institutions that are foreign to the "people." Thus, for example, the judiciary desires a written law by which to measure the acts of the government that might work against the will of the sovereign people. Likewise, the flaw under the British constitution was not that the people could not match their ideal selves but that the British governors attempted to introduce innovations into the colonial arrangement. James Madison was representative in noting that "parchment barriers" could not contain the determined will of a popular majority within a republican system. The value of a written constitution did not lie with its rather limited potential to restrain the people, but with its utility in restraining their agents.[11]

A written constitution need not uproot the old regime and set down promises for a bold, new regime to come. While working real changes, the Constitution of 1789, especially in the phrases favored by aspirationalists, followed well-beaten paths. Most of these "transformational" passages were in fact the product of the anti-Federalists who sought to preserve the achievements of the Confederation in the new Union. The French Revolution drew from Rousseau's conceptions of a collective will emerging from a unitary and ideal sovereign people, seeking an emancipatory freedom from within capable of fomenting an essential transformation of the citizenry in constituting themselves as members of the collective. The American constitutional experience drew from rather different ideas.[12] The American constitutional contract did not so much transform the people as free them from external impediments, throwing off the decayed institutions of the old nation in favor of better structural mechanisms for preserving ancient principles.

Finally, it should be noted that the transformational effects of a constitutional document need not produce further transformational readings. Aspirationalists assume that changes produced by the document initiate a cycle of further changes, sealing off the past as the constitutional text unrolls into the future. Thus, for example, Justice William Brennan contended that we can read the Constitution only as "Twentieth Century Americans," viewing the text through a "prism refracting all we perceive."[13] To some degree, such contentions depend on hermeneutical theories, but they provide an added element in connecting these theories to assumptions of aspirational transformations. Although it is certainly true that two centuries of constitutional government have witnessed and produced significant changes in the political, economic, and sociological landscape, these changes have not necessarily produced an essentially new type of person incapable of reading the text as the founders did. Changed conditions do not necessarily result in changed subjects or changed perceptions. To the extent that such radical transformations have occurred, they could provide little justification for consciously seeking to adopt appropriately "more advanced" behavior. Further, past transformations do not necessitate future transformations. Rather than displaying a steady evolution as new interpretations lead to even more innovative insights, the construction of the constitutional text has often circled around the same disputes or held fast to the same position for years and decades.[14] Far from being a necessary feature of written constitutionalism, transformative aspirationalism appears to be dependent on the conscious adoption of a particular interpretive approach.

ASPIRATION AND REAFFIRMATION

The second argument for the text as promissory note posits that the Constitution must be continually reaffirmed in order to function as supreme law. Generally speaking, the demand for contemporary ratification of the Constitution is incongruent with the text as inherited. Proponents of a contemporary reaffirmation provide a strangely truncated understanding of the Constitution, one that is only capable of addressing selected portions of the document. Consideration of such specific arguments and the philosophical theories that motivate them reemphasizes the subjective nature of the constitutional text and the need to take into account its historical character.

There is more to salvage in this version of aspirationalism, but again the strong argument fails on several counts. First, there is its tendency to divide the constitutional text into numerous individual clauses, though often reconstructing a seamless constitutional theory from these selected pieces.[15] One result of such selective theorizing is that the text that must be "reaffirmed" is approached as if it were unrelated to a larger governmental structure or greater foundational document. The compromises and trade-offs constitutive of both normal politics and the original document are cast aside in the interest of constructing a theoretically consistent and morally worthy text. This emphasis exaggerates the already-present tendency of the judiciary to pursue absolutist policies at the expense of less-favored, but legitimate, interests.[16] A further difficulty with this piecemeal approach to the Constitution is that it neglects and has difficulty accounting for constitutional features incapable of being rendered in moralistic terms. Whole sections of the original Constitution and even elements of the Bill of Rights are reduced to a secondary status in this account, uninteresting for exposition and insubstantial when confronted with antagonistic concerns.[17] Moreover, this approach offers a series of false choices when setting up the supreme law for reaffirmation, for the current populace is urged (hypothetically only!) to ratify once again fundamental principles but this time disaggregated from the original package. We are asked whether current cultural mores would favor more liberty, more equality, more privacy without the counterbalancing questions of how such goals are to reconciled with one another, how they are to be reconciled with other important but less sublime goals, and how they are to be realistically institutionalized, to say nothing of the costs of such change and the reshuffling of constitutional values.

If the Constitution must be constantly reaffirmed in order to continue to serve as the supreme law of the nation, then the aspirationalists' almost exclusive concern with a mere handful of constitutional provisions appears seriously inadequate. We are often urged to reconsider our commitments to equal protection and due process and what forms of those commitments we would now ratify, but by the aspirationalist logic of continual ratification, we (the Supreme Court) must equally reconsider our support of such issues as the minimum age and native birth of the president, native-birth citizenship, presidential term limits, unicameral treaty ratification, and supermajority voting requirements for treaties or even for constitutional amendment.[18] If such provisions do not meet our current best conceptions of a good society, must they not also be regarded as constitutional "contradictions" and therefore not really part of the fundamental law?[19] Should the courts refuse to participate in such insufficiently just provisions, for example, by denying citizenship rights to American-born children of illegal immigrants? Although aspirationalists have little difficulty imagining an ever-expanding realm of rights provided through judicial interpretation of favored constitutional clauses, the prospect of similar judicial determination of institutional mechanisms that befit current public moods (or how such aspects of the fundamental law fit into the aspirational model) is discreetly ignored.[20]

These difficulties offer a reminder that the Constitution is more than a statement of principles; rather, it is a historical compromise reflecting numerous interests, principled and otherwise. A sweeping collection of political tenets may seek to be all-inclusive, but a governing constitution may not. In such a historical document, the appropriate product of compromise among the great interests of the proposed nation, there will necessarily be some political losers who are unable to codify into the fundamental law all that they desired and who perhaps even witness deeply antagonistic provisions included in the final document. The existence of excluded, marginalized, or otherwise incompletely represented interests should not necessarily undermine the authority of the Constitution, for no such document can be realistically measured against a multitude of independent and ideal scales. Ultimately, a system of governance must be accepted or rejected as a whole.[21]

The Constitution also operates at a lower level of abstraction than could be consistent with the supreme moral instrument envisioned by the aspirationalist argument. Rather than being designed to represent the best ideals of justice of an evolving society, the document is fundamentally political and marked by specific historical, political, and institutional concerns, creating a framework for future political struggle, not a blueprint for an ideal society. For a text that is primarily to serve as a vehicle for ahistorical conceptions of justice, specific prohibitions against ex post facto laws, bills of attainder, the denial of habeas corpus, titles of nobility, the quartering of soldiers in private homes, or requirements for jury trials in cases involving over twenty dollars and the relinquishment of fugitive slaves to their owners seem misplaced.[22] Such provisions suggest a document primarily concerned with settling particular, historically contingent political disputes. Such specific prohibitions would not only be superfluous in an aspirational text but positively harmful since they could be read as limiting its otherwise general nature. A truly aspirational document should be pitched at a much higher level of abstraction, fully accommodating the changing conceptions of the moral majority.

The drive to require that the Constitution be held up to shifting moral standards in order to be regarded as fundamental law in part derives from recent Kantian influences in political philosophy. This tradition locates authority and moral obligation in the perfection of the moral ideal.[23] That which does not conform to the ideal, under this conception, is merely contingent and therefore not obligatory and without the requisite normative weight to require allegiance. The existence of a written constitution is actually incidental to this doctrine, since a supreme law always exists and is always the moral ideal, regardless of the existence of any constitutional document. If a written constitution is introduced into such a system, however, it is the document that must be tested against the ideal fixed standard. Kantian theory dictates that the moral ideal be preserved; American political and legal culture requires that the written Constitution be preserved. The American Kantian reconciles these two requirements by affirming the aspirational text, the vision of the "perfectible" text that reflects the preconceived moral ideal.[24]

The Kantian approach to the supremacy of the Constitution is untenable. Although such "thought experiments" may be occasionally useful for highlighting aspects of political theory, they are ultimately unrealistic for approaching a political document such as the Constitution. The Constitution is thoroughly scarred with the evidence of its birth and does not conform to a model of moral idealism. Further, it is unlikely that any functioning governing construct could meet such ideals. Consensus is only likely to be gained by one of two paths, through compromise or a retreat to higher levels of generality. Neo-Kantian theories pursue the ideal of consensus in the guise of rational agreement but largely close off the avenue of gritty compromise, for fundamental principles are not properly subject to compromise. The only alternative remaining is to pitch political principles at a high level of abstraction and to exclude from the community those "few" who will not accept the results.[25] The actual Constitution pursues agreement along both paths and equally significantly eschews strong notions of substantive consensus. The Constitution's own provisions for ratification and amendment diverge from the Article of Confederation's unanimity requirement, locating supremacy not in universal recognition of the document's inherent rationality but in its practical acceptability as a workable alternative to the previous constitution. As its framers recognized, no constitution will be able to meet the high standard of best conceivable text.[26]

Such forms of aspirationalism also suffer from an indeterminacy of their own. One need not fall into the excessive skepticism expressed by John Hart Ely's fear of a Supreme Court declaring "We like Rawls, you like Nozick. We win, 6–3" to question the degree to which such political philosophers can be drafted into service to provide detailed guidance for constitutional decision making.[27] The difficulty is not that moral philosophy is bankrupt or that moral reasoning a shell game hiding a naked will to power but that abstract theories developed for other purposes do not provide clear guidance for jurists seeking to interpret constitutional language designed to convey other intentions, other meanings. Political philosophy can provide useful information for both guiding constitutional politics and informing constitutional theory, but it is unlikely ever to provide the conclusive moral knowledge required by the aspirationalists to condemn, consecrate, or illuminate current textual language. There is a reason why John Rawls had little to say in *A Theory of Justice* about such traditional liberal concerns as particular institutional forms and methods of adjudication.[28]

Finally, the neo-Kantian aspirationalist requirement that the Constitution meet its standards of justice to constitute supreme law is simply unpersuasive, not only as a description of the constitutional document but also as a vision of what the supreme law ought to be. The Constitution does not claim to provide the sort of comprehensive guidance Kantian theory is designed to elucidate. The authority of the Constitution does not extend to all aspects of life but delimits the legitimate activities of those performing certain political functions. A judge need not conclude that a constitutional provision is the best possible in order to feel bound in his institutional capacity to carry out its terms, for the power and authority of the judicial role only exists within the institutional schema created by that Constitution. The judge, as judge, is not elevated above that structure for the purposes of setting new constitutional preferences. In providing mechanisms for its own amendment, and in being embedded in a larger political theory accepting revolutionary changes in government, the Constitution defines the limits of its own claims to supremacy. The document does not suggest itself as the final word on political theory and practice, as the aspirationalists contend, but indicates the manner of operation of a given set of political structures. The construct as a whole may fall short and require replacement, but the supremacy clause serves as an internal structure for as long as that construct remains in effect.[29] Supremacy and political obligation are contextually embedded concepts, not properly subject to the abstract testing of the neo-Kantian aspirationalists.[30]

The desire to seek a reaffirmation of constitutional provisions also can be grounded in Lockean theory.[31] Where the Kantian desire for continual reaffirmation of constitutional supremacy seeks a moral absolute, the more pragmatic Lockean tradition requires that a given constitutional regime be able to gain the consent of its citizenry. Although the process of gaining actual assent from individuals forms the model for the Lockean understanding, the critical feature of Lockean political obligation is less the giving of consent than the reasonableness of the means and especially ends of government.[32] Thus, the Lockean aspirationalist test of constitutional supremacy is neither in the demonstration of actual popular consent to the document nor in a logical proof that the Constitution embodies the best conceivable moral vision;

rather, it is in the plausible argument that the Constitution represents a rea-sonable political vision. This form of aspirational reaffirmation has the advan-tage of setting a lower test for constitutional obligation. The Lockean gov-ernment need not be the best conceivable but only consistent with reason. Moreover, the Lockean calculation must take into account the degree to which the present Constitution differs from the preferred, the degree of harm caused by this difference, the dangers attendant to change, and the availability of suit-able alternatives.[33]

Nonetheless, the Constitution must ultimately be compatible with reason if it is to be binding, and Lockean aspirationalism still requires that constitu-tional provisions be interpreted so as to be consistent with current standards of reason. Unfortunately for aspirationalists, Lockean theory does not suggest the kind of non-originalist interpretive approach required by the Kantian model. Though any constitution should be reasonable to remain viable over time, it is doubtful that any originalist interpretations of the amended aspects of the Constitution fail to meet this standard.[34] Politically preferable inter-pretations may be imagined, but Lockean doctrines give little support for such "best light" judicial constructions. Further, Lockean theory suffers from an even greater indeterminacy than Kantian theory. Partially because the former approach is more contextually situated, and thus capable of greater specificity, it is also prone to greater variation. The reasonable interpretation developed under a Lockean approach is likely to be a set of possible interpretations, not a single answer, which again undercuts efforts to replace the originalist under-standing with the "preferable" aspirational one. Finally, calls for a Lockean reaffirmation of the Constitution on non-originalist terms are best addressed to the nonjudicial branches and can therefore be accommodated by an expanded originalist theory. Though securing actual consent is not the sine qua non of Lockean theory, recurring to the people is clearly the preferred method for ascertaining what constitutes current standards of reasonable-ness.[35] Lockean theory does not simply track public opinion polls; the key is in rational deliberation on political ends, not simply in current moods. Thus, a developed Lockean approach can elucidate rational principles that can chal-lenge, as well as affirm, current public opinion. Nonetheless, the impetus of Lockean theory is to increased popular deliberation, not the displacement of fundamental issues to a further remove of elite decision making.[36] If the Con-stitution is to be interpreted aspirationally, this colloquy should be reflected in more representative bodies.

For the aspirationalists, the failure of right reason to construe a constitu-tion worthy of supremacy undermines any effort at constitutionalism what-soever. They are forced to agree with Paul Brest's dictum that consent is "not an adequate basis for continuing fidelity to the founding document," and an imagined "history of continuing assent" indicates the "questionable authority of the American Constitution."[37] This fear can in part be alleviated by recognizing that alternative models of political authority exist that do not require the judgment of ahistorical reason to confirm the supremacy of the Constitution.[38] Disassociating constitutional supremacy from judicial rulings can further reduce it. As moral agents and political actors we may indeed strive to make the Constitution worthy of our most fervent commitments in carrying out activities pursuant to it, but such a constitutional supremacy is not equivalent to the interpretive gloss provided by the Supreme Court. In a regime characterized by institutionally diverse interpretive standards, as is being argued for here, judicial pronouncements need not be "supreme" in the ultimate and final sense assumed by aspirationalist arguments and occasionally by the Court itself.[39] Constitutional supremacy within the legal system need not require that judicial interpretations of that document reflect our current aspirations, only that the regime as a whole be capable of incorporating those concerns.[40]

The "perfectionist" impulse, which seeks to find current aspirations already written into the text, sets the stage for an unending revolution of judicial interpretation and reinterpretation. The American constitutional model assumes that political compromises can be fixed in the text and be binding until the text is replaced and not just reinterpreted.[41] Such written constitutions do not gain their legitimacy from the "perfect" quality of the common law, which is "unchanging" and yet capable of embodying contemporary notions of justice, but from the acceptance of the binding quality of a historical founding moment.[42] If a written constitution requires reaffirmation to remain in force, then it is the reaffirmation of constitutionalism and the rule of law, not of this particular constitution or this particular law. Beyond that, the text may simply have to be replaced.

Determinacy, History, and the Text

The third alternative to an originalist approach to a written constitution focuses on the supposed indeterminacy of texts. Although there are certain important lessons to be drawn from this literature, such claims are persuasive only in a tempered form that does not threaten the possibility of originalist interpretation. Answering these claims requires a more complete examination of the relationship between linguistic conventions and textual usage. Is the meaning of a text determined by linguistic conventions? If so, is there any principled way of choosing among available conventions? Can a single, determinate meaning be attributed to a text, even if multiple meanings are possible according to dominant conventions? Detailed consideration of these arguments further demonstrates that specific texts necessarily convey the intent of specific authors and that interpretation is the effort to discover that intended meaning.

GENERAL RESPONSES

In evaluating the effectiveness of these arguments as an attack on originalism, the consequences of indeterminacy for originalism must be clarified. A successful claim of radical indeterminacy, in which judges necessarily could not locate any fixed meaning in the text, would thoroughly undermine the originalist case, along with much of current legal theory. A less successful claim of only partial determinacy would also have consequences for originalism, but they are much less severe. Partial indeterminacy would not disqualify originalism as an interpretive method but would rather limit its sphere of influence. As I argue here, originalism is the only interpretive strategy available to authorize judicial action. To the extent that originalism cannot guide judicial consideration, there can be no action. Other political actors, who are capable of embracing other interpretive standards, would have to fill the gap with their own constructions of the document. Where the judiciary cannot ground its decisions in an originalist understanding, it is forced to defer to the constructions of other branches. Thus, the greater the indeterminacy in an originalist text, the greater the judicial restraint must be. Judicial review can thrive only where the text is determinate; but it can exist as long as some areas of determinacy can be found.

Moreover, the nature of judicial review requires only a partial determinacy. Judicial review is an essentially negative enterprise, concerned with delimiting a sphere within which unspecified positive actions may be taken. The requirements of such a task are far less demanding than that necessary to the critical exegeses or philosophical investigations primarily considered by theorists of indeterminacy.[43] Likewise, the historical investigation of the judiciary is limited to answering a given question. An attempt to comprehend the overall historical context of the founding may well be subject to perpetual disagreements, but the narrower requirements of the judiciary can avoid many of them by pursuing an interpretive strategy keyed to a more directed historical investigation.[44]

The burden of an originalist response, therefore, is to undercut the claim of radical indeterminacy, not to demonstrate the possibility of absolute certainty or complete determinacy. An important step in doing so is the recognition that legal writing, of which the Constitution is an example for the judiciary, is more contextualized than the literary writing around which indeterminacy theories developed. Political texts address historically specific problems, which not only guide the writing of the text but also provide inescapable guidance to the reader. Literary texts create an imagined universe with only a limited connection to the real one of the author; the political text maintains a much closer relationship to external events. The problems that motivated constitutional clauses, the intellectual background of such clauses, alternative solutions to the same political problems, and contemporary responses to interpretive questions exist for political documents, though such background is usually unavailable for literary texts. As the available evidence to inform interpretation is increased, the text appears increasingly determinate. Further, the institutional setting of judicial construction, in which material results necessarily follow from legal writing, provides greater incentives for clarity of communication for legislators than for authors. Again, the legal context does not reward ambiguity as the literary context often does. Thus, there is every reason to expect legal writers to provide the contextual evidence necessary to make their intentions relatively clear.[45]

Such aspects of legal texts suggest that writing is not as uniquely subject to indeterminacy as some theorists suggest. Though writing is supposed to be more decontextualized than speech, in which speaker and hearer share a common context and thus referential perspective, and the speaker is readily available to clarify unclear statements, the distinction is not as sharp as those factors suggest. Space and time may also separate participants in a dialogue, attenuating the shared context; and unwritten discourse does not necessarily allow for interrogation, nor does the possibility of questioning ensure any greater clarification. Conversely, writing can actually be the means for conveying greater contextual information, or more refined ideas, than ordinary speech. The mere absence of a shared physical context between writer and reader does not make it an essential or a debilitating aspect of writing but is only a contingent feature that may or may not become critical to interpreting a specific text.[46]

Even within their own disciplines, the various theorists of indeterminacy have largely backed away from the radicalness of their early claims, though, as is often the case, these qualifiers have not blunted their own rhetoric or affected their perception within other disciplines. In the case of reader-response criticism, this strategic retreat has led Stanley Fish to move from his original advocacy of individualistic reader subjectivity to the interpretive communities already discussed. Though his current position is still problematic from an originalist perspective, it is a much weaker claim than that of his earlier writing and provides substantially less support for those advocating the radical indeterminacy of the text.[47] More puzzling are the qualifications to various poststructuralist texts. These supplements are not meant to mark a change of position, as in the case of Stanley Fish, but are simply placed in the text alongside claims to a revolution.[48] It soon becomes evident that these theorists cannot sustain their explicit claims that the texts somehow "deconstruct themselves" in such a way that indeterminacy cannot be avoided or mitigated. Rather, these theorists slip to a much more reasonable, though still questionable, claim that texts can be made indeterminate through a series of purposefully chosen analytical maneuvers.[49] Accepting deconstruction as a form of analysis makes its irrelevance for judicial interpretation much clearer, for the judiciary has never been viewed as a proper forum for dissecting legal texts for the purpose of exploring their origins or intellectual implications. If deconstruction is a form of analysis, then it constitutes a procedure distinct from and secondary to forming an understanding of a text. Though deconstructionist opponents of originalism assert that the text is too unstable to support any determinate interpretation, poststructuralist practice indicates that even these critics recognize the relative stability of texts. Poststructuralists choose to subject these texts and their interpretations to a more modest destabilization of received meanings and a further form of analysis that provides insights apart from textual meaning in the standard sense.[50]

In part, such moderation of earlier radical claims is necessary because of the recognizable connection between language and an independent reality. These theories of radical indeterminacy do not rest on an idealist position that there is no material reality but rather assert that material reality is heavily, if not wholly, mediated by social conventions and can support innumerable equally plausible interpretations. Even this latter position is vulnerable, however. It is instructive, for example, that Michel Foucault must turn to a mythical categorization in order to make his point that classification schemes are possible that seem wholly incomprehensible from other perspectives.[51] Though the mind may access reality through language, it is not clear that linguistic categories may be designed in wholly alien ways. Those who assert such freewheeling categorization tend to look for an absent one-to-one correspondence between different classificatory schemes,[52] but the material reality behind language dictates that most concepts will be represented in every plausible linguistic system, though more or less efficiently.[53] One might imagine a society with no notion of "mind," for example, but the vast majority of mental concepts are sufficiently rooted in material reality to constitute linguistic systems, rather than the other way around.[54] Although it may be misleading to refer to a reality that we can access "behind the back of language," it is nonetheless the case that mental constructions are not wholly arbitrary and respond to material stimuli, and thus are capable of comparison and correction.[55] Our world is not simply "interpretation all the way down," for there are footholds along the way with which we can adjust our interpretations and question the social constructions within which we normally operate.

Partially as a result of being attached to a common material reality, our social conventions are not radically incommensurable. Each of the theories of indeterminacy depends on some version of the claim that having adopted a given interpretive community, interpretive tradition, or language, an individual is completely excluded from all others, able to address them at all only in the inappropriate terms of one's own conventions. In response, we must admit that we can only understand a text as we understand it; that is, there is no way to step outside our context in order to check its accuracy. Ultimately, Fish, Hans-Georg Gadamer, and the others are correct in claiming that there are only interpreted truths. Yet there are two difficulties with the claim as they make it.

First, the fact that we can only interpret in accord with our own best understandings also entails that we can only understand a text's differences from ourselves in our own terms. The only way we can rationally hold, for example, that the founders were different from us is if we can understand those differences and elucidate how exactly they differ. But if we can define how they are different, then we must be capable to a significant degree of understanding them. We must hold an extraordinary amount of knowledge in common in order to convey anything at all, even the fact of our difference. This capacity for recognizing difference entails that the differences are not in fact radical, that they are not so extreme as to prevent translation or interpretation. Though we cannot know with certainty that the founders were like us, we also cannot comprehend how they could be wholly different. The practical result is that originalist interpretation is unaffected, for we must behave as if understanding is possible. We could not know and could not change our practice if it were not.[56]

The second difficulty with the claim as presented is its use to contend that, since the text's original context is unavailable to us, there are no consequences to the choice of interpretive method.[57] "Anti-theory" theorists contend that since we cannot know interpretive conventions other than our own, theories about interpretive method cannot affect our actual interpretations. In the end, an originalist will behave like any other judge. At most, theorists can only use the rhetoric of theory to gain political advantage. Such claims are problematic and contradictory in that even as they deny the knowledge of alternative interpretive conventions, they continue to suggest an awareness of those alternatives' essential difference. Although claiming to possess no useful knowledge of the past, they imply that present interpretations of historic texts are distorted and too contingent to satisfy originalist requirements.

More significantly, such claims erase meaningful distinctions on the grounds that they are all part of the same context.[58] Though texts may only be approached through interpretive assumptions, such assumptions need not be of a piece. The mental context within which we approach a text is not simply a web of equal beliefs but is composed of interconnected series and levels of beliefs that are amenable to different degrees of change. In approaching a new text, one does not simply read off one aspect of one's preformed expectations about it, for the interpreter is capable of recognizing true differences between expectations and the text, background assumptions, and confronted statements. In such circumstances, the reader can recognize evidence external to the text in question, for interpreted events differ from one another even though all are interpreted. If interpretive beliefs, conventions, traditions, and so on are multilayered, then aspects of a text can seem genuinely strange and in need of further effort, that is, different forms of evidence and modes of thought, to interpret. Such additional information does not simply feed into the same interpretive circle but joins a dialectic as different forms of evidence are consulted and brought into play in order to constitute a new understanding with which to interpret the text.[59]

This dialectical conception of the interpretive process has the advantage of giving interpretive weight to different texts and forms of evidence. Moreover, it indicates a point that theories of monolithic interpretive conventions overlook, that it affects interpretive practice and results if the reader seeks to elucidate the constitutional text by looking to historical documents instead of consulting recent moral theory. Though the interpretive enterprise may necessarily be about illuminating textual intent, it does matter to interpretive practice whether that fact is emphasized and where evidence of intent is found. The interpretation proffered will vary widely depending on whether the interpreter looked to the ratification debates, the intellectual context of the founding, the centuries-long republican tradition supporting it, or the recent liberal theorizing resulting from it. Differentiating between these forms of evidence by turning to individual, intentional agents provides the basis for elucidating an originalist document and for distinguishing between different contextualist interpretations. Despite the rhetorical spin of Ronald Dworkin and Fish, we are not all "originalists" now. It makes a difference as to how we try to understand the intent of the author.

A final general response to theories of indeterminacy should be offered, reestablishing the identity between the text and authorial intent. Each theory of indeterminacy assumes that the text can be logically separated from the context of its writing and from the intent of the author, that the text is somehow autonomous. This assumption is flawed. The written text is identical to the author's intent; there can be no logical separation between them and thus no space for an autonomous text capable of adopting new contexts. As is readily conceded by indeterminacy theorists, writing presupposes an intentional agent who can give it meaning. The text is not inherently meaningful but requires active intelligence to breathe life into barren marks. Indeterminacy theorists move from this assumption, however, to the claim that the absence of the writer gives the text autonomy, so that the reader must supply meaningful agency. This claim does not follow from the original assumption but represents a transformation of that assumption—imagining that the text as text continues to exist in the absence of the intentional agent who created it. In fact, textuality is meaningful only if the originating agent is not truly absent from the text. A "text" that is completely autonomous of its writer ceases to be a text at all; that is, it can no longer be interpreted as a meaningful sign. The creative "reader" can write a new text atop the old, as a painter might paint over an older painting, but such acts cannot be regarded as interpretation and bear no relation to the original text.[60]

The connection between a written text and an intentional producing agent can be seen through an example. As explicated by Steven Knapp and Walter Benn Michaels, we can imagine coming across the first stanza of Wordsworth's "A Slumber Did My Spirit Seal" etched in the sand of a beach. As we watch, a wave washes across the words and in its wake leaves the second stanza of the poem.[61] Having seen the first lines of the poem already in the sand, we naturally take it to be a text subject to interpretation and left by some unknown author. Witnessing the source of the poem in the motion of the waves, however, necessarily changes our conception of the nature of the text. We must conclude that either the ocean is a sentient being or that the marks in the sand are a natural phenomenon that only coincidentally resembles a familiar English poem. In the first case, we would feel justified in interpreting the text as communicating meaning; but in the second, we could no longer accept the marks as constituting a text supporting interpretation. Without an intentional agent behind the marks, the very concept of a text or of interpretation becomes nonsensical. Although we might now be interested in explaining how the ocean movements produced such precise marks, we could not seriously attempt to understand the meaning of those marks.[62] Consideration of astrological signs should make this clearer. The wave poem consists of marks that qualify as known, phonetic linguistic types, but astrological signs are com-

posed of patterns of stars that can be imagined to form a given graphic symbol. The stars are clearly not trying to tell us something, and the arrangement
of the stars clearly precedes our construction of a system of symbolic meaning. Though we may appeal to the stars to substantiate our configured images,
we cannot be said to be "interpreting" the stars. The meaning we find in the
stars is imposed by the system of meaning we have constructed around them,
and it is this system that we interpret. The text cannot exist independently of
the intentional agent who has infused it with meaning. Without the astrological system, the stars are simply stars. In reading the stars, the stargazer is interpreting an astrological text created and given meaning by human authors.[63]

It can be argued that even though the language system that makes certain
marks meaningful must be formed by intentional agents, no agent is necessary
to produce a given text that activates those preexisting conventions. Intentionless meaning is impossible, but a given text may still be autonomous of its
author.[64] In this reading, intentions enter the system through the construction
of linguistic conventions, not through the construction of a particular text.
Knapp and Michaels have responded that we would clearly reject a linguistic
convention that substitutes the antonym of each word in a text, because the
results would not plausibly guarantee "any degree of proximity to the author's
intention."[65] As Gary Iseminger notes, the example is inadequate since proximity of meanings is not critical to the functioning of linguistic conventions.
The posited antonym rule does not fail simply because it generates meanings
that do not seem "close" to the author's intentions, or to one another.[66] Com-
plimenting someone on her fine "case" can conventionally refer either to her
briefcase or her state of pneumonia, and though both meanings are equally
semantically valid, they display little "proximity" to one another. The point of
the antonym-rule example, however, should be that the application of conventions to a given utterance is evaluated by their capacity to locate the utterer's
intent. The proximity of generated meanings is not crucial to evaluating linguistic conventions, but their ability to clarify the author's intentions is.

Determinacy need not arise from linguistic conventions alone. A language
may quite reasonably consist of conventions that each produce multiple
widely divergent meanings; but the interpreter's concern is with the meaning
of particular statements, not with the results of linguistic conventions operating in the abstract. For this purpose, the pursuit of conventional meaning
must be rejected if it leads away from authorial intent rather than toward it.
As native speakers of English, we may be quite confident in our grasp of the
language's conventions and know that the shouted word "fire" is in itself conventionally ambiguous. We might, therefore, assert that "fire" possesses a
"semantic autonomy," a known dual "word meaning." Nonetheless, we could

not reasonably assert the ambiguity of such an utterance in the face of a clear intent. We could not, for example, maintain that the fire text really means that there is a fire in the theater when confronted by an utterer shouting to a line of soldiers pointing rifles.[67] The convention is useful for discovering meaning, but it does not itself define meaning for the purposes of final interpretation. The semantic correctness of shouting "fire" in either context does not make both equally correct interpretations of a particular use of the word. Moreover, if we are actually in a theater and a moviegoer jumps out of his seat, slaps his pants, and shouts "fire," quickly emptying the theater, we could not conclusively assert that the shout meant that there was a fire in the theater. If the shouter afterward explains that in fact his seat contained a nest of fire ants, which had stung him and sparked the spontaneous outburst, and subsequent investigation produces no sign of fire but does locate such a nest, it would clearly be unreasonable to maintain that his shout in fact meant that there was a fire in the face of a clear contrary intent.[68] This conclusion establishes the ontological identity of text and authorial intent, but it is silent on the epistemological point of how that intent is to be discovered. It may well be the case that the interpreter has no interpretive tools other than well-established linguistic conventions to apply in trying to find the meaning of the text. In such a case, the only discoverable meaning may be its conventional meaning, but as always this could only be a provisional conclusion until better evidence indicated the correct meaning of the text. The interpretive convention does not define meaning but aids in discovering it.[69]

Two additional consequences follow from this discussion. First, since a text requires an activating intent to give it meaning, the absence of intent signals the absence of textual meaning. Though the marks written may correspond to conventionally recognizable words, the text in fact has no meaning, regardless of whether it was written by waves, a lucky monkey sitting at a typewriter, or a person. This point achieves particular relevancy in relation to the issue of whether a legislature, or a series of ratifying conventions, can have a collective intent, including the specific case of legislative compromises. Analytically, the concept of collective intent creates no difficulties. Textual meaning is formed in the same way regardless of the identity of the author. The real difficulty of collective intent is in its empirical discovery, not in its conceptual viability. To the extent that the founders could genuinely not achieve a common understanding as to the meaning of particular textual provisions, these provisions must necessarily remain meaningless.[70] If two parties agree that at an appointed time one will "fire," and yet they have unstated but divergent understandings as to what is entailed by that agreement (one assumes combustibles will be ignited, the other that an employee will be terminated), then in fact they have not "agreed" to anything at all. Actions may result from the putative agreement, but the original contract itself had no linguistic meaning, as opposed to a motivating force. In the case of the founders, it is unlikely that terms used in the constitutional text had literally no commonly recognized meanings. Far more likely is the possibility that the founders had divergent motivations for supporting given textual language and expectations about its later use and that they differed in the particulars that they imagined falling under the principles being ratified. Such disagreements do not themselves affect the meaning of the terms, but they do make the task of discovering those meanings more difficult. To the extent that a core of common principles can be found, the text has meaning, though the consequences of those principles may be in dispute.

The very nature of language as a non-natural means of communication requires that something like collective intent be both possible and common. Since words do not have some "natural" meaning but gain meaning through the shared experiences of interacting individuals, the very use of language assumes that the same meaning is cognizable in multiple minds. Even though we do not normally express the same thoughts in the same words, we must be capable of doing so in order to discover another's intentions at all, that is, to use language. Such a capacity ensures the possibility of collective intent; the use of a common text by multiple individuals suggests the likelihood of such an intent. There would be little point in framing a common instrument if the drafters never sought to unite the meanings of those words. The process of negotiation and compromise that marked the framing process indicates that the authors of the Constitution were making efforts to unite behind a single text and that changes in the text were made in order to bring it more in line with general thinking. This is not to contend that all were satisfied with those changes but that such negotiated amendments create a presumption that all understood the language being used. The difficulty for an originalist Court is not whether such an intent could exist, but how to single it out from the evidence at hand. The pursuit of intent, collective or otherwise, requires judgment as to the utility and veracity of the available evidence, how statements of specifics shed light on the underlying principles of a general clause, how principles are to be applied to present circumstances, and so on. Various conventions of interpretation have been adopted in order to make the interpretive task easier in the face of such evidence, such as limitations of parole evidence in construing contracts. Such qualifications go to the difficulty of discovering intent, not to the question of its existence.[71]

Such interpretive conventions point to a second implication of the intentionalist analysis, that though our meaning is identical to our intentions, we may still fail to express what we wanted to say such that others can understand it. Such failures lead to the common fact that we sometimes change our text to make it "mean" what we originally wanted. Such experiences can be accommodated within this analysis in three ways. The first instance happens when we intend to use a given convention but fail to do so successfully. For example, a student required to translate a passage on a foreign-language test may be capable of conveying the gist of the passage and yet be incapable of correctly using the appropriate grammatical forms. While his text has expressed part of his intention it has not embodied it completely; he has failed to express his intent. His intent not only included the substance of the statement but also its form. Thus, given the opportunity, the student would rephrase his translation in order to fulfill his original intent.[72]

The second instance of such rephrasings occurs when we restate our original text in order to clarify its meaning to the reader. In this case, we in fact did fully express our intent in the original utterance. We failed, however, to satisfy our goal, or motive, which was to communicate information to another. In order to make our intention clear, we may wish to rephrase it, perhaps employing more conventional usages in the new text or simply expanding it appropriately. In such cases, we could correctly preface our new remarks with "what I meant was." The qualifier indicates that we have not changed our intent with the new text, or even that the old text did not embody our intent, but that we are simply explaining our original text for the other's benefit.[73]

The third instance transpires when the author genuinely changes meaning with the rephrasing. Such rephrasings may better convey our current intentions, but they do not convey our original intent. The Socratic dialogues are representative of such reformulations. Upon having the implications of their positions made clear, Socrates' interlocutors were forced to abandon their original positions in favor of others. Socrates demonstrated conflicts in their commitments, which had not been previously made explicit, and thus required the Athenians to remove these inconsistencies in order to reconcile their practices and beliefs with their most fundamental commitments.[74] These various instances of when we change our text to accord with our intentions indicate that there can be connections between conventions and intent but that such links are either epistemological or else a special case of the identity of intent and textual meaning. We can correct or explain our text, but neither requires that we have said something other than what we mean.[75]

A final point to be made about this understanding of intent is that it does not presuppose a Humpty-Dumpty theory of language.[76] The preceding claim is not that speakers can routinely make utterances that seem to invoke known conventions but that in fact secretly violate them, as Humpty Dumpty wanted to do. Ultimately, meaning must be communicable. Often the easiest way to communicate is to follow shared linguistic conventions, but the violation of such conventions does not abrogate intent. A Humpty-Dumpty language would provide no clues to textual meaning, other than subsequent definition by the utterer. Clearly such a language would not be viable, for the reasons Wittgenstein pointed out. Conventions cannot be knowingly invoked and yet meaning defined through internal assertion, like a child secretly crossing his fingers while making a promise. Under such pressure language itself would break down, for intentions would purposefully be kept internal. The point of originalist theory, however, is that intentions are not hidden away in the mental world of the speaker but are in fact externalized in the text itself. Although such externalized intentions may or may not follow conventions or empirically be discovered, they are in principle discoverable. Humpty Dumpty's utterances were not even theoretically interpretable, not because they violated convention but because they were constantly subject to unverifiable post hoc decree.[77] When intentions are externalized in language, however, the text and authorial intentions are identical, leaving no space for the interpretation of an autonomous text.

Consideration of the problems of language raised by indeterminacy theorists has afforded the opportunity to clarify the relationship between writing and authorial intent. This more detailed consideration of that relationship indicates that a text cannot logically be separated from the intention of the person who wrote it. "Interpretation," if it is to have any meaning at all, is the effort to discover the author's intentions embedded in the text. Linguistic conventions do not define the meaning of a given text but serve as aids in the search for the author's meaning in using a language. Examples of language taken in the abstract may well be indeterminate, but a specific utterance made by an intentional speaker is not. Intentions may be difficult to discover in practice, but they are not in principle separable from a given text. Although the indeterminacy theorists are right that language is conventional and that we do not have unmediated access to authorial meaning, it does not follow that we cannot distinguish among conventions and make reasonable judgments as to an author's intended meaning.

SPECIFIC RESPONSES

The preceding considerations address assumptions and arguments common to all the various theories of indeterminacy posited in chapter 3. In addition to these general criticisms, however, a number of specific responses to individual schools of thought should be offered. In doing so, I specifically examine structuralism, poststructuralism, and historical hermeneutics. Reader-response criticism, focusing on determinate but not fixed texts, has been adequately addressed. Reader-response has made an important point in emphasizing the artificial nature of textual interpretation, but the additional aspects of the theory asserting the freedom, incommensurability, and internal flatness of interpretive conventions are largely false and cannot threaten the possibility of originalist interpretation.

These same features mar structuralism, but some additional problems should also be noted. Foremost among these is the problem of defining meaning strictly through difference. This feature of structuralism is retained by poststructuralism and grounds both theories' understanding of language and how it is to be interpreted. As stated by structuralism's founder, Ferdinand de Saussure, "In a language there are only differences, and no *positive terms*."[78] Meaning cannot be derived purely from a system of differences, however. A simple example of a three-term universe composed of the signs x, y, and z should make this clear. If meaning is defined without positive reference, such that x is only known to be not-y and not-z and so on, the terms remain ultimately meaningless. No substantive concepts can be developed from such a closed system, even if additional terms are included in the system or different, but still purely arbitrary, signifiers are used.[79] Without some reliance on positive terms, and thus some external reference, meaningful signs cannot be formed. Rather, meaningful signs develop through the relationship between language and reality, in which arbitrary signifiers are linked to nonarbitrary signifieds, constituting a relationship that is responsive to nonlinguistic elements and is not open to free, idealistic play. Both language and mental concepts are relatively fixed.[80]

Structuralism also fails by regarding specific utterances as nothing more than *parole,* or instances of the larger *langue* that is the true focus of analysis. By adopting this perspective, structuralism has already excluded intentions from its consideration, for specific statements are construed simply as part of a community's general linguistic competence. Any given statement always already exists as a potential statement, given the rules of the language, and is thus already decontextualized by the procedures of the theory. Such an approach ignores the difference between actual statements and potential ones. The key to understanding language, and specifically to understanding a communication, is to see an utterance realized in context.[81] Though the English language may be manipulated to produce innumerable sentences, it is only manipulated by intentional agents acting within specific contexts for identifiable purposes. Thus, contextualized utterances have external references as a result of their use; mere linguistic possibilities may not.[82] Further, the same grammatical sentence may be used in different utterances to signal wildly different concepts, and the same concepts can be expressed without drawing from those formal language structures at all. Structuralism's tendency to view texts as autonomous units is a by-product of its analytical divisions, but such a division of text from writer mischaracterizes language and mistakenly imposes the imagined autonomy of theoretical analysis on the actual utterances of situated communication.

Poststructuralism is, if anything, even more dependent than structuralism on the assumption that language is composed of terms defined purely through difference and without positive content. Without this assumption, the deconstructionist demonstration that these systems of differences can be destabilized appears highly artificial. The deconstructionist problem is a false one, for the strong oppositions deconstructionists seek to locate are a product of their own methodology. The demonstration ceases to be impressive, and ceases to suggest radical indeterminacy, as soon as it is realized that the oppositional systems of difference deconstructionists envision are pitched at such a high level of abstraction as to be meaningless, are not the logical core of others' thought, and do not threaten the foundations of linguistic systems that recognize the possibility of positive terms.[83]

In addition to assuming that all meaningful signs depend upon systems of oppositions, poststructuralism also assumes that interpretation requires unmediated access to the writer's intentions, "origin," or "presence" in order to be determinate. In part, the loss of origins is a function of deconstructionism's embrace of meaning through differentiation. In a sign system without positive terms, each individual sign constantly refers to all other possible signs in order to gain any meaning at all, and yet all those signs refer to all others in a vicious circle of self-reference.[84] The lesson to be drawn from this difficulty is that structuralism's conception of language is deeply flawed. Unable to give up on structuralism's deepest assumptions, however, poststructuralism instead uses this constant system of reference to argue that the reader can never isolate a single term and access its meaning. The "origin" of meaning is constantly displaced to the remaining terms. Abandoning the notion of a language system without positive terms avoids this endless chase, for signs are then recognized as having relatively stable points of reference outside the language system.

Moreover, poststructuralism's absence of origins reflects the realization that the perceived signs do not provide unmediated access to the speaker's thoughts. Without the "presence" of a mind in the text, the marks on the page seem empty and thus capable of being freely filled by the interpreter.[85] Though it is clearly true that a reader or hearer only has access to other minds through the sometimes problematic medium of language, other theories have long been constructed with such an assumption but without concluding that inde-terminacy was the inescapable result.[86] An originalist interpretation of the text does not seek to locate the intentions lurking "behind the text," to reimagine and recapture its "origins," but pursues the intentions embedded in the text and conveyed through it. The misguided quest for origins treats the text itself as an empty object to be manipulated by whoever comes into contact with it, nothing more than a signal of another. In fact, the text is not simply a sign of others, but a sign from others, conveying meaning in itself and not merely pointing to something behind it.

Finally, poststructuralism's unusual reliance on linguistic conventions should be recalled. For deconstructionism, the difficulty with establishing the determinacy of a text is not the insufficiency of conventions to define mean-ing but the profusion of conflicting conventions that overwhelms a given writ-ing or speaking context and sets the text free.[87] Like structuralism, viewing the text as a *parole* rather than as an utterance, poststructuralism analyzes words as triggering multiple linguistic conventions that alternately[88] give new mean-ings to the text. Recognizing that texts do not exist independently of an acti-vating agent, however, undermines this perspective. Once texts are perceived as utterances, rather than decontextualized examples of possible speech, the context of the writing or speech becomes integral to the text itself.[89] Linguis-tic conventions cannot take over a text and strip it of its contextual meaning, for such conventions only exist for the purposes of aiding the writer and reader in the effort to convey and interpret meaning. Not only are conven-tions not controlling, they are not even necessary for communication.[90] Thus, conventions must be selectively applied in the interest of elucidating intent. Continuously to employ potentially applicable conventions at random is to confuse the specific text at hand with a collection of unrelated words, the par-ticular instance with a general type.[91] Textual meaning is not permanently deferred as additional, equally applicable conventions are applied. All possi-ble conventions are not equally applicable.[92]

Last, we turn to the specific difficulties with historical hermeneutics. Many of the elements of the critique of such theories have already been provided. A number of these theorists rely upon notions of incommensurable conven-tions that cut the present interpreter off from the past context of a text. Like-wise, they too contend that interpretation is wholly convention-bound, trapping interpreters within their own assumptions and weakening or elimi-nating their capacity to accept the divergent assumptions of strange texts; or they contend that language operates independently of reality, allowing lin-guistic conventions to differ wildly from person to person or time to time.

These and other considerations indicate how far we must go from such theories in order to interpret properly a historical text.

Such considerations lead to the conclusion that the model of the "hermeneutical circle" relied upon by such theorists of indeterminacy is essentially flawed, or at least misleading. As developed by such writers as Gadamer, the circle traps the interpreter within his own inherited traditions and conventions. The circle becomes vicious as it provides standards for objective interpretation within a given convention but cannot provide the basis for any debate between conventions.[93] As interpretation depends upon the resources of an interpretive tradition, it cannot exceed that tradition. Yet interpretation is not so dependent on conventions. It often requires the interpreter to go beyond existing conventions, which can only provide a provisional basis for interpretation at best. This creative aspect of interpretation does not free the reader to discover just any meaning in the text but indicates that interpretation is an individual skill that cannot be reduced to following tradition. In order to do justice to the text, the reader must revise received conceptions about the text and interpretive method in order to discover the meaning uniquely communicated by the individual text. If a text is not completely alien to the reader, neither is it so familiar as the idea of an all-encompassing tradition suggests. Traditions are not as unified, and thus not as informative, as Gadamer suggests; but at best they provide a partial aid for approaching a text, to be surpassed as interpretation truly begins. The resulting interplay between text, interpretive conventions, and reader provides the resources for approaching the original meaning of the text and not simply a reconstruction in accord with currently held conventions.[94]

The defect of this hermeneutical approach can also be seen in Gadamer's idea of a "fusion of horizons" between reader and text. Though this idea is supposed to provide a basis for taking into account the intentionality of the text, in practice it is far too weak a reed to provide such support. Gadamer hopes to preserve some sense of the potential strangeness of the text, but his Heideggerian assumptions about the historicized nature of human understanding prevent him from giving full weight to the text. In those terms, humans are incapable of holding anything constant through time. Thus, although the marks on the page are preserved into the future, the meaningful context of those marks is lost in the past, or at least transmitted only through an ever-changing interpretive tradition that contains as much of the present as it does of the past. Given such assumptions, the text can provide little resistance to the reader's interpretive presuppositions. The only interpretive conventions available are those supplied by the reader; Gadamer's "fusion" more closely resembles immersion, as the decontextualized text is brought into contact with the overwhelming context of the reader.[95] The only way to preserve the text's independence is to recognize that it carries the author's contextualized intentions with it. Once such embedded intentions are recognized, the metaphor of fusion fails at both ends, for the text can contribute nothing to the fusion without intentions, and yet the need for fusion is removed once intentions are made available.[96] The idea of conceptual fusion self-destructs as soon as textual content is taken into consideration, requiring that we abandon the metaphor in favor of a more accurate description of textual interpretation.

Gadamer's claim that textual application is essential to understanding, and thus that meaning changes with each application, is equally problematic. Although he is quite correct that the specific application of textual content will change over time, he is wrong to see application as inseparable from understanding. In the first instance, this contention conflicts with the everyday experience of interpreting text. Though some texts might require the reader to form a particular, concrete idea from reading a more abstract text, as a reader may imagine a face for a novel's protagonist, this is not an essential aspect of reading all texts.[97] Quite often, in fact, we must formulate and understand a general principle before specific applications can be considered, let alone resolved. Even in the case of devising examples of "what we mean" by a phrase, we nonetheless do not regard the examples as essential to the meaning of the clause but as contingent illustrations that may make our understanding easier to explain. Such attempts at explanation may feed back into greater understanding, especially if our applications are questioned by others and we are forced to reconsider them, but understanding and explanation remain distinct components of interpretation. Further explanation offers an opportunity for modifying our understanding but is not a prerequisite to it. Our understandings are not set, in the sense of being unrevisable in the face of error, but neither are they essentially tied to applications such that every application results in a new, equally valid, and potentially contradictory understanding.

To the extent that we do apply texts to specific situations even as we understand them, the two activities, application and understanding, are still analytically distinct. The process of application may help clarify our understanding, aid in our explanations of what we understand, or deepen our understanding by extending the logic of our thoughts in ways we had not previously considered. None of these uses of application, however, requires that the text take on new meaning with each application. Even after an application is made, the meaning of the text remains the same, though it is now more explicit. A historical, legal text such as the Constitution will undoubtedly extend to new situations over time, whether because entirely new fact situations arise[98] or because political change has brought certain aspects of the text into greater prominence.[99] Each additional application may well extend our inventory of knowledge of the text, allowing us to perceive new difficulties or implications that were previously hidden and to expand our inventory of particularized meanings encompassed by the general terms of the textual language. But consistent interpretation will not produce contradictory meanings, for example.[100] Each generation must read the Constitution for itself and its own concerns, but such situated readings do not produce new texts; rather, they fill in the text that has always existed. The application of the text expands along two dimensions, as particular meanings of a general text are cataloged and as the known meaning finds new significance, and such expansion will presumably continue into the future. Such additional applications suggest neither that we have gone beyond the original intent of the text nor that the meaning of the text changes over time as it is applied to new contexts.[101] The text, along with all its interpretations, is contemporaneous, not because it always changes with the times but because it is fixed and thus serves as a standard against which to measure various interpretations.[102] Though applications of the text constantly highlight additional aspects of textual meaning, and perhaps even correct earlier interpretations, such applications cannot produce new texts or new meanings inconsistent with the original intent of the text.[103]

To frame the issue more graphically, an originalist seeking to salvage a soiled painting would gradually clear away smudges in order to see better the original portrait beneath. As layers of dirt are removed and the canvas and paints tested, details emerge to deepen our perception of the figure who was always vaguely visible, and occasionally false marks are removed to reveal the original underneath. A Gadamerian interpreter, on the other hand, would not be seeking to deepen our understanding of the artist's portrait by revealing details contained in the original. Rather, he would seek to expand the artist's vision for the new audience, adding new details with fresh paint, multiplying the portraits appearing on the canvas.[104] One can imagine such an extreme Gadamerian interpreter operating like a computer that must reconstruct an image from existing fragments. Gadamer tends to assume that every image is highly fragmented, so the computer would be very active in rearranging and supplementing these fragments, drawing upon a data bank of interpretive tradition. One must ask how the fragments themselves are discovered and identified in order to be fed into the interpretive machine.[105] The recognition of these fragments is the process of interpretation, as defined in this book. Filling in the remainder of the image around these fragments is construction, requiring an additional process and system of analysis. Although the image formed by the originalist text may on occasion be relatively fragmented and require active construction, there is little reason to assume a priori that all texts are radically fractured so as to leave no role for interpretation narrowly defined.

Similarly, if a law passed in the late nineteenth century prohibited "vehicles" from a designated wilderness area in order to prevent environmental degradation to a place that lawmakers think should be available to future, increasingly urban generations, it would clearly prohibit horse-drawn carriages. Automobiles, having not yet been invented, could not have been included within an original listing of prohibited vehicles; however, the general law excluding "vehicles" rather than a list of specific vehicles embodied an intentional principle that is just as subject to originalist interpretation as a specific list. Additional applications of the principle to motor vehicles would deepen our understanding of the principle, by adding to our mental inventory of included examples, but would not expand the principle beyond its original intentions. If a twenty-first century judge were to determine that foot traffic must also be prohibited in order to secure the area in its "natural state," such an application would clearly go beyond the original intentions of the text. It would not simply deepen the statute's understood meaning but would also expand it to secure better its perceived aims. The judge might be reading the statute in its "best light" in accord with twenty-first-century standards, reaching a fusion of nineteenth-century and twenty-first-century horizons, but he would clearly be overriding the intentions embedded in the text in favor of new meanings. Such an interpretation would bear a relation to the original intentions, but it would clearly not be an originalist interpretation.[106] The originalist seeks to deepen our knowledge within the confines of the text, for example by bringing to bear additional historical evidence as to the founders' intent. Gadamer seeks to expand the text, reconfiguring its original confines, for example by appealing to current moral theories that operate within the same liberal tradition as the founders.

Hermeneutical theories are particularly concerned with historical texts, focusing on the difficulty of recapturing temporally distant minds. Related concerns have penetrated historiographical writing, leading some commentators to argue that the writing of history is necessarily distorting and creative. In part, such concerns again result from a misconceived reaction to antifoundationalist claims.[107] Like reader-response criticism, for example, such historiography finds the inability to gain unmediated access to historical evidence to be critically damaging to the entire enterprise of writing history.[108] Such unmediated access to "given" facts is unnecessary to objective interpretation, however. Such assumptions are not even necessary for recent historiographic theory.[109] Though such concerns are overstated even in the case of comprehensive, sweeping histories, the particular needs of originalist constitutional interpretation reduce any difficulties even further. Requiring only a limited historical investigation to answer a specific textual question, originalism constrains the historical interpretation, structuring the historical field so as to distinguish different levels of historical evidence and to provide the footing for relatively objective evaluation. The originalist need not employ entire historical epochs nor attempt to recapture the full context of the founding. For the purposes of the narrow task of constitutional interpretation, a more limited historical context can be reconstructed, evaluated, and comprehended.[110]

Such historiographical thought shares a second assumption with other theories of indeterminacy, that experiences exist in an undifferentiated stream and therefore any meaning found in historical studies is imposed by the historian, external to the inherently meaningless history itself. As applied to historical research, this assumption has three critical difficulties. First, history is in fact experienced as meaningful. We do not encounter an infinite stream of undifferentiated stimuli but a variegated universe of distinguishable parts and significances. The historian does not approach a blank slate upon which he can draw any pattern at will, for his subject matter, human history, already contains recognizable patterns. To this degree, historical writing does not distort experienced reality but accurately represents it. Though sound waves are necessary elements to the experience of hearing, for example, experienced reality does not normally consciously include sound waves but already interpreted sounds. To begin with sounds as a basic unit of historical evidence is not an arbitrary, ideological, or imaginary choice. It is rather an accurate representation of human reality.[111] The fact of an experienced structure resists the creative play of historical representation, constraining the forms of interpretation that the written history may reasonably take.[112]

A second problem with assuming an undifferentiated stream of experience is that it misrepresents the nature of historical evidence, especially the evidence necessary for originalism. Proponents of the fictional nature of historical representation posit a historical inquiry building up from the most basic units of sensory experience.[113] But the historian does not only encounter inventories of historical facts that must then be provided with a narrative structure. The historical evidence itself is often already arranged in recognizable patterns, interpreting events in accord with their own conceptions of significance. The constitutional interpreter's task is less to construct a meaningful reality from a mass of trivia than it is to arbitrate among competing representations, whether those of the contemporary subjects or of other observers, and modify those representations as necessary.[114] The interpreter is confronted with a historical context already filled with meaning. Such already contextualized data is more resistant to the pull of the historian's preconceived interests, drawing the historian into the original context rather than presenting him with atomic elements free for manipulation.

Finally, it should be recognized that not only is history experienced and presented as meaningful but that human history is in fact meaningful to both the participants and its observers. Though human action may give rise to unintended results, the actions themselves are intentional, and thus meaningful, from their origin.[115] A key aspect of explaining historical human actions is the reason for those actions. It is those reasons that fit isolated actions into patterns and form an essential element of the action's cause.[116] Indeed, intentionality is crucial to even distinguishing human action from mere events.[117] Although a natural history may be able to describe a succession of causal events, a human history that excluded consideration of the intention embedded in action would seriously misrepresent the nature of human activity, improperly assimilating human to natural history.[118] In order to realize fully the inherent meaning in historic activity, and especially in historic texts, the historian must recover the intentions embedded in action.[119]

Historical research provides the context for understanding the language used in the historical document.[120] The goal of such interpretation is to be able to place the utterance within its historical context, clarifying the purpose of the utterance, the discursive forms that it shared, and how contemporaries received it. Like speech-act theory, from which much of this historiographic argument is drawn, such a concern with context can lead to many of the same problems of excessive reliance on linguistic conventions that characterized theories of indeterminacy.[121] The desire to contextualize a given utterance can easily lead to a focus on the context to the exclusion of the utterance, with the result that the text is trapped in a distant world with little relation to the present situation. Where hermeneutical theories would conclude that such an isolated text must be updated by drawing it into the present context across the bridge of an interpretive convention, speech-act historiography offers no mechanism for crossing between past and present contexts and thus risks idle antiquarianism.[122] Textual intent can be recovered without complete dependence on linguistic conventions, however. Speech-act historiography can be readily modified to take into account these lessons, employing linguistic conventions as an aid for discovering meaning rather than as a determinant of it. Such a modification retains this theory's concern with contextualizing historical texts and accepting them as intentional utterances but amends its methodology to recognize the limitations of conventions as surrogates for authorial intent.[123]

The flaws in the various alternative readings of the nature of the written

Constitution have now been demonstrated. Although the writtenness of the Constitution authorizes the judiciary only to pursue an originalist interpretive method, there are additional implications of the written text that must be taken into account by a complete originalist theory. In addition to considering and refuting various theories of textual indeterminacy, originalism must expand its vision to establish the framework for constitutional interpretation outside the judicial branch. It is in these political arenas that originalism can accommodate the political aspects of the constitutional text and any aspirationalist implications that may be drawn from the textual language. Strong versions of these theses, which would require the judiciary to interpret the Constitution as a political referent or as an aspirationalist text, must be rejected as flawed, however.

Similarly, various theories of textual indeterminacy have been considered and rejected. Even though the claims of radical indeterminacy made by proponents of such theories have been found implausible, some lessons can be drawn from these discussions. The confrontation with such theories forces originalism to clarify its understanding of authorial intent and its relation to the text, including a recognition that constitutional interpretation requires active involvement by the judge in order to elucidate the meanings embedded in the text. At the same time, it emphasizes that originalism is not seeking to look "behind the text" but is seeking the necessary evidence to make sense of the text itself. As a particular act of writing, the Constitution has a meaning conveyed through its text. The test for the interpreter is in discovering that meaning. The tools that might be appropriate for interpreting any given text are variable, but the goal of interpretation is always the same. The appropriateness of interpretive tools must be measured by their ability to advance the goal of understanding the intentions of the author of a given text. Further, such indeterminacy theories emphasize that textual language can be perceived as autonomous of the founding intent or context. Such perceptions are misguided and inappropriate for true interpretation of textual meaning, but they are well enough grounded in common experience to suggest the interpretive strategies other constitutional actors are likely to adopt. Though the judiciary must reject such strategies for its own purposes, other interpreters may well embrace them to guide their own constitutional construction, as political ideals are built upon a vision of the Constitution and ultimately settled into institutional practice.

5. Popular Sovereignty and Originalism

In our exploration of the nature of a written text and its implications for a jurisprudence concerned with interpreting the Constitution, the arguments considered have been essentially internal. The binding authority of the existing Constitution was assumed. The desirability of a project of judicial review based on interpreting that fundamental law was taken as axiomatic. Given that foundation, we have been concerned with drawing out the implications of the commitments that we have already made and to which we at least putatively continue to adhere. The judicial task of interpreting the Constitution was found to require an originalist methodology, and unless we are willing to abandon either the written text that we have inherited or the interpretive role of the courts, then we should renew our commitment to originalism.

This justification for originalism is incomplete, however. Although fully sufficient to justify the unique authority of an originalist jurisprudence, it does not fully respond to the more radical doubts raised about the practice of judicial review. Moreover, this basic justification for originalism does not exhaust its foundational claims. We must also consider American constitutionalism from an external perspective. Suspending our existing practice of judicial review based on textual interpretation, we must ask why the Constitution itself should be taken as authoritative.

Certainly there have been prominent political actors in American history who have rejected the claims of both the judiciary and the Constitution to political authority. It has become an accepted starting point of constitutional theory to demand not merely that the judiciary justify itself in terms of the Constitution but that the Constitution justify itself in terms of political theory. Even a relatively conservative theorist such as Cass Sunstein, who begins his analysis noting that "everyone agrees that the Constitution is law," quickly accepts the notion that "ultimately obedience is justified, if it is, for some amalgam of substantive political reasons."[1] Other, more radical theorists simply begin with the latter point, assuming the "questionable authority of the American Constitution" and working from there to identify how the exercise of judicial power can "contribute to the well-being of our society."[2] Such concerns are not unreasonable. We expect judges and lawyers, when acting in their official capacities, to adhere to their best understandings of the requirements of this Constitution. It is the role of the constitutional theorist not only to grapple with the full meaning of the Constitution but also to examine the nature of constitutionalism more generally and the normative basis for any particular expression of it. Perhaps more important, elucidation of such normative underpinnings will help demonstrate the interpretive method most conducive to realizing those substantive values. Questioning the authority of the Constitution does not simply reaffirm our faith in the existing text, but it also informs us as to what that faith requires. Originalists have been guilty of overlooking this latter point and of being too quick to dismiss critics as subversive of the constitutional order. More extensive examination of originalism from this perspective is necessary, not only to convince critics and to continue to engage in the dialogue over constitutional meaning but also to elucidate constitutional practice.[3]

The external perspective developed here seeks to ground the authority of originalist jurisprudence, and the Constitution itself, in a theory of popular sovereignty. Originalism is justified not only because it was implicated in the choice of this kind of constitution, a written text. It is also justified because it is implicated in the very possibility of constitutional choice. The fact that the Constitution arises not from "accident and force" but from "reflection and choice" entails an originalist method of preserving that Constitution.[4] By construing the Constitution in terms of the intent of its creators, originalism both enforces the authoritative decision of the people acting as sovereign and, equally important, preserves the possibility of similar higher-order decision making by the present and future generations of citizenry. In doing so, an originalist Court avoids the countermajoritarian difficulty by adhering closely to its authorized role entailed by the binding written text. Moreover, it subsumes the difficulty within a larger democratic theory. The Court is not simply an antidemocratic feature of American politics but is an instrument of the people in preserving the highest promise of democracy. This reconceptualization of the foundation of judicial review has important implications for its practice and for the limits of its purview.

Traditional defenses of originalism often employ some version of a popular sovereignty argument. Indeed, this type of argument formed the basis for the original justifications for judicial review. John Marshall argued that "the people have an original right to establish, for their future government, such principles as, in their opinion, shall most conduce to their own happiness. . . . The authority, from which they proceed, is supreme," and therefore, "the legislature may [not] alter the constitution by an ordinary act."[5] Previously, Alexander Hamilton had made a similar argument, contending that "the Constitution ought to be preferred to the statute, the intention of the people to the intention of their agents."⁶ Such justifications have been embraced, with little elaboration, by originalists. Employing a positivist framework, originalists contend first that the legal order depends on the identification of a sovereign will that establishes legal rules to be applied by the courts. In a republic, the people are taken to be sovereign, and the written text of the Constitution is taken to be the durable expression of their will. Second, the durable will of the founders is authoritative because it represents the formal consent of the governed to the government, as they voluntarily accept the future application of coercive force to restrain individual citizens and government officials. The Constitution maintains "popular consent to limited government." Finally, the judiciary is the designated enforcer of that embodied popular will. Thus, "Society consents to be ruled undemocratically within defined areas by certain enduring principles believed to be stated in, and placed beyond the reach of majorities by, the Constitution." The judiciary gains its authority by objectively applying those principles to which the people consented at the founding. Abandoning originalism allows the judiciary to impose value choices that have not been authorized by democratic action.⁷

As expressed, however, this justification is inadequate. The primary difficulty is not that the theory is obviously wrong but that it is underdeveloped. As such, it leaves critical questions unanswered and is not yet persuasive. A fully developed originalist theory of popular sovereignty needs to answer several questions.⁸ First, how can the sovereign will be embodied? Note that this is not a question of how the sovereign will can be interpreted, as the tools for answering that question have already been provided. Rather, this issue focuses on the nature and purpose of the concept of sovereignty and whether the idea of a durable sovereign will is sustainable. Second, how can the sovereign will be alienated from the sovereign? This refocuses the first question. The general problem of the durability of the sovereign will has a particular force in relation to a conception of popular sovereignty, for the latter concept raises the difficulty of how the people can simultaneously act as both rulers and the ruled. If the people are sovereign, and the Constitution is the creation of the people, then how can the text be binding? Third, how can the sovereign itself endure over time? Unlike the previous questions, which focused on the durability of the particular will of the sovereign, this focuses on the difficulty of identifying the sovereign actor over the course of time. Fourth, how are we part of the sovereignty that created the Constitution? How does the idea of popular sovereignty create a political authority over us, given that the individuals who compose "the people" are not the same as those who explicitly consented to the Constitution in the late eighteenth century? Finally, why is the judiciary singled out as the special organ for enforcing the sovereign will against the other branches of government? In other words, even if popular sovereignty explains the Constitution and limited government, how does it authorize the judiciary as the final interpreter of constitutional meaning? Generally, originalists have not sought to answer such questions but have been content to assert that originalism rests on the widely supported foundation of consensual government. On the one hand, this assertion has proven inadequate to defend an originalist method against other conceptions of the requirements of consensual government or against theories that downplay consensual government in favor of some other political foundation. On the other, the lack of theoretical specification has contributed to some confusion over the nature of originalist theory itself. Further consideration of a theory of popular sovereignty can reduce these difficulties and strengthen the case for an originalist jurisprudence.

The Idea of Sovereignty and the Active Sovereign

Before embarking on a discussion of popular sovereignty in the American context, it is worthwhile to consider briefly the history of the idea of sovereignty. Although not particularly detailed or historically rich, such an outline may provide some perspective on the American use of the term and the degree to which the idea is well suited to it. It is quite possible that sovereignty twists American constitutionalism in a different direction from one we would imagine or that the concept of sovereignty cannot bear the weight placed on it by American constitutional theory. Although I do not go so far as that, I do suggest that we need to qualify our use of the term. The development of the idea of sovereignty raises difficult questions about the need for activity and decisiveness by the sovereign, the possibility of alienating sovereignty and the relationship between the people and the government, and the necessity of interpreting the sovereign will.

BODIN, HOBBES, AND THE INVENTION OF THE SOVEREIGN PRINCE

The modern doctrine of sovereignty originated with Jean Bodin in the sixteenth century. Bodin captured the political change taking place as Europe emerged from the medieval period and feudal and ecclesiastical structures of authority began to break down. The modern European states undermined the traditional division of power in favor of a centralized government claiming direct vertical authority over every individual subject. The loose hierarchy of overlapping authorities, each claiming certain rights while respecting its own particular obligations, gave way to a monarch who recognized no mediating authority and demanded that the traditional groups fall into line as merely derivative institutions within the prince's extended body. Political and social authority became indivisible, responding to a single sovereign will, allowing for the imposition of order domestically and the clarification of relations internationally.[9]

Bodin's sovereign is essential to the very existence of a commonwealth, for without that unifying authority, the polity would split apart into uncontrollable factions. The sovereign provides unity across time as well as across space and political subject matter. Although individuals may pass over the course of time, the sovereign remains, defining a people as a continuing body. A ship is not defined by its parts, which are "no more than a load of timber," but by its organization and common purpose, by the continuity of a keel and tiller.[10] For Bodin, the sovereign is not simply a symbolic force but must take an active role in constituting the people, welding them into a unity. The creation of order in the midst of chaos is the function and identifying feature of the sovereign.[11]

This act of creation is never final, however. Bodin offers no historical moment of "founding" that creates a sense of permanence and stability and that might allow the transfer of power from the founder to lesser, conserving administrators. The founding moment is continually relived, and each communal decision raises the specter of renewed conflict from which a new order could emerge. Internal and external threats to the cohesiveness and stability of the commonwealth put constant pressure on the sovereign, whose task is not to create a perpetual order but to manipulate the political environment in order to put off the day of reckoning as long as possible.[12]

The innovative feature of Bodin's sovereign was that he was a true legislator in that law gained its authority from the force of his will rather than from its connection to an autonomous order of natural law. The separation of law and truth allowed disagreements over religious principles to continue without directly threatening the foundations of the state. Political power could be enhanced to achieve other goods by depoliticizing unsettled moral disputes, by distinguishing the "common interest" from the private. This strategy drove the jurisdiction of the commonwealth increasingly to necessities, such as "sustenance and defence," instead of to higher goods.[13]

Having limited the sovereign to subjects of common interest, however, Bodin could brook no dissent, for disagreements undermined state authority. If sovereignty exists through the creation of order, its defining feature is the ultimate authority to make law, the power to impose order.[14] Bodin makes clear, however, that the legislative power is in essence the power to decide. The capacity to render a decision, to resolve conflict, marks the sovereign as the supreme authority. Settling disagreements prevents the escalation of conflicts into more serious social discord while reaffirming the existence of a sphere of commonality shared among the diverse members of the commonwealth.

Several implications follow from this necessity. For Bodin, legislative assemblies could not be stable sovereigns. Disagreements within the legislature would undercut the decisiveness essential to the state; therefore, assemblies would eventually be led to turn power over to an executive, who would in fact become the new sovereign.[15] Second, the sovereign could not rule by power alone but must maintain authority over his subjects. No individual could effectively control the populace through the direct exercise of force. As a result, sovereignty is a legal and political concept, not a purely sociological one. The concern is with the rightful exercise of power, not the mere capacity to influence events.[16] Third, although the sovereign must employ agents, he cannot delegate the power of decision without transferring his own sovereignty. Bodin illustrates this with the example of magistrates. Although the magistrate issues binding edicts, he cannot be considered sovereign because those edicts have limited jurisdiction and force. They are derivative of the sovereign's authority and limited by him. Moreover, officials with any significant autonomy or power can only be allowed to hold office for limited terms, ensuring that the sovereign can examine and replace subordinate officials in order to preserve their adherence to his will.[17] Most significantly, the sovereign is obliged to hear all appeals from the magistrates, thus actively exercising the sovereign will either to certify or reject the agents' particular interpretations. The final hearing of all disputes is so essential to the very nature of sovereignty that the sovereign cannot evade this responsibility, either through the denial of all appeals or through the delegation of the hearing of appeals, without transferring sovereignty itself to the court of last resort.[18]

Similarly, the sovereign cannot undermine his own authority. The preconditions for decisiveness must be maintained in order to maintain sovereignty. Some preconditions are logical, but others are sociological. Such precepts include that the sovereign cannot contradict himself and therefore cannot be bound by his own prior laws. Likewise, two absolute authorities cannot exist simultaneously in the same jurisdiction; one must emerge as superior to the other. The necessary preconditions to sovereignty could also be more restrictive. Bodin argues that the sovereign cannot, for example, violate the fundamental laws that constitute his own power. A particular entity is sovereign only by virtue of his command over the commonwealth. The dissolution of the commonwealth, the modification of the constitutive codes of his own office (such as the order of succession), or the violation of the natural law upon which his own order is modeled are beyond his legitimate power. Although Bodin provides no mechanisms for preventing such actions, they contradict the authority of sovereignty and deprive the prince of his station. Even more specifically, Bodin contends that the sovereign must consult advisers and his subjects, even though their actual consent is not necessary to the validity of the law. Such consultations are a necessary part of building and maintaining political authority and therefore of sovereignty. The decision itself, however, can reside only with the sovereign.[19]

Thomas Hobbes carried Bodin's absolutist project even further, fully integrating the republic into a single sovereign entity. For Hobbes, the constituent elements of the civil government are not Bodin's and Aristotle's familial household, but the individual.[20] As a consequence, the relationship between the individual and the sovereign is established more firmly, without mediation or qualification.[21] Central to this vision is the essential commonality of all men, their basic equality, which structures Hobbes's understanding of the nature of the problem of politics. Equality is not the end of government but the social problem that requires government. Equality means that no individual can be singled out from the crowd for any inherent qualities. To the extent that an individual is valued, it is a function of transitory desires by others. A change of mass taste could throw even the most honorable individual back into obscurity. Moreover, equality means that no individual can distinguish himself from the crowd by vanquishing others. Scarcity of resources, both material and social, mandate interpersonal conflict, but equality ensures that the conflict cannot be resolved. Any gain is temporary and unstable. Thus, contrary to Bodin, Hobbes provides no avenue for an individual to emerge to claim political authority. The lack of differentiation among men prevents anyone from recognizing a superior, preventing the imposition of order.[22]

This profound equality of man sets the stage for the integration of the commonwealth into a single entity, without division between the governors and the governed. The commonwealth simply is "One Person, of whose Acts a great Multitude, by mutual Covenants one with another, have made themselves every one the Author, to the end he may use the strength and means of them all, as he shall think expedient, for their Peace and Common Defence." The sovereign is "he that carryeth this Person."[23] The personality of the commonwealth is literal, though "artificial."[24] Unity is achieved through the capacity to contain the expression of desires. An individual is no less singular for being composed of multiple, conflicting desires. Likewise, "It is the *Unity* of the Representer, not the *Unity* of the Represented, that maketh the Person *One*."[25] In order to impose order on the chaos of conflicting individual desires, the sovereign cannot simply mirror that chaos. The individual authors the sovereign acts by participating in the sovereignty, not by specifying the ultimate decision.[26] The sovereign is valued for his decisiveness, not for his decision. It is this decisiveness itself that creates commonality among conflicting individuals. The need for decision is universal; the decisions themselves expand the sphere of universality.[27]

Hobbes has the same fear of instability as Bodin. The sovereign must be constantly active to prevent division. Legislatures open the possibility of discord by suspending the moment of decision. By emphasizing the contingent quality of government actions, legislatures encourage the formation of factions that do not accept the authority of the legislative majority. Legislative politics highlights the lack of prior consensus and therefore undermines the acceptance of the ultimate decision. Having contested the appropriate rule, the minority is clearly not the author of the eventual legislation. It can be brought to acquiesce in the result only through coercion, not through acceptance of sovereign authority.[28] Hobbes thus favors a monarchy because, unlike a legislator, the monarch has no private life. The latter has no interest independent of the commonwealth; the sovereign prince's identification with the commonwealth is complete. The legislator necessarily drives a wedge between the sovereign and the commonwealth, for he contains both as separate facets within his own being.[29]

As with Bodin's, Hobbes's sovereign is always active, ensuring the decisiveness that constitutes the commonality within the state. With the breakdown of the medieval religious and political order, politics could be maintained only by reconstituting an area of agreement. Whereas Bodin merely separated law from morality, Hobbes reduces morality to law. Reversing the natural lawyers of the medieval period, Hobbes eviscerates the content of morality in order to identify it with law.[30] As a result, his sovereign is even less restrained than Bodin's.[31] The sovereign created commonality through a shared language of authority. Agreement was reached not necessarily by eliminating dissent but by representing it as prior to the expression of the sovereign will rather than as constitutive of it. At the heart of the modern state lies the Leviathan that unites the essential attributes of sovereignty in a single entity capable of decision. Further, not just the "sovereign," but the sovereign will is at the core of political power. Without will, there can be no power; the separation of sovereignty from the sovereign will is meaningless.

THE RISE OF CONSTITUTIONALISM: LOCKE AND MONTESQUIEU

The absolutism of Bodin and Hobbes was immediately opposed, and new constitutionalist theories were gradually successful in justifying restraints on the monarchy without returning to a feudalistic decentralization. One aspect of this movement was the avoidance of the term "sovereignty" itself.[32] Nevertheless, important elements of the concept were retained, even if the despotic connotations of unlimited power were rejected. A primary achievement of this movement was the effort to separate government officials from the source of sovereign powers and to regulate their use of them.

Popular sovereignty began as the claim that government officials were merely agents of the people and thus ultimately were obliged to serve the popular will. The reconception of government officials as mere agents or ministers of the people's will shifted the significance of the ancient doctrine—that the good of the people is the highest law of government—from defining the proper end of government to rendering its legitimacy contingent. Stripping the government of sovereignty and placing it with the people gave operational significance to the precept, for it justified a right to revolution to depose leaders who did not serve as faithful agents. Such a doctrine was already developed by the sixteenth century when Bodin argued that it was excessively destabilizing.[33]

As legislative assemblies gained political ground, they increasingly came to be seen as the representative of the people in the government, especially in England. The doctrine of popular sovereignty was, therefore, easily associated with parliamentary sovereignty. Violations of the king's obligations to the people authorized the legislature to exercise the popular authority to depose him and to institute another in his place. This theory had the advantage of locating the power in an actual government organ rather than in a diffuse populace, thereby rendering it active. The parliament not only could effectively exercise the right of revolution, but it could also readily assume the other marks of sovereignty such as lawmaking, initiating war, and so forth. Though placing a check on the king, the empowerment of Parliament threatened to undermine constitutional limitations on government power to an even greater degree.[34] The question then becomes whether this is an avoidable outcome.

John Locke circumvented the ruthless logic of Hobbes by positing a more social human nature than the mechanical materialism assumed by the latter. For Locke, God speaks to each individual personally, communicating His will by the light of Reason. Every person can recognize His law, and all are responsible for their interpretations of it at the final judgment.[35] Conflict arises less from inherent antagonism than from error in judgment. Although the "inconveniences" of such errors necessitate the erection of the state apparatus, the basic sociability of man lessens the need for government activity and creates the possibility of restraining government officials.[36] Bodin's sovereign was constrained only by his pragmatic assessment of the limits of his power; Hobbes's was less constrained than satiated, by rendering his interests coterminous with the states. The necessities of politics and the rapacious nature both of the governors and the governed made additional constraints unworkable. The internal guidance of reason, however, allows in Locke for the new possibility of trust—of agents not to abuse their office and of subjects not to destabilize the government.[37]

Locke's community is of two types. Individuals enter into social relations among themselves within the state of nature. Thus, such social institutions as money, property, and family exist independently of the state. Individuals also enter into a political community. The popular sovereign is here self-defining. Individuals singly enter into it, and in doing so they constitute a common sphere, become a people. Once formed, this political association gains the capacity to intrude on all other social arrangements.[38] If internal communities have independent existence, they are neither autonomous of state power nor foundations for state authority. As with Hobbes, Locke's sovereign enjoys unmediated access to individual citizens. Similarly, Locke's civil society exercises all the powers Bodin lists as characteristics of sovereignty.[39]

Although the individual consents to the creation of the sovereign, and thereby assumes responsibility for its subsequent actions, individual authorship of the sovereign will remains metaphorical. For the minority, the sovereign will is still imposed from without, requiring a personal submission to internalize the common judgment. The "*consent of the majority* . . . [is] received, as *the act of the whole,* and conclude every individual."[40] Although the popular sovereign may remain active in the form of a collective assembly of all citizens, the community is more likely to appoint agents to perform political functions. In doing so, however, the sovereign community becomes passive. With the establishment of a permanent government, the appointed political officials become supreme, exercising all the prerogatives of sovereignty without recurring to an outside will. The authoritative political will becomes the will of government officials. The popular sovereign regains its place of authority only through the force of arms.[41] Once the commonwealth is formed, the unitary voice of the sovereign speaks without qualification for all citizens. When political power is transferred to an agent, it is transferred in an indivisible block; and upon making the exchange the transferring party is completely disempowered relative to the objects of political authority. In delegating power to the legislature, the sovereign neither leaves instructions nor holds back part of its available powers.[42]

In developing his theory, Locke foregrounds the limitations on sovereignty. The civil society is formed for a purpose and the restrictions of natural law are relatively substantial. Nonetheless, the sovereign remains active, unitary in will, and unchecked by an external power. Locke does advance two significant propositions. Because sovereignty is located in the people, more than one agency can be authorized to exercise political power. Thus, the executive and the legislature can be independently authorized, so that neither relies on the other for its legitimacy and power. The advance is limited, however, since each agent remains unbound when acting. The executive is either wholly subordinate and ministerial when executing the law, or wholly supreme and unchecked when exercising prerogative.[43] Second, by locating sovereignty outside the government, Locke suggests the contingent nature of any given government and the possibility of reconstituting it. Legislative representatives are not themselves the people but merely act for them; therefore, the legislature does not have the authority to restructure constitutional arrangements. In this, Locke was more radical than his fellow Whigs, who accepted Parliament's right to depose King James II and to reform the monarchy under William and Mary. The continuing difficulty, however, was in defining the relationship between the people and the government. Although Locke asserts that the former exists in perpetuity alongside the latter, only the latter has institutional form, actively exercises power, and possesses political discretion. The tension is not resolved, and the right of revolution simply confounds the problem as the populace factionalizes until the sovereign will emerges only after the "appeal to Heaven."[44]

Montesquieu's work in the mid-eighteenth century offered a further modification of sovereignty that embraced a more far-reaching constitutionalism, including a real division of power.[45] Like Locke, Montesquieu suggests that man is by nature sociable and relatively pacific. He agrees that even natural man is governed by the rules of "fairness," though error in judgment can cause discord. Moreover, far from being confident in his ability to challenge others, natural man is uncertain of his own powers and fearful of being defeated. Only society provides the confidence and motivation for sustained conflict.[46] Thus, the absolutist and violent sovereign recommended by Hobbes is necessary only as a result of flawed social and political institutions; a better-designed society reduces conflict and lessens the need for the exercise of political power. Although Locke recognized the need for the socialization and education of children in order to maintain his liberal polity, Montesquieu vastly expands and politicizes this transformative element of republicanism. The shaping of human psychology is taken as a constant and basic function of political institutions, and one crucial to the success of popular government. The sovereign is always active, but now the activity is partially sublimated.[47]

Montesquieu accepts that the sovereign must possess a single will. Individuals are incorporated into the state, for "individual strengths cannot be united unless all wills are united. The union of these wills . . . is what is called the CIVIL STATE."[48] In a republic, this integration occurs at an individual level. Each citizen is both monarch and subject. The individual "can be the monarch" only through voting, yet it is the collective will, not the expressed individual will, that is controlling. The individual's role as monarch is contingent upon his agreeing with the "people as a body," for the "sovereign's will is the sovereign himself."[49] One cannot remain sovereign and be separated from that will. The integration is achieved not merely through voting but through embracing the law as an object of "love." Virtue unites the twin elements of citizenship, freely accepting the law as one's own in that it is taken as a "rule" but not as a "constraint." The loss of virtue would lead to the resistance of the laws, which in turn would signal the collapse of republican government since the sovereign power cannot be distinguished from the law's subjects. One must undergo a "renunciation of oneself" in order to accept the sovereign will as one's own. The only available alternative is the centralization of lawmaking and the external imposition of force by the government.[50]

The unity of will underlying government allows for the division of powers within it. Indeed, separation of powers is a necessary adjunct of republicanism for Montesquieu because it prevents the formation of a division of wills between the populace at large and their agents in government. Although each government official is an agent of the people, the legislature is their direct representative, embodying the community within itself. It is this very representative quality, however, that necessitates the separation of powers. Both judging and executing the law requires particularity and immediacy, but neither allows for any creative power of its own. Having the legislature serve as judge or executive would require that it become less representative and more singular in order to conduct those essentially ministerial and nondeliberative duties, thereby corrupting the legislature and diverting it from its central purpose.[51] Montesquieu, therefore, provides the basis for a functional separation of powers but does so by once again elevating the legislature to a place of supremacy. He avoids collapsing his theory into a notion of legislative sovereignty only through the idea of virtue, which creates an identity between the will of the popular sovereign and the will of its legislative representation.

The constitutionalism of Locke and Montesquieu indicates the two directions of popular sovereignty. Either the sovereign constitutes a government but then delegates discretion and power to its agents, or it is embodied in the government by identifying the popular will with legislative outcomes. Sovereign power is not constrained per se; rather, the burden of its weight is reduced. The citizenry does not feel the weight of government because conflict is largely eliminated through self-restraint. Similarly, questions of interpretation either do not arise in these theories or are referred directly and constantly to the sovereign for a new expression of his will. It is unsurprising, therefore, that such theories of popular sovereignty easily became mere legitimating devices for the exercise of government sovereignty.[52]

ROUSSEAU AND THE CENTRALIZATION OF THE POPULARIZED SOVEREIGN WILL

Jean-Jacques Rousseau goes further than previous theorists of popular sovereignty and in so doing returns the theory full circle. As with previous theorists, Rousseau attempts to integrate the state fully, especially by overcoming the division between the people and the government. Yet he also seeks to escape Hobbes's solution of enclosing everything within the body of the prince. Thus he builds upon the republican example of implanting an external sovereign will within each citizen. Division is overcome by reducing the citizenry to a single unit. For Rousseau, man is naturally peaceful but corrupted by society and bad governments. Founding civil society on proper principles both controls men and renders them more controllable.[53]

Unlike constitutionalists such as Locke and Montesquieu, Rousseau is explicit that the sovereign is absolute and indivisible. There can only be one supreme will. Rousseau's focus is on the location of sovereignty, not on efforts to divide or check it. His sovereign encompasses the citizenry, not as an aggregate of individuals but as a new collective people. Each person "gives his entire self" and "instantly, in place of the private person of each contracting party, this act of association produces a moral and collective body, composed of as many members as there are voices in the assembly, which receives from this same act its unity, its common *self,* its life, and its will. This public person, formed thus by the union of all the others . . . now takes [the name] . . . *Sovereign.*"[54] Thereby, Rousseau centralizes power and authority in the people, not in the state apparatus. Likewise, he invests the sovereign people with the energy necessary to direct and oversee the actions of its agents. The sovereign people do not come into existence in order to transfer political discretion to agents, for "power can perfectly well be transferred, but not will." It is the sovereign itself that retains the legislative power. The government consists only of "magistrates," who may not "make laws" but only give "force" to the established sovereign will.[55]

In order to make this system operative, citizens must face an internal duality that allows the commonwealth to be integrated but that requires submission of internal private passions to the common will. Rousseau draws out what was merely implicit in Montesquieu, arguing that the private interests of individuals' particular wills have no bearing on the sovereign general will of the people as a whole. Although the general will is illustrated by a voting procedure, it is not determined by voting. Each vote expresses an opinion as to the content of the general will instead of expressing a policy preference. As such, the sovereign will reflects what is truly held in common by the people rather than what is desired by particular individuals. Members of the out-voted minority are not suppressed as being against the general will but are educated by the outcome so that they realize their opinion was mistaken. Ulti-mately each citizen is and wants to be sovereign and thus "consents" to, or authors, the sovereign's judgment. The sovereign's will is the citizen's will, but the former is known before the latter. Under the best of circumstances, the true citizen simply knows the general will, without the need for discussion or explicit consideration. The individual communicates with the sovereign with-out the necessity of turning outside of himself; at the same time, the sover-eign imposes his will without the need for external mechanisms of coercion.[56]

The sovereign requires, nonetheless, some physical instrument by which to particularize and execute its will. Political instruments are necessary to bridge the gap between the generalized and abstracted will of the sovereign and the material objects of the world. The "act that institutes the government is not a contract but a law," which signals that the officers so instituted are merely magistrates concerned with interpreting and implementing that law, applying the general to the particular. The "inherent and inevitable vice" of politics, however, is that the magistrate "acts incessantly" to undermine, or alter, the law established by the general will. Electoral accountability is an insufficient check, since elections cannot replicate the general will and rep-resentatives are never the sovereign itself. Rousseau recommends the peri-odic reformation of the sovereign assembly, which can then reconsider, reemphasize, and reestablish its authoritative will. Such moments clarify the expression of the general will and correct deviations from it.[57] The correct understanding of the general will is less one of interpretation, however, than of perception. The general will is always available to be consulted and always actively impinging on the mind of the citizen, but it can be eclipsed by con-cern with individual private interests. The critical problem is not one of interpretation but of good faith. The periodic assembling of the sovereign undercuts government claims to be the authentic representative of the sov-ereign will and publicizes deviations by reasserting the authoritative expres-sion of the sovereign.[58]

THE CONSTITUTION, DIVIDED SOVEREIGNTY, AND
JUDICIAL REVIEW

This brief sketch clarifies the task that the founders set for themselves. It also indicates both the possibilities that exist in the example of the founding and the theoretical limitations that constrained the founders. Consideration of popular sovereignty in the founding is primarily illustrative of an approach to the Constitution. It indicates the tradition within which the Constitution can be located and of which it is an expression. Further development of that tradition can provide the justification for our continued adherence to the Constitution and the normative value of an originalist jurisprudence.[59]

As the American Revolution approached, the colonists attempted to divide and limit the sovereign powers of the British government. Parliament was pictured as constrained in its powers, and the colonial governments were elevated to a status of sovereignty on par with the British within an imperial federal structure. The British response that there could be no *"imperium in imperio"* was eventually persuasive, although the posited location of *imperium* in Parliament was not. By the time of the Revolution, sovereignty was conceptually reunited in America, but in the sovereign people who authorized government institutions.[60] The idea of popular sovereignty has certain advantages from the perspective of separation of powers, since it allows for the specification of numerous separate agents of the single sovereign. Both separation of powers within the federal government and the division of powers between general and state governments become readily explicable, given such a conception of sovereignty, since none of these particular functionaries can be regarded as sovereign. Similarly, popular sovereignty allows for the establishment of a limited government enforceable by judicial review, since the legislature can claim neither sovereign authority over the Constitution nor supremacy over the courts. Judges are as much the people's agents as are elected representatives.[61]

The American application of theories of popular sovereignty made several advances, but it was also entangled by the confusions of the developed theory. Clarifying both provides a starting point for the adequate development of a theory of popular sovereignty and its relationship to originalism. Driven by the necessity of the hostility of the state legislatures and by theoretical and political concerns to ground the new federal constitution in the authority of the people, the Philadelphia Convention both represented and contributed to the implementation of popular sovereignty through the mechanism of popular convention. This move was of no small significance.

The contrast between the king, or the king's gubernatorial representatives in America, and popularly elected legislatures had contributed to a conception of legislatures as being the representatives of the people against the government, as opposed to the representatives of the people in government. As the monarch's power was reduced in Britain and eliminated in America, the nature of the legislature relative to the government was obscured, effectively strengthening the authority of the government by erasing the distinction between government and society, legislature and people. Although the device of popular convention did not and could not go so far as to assemble the whole people, as Rousseau had directed, it did make a sharp distinction between government and society and emphasized that ultimate political authority resided in the latter. It also suspended the regular legislature's claim to represent the people; legislative representation was limited and contingent. The promise of the American constitutional experiment was not that it realized the possibility of the social contract, making historical what had previously been regarded as merely hypothetical. Britain's own Glorious Revolution belied the claim of American exceptionalism in this regard. Britain failed to preempt the American example only because of the failure of political leaders properly to conceptualize their revolutions and the subsequent state. The Levelers and Whig radicals such as Locke had urged the institutionalization of a distinction between Parliament and people, but parliamentary advocates had rejected their theories and implemented others.[62] The resulting legislative sovereignty set the stage for the American Revolution. Thomas Jefferson's caution that the revolutionary state legislatures should not draft their own constitutions was not merely philosophical quibbling but an attempt to define the fundamental nature of the new republic and was consistent with his other efforts to ensure popular control over the new constitutions.[63] The founders undermined government absolutism not by adhering to contractarian theory but by adopting a particular version of that theory that institutionalized the derivative and qualified nature of government authority.

If the convention device undercut claims of legislative sovereignty, it did not dispel them. The active nature of concepts of sovereignty continually reinforced claims of government supremacy. Many of the supporters of the Constitution followed the path of Montesquieu by seeking to use popular sovereignty as a legitimating device for government rather than as a genuine alternative to government authority. They were hampered by continuing theoretical confusions and emboldened by the desire to establish an energetic new government. James Madison carefully distinguished democracies from republics, noting that the former are "spectacles of turbulence and contention" but that the latter are governed by "representatives or agents" who "refine and enlarge the public views." The new government is to "derive all its powers" from the "great body of the people," but the popular connection to the government would be mediated and temporary. Madison described popular consideration of constitutional provisions in the same terms as democratic government. The "appeal to the people" is disruptive to the "public tranquility by interesting too strongly the public passions." The people were to serve as the "only legitimate fountain for power" from which the Constitution is "derived," but after ratification the government should strive to cultivate the "prejudices" of the masses to revere the new Constitution and government as essentially without defects. Presumed constitutional perfection allowed for presumed tacit consent to the government, creating "a timeless form of politics" in which the Constitution always already "existed entirely in a theoretically perfect present."[64]

Despite Madison's later efforts to distinguish between the sovereignty of state governments and that of the people of the states, his terminology as Publius indicates that sovereignty could be readily attributed to governments, state and federal, once they had been constituted by the people. The Constitution, therefore, creates a "divided sovereignty" in which the general government is sovereign within its "vested" powers and the state governments are sovereign in their "residual" powers. The power to resolve disputes between the two sovereigns is "established under the general government." The people yield entirely, although the "constitutional road" of Article 5 amendment remains "open" to them for "certain great and extraordinary occasions." Despite the fact that some thirty-one constitutions had been created and employed between the Revolution and the ratification of the Constitution without the rise of anarchy, Madison regarded further constitutional changes as "of too ticklish a nature" to repeat.[65]

Even before ratification, the Federalists embarked on a concerted effort to reinterpret the nature of American government, displacing the sovereign people from the temporal realm. The people were less often referred to as "sovereign" and demoted to the status of a mere "source" of power, a legitimating device. The implications of the phrase "popular sovereignty" became "more tenuous and less complete in scope" as it lost its relationship to the actual formation of constitutions and became the hypothetical wellspring for government action. In keeping with this theme, the Federalists portrayed the founding as a unique and critical moment and the founders themselves as more than merely human. The founding moment of constitutional creation became less real and more mythical, less a historic event that could be repeated than a miraculous aberration to be worshiped.[66] Such efforts were not without effect. As the founders were passing from the political scene, John Marshall emphasized their enduring role. Although declaring the Supreme Court to be the ultimate interpreter of the Constitution, Marshall also asserted that the state and national governments were "sovereign," supreme within their spheres of action and armed with all the accoutrements of sovereignty. The durability of the Constitution was shifted from being a hope and an expectation to being an axiom, with the result that the Court and Congress were given the task of ensuring that the Constitution would "endure for the ages" by being none too restrictive on government officials.[67]

This Federalist reimagination of constitutional government was not merely a cynical grab at political power; it was also a function of the confused concept of sovereignty. The history of the concept indicated that the sovereign must be active, to respond to changing circumstances and to reassert his will. Certainly, the parallel use of sovereignty in terms of international relations left no room for the reality of a "popular sovereign," who could not enter into diplomatic relations with other states. In the international arena, the government was always the sovereign.[68] Such concerns carried over into the domestic realm, in which the sovereign faced threats of internal disorder. The transfer of political discretion was equivalent to the transfer of sovereignty itself; therefore, Rousseau derided the British people for thinking that "it is free," when "it is free only during the election of the members of Parliament. As soon as they are elected, it is a slave, it is nothing." Similarly, British observers questioned the reality of the American exception, noting that "a monarch who slumbers for years is like a monarch who does not exist." The slumbering popular sovereign was contrasted unfavorably to the "ever-wakeful" Parliament.[69] Americans, such as James Wilson, who were more influenced by Rousseau and sought to emphasize the popular sovereign were nonetheless stymied by the reality of representative government. Warping Rousseau, Wilson celebrated the "sovereignty" that inhered in the people when they exercised their suffrage; but in doing so, he obscured when the people changed the Constitution itself, not just particular government agents, and how the unelected judiciary could still be an agent of the sovereign.[70] The founders thus opened the way for the further development of a theory of popular sovereignty, but they remained mired in theoretical difficulties that tended to lead to claims of government sovereignty. Although such difficulties cannot be fully resolved here, it is possible to reconstruct a theory of popular sovereignty that can ground the authority of the Constitution and indicate why an originalist jurisprudence can play an integral role in maintaining that sovereignty.

Rethinking Popular Sovereignty

At root, a theory of popular sovereignty is a version of a theory of democracy. Its concern is limited to the foundational elements of normal government institutions and the requirements of consensual government. There are various ways of thinking about both democracy and popular sovereignty, however. In the American context, the historical stability of the Constitution and the government it created has led to a shifting of perspective as to what popular government requires. At the level of suffrage, the demands of democracy have been gradually expanded, embracing a large segment of the population within the ranks of full citizenship. At another level, however, the conception of popular government has been thinned over the course of American history. Democracy has been reduced to the casting of ballots for elected officials while other elements of citizenship, from jury duty to lobbying, have been compartmentalized as subsidiary activities of government administration, chores to be avoided or delegated to specialists. Although the value of this shift in understanding is ambiguous, it has led to at least one clear problem. The flattening of popular governance has blurred the distinction between the government and the sovereign, administration and high politics. The reassertion of this distinction would emphasize that the Constitution is not something we have, but something we make. The critical question then becomes who "we" are.

CONSENT, LEGITIMACY, AND RESPONSIVENESS TO THE POPULAR WILL

We consent to government by authorizing its existence, that is, by constituting it.[71] In doing so, we define what the government may and may not do, who will compose it, and how they will reach decisions and take actions. In this way we both empower and constrain government. We empower it by authorizing it to act as our agent in order to serve our interests. This empowerment is not merely formal, for in constituting a government we permit it to seek out our interests and speak in our name. This capacity to represent us gives the government powerful leverage to redirect our resources and to employ violence against us as individuals and for us against others. It is this claim to be serving the citizenry that has given most modern states an unparalleled power over our lives. This delegation of authority requires the imposition of substantial restraints on political officials, which both limit the actions that may be taken and specify how and by whom those actions are to be taken. Ultimately, these constraints are concerned with countering the government's claim to popular authority. They are realized when it becomes evident that we have not authorized the government to do what its officials want to do. The creation of a constitution, therefore, is a people's highest expression of its consent to the government. It is the embodiment of the popular will that rules government officials as they attempt to rule the populace. The difficulty with this vision comes with the fact that the power of making constitutions has been largely left unexercised in the United States in recent history.[72] If constitution making is the fullest and most explicit expression of consent to the government, how can our government continue to be regarded as consensual? Alternatively, what does popular sovereignty mean in this context? I hope to rescue the idea of consensual government by rejecting the reliance on tacit consent and suggesting an alternative formulation of "potential sovereignty."[73]

The starting point for reviving the ideal of consensual government is the rejection of the legitimating authority of tacit consent. This concept is designed to address precisely the problem of the absence of actual, express consent to government. Not only did we not participate in the ratification debates, but a large proportion of the population of the time did not; and of those who did, many opposed the Constitution. Tacit consent purports to provide a rationale for obligating those of us who, by chance or choice, have not made their approval of the government explicit. Tacit consent can operate in two forms: either our actual behavior is construed as an indirect expression of consent, or it is assumed that we would consent if asked because the government is a good one. The first has been tied to a wide variety of activities, from residing within a political jurisdiction to taking advantage of the benefits of government to refraining from voicing objection to government actions. Perhaps most significantly, we are taken to have consented tacitly to government action if we continue to vote for government officials (and thus presumably accept the validity of the voting outcomes) and if we fail to pass constitutional amendments to reverse government action at odds with prior interpretations of existing constitutional requirements. If these mechanisms for disciplining government officials are maintained, then government actions possess a presumptive authority, which can be expressed in constitutional terms.[74] The second version of tacit consent has been employed by contemporary neo-Kantian political philosophy, such that government is authorized and limited by reference to what we, given various limiting conditions, would want it to do. The Constitution gains its authority through its adherence to those standards, and it is to be interpreted now so as to realize that hypothetical construct.[75] Although I primarily consider the first type here, neither provides an acceptable foundation for constitutional authority as enforced by the courts.

The questionable authority of tacit consent can be laid bare relatively briefly. In general, tacit consent fails because it turns the very notion of consent on its head. Since the goal of consent theory is to ensure that government derives its authority from the conscious choice of the individuals it is to govern, the introduction of tacit consent undermines this purpose by positing the existence of consent where no deliberative choice has been made. In part this is a function of incorrectly interpreting nonpolitical actions as deeply political, such as residence or the acceptance of government benefits.[76] More troubling, however, is that this error is also a function of employing the wrong consensual context and theoretical perspective. The vast majority of normal political activity does not take into account the contingency of government authority but operates against a background of assumed authority. The choice implied by our behavior is about what policy this government should adopt, given its existence and activity, not about whether this government should continue to exist in its present form. The adoption of tacit consent implicitly transfers the locus of sovereignty away from the existing citizenry. The power of creating government is lodged elsewhere because the possibility of current re-creation is not seriously considered. The motivation for adopting the tacit consent approach is to gain legitimacy for existing de facto government practices, biasing the outcome in favor of approval and yielding the constitutional authority of initiating new government practices to the government itself.[77]

The failure of tacit consent to replicate consensual government can be seen in the example of voting.[78] John Plamenatz, for example, has argued that the "citizen who votes at an election is presumed to understand the significance of what he is doing, and if the election is free, he has voluntarily taken part in a process which confers authority on someone; . . . he consented to the authority of the man elected."[79] In the American context, this argument is particularly troubling, because elections are held within a given framework. Elections do not confer general political authority. A particular individual is elected to fill an office that has been previously constituted. In gaining the office, the individual gains only the existing authority of the office, including the limits on that authority. Government officials cannot bootstrap themselves into a position of reconstituting their own offices by pointing to an electoral mandate that only exists by virtue of the prior existence of that office. Moreover, the same concern with background conditions again applies to the specific context of voting. The voter in a normal election does not face the issue of the continuation of government authority but must choose between candidates who seek to govern under that authority. This expression of preference is constrained by the knowledge that there will be a victor who will make use of government resources to create immediate policy.[80] Similarly, government alteration of constitutional requirements cannot be assumed legitimate simply because no amendment is ratified to reverse the change. Both the existence of a written constitution and the specification of a supermajority to amend it are indicative of the continuing locus of sovereignty in the people themselves. Amending the Constitution is difficult not only to enhance stability but also to ensure that there is widespread and deliberate support for the change. Deriving tacit consent from a failure to amend grants the government a positive authority that could only have been demonstrated through the populace's active engagement with the constitutional text.

Such concerns can be expanded to indicate why there can be no government sovereignty under a popular regime. The transfer of sovereignty to government institutions has been a recurring problem in theories of popular sovereignty. Although not usually expressed in terms of sovereignty, the problem emerges in modern form in theories that advocate loosening the bonds of constitutional law so that government officials may have a freer hand to represent the current popular will. The sovereign power of constituting the fundamental law is effectively transferred to government officials who are then authorized to reconfigure its requirements, either through "interpretation" or mere policy making.[81] Perhaps the most obvious difficulty with such claims is that the government is only imperfectly representative of the people and that those imperfections are particularly relevant to considerations of authority for constitutional revision. Both the legislative agenda and the resulting legislation are partially autonomous of the broader populace. Much of the government's normal policy making takes place outside the context of considered public opinion.[82]

It must be emphasized that my claim here is not that the government is unresponsive to the popular will. There is every reason to think that the government is highly responsive to the electorate. That responsiveness, however, is geared to the particular purposes of policy making within the context of government authority. Government officials only rarely question their own authority to conduct policy and accomplish their goals; their primary concerns are immediate and relatively concrete. The critical point is not whether government resists the popular will, but whether it adequately represents the people for constitutional purposes. To this degree, government institutions are problematic because they are both unfocused and semiautonomous. In supporting a particular candidate for office, few voters deliberate on constitutional issues, for the good reason that the Constitution is not directly implicated in normal political elections. Likewise, political officials are faced with myriad concerns related to the daily operation of the government. The Constitution provides the context for their actions but is not itself the object of their deliberations. Further, members of the government have an interest in maintaining the status quo, in a broad sense—that is, officials may seek to change particular policies, but they are reliant on the stability of the overall political structure. Existing formations of political agendas, leadership structures, issue networks, and political resources provide both a foundation for the careful making of policy and an interest in limiting reform. Such resources are not shared by the populace at large, which does not engage directly in policy making. Such a desire to preserve existing political structures may or may not be representative of the larger citizenry, which is not part of the political class. The government as a whole serves a particular function in the constitutional system, which is to make policy. The distinction between the needs and tendencies of policy making and the sovereign authority to constitute government motivates the separation of the government from the sovereign.[83]

The division between the government and the sovereign can also be seen in the continuing existence of constraints on the former. Few of those individuals who would replace inherited constitutional authority with some form of democratic deference to current government officials would accept that government power is free of all nonelectoral restraints. The constitutional tradition of limited government is simply too strong to accept the type of government sovereignty advocated by Blackstone, even as the distance between government practice and constitutional requirements is reduced in favor of the former.[84] The recognition of some constraints on current representatives indicates the continued sovereignty of the people outside the government. A theory of tacit consent, however, can make little sense of such inherited restrictions. Thus, for example, Samuel Freeman, an advocate of Rawlsian hypothetical consent, considers the state representation guaranteed in the U.S. Senate to be contrary to the constitution to which we would consent, yet recognizes that the government could not simply ignore or alter that textual provision.[85] Such limitations on government authority are embarrassments to theories that rely on tacit consent, for such a government is legitimate only to the extent that it is responsive to that posited popular will. If geographic representation in the Senate does not receive our current (tacit) consent, then it is illegitimate. Mere inclusion of the guarantee in a text cannot save it, for our "Constitution," the authority for our political practices, is determined by what would garner our current consent, not by what is included in a piece of parchment. Deference to disfavored textual provisions makes little sense when the appropriate method of textual interpretation and the extent of textual authority are the very issues at question in developing the theory.[86]

The concept of potential sovereignty better represents this basis for constitutional authority. Like tacit consent, potential sovereignty is concerned with ensuring the consensual foundation of government. Unlike tacit consent, however, potential sovereignty does not assume that such consent exists at all moments to authorize current government actions. More concretely, it does not assume the existence of present agreement as to the content of the sovereign will. Perhaps more clearly, it does not assume the existence of a currently active sovereign. In order to make tacit consent meaningful, government officials, whether judges or legislators, must not only assume that the people at large agree on the nature of the government to which they would consent but also that the existing government is consistent with that hypothetical one. Government officials must constantly imagine a sovereign will and then claim to speak for it. It is much more plausible to assume that there is no existing sovereign will, that there is no consensus as to what the Constitution should be. Most people have not thought seriously about what government they would authorize. Even fewer have had the opportunity to debate such issues and to be confronted with antagonistic views with which they must reach agreement. The arrogance of theorists of tacit consent is that they presume that if asked, intelligent citizens would agree with them—and therefore it is unnecessary to ask. Potential sovereignty presumes that there is no such agreement and that there could not be until the people are actually called upon to deliberate on specific constitutional proposals.[87] Consensual government does not require the imagination of a current consent; rather, it requires that government receive authorization for its actions. The Constitution provides that authorization. Government action requiring different authorization would require another such expression of consent. The government was set in motion by consent, but it need not demonstrate our continuing consent in order to remain in motion. It is enough that it not change course, or even stop its motion, except by our new consent.[88] The implication is that the founders initiated the Constitution, which remains valid and binding not by virtue of their right to govern over us but by virtue of the "historical accident" that their text is the most recent expression of consent. "The constitution remains legitimate only because all alternatives lack legitimacy."[89]

By emptying the Constitution of any current positive authority, we can recognize the true basis of its continuing legitimacy. The Constitution is not binding in a strong sense. We have not vested it with authority. Rather, it is binding in a weaker, but still sufficient, sense, in that it represents our potential to govern ourselves. By accepting the authority of the Constitution, we accept our own authority to remake it. The existing Constitution is a placeholder for our own future expression of popular sovereignty. As such it performs an important function. It is not simply a vacancy but an instrument that maintains a political space. We can replicate the fundamental political act of the founders only if we are willing to recognize the reality of their act. Stripping them of their right to constitute a government would likewise strip us of our own.

The reality of this reciprocating relationship can be seen more clearly by considering the duty imposed on government by the idea of potential sovereignty. The fundamental obligation of government officials under a correct theory of popular sovereignty is to respect the limits of their trust and not usurp the constitutive role of the sovereign. Transitory errors and abuses of government are of little significance compared to the usurpation of the right to define government powers, for this right is at the core of limited government. Potential sovereignty, therefore, imposes the duty on government to retain a democratic openness and the capacity to change constitutional forms in accordance with the popular will. By contrast, tacit consent empowers the government to act on the presumed will of the people. The former assumes uncertainty where the latter posits certainty. The former directs government to assume that it possesses no authority; the latter directs it to assume that it possesses full authority. The goal of popular sovereignty, thus understood, is not to create anarchy but to undermine government confidence.

In *McCulloch,* John Marshall prefigured the modern confidence in the authority of government. In upholding the power of the federal government to create a national bank, Marshall largely reversed the assumptions of the enumerated powers, at least in cases where "the great principles of liberty are not concerned."[90] Although the historically significant and much abused power to create corporations had not been explicitly granted to the federal government, Marshall found such a power to be implicit in the constitutional scheme. He insisted that the national government was a real government, in contrast to the head of a mere league or confederation. As such, the federal government possessed the necessary attributes of sovereignty, including such traditional powers as the ability to incorporate. A firm believer in the capacity of government to do great good on the public's behalf, Marshall contended that the federal charter should be construed generously to empower government. The Federalist justice could see no gap between the people and its governmental representatives, and as a consequence he could see no point in questioning the power claims of that which was "emphatically, and truly, a government of the people."[91] The possibility of constitutional impediments to the abuse of power, beyond the direct violation of specific individual rights, is ignored. The emphasis on the sovereignty of the government lowers the barrier to the discretionary use of political power.

It is the assumption of the necessity of an active sovereign, of a constantly legislating will, that required the transfer of sovereignty from the people to the government. The unquestioned foundations of government power, "derived from the people," allow the actual will of government officials, whether legislator or judge, to replace that of the people, for admittedly the people are not present. In order to draw upon the authority of popular consent, however, government officials must be made to demonstrate the authority for their actions.[92] In the absence of a present sovereign that demonstration can be made only by reference to the Constitution.[93] Political officeholders, there-fore, are chosen by the electorate, but they are agents of the sovereign people. The limits of their trust are defined not in the tea leaves of election returns but in the objective presence of the constitutional text. Constitutional inter-pretation becomes the first task of government officials, the necessary condi-tion for positive government action.

DEMOCRATIC DUALISM

The underlying assumption behind the notion of potential sovereignty is that "the people," in their sovereign capacity, do not always exist. Therefore, the people do not and cannot be understood to renew constantly their con-sent to the government and its constitutional form. Rather, the people emerge at particular historical moments to deliberate on constitutional issues and to provide binding expressions of their will, which are to serve as fundamental law in the future when the sovereign is absent. Between these moments, the only available expression of the sovereign will is the constitutional text, and government agents are bound by the limits of that text. Such agents are not without popular authority, but they possess political authority of a dual nature. They are chosen by and responsible to the electorate in order to ensure the faithful care of the public good, and they are empowered by the sovereign people to use the resources of government to fulfill specified ends. This dual authority speaks to different aspects of the political trust and is granted at dif-ferent times and by different manifestations of the citizenry. Moreover, these dual aspects of authority are hierarchically ordered. The former specifies the wielder of political power; the latter specifies the nature of that power. The first specifies the policy of government; the second legitimates the govern-ment itself. The achievement of popular sovereignty is to separate these two elements of politics, distinguishing between the constitutional and the merely administrative. The continuing threat to self-government is the tendency to reunite these elements in the hands of the governing officers.[94]

Rousseau thought that freedom, which for him was largely equivalent to a form of self-government, could not be realized without a permanent assem-bly of all the citizenry. The implication of this assertion, of course, is that free-dom cannot be realized in a modern nation-state. The defect in representative government that he diagnosed is the tendency of the representatives of the peo-ple to regard themselves as equivalent to the people. To the extent that they do so, they gradually bring under their own control the power to make the fun-damental law, consolidating sovereignty in fewer hands.[95] Protection of the principle of dualist democracy recognizes this tendency and resists it. Dualism maintains the distinction between the sovereign lawmaking power and the governmental administrative power, regardless of the particular form of government that exercises the latter. The fact that the American government is relatively representative has obscured the distinction, even though a prime actor in governmental constitutional change is the judiciary, which is the least representative component of the federal government.[96]

Moreover, that the constitutional lawmaking power was most authoritatively exercised by a "popular" convention composed of representatives of the people, and not the people themselves, has further undermined the distinction. In 1788 Noah Webster observed of his own state that "a distinction between a *Convention* and a *Legislature* is . . . a palpable absurdity . . . for there is no constitution in the State, except its own laws, which are always repealable by an ordinary Legislature." A constitutional convention is "no more than a Legislature chosen for *one particular purpose* of supremacy; whereas an ordinary Legislature is competent to *all* purposes of supremacy."[97] This analysis neglects, however, the distinction between fundamental law and regular legislation. The legislative power is delegated to Congress under and by the Constitution, and therefore the fundamental lawmaking power cannot be regarded as part of that legislative grant.[98] The essential aspect of sovereignty is not delegated to the government but is retained by the people, and as such it is actually absent from the political sphere. The temporal absence of such retained powers tends to make them invisible. Thus, Marshall and Madison neglected to account for them in dividing the sovereign powers between those delegated to the general government and the "residual" lodged with the state governments.[99] It is, nevertheless, this very removal of the constitutive power that renders popular sovereignty possible, for in its absence it leaves behind only the traces of its presence in the form of a text. The text alone is present in normal politics, and therefore no organ of the government is authorized to speak in the name of the people. The sovereign people are not present.[100]

This absence, however, not only renders the popular sovereign difficult to perceive, but it also renders its will difficult to enforce. It was for this reason that James Wilson advised the Pennsylvania ratification convention that "our constitutions are superior to our legislatures" as the people are to the constitution. But the power in the latter case was actually the greater "for the people possess, over our constitutions, control in act, as well as in right."[101] In the absence of a popular convention, the sovereign will can only be controlling in right; the active power of enforcement is missing, or at least delegated in trust. In writing a constitution, the people have separated fundamental law from the source of political power, just as they have separated powers within government and between levels of government. Moreover, the drafting of an enduring text also serves to divorce the objective, historic will of the people from the subjective, fluctuating will of the electorate.[102] Recognizing these separations is the first step toward maintaining them.

There are a number of reasons for valuing this division between constitutional and normal politics. First, it sustains self-government but puts fewer demands on the citizenry than the kind of continuing constitutionalism advocated by Rousseau. As he recognized, few societies could ever be capable of maintaining the high level of political commitment required by his republic. The people cannot be constantly assembled; public virtue cannot always be kept at a fevered pitch. Such theorists as Rousseau and Montesquieu were correct to note that a republic cannot sustain itself without a certain minimal level of public virtue that prevents legislation from degenerating into corrupt bargains and lawful behavior from being dependent on the use of state coercion. But the heightened degree of virtue wished for by those theorists that would create an identity between self and polity and replace self-interest with an other-regarding ethos is unrealistic. Moreover, the good life cannot be simply identified with the political life, and individuals need to be free from politics in order to pursue other diverse goods. Dualism respects this by limiting the times in which society places heightened demands on citizenship. Under normal circumstances, the concerns of politics can be delegated to others or engaged in with limited energy. The basic framework of government is settled, and individuals can order their lives within the security of a stable political system in which the fundamental decisions have already been made. Although important decisions may arise within that framework, those are likely to be more specialized and inherently contained in their implications. Participation in government administration may be desirable, but it may also be expendable. Distinct moments of higher lawmaking, however, potentially require much greater attention, as they unsettle expectations about the future direction of the government itself. Although an individual may still opt out of this constitutional discourse, the risks are potentially higher and certain costs are guaranteed. Self-government is not only useful for the protection of private interests but is ultimately essential to human dignity. Refusal to participate in moments of constitutional formation may threaten personal interests and definitely reduces the personality.[103]

In addition, dualism recognizes the reality of distinct moments of self-government. Dualism not only allows individuals to stop "acting like citizens" and turn to nonpolitical affairs, but it also prevents government from reducing the sphere of self-government. The flattening of democracy to a single level does not enhance democratic values but undermines them. The reality of nonpolitical concerns means that the citizenry is not always fully engaged in politics, and therefore a government that claims the full authority of the people is claiming more authority than it rightfully possesses. Such claims, if unchecked, in turn pervert politics, desensitizing the people to their true role in government and expanding the power of the government to act against the people. Such effects are myriad. The effort by government officials to make plausible their claim to popular authority leads to a constant heightening of political rhetoric, with its consequent baleful influence on policy making and political life. Every policy dispute must be imagined in terms of crisis and war, and political opponents must be vilified as enemies of the people. The turbulence of democratic politics feared by the framers becomes particularly intense if its democratic pedigree is uncertain, and greater efforts must be made to create the illusion of authority in order to convince political opponents that the people not only have an opinion but have demanded with their sovereign will that a tax deduction be given for business entertainment expenses.[104]

Likewise, once policy debates are portrayed as reflections of sovereignty itself, the set of measures available for government use is expanded. Actions regarded as unacceptable and burdens on the populace become "necessary and proper" if government officials are regarded as fully authorized to act for the sovereign people and exercise their own discretion in serving the public good. Specific constitutional authority becomes less important if it is possible to invoke public necessity as the raison d'etat of daily democratic politics and if transitory policy disputes become the "moral equivalent of war." Constitutionalist restraints are loosened in the face of the sovereign himself acting for the public good, a regression to the earliest theories of sovereignty and the unencumbered delegation of the public trust. Instead of recognizing the possibility of consulting the people and acquiring their consent to changed governmental forms, officials merely assume that their own elevation to office is an adequate mandate.

It is important to note that the value of constitutional politics does not arise from any posited elevation of public virtue to be found during such moments.[105] Rather, the critical feature of popular sovereignty is the authority to decide. The basic fact of governance is that the power to decide constitutional forms must be lodged somewhere. Democratic dualism rests on the claim that this power of decision should reside with the people who must live under those constitutional forms. Although there are reasons to believe that such moments of decision would include genuine deliberation, the right of the people to govern themselves does not arise from what they decide but from who they are, the subjects of government. A space remains for the people to err in their formation of a constitution; but if they do, it is their error, its costs will be borne by them, and they have the capacity to correct their creation. The possibility of error may suggest that sovereignty should be removed from their hands and lodged elsewhere, or that the idea of sovereignty should be abandoned in favor of a different conception of constitutional authority. Such responses would be misleading, however.

Constitutional requirements are ultimately a matter of choice and will. Although reason, at least, has much to say as to the correct form a constitution should take, it is not conclusive in and of itself. The rights due to individuals, the goods to be achieved for them through government, and the instruments of government necessary to do both are subject to disagreement and controversy. In part such controversy arises from the fact that there are multiple correct answers; there are multiple ways to formulate individual rights and several reasonable responses to the inherent trade-offs of politics. And disagreements arise in part as a result of the limitations of reason. There may be determinate right answers to some political questions, but we do not agree on what they are. Given such disagreements, the burden of decision must fall somewhere, and there is little reason to believe that it is better lodged with government officials than with the people more broadly. It is both dangerously overconfident to regard the government as more fit to reach such decisions and unjustly belittling to regard the people as unfit to rely on their own judgment.[106]

The second difficulty with the rejection of popular sovereignty is that it assumes that good government can be maintained without the authority of the people. A basic judgment of democracy is that government cannot save the people if they are fundamentally corrupt. A critic of democratic dualism has contended that "more is at stake than the scope of judicial authority. We want to know if 'the People' can do anything they like."[107] But in fact the scope of judicial authority is precisely what is at stake. The task of constitutional theory is not to design the best possible world but to consider constitutional forms. The critical issue is not whether the people can make mistakes, but whether the judiciary can save us from our mistakes. The history of the American judiciary is not encouraging in this regard. The standard example of the constitutional protection of slavery is indicative of the limits of judicial power. Political action, not judicial construal of constitutional terms, ended slavery. More recently, the judiciary has not proven to be a firm barrier against public fears of radical subversives, the governmental emasculation of private property, or the segregation of the races. Although the courts have undoubtedly been significant in making isolated gains in the enhancement of public life, they have also been instrumental in abuses; and many of their most celebrated advances have depended on underlying political changes to make them possible. Although the people may act in ways that justify resistance to their decisions, the judiciary is a thin reed upon which to rest one's hopes for political salvation in a corrupt world.[108]

Even assuming that the judiciary could operate as a truly independent force in the governmental realm and act decisively against the public will to impose a different constitution on the populace, such actions could hardly be judged worthy of celebration and political legitimacy. Judges are not simply private citizens well positioned to prevent public harm. They are public officers, invested with political authority by virtue of the people's constitutional law. Use of the instruments of that office in the interest of advancing a better constitution over the people's will can only be regarded as an abuse of power. The persuasiveness of such claims relies heavily on the obfuscation of the violence at the heart of the judicial power.[109] For a judge to issue an edict in contradiction to the known law in the interest of his own, perhaps correct, theory of justice, he would be seeking to employ the tools of public coercion against the public itself.[110] The underlying reality of such actions can be highlighted through a more immediate and extreme example. A police officer may be completely convinced that abortion is murder and that a just system of laws would prohibit it. As a result of these beliefs, the officer not only views himself as incapable of enforcing current abortion laws but believes that he must take positive action to resist them. Granting the accuracy of his position, we may agree with his moral conclusion. If the officer were to refuse to resign his position, however, but instead "arrested" abortionists and incarcerated them at the point of his service revolver, we would rightfully regard him as illegitimately acting "under the color of law" but without actual political authority. The officer's crime is compounded by his use of the instruments of the state to achieve his own ends, his continued pretension to legal authority in acting against that authority. Such would be the judge's position in determining that the people were in error in drafting their constitution and in seeking to correct that error through his official activities. The rejection of democratic dualism because the people may make mistakes is not the rejection of human fallibility but the substitution of one set of fallible political actors for another.[111]

Although the authority of the popular sovereign does not depend on the truth of its will, there is reason to think that the results of its deliberations will be reasonable.[112] Nothing about democratic dualism requires the divorce of reason and will. Rather, it insists upon the necessity of popular will in support of reason. Neither is dispensable to political authority, but reason gains its force through its acceptance by the sovereign. The founding itself cannot be characterized as a moment of complete public virtue and the rejection of self-interest and factional disputes. Nonetheless, historic instances of constitutional politics such as the founding are moments of deliberation and are, at least, open to reason. The outcome of such moments of higher lawmaking are not predetermined or simply reducible to social forces, but both rely upon rational argument and gain their authority through that reliance. Democracy is open to the philosopher, even if politics cannot be reduced to a philosophical exercise.

The effects of pure self-interest are likely to be reduced by the nature of constitutional deliberation. Constitutions are not concerned with the resolution of an immediate policy dispute but with the framework within which both immediate and distant concerns will have to be resolved. If constitutional framers are not placed in a Rawlsian original position, they still do not know at the moment of decision the full effects of constitutional forms in the future. Constitutional actors, therefore, must consider not only the likely effects of constitutional forms on their immediate interests but also on their possible interests at some point in the future and on the interests of their posterity. The very permanence of constitutional changes, as opposed to mere legislative outcomes, necessitates a broader perspective by those engaged in the deliberations. Similarly, the generality of concerns that arise in the formation of a constitution weakens the connection between constitutional outcomes and particular, individual interests. Although some individuals may have an immediate stake in aspects of the constitution, other aspects are unlikely to so concern them, and therefore their deliberations on those aspects will be less partisan. The Philadelphia drafters themselves emphasized this aspect of their own and the ratifiers' deliberations by explicitly noting that the Constitution was to serve for "ourselves and our Posterity." In doing so, they strove to convince themselves to consider more than their own immediate interests and to draft that which would be most just. To this degree, constitution making partakes in an even more emphatic way of the general virtue of legislating in a rule of law, in that the results must be written in general terms and applied by another.[113]

The fact that the constitution will be controlling not just today but also tomorrow directs the sovereign to consider those likely effects as well, pushing him toward a more universal perspective. This effort requires, however, that the sovereign deliberate on the constitution itself. One of Madison's fears of a periodic convention to "interpret" the document was that such conventions would not be able to escape the partisan disputes of the moment.[114] The separation of government from the sovereign power to make constitutions helps lessen this effect, however, as does the lengthy and difficult process of gaining approval for textual change. Such devices help focus deliberation on the fact that it is a constitution that we are making, with all the responsibility that entails. Although such efforts cannot ensure that temporary disputes do not carry over into the constitutional realm, they do help mitigate the risk. Democratic dualism is to be valued not because it will ensure the creation of the best conceivable constitution but because it is the best means available for creating a good governing document.

THE REALITY OF THE POPULAR SOVEREIGN

The value of dualist democracy still leaves a certain dissatisfaction with the notion of popular sovereignty as a realization of consensual government. Accepting the idea that government must ground its authority on the consent of the governed, how does popular sovereignty realize this ideal? Why are constitutional conventions any more authoritative than mere government legislatures, and how do they come to speak in the name of the people? Not only do conventions include a sliver of the total population of society, but the founding conventions in particular were not even selected by large portions of the founders' own population and certainly were not selected by us. Three recent commentators have characterized popular sovereignty as a "fiction," a "myth," and a "metaphor," none of which seems conducive to promoting it as the basis for constitutional authority.[115] The challenge of such a theory, therefore, is in establishing why we should accept its reality.

Perhaps the first step in recovering the reality of the popular sovereign is in explaining why such characterizations of the idea as fictional are actually useful to clarifying, and not just dispelling, the concept. In order to do so, I adopt the metaphorical label.[116] Although "fiction" and "myth" grasp at the same underlying concept, they have unfortunate negative connotations. Popular sovereignty is a label for a story we tell about ourselves, indicating both how we think our system functions and how we think it ought to function. The persuasiveness or compelling quality of the story derives from both how desirable the normative goal is and how well it comports with our experience of actual politics. That this is a government "by the people, for the people" is not literally true, but it is true enough that we can adopt it as our regulative ideal. The fact that it is not literally true does not make it any less capable of justifying the political system, as long as the separation between the ideal and the reality does not become too great.[117] To this degree, popular sovereignty is a metaphor for our constitutional order. Our Constitution is like self-government, but it is not actually self-government.

Such metaphorical relations, however, are neither pernicious nor unusual. In a political context, the notion that an elected member of the legislature "represents" her district, or that in casting a vote "I elect" "my" legislator, is equally metaphorical. My elected representative differs from me in innumerable ways, both trivial and significant, not least in that she influences the outcome of the legislative process and I do not. Nonetheless, the idea of representation binds us together, reminding us both that she is not an independent actor but must be responsive to my will. Within limits, she must behave as if she were my representative in the government and not inform me that in fact I am but a single voter out of hundreds of thousands, that rationally I should not even bother to vote at all, and thus my opinion means next to nothing to her (especially given that I am not a member of her party, contributed nothing to her campaign, and did not even cast my vote for her in the last election).[118] If she were to do so, it is of less importance that she might change her voting behavior than it is that she would be sacrificing the authority of the government over me. In a fundamental sense, she would cease to be part of "my government" and simply become a coercive force in the world. This relationship is not unique to politics, however, but is basic to our social and mental structure.[119] Language itself is rooted in metaphorical relations, in which I accept that my words are like the objects in the world that they represent, that the phrase "two plus two equals four" has some relation to the handful of apples sitting on the table, that "I" is a meaningful term, and that I "am" an American. To recognize that the ideal of popular sovereignty is not literally true is itself uninteresting. The more important question is not whether we are literally members of the popular sovereign, but in what ways our membership is real and significant.

There are a number of ways in which the popular sovereign gains substance for us. Most fundamentally, it does so through our engagement with it. By engaging in constitutional meaning, by entering into a discourse as to what the text means and what kind of constitution should govern us, we are drawn into the sovereign. Hobbes provides an entry point for such an analysis. For him, the essential role of the sovereign is to bring order to a chaotic world. That order is only partially physical, for the physical depends upon the mental. Therefore, Hobbes's sovereign must assert his control over language itself, defining "justice," among other things, in terms of the sovereign will. The sovereign rules his subjects by defining the available rules; he can only be measured and found wanting if someone else controls the measuring stick. The sovereign gains authority by convincing the subjects to adopt his understanding of authority; Hobbes persuades us to construct the Leviathan by drawing us into his imagined world of a war of all against all. Taking the example of Hobbes himself rather than that of his sovereign can reduce the Leviathan's absolutism. The sovereign imposes definition, but Hobbes persuades us to adopt his definitions. The sovereign seeks to monopolize discourse; Hobbes invites us into a common discourse. Still, Hobbes is no less authoritative. He is successful precisely to the degree that we seriously engage him, accept his questions as the relevant ones to ask, and conduct the conversation on his terms.[120]

Similarly, "The Constitution is binding to the extent that it continues to make a political people by providing the grammar by which they speak authoritatively about their public values."[121] Perhaps more fundamentally, the popular sovereign is real precisely to the extent that we engage in the common enterprise of constitutionalism. As an expression of the sovereign will, the Constitution is binding, not because we currently accept its particular terms in their entirety but because we accept its project, its grammar.[122] The Constitution, therefore, is a token of our capacity to engage in constitutional discourse. Its authority hinges on our continuing willingness to do so. Abandoning that form of constitutionalism, self-governance, would undermine the basis for the entire document, not just its particular terms. The popular sovereign is real because we form it through the acceptance of a public sphere, a common interest in constitutionalism. We are part of the popular sovereign because we accept that common interest and help construct it, either explicitly or implicitly. We join with the founders because we accept that we too could be founders. In doing so, we accept their inheritance. In ratifying the Constitution, the founders did not seek to govern us from beyond the graves; rather, they sought to secure for us the right to govern ourselves.[123] By accepting the authoritativeness of the Constitution, we accept our right to devise a new constitution and incidentally become authors of the old.[124]

As with all sovereigns, the popular sovereign of the Constitution is self-creating. The gap between chaos and order can be bridged only through a singular act of will. Despite efforts to naturalize "the people," they remain diverse. Their commonality is created through assertion, although not through an empty assertion. We are not just said to be a common people; we are brought to recognize our commonality. John Jay was not merely being naive in contending in the *Federalist* that this is "one connected country" given by Providence "to one united people" possessing the same ancestors, language, religion, customs, political principles, and history, just as Hobbes was not being naive in contending that men were isolated individuals prepared to battle every other individual to the death for honor and goods. Rather, both men were concerned with creating the rhetorical basis for a common people. That the Americans were not really one united people is of less importance than the fact that they could think of themselves as such, and that nationalists such as Jay were ultimately successful in persuading the citizenry to embrace his vision rather than that of other "politicians" who "insist that this opinion is erroneous" and who advocate the "new doctrine" that the Americans are actually many peoples deserving of separate governments.[125] When the Constitution speaks in the name of "We the People" and specifies that "the people" will ratify the document through special conventions held in each of the states, it designates its own authority and creates the people itself.[126] There could be no response to Patrick Henry's question as to who authorized the Philadelphia Convention to speak in the name of the people, since there could have been no such authorization.[127] The people did not exist until they constituted themselves through the action of forming a constitution. The success of a constitution, though not necessarily of this Constitution, marked the reality of the sovereign people.

Moreover, having designated the relevant "people," the Constitution has also modified their composition since the founding. There are no natural barriers delimiting the extent of the populace. Jay attempted to naturalize such boundaries, but the attempt rings artificial to modern ears. His particular metaphor has lost its force. In arguing for the strengthening of the Union, Jay noted, "It has often given me pleasure to observe that independent America was not composed of detached and distant territories." It was instead "one connected country."[128] The image was persuasive, but it does not specify how we know that America is not composed of "detached and distant territories." Is physical contiguity sufficient to demonstrate the existence of a single country? Is Hawaii less a part of the United States, or Maui of Hawaii (or Manhattan of New York), by being separated by water? The answer depends on the persuasiveness of the image of the nation. Similarly, since the founding, the people have modified themselves, expanding the rights of full citizenship to include blacks, women, the poor, and young adults.[129] In doing so, the people have less expanded the composition of the popular sovereign than it has extended and reinforced the bonds within the sovereign, strengthening the reality of its own existence.[130]

As the initial discussion of sovereignty indicates, the sovereign gains his political authority by his claim to represent the whole of the people. The sovereign is not a partial entity, representing a single class or subunit of society against the rest but claims to encompass the whole. It is this aspect of popular sovereignty that connects it to the ideal of self-government. We are each an author of the sovereign's actions, because the sovereign acts for each of us equally as part of the whole. This necessity of speaking for the whole leads to further consideration of the nature of the popular sovereign. The constitutional conventions obviously did not physically include the entire populace. Moreover, acceptance of the Constitution was not unanimous, nor could it have been.[131] We therefore need to clarify the sense in which the popular sovereign includes the whole. First, the will of the sovereign encompasses the whole because the whole embraces that will, even if only post hoc. As Rousseau noted, the general law is expressed through majority voting, but the minority authors that law by accepting it as their own. Although Rousseau suggests a certain mystical element to this enterprise, his essential point is sound. The continued rejection of the general law by the minority indicates that there is in fact no common society between the majority and minority; they do not form a single people and therefore possess no common sovereign. The minority would recognize no greater claim of the constitutional government over it than the claim of a geographically foreign government; both are equally alien.

In an important sense, this acceptance of the sovereign will is not just the acceptance of the decision procedure but is an acceptance of the particular outcome itself. The minority does not "author" majority rule; it authors the general will. Thus, less clearly than Rousseau, Locke and Hobbes require that each individual consents to the sovereign and accept his authority. Only after that authority is established can the sovereign make particular decisions that are contrary to the will of particular individuals. The constitutional decision requires the whole, but subsidiary administrative decisions may be partial. There is no sense in which the minority could say, "You won this vote and got your constitution; but we'll be back tomorrow and we'll see who wins then." The commitment is not to a continuing decision procedure.[132] Each constitutional decision is regarded as final, even if it actually has to be remade at some point in the future. There can be no recognized tomorrow in which the constitutional vote is retaken and a different outcome reached. The constitution is accepted as necessary, even if it was in fact a contingent result. The artifice of the decision must necessarily be hidden.[133] The astonishing acquiescence of the anti-Federalists to the result of constitutional ratification could only come from their acceptance of the Constitution itself. The anti-Federalists could just as easily have refused to attend the state conventions, or called new ones immediately after the ratification votes of the first, or turned to the regular state legislatures as alternative representative institutions authorized to reach a different result, or simply taken up arms against the new federal government. The fact that they did none of these things is indicative of their acceptance of the Constitution as written as the authoritative expression of the popular will, binding themselves as well as their opponents.[134] For many anti-Federalists, the Federalists had tried to bind the hands of the states too tightly. Popular state conventions, they argued, could not be limited to simply ratifying a text but should be regarded as creative in their own right and as an intermediary stage in a continuing process of constitutional negotiation. Ultimately, the anti-Federalists were not convinced of the naturalness of the ratification scheme; they were convinced to accept the authority of the Constitution, including Article 7, creating this ratification process. The authority of the conventions was as much a product of their success as it was a condition for that success.[135] The outcome of the conventions was not just the Federalists' Constitution, but the American Constitution. Both sides in the ratification debates were required to make that intellectual leap and accept the government as their joint creation.[136]

The minority is also embraced within the sovereign through the deliberative quality of the constitutional decision. The majority cannot simply impose its will on the minority through strength, even if that power is only the strength of votes. Rather, the majority must open itself to the minority by engaging it in deliberation. Even if the minority is ultimately unconvinced and there remains disagreement when the final vote is taken, the minority has been accepted as internal to the whole and not as an alien element simply to be defeated. The process of constitutional formation cannot be guided by the slogan "to the victor go the spoils," for genuine efforts at conversion and reconciliation are integral to the process of gaining political authority over those who are finally outvoted. The majority, therefore, must be willing to put the ultimate constitutional outcome in doubt. By opening the constitution to deliberation, its shape is put in jeopardy and is dependent on the capacity of the majority to sustain its support in the face of argument. Convention delegates need not be considered disinterested, but they must be willing to justify their position and attempt to persuade other delegates.[137]

Partially for this reason, political factions are inconsistent with constitutional deliberation. Such factions are dangerous precisely because they are preformed, and therefore closed. Their positions are not subjected to external challenge but are asserted against others. Although subgroups may form within the convention to advocate for given positions, no organized interest may "capture" the convention in order to impose its own constitutional choices against the interest and will of the remaining citizens.[138] The existence of such factions in the normal legislative process helps undermine the government's claim to be a direct representative of the sovereign.[139] Such devices as extralegislative caucuses and party-line votes violate the basis for determining the sovereign will. In such cases, party members support a given position in the convention for reasons external to the position itself, in the interest of party discipline, for example. The outcome of the vote would be predetermined and not open to public deliberation. The result would depend on the strength of faction, not on the strength of reason. In such instances, the sovereign will cannot be representative of the whole but is explicitly the rule of a partial society over the whole through the instrument of law. The constitutional law then becomes an instrument of dominance rather than an expression of political authority. The ratification of the Constitution provides an explicit example of such openness. The initial election of delegates to the ratification conventions favored the opponents of the Constitution. An immediate majority vote based simply on the strength of numbers would have found the Federalists in the minority. In order to win ratification, proponents of the Constitution necessarily had to "convert" some of their opponents. In allowing such deliberation, the anti-Federalists threw the outcome of the conventions into doubt and eventually lost control over the results. In doing so, however, they enhanced the authority of the adopted Constitution.[140]

Such an emphasis on the wholeness and representativeness of the sovereign will recalls the necessity of unity in the sovereign. The sovereign must be one not only to be decisive but also to include the entire people within its terms. Division within the sovereign would also indicate division between the sovereign and part of his subjects. Unity suggests its own problems for the notion of popular sovereignty, however. A posited need for unity suggests that the sovereign must either be exclusionary or unreal. In order to secure its internal homogeneity, the sovereign must eliminate or paper over its own dissenting elements. Further, a requirement of unity, or unanimity, indicates the impermanence of the sovereign. Government only becomes necessary when such unanimity breaks down, but that would also require the dissolution of the sovereign and the end of political authority.[141] Alternatively, unity undermines durability because there is no basis for requiring duration. An individual cannot bind himself, for in each moment he exists anew with a fresh will. A unitary sovereign cannot contradict himself because there is no common basis for comparing two expressions of the sovereign will; each exists independently of all others. The possibility of a binding will, of contractual obligation, can only exist in the presence of diversity, with its possibility of conflict.[142] Finally, unity may be achieved by excluding the basis for dissent, instead of excluding the dissenters themselves. Thus, a hypothetical sovereign can be imagined that is composed only of purely rational individuals who are stripped of their individual differences. In essence, the sovereign will is determined by a single, constructed rationalist. Only in this way can the true basis for agreement be discovered and the sovereign will articulated.[143]

Each of these objections misconstrues the nature of the unity of the popular sovereign. The sovereign must be united in will, not in being. The neo-Kantian construction of a singular representative of the polity is an atavistic return to the Hobbesian artificial person who can exercise sovereign discretion. Similarly, the other objections derive from a Hobbesian identification of act and will, the necessity of an active sovereign. The separation of power from law, however, suggests that the necessary unity is not to be found in the decision makers but in the decision. The sovereign embraces the whole people by appealing to what they can hold in common. But they may only share the will itself, not the interests and motivations that formed that will. The possibility of commonality in diversity thickens the idea of popular sovereignty. The sovereign need not be extracted from the people in order to create unity, but unity must be reached through common agreement. The people come from divergent positions to a point of agreement. As the embodiment of that momentary agreement, a constitution is stable. Moreover, as an agreement among diverse actors, that sovereign will is binding even when those actors reassert their diversity. A constitution is not simply a "precommitment" of the sober founders hoping to bind their irresponsible offspring or later selves.[144] The Constitution is also an actual contract, an agreement among diverse parties with real and separate interests. The capacity to compromise and to make trade-offs allows them to form a common ground, even though their individual interests may be antagonistic to given parts of that to which they have commonly agreed. "We the People" exist through our capacity to reach a common agreement, to form a common Constitution. But we need not be viewed, and in fact do not exist, as a single unitary social organism.[145] The Constitution recognizes both our diversity and our unity. By reaching agreement and committing our collective will to writing, we define the boundaries of how we can effectuate that diversity through government. In seeking our particular goods under the Constitution, we are bound by how we collectively have agreed to rule each other and be ruled in turn.

The idea of popular sovereignty in particular has served to undermine the durability of constitutions by indicating that each generation must itself consent to the government. Past generations are thought to be no more able to bind future generations without their consent than some individuals may bind others. The result is a discontinuity in the popular sovereign. Each generation is assumed to be a self-contained unit. Renewed consent can be achieved only by reconceptualizing the sovereign as an organic whole that includes the past and future as well as the present, by reintroducing the notion of tacit consent, or by providing mechanisms for renewed expressions of positive consent.[146] A theory of potential sovereignty adopts the last strategy, but with modifications and qualifications. It is unnecessary to build an expiration date into the Constitution in order for it to satisfy the needs of consensual government in the context of generational change. It is, however, separately necessary to recognize that each generation is not fully independent from earlier ones, and that this has an effect on the nature of constitutional authority. The founders' constitution gains authority over us by giving us the capacity to reject it.

The Constitution gained its initial authority from the consent of those who would be governed by it through the mechanism of ratification. It continues to enjoy authority over us, who did not ratify it, by virtue of its own commitment to self-government. Unlike the early constitutions adopted by the newly independent states, the Constitution does not claim to be eternal but is silent as to its own duration and provides a framework for its own modification. In doing so, it implicitly minimizes its own authority in order to strengthen the authority of the popular sovereign that lies behind it. It is not the Constitution that grounds the nation, but "We the People" who expressed our will through the text. The durability of the text is conditional on the people's not replacing it. This is the fact of popular government that such early texts as the Articles of Confederation and the first state constitutions attempted to bury and that Federalist hagiography attempted to rebury after ratification. Despite such late efforts, the text itself highlights its own origins, including the terms of its own implementation within itself—creating a brief, public record of the temporality of the sovereign will. Each generation is therefore reminded of its own capacity to refound the nation on its own terms. Moreover, by providing not only for amendment, but also for a larger democratic governing structure, the Constitution draws subsequent generations into its own discourse. Although the Constitution could be rejected in its entirety and its authority replaced, its capacity to accept amendment seduces radical movements into becoming merely reformist ones. More broadly, by guaranteeing the underlying basis for sovereign deliberation, the Constitution almost ensures that later generations will build on its foundations in any future constitutional project. As a result, the founders' constitution serves as the cornerstone for the nation's continuing constitutionalism, ensuring its own authority through both its necessity and its adaptability.

This ability of the Constitution to structure future constitutional discourse, and therefore to ensure its own viability, points to a difficulty with the concept of generational change. Each generation does not begin ex nihilo. Indeed, the very idea of a distinct generation is highly abstracted from the concrete circumstances in which a real citizenry emerges. The present has not appeared on the political stage unburdened by the past, free to form its own government as if on a blank slate. Rather, the present is dependent on the past. It is born with obligations to the past. Consensual government depends not on the freedom from such obligations but on the voluntary acceptance of them. The past both structures the present's choice and influences the choice that will be made. By placing its own example in the foreground, the Constitution limits our perspective, and thus limits our choices, just as the British constitution and common law did for the founders. By elevating the notion of the popular sovereign as a distinct political authority independent of government, the Constitution provides us with a basis for deliberation on fundamental political issues.[147] These claims suggest that a judicial challenge to constitutional authority in the interest of creating space for the judicial choice of fundamental values badly misconstrues the nature of constitutional authority. The Constitution is not simply a text to which we have not consented and which therefore can be cast aside in favor of some preferred alternative. Rather, continuing constitutional authority is a basic fact of American governance. Its authority is not dependent on judicial demonstration of its continued acceptance by the populace. Instead, the essential point in need of demonstration would be its lack of authority, its replacement by some authoritative act of the sovereign with a different instrument of governance.[148]

These observations indicate that there is a dual responsiveness in the popular sovereign. Sovereign deliberation serves as a bridge between reason and interest. The result of that deliberation gains its authority not only from being good but from being willed by those who must live under it. There is an electoral connection in the device of popular conventions. The conventions served to historicize and particularize sovereignty. The popular sovereign was active in a particular moment and was composed of actual individuals representing an interested citizenry. As a result, the national good could not simply be asserted but had to be demonstrated to those who held different opinions and would potentially be harmed by government actions. The sovereign will contained in the Constitution was not to serve as a mere ideal; rather, it was to serve as the source for actual governing institutions. In order to gain the acceptance of actual citizens, the document appealed to their current and future interests, to "the people" that they were as well as to the people that they wanted to be. Convention delegates deliberated from a situated position, and though they were willing to compromise their own immediate interests, they were neither willing nor able to ignore them. The popular sovereign did not rule for the good of the people but governed in accord with the will of the people. The people were to determine for themselves their own good.

Although the popular will is a necessary component of sovereignty, it is not exclusive, and the popular will is not antagonistic to reason. The formation of the Constitution depended on popular deliberation, and it was drafted and ratified on the basis of the persuasion of the whole, not the assertion of a part. Thus, if the popular sovereign did not immediately reflect the will of the minority, the former was nonetheless responsive to the latter. Dissenters were not excluded but were invited to engage in a common project. The addition of the Bill of Rights to the Constitution is indicative of this responsiveness. Although not satisfying all possible anti-Federalist objections, the addition of the first amendments completed the larger ratification process, expanding the foundation of the text so that the final product was as much the work of the opponents as the initial text was of its proponents. The formation of the document as a whole was therefore open not only to the convention delegates, or even to the voting citizenry, but to all those who could deliberate on the basis of the governing order. Popular campaigning, pamphlet and newspaper commentary, and barroom discussions demonstrated the expansiveness of the deliberative process and the inclusiveness of the popular sovereign. Such informal debaters did not possess a vote on the final passage of the Constitution, but neither were convention delegates sequestered from such public discussion.[149] The conventions were to focus and elevate the public reasoning, not substitute for it. The authority of the conventions to act as agents for the people depended on their capacity to justify themselves to the citizenry and to represent their concerns in a smaller forum. The capacity of the people to participate in the deliberations "at a distance" helped forge a political community. If the conventions were not simply microcosms of that larger community, they were the active extensions of it.

The idea of the popular sovereign offers the possibility of democracy, and it is this possibility that creates constitutional authority. The people as a sovereign entity are not present in the government operations under the Constitution, but the spirit of their existence animates the whole. It is this spectral presence—the actual consent of the past and the possible consent of the future—that grounds the Constitution. The current populace does not and need not actively reconstruct the sovereign will at all times in order to maintain the authority of the Constitution. By placing it in motion, and retaining the capacity to modify or replace the inherited text, the people have provided the continuing basis for constitutional government and for meaningful consent to government. Maintenance of the Constitution secures the authority of the people for the present and the future.

Originalism and Its Relation to the People

This discussion of the nature of popular sovereignty and constitutional authority provides the basis for valuing the Constitution. In doing so, it also provides instruction as to the proper method of interpreting that document. Originalism is not an accidental addition to the constitutional framework but a necessary component of the Constitution's own vitality. At minimum, originalism is supportive of constitutional authority. At most, the rejection of an originalist method would undermine the basis for both judicial review and adherence to the Constitution itself. Originalism advances democratic values not through a majoritarian endorsement of judicial restraint, as some would have it, but through the maintenance of popular sovereignty as a governing ideal.

Ironically, the idea of popular sovereignty suggests a particular role for the judiciary in the constitutional system. Although the judicial obligation to engage in constitutional interpretation is not unique to the courts, since each branch is bound by the sovereign will, the judiciary nonetheless is functionally elevated above the other branches in terms of its specialized capacity to interpret that will. First, the independence of the judiciary from the normal realm of electoral politics enhances its capacity to act as a conservative element in the constitutional system. Judicial isolation from normal electoral forces makes the judiciary particularly ill suited to gauging the current mood and interests of the electorate. The judiciary's sources of information are limited in this regard, as are its incentives to ascertain and react to shifts in public opinion. Given the fact that the government is not directly representative of the sovereign, such distance from common governmental forces can assist judges in focusing on the text of the law rather than on the interests of politics. As Madison noted, under the Constitution both government officials and individual citizens are likely to be caught up in partisan, factional disputes over particular issues of policy. The republican challenge is to provide a mechanism that can stand apart from such partisanship and enforce the general will against the particular. The judiciary serves as such a less-interested forum.[150]

In addition to the advantage of independence, the judiciary benefits from its legalistic nature. It is practiced in applying the law, requiring both specialized skills and a detached disposition to discover the requirements of the law and to determine its applicability in given circumstances. The embodiment of the sovereign will in a constitutional text creates an independent law that is binding on the government. Rather than govern by its own hand, the popular sovereign must rely on agents who hold political power in trust and on rules that authorize and bind those agents. The maintenance of a government under law implicates a judicial body to enforce that law. Moreover, since the constitutional law is directed primarily to the government itself, government officials become interested parties in disputes over constitutional meaning. Driven by their own immediate goals and political mandates, government officers are likely to strain at the limitations placed on their powers. Being uninvolved in most such disputes, the judiciary serves as a relatively neutral arbiter to examine objectively the terms of political office and to sustain the distinction between the sovereign people and their government.

Finally, by relying on the persuasiveness of reason to assert its own authority, the judiciary reinforces the independence of the sovereign. This claim must not be misunderstood. The judiciary does not and cannot re-create the sovereign deliberations on the appropriate constitution. The judiciary can speak neither for nor to the absent sovereign. As a part of the government, the judiciary is merely an agent of the sovereign, not its representative.[151] Judicial authority comes from its functional expertise, not from its special constituency. Judicial reasoning supports the authority of the sovereign because it indicates the need for government to justify its own authority in terms of an external source. Elected officials tend to subvert constitutional authority by elevating the authority of their own electoral mandates, but the judiciary does not possess a popular base from which to challenge other officials.[152] Thus, the judiciary potentially exemplifies the inherent lack of government authority. The judiciary's particular claim to authority can come only from the accuracy of its efforts to interpret the Constitution. In doing so, the judiciary serves as a reminder of the absence of the sovereign and the presence of the law. The judiciary counters political power not with reason simply, but with the authority of the Constitution. It is the inherent weakness of the judicial position that renders it most conducive to preserving the integrity of constitutional requirements. Such arguments do not support a unique capacity in the courts to engage in constitutional interpretation, but they do indicate a special obligation by the courts to interpret the fundamental law and a particular reason for respecting their judgment.[153]

Given the need for judicial interpretation of the Constitution, popular sovereignty also dictates the adoption of an originalist method of interpretation. Much of the support for an originalist method is implicit in the previous discussion of the nature of popular sovereignty, but a few points should be made explicit. The fundamental basis for the authority of originalism is its capacity to retain a space for the popular sovereign. From its earliest formulations, popular sovereignty meant the right of revolution. Such a right was grounded on a view of government officials as mere agents of the people. This conception of government elevated the good of the people to being the ultimate end of government. Further, it specified that the people themselves were their own judge of what constituted the *salus populi*. Public officials could not only be tyrants who positively violated the public good; they could also be usurpers who asserted their own authority to determine the public good. In the American context, the right to revolution was rationalized and structured in the right to make constitutions. The authority to constitute government is prior to and more basic than the authority to replace its members. Revolutions are not simply rowdy elections but are reorderings of the political society. Sustaining the authority and possibility of popular sovereignty requires preserving that right to constitute government. Originalism preserves that right by enforcing the terms of the known sovereign will, and in so doing it protects a space for a renewed exercise of popular constitutional deliberation. By enforcing the discoverable intentions of past expressions of the sovereign will, originalism both requires the renewed expression of the sovereign to change constitutional meaning and renders the possibility of such expressions meaningful by making them legally significant.

Within this broader framework, several subsidiary supports for originalism can be indicated. First, it maintains the separation between the sovereign and the government and thereby secures the primeval check on government action. It does so both by denying the identity of the sovereign will and government actions and by denying the capacity of government to modify constitutional terms. Other methods of interpretation implicitly erase such distinctions. Interpretive approaches that allow judicial restraint in relation to some parts of the text implicitly assert that the other branches of government directly embody the deliberate popular will relative to those aspects of the text. Similarly, methods that authorize judicial activism in disregard of the intentions of the founders implicitly cast the Court itself in the role of the sovereign, authorized to remake constitutional meaning in accord with some preferred conception of the political good. In either case, consensual and limited government is undermined, replaced with a selective reordering of constitutional values by government officials who claim an authority superior to the fundamental law under which they hold their offices. Originalism insists that government has no intrinsic authority; other approaches position government officials as autonomous political actors. By depending on the authority of the constitutional conventions to define constitutional meaning, originalism indicates and draws upon the constitutional foundation of popular sovereignty—that the people alone determine the higher law.

Second, originalism preserves the universality of the popular will. Other methods of constitutional interpretation ultimately claim direct access to the source of the popular will, whether reason, the natural law, the prerequisites of democracy, or the public good. Only originalism adheres to the sovereign intent alone. In doing so, originalists need not claim that sovereign deliberations are purely a matter of will, of power politics with no relation to external concerns or values. Indeed, the worth of popular sovereignty arises from its connection to external sources of value. Originalists must maintain, however, that such political influences gain their legal authority through their adoption by the people. In part, this derives from the people's right to be governed only in accord with their own consent, even if substantive goods could be achieved by ignoring their wishes. It also derives, however, from the ambiguity and indeterminacy of such external sources of political action. The selection of a particular constitutional form must always depend upon the exercise of judgment and choice. Originalism insists on the people's right to make that choice. Further, in the case of error in judgment, popular sovereignty recognizes no other body with the authority to substitute its own judgment for that of the people. Although the people may be fallible, democracy rests on the claim that there is no identifiable group that is less fallible or has the right to impose its judgment on others.

Third, originalism preserves the effectiveness of the popular will. The ideal of popular sovereignty would be meaningless if others could set the actions of the sovereign aside. The abandonment of an originalist method depends on just such a capacity, at least by the judiciary. By enforcing the original terms of the constitutional contract as articulated by its authors, an originalist Court ensures that the efforts of the sovereign are not in vain, that its will is effectuated in its absence. Self-governance becomes an empty phrase if the intentions of authoritative popular bodies can be disregarded. From another angle, originalism secures the effectiveness of a future expression of the popular will. By maintaining the principle that constitutional meaning is determined by its authors, originalism provides the basis for future constitutional deliberation by the people. Present and future generations can only expect their own constitutional will to be effectuated if they are willing to give effect to prior such expressions. The abandonment of the principle that past decisions control the future until replaced by a new decision marks the abandonment of popular government itself. Unless we accept the authority of the past, we cannot assert our own authority over the future, whether understood as a matter of decades or as a matter of weeks. By enforcing the originalist meaning of the Constitution, the judiciary preserves the mechanism for our own efforts at constitutional creation.

Finally, originalism insists on the reality of consent. By abandoning the notion of tacit or hypothetical consent in favor of an ideal of potential sovereignty, originalism erects a bulwark against the seductive pressure to replace the will of the people with the will of their governors. The American advance in constitutional practice was to realize popular sovereignty as a concrete force in historical time. Popular sovereignty ceased to be a hypothetical construct by which to measure government action and became an actual device for self-governance. As such, control over the definition of the popular will shifted from the governors to the people themselves. The time that has passed since the drafting of the main body of the present Constitution has once again obscured the reality of popular sovereignty, resulting in the gradual encroachment of hypothetical constructs of one sort or another manipulated by those individuals in possession of political power. The elevation of such constructions not only replaces the particular founding of the Constitution but also replaces the very idea of actual popular government. By enforcing the content of the last expression of popular consent to the government, originalism insists that consent cannot be assumed but must be obtained from those people who will be subjected to government power. Thus, even if the founding becomes more distant, it at least remains temporal, and as such its promise remains both temporal and immediate.

An originalist judiciary is not placed in the position of facing backward and looking entirely to the past. Rather, originalism begins with history as the source of enforceable law, but its constitutional vision is to the future. Originalism is not driven by a fawning celebration of historical figures but by the patient waiting for renewed popular deliberation on constitutional form. The past is remembered and preserved in order to sustain the constitutional faith in the possibility of a return of the popular sovereign.

In the meantime, originalism respects the limits of legal authority. It should be recalled that the sovereign will represents that which is held in common by the citizenry. The imposition of force in keeping with the sovereign will is justified because of the authority of the sovereign, its representation of the whole. The courts gain their own legitimacy through their adherence to that law—that is, by enforcing the law that was formed not simply by a will outside the judges' own but by a will held in common by all. The authority of law falters precisely where that general agreement breaks down. Further efforts by the courts to fill remaining gaps in the law represent political choices not only in the sense that they depend on something more than can be provided through examination of the law, but also because they move outside the realm of legal authority. Gaps in the law indicate failures of agreement, points at which there was no consent given to the government and in which government does not have authority. Traditional theories of sovereignty eliminate such gaps through the maintenance of an active sovereign. The sovereign prince was always available to assert his will and to impose order in the face of disagreement. The supreme legislative authority could always be located to provide a new expression of the authoritative will to address unforeseen circumstances.[154] Such gaps cannot be eliminated in the American context, for the popular sovereign is not present and active to render new decisions. The popular sovereign as constitutional author can leave only the law, with whatever gaps it contains.

The necessity of operating in such gaps suggests the need for introducing the notion of a partial sovereign. Where interpretation fails to provide guidance for governing, and the true sovereign is absent to provide an authoritative extension of the inherited constitution, the partial sovereign serves in the breach through the mechanism of construction. Although it is unnecessary to address this topic fully here, it is useful to note briefly that the partial sovereign occupies an uneasy position between the full authority of the sovereign and the complete absence of political authority. The idea of a partial sovereign recognizes the potential need for government action when the constituting law is uncertain, but it highlights the inadequacy of any resolution. The filling of such legal gaps can only be undertaken in conscious recognition of both the absence of legal meaning and the partiality of its substitute. The author of constitutional constructions is partial in three ways. Constructors are partial because they are not fully authorized to take action. Only the Constitution, as an expression of the consent of the governed, can authorize political action. Therefore, action in areas of indeterminacy can only be regarded as contingently legitimate. The basis for such actions is always uncertain and turns on something outside the sovereign will.[155] The introduction of this external element indicates the political nature of the task and the inappropriateness of its pursuit by the judiciary with its limited access to external sources of authority. In constructing constitutional meaning, political officials take up the basic material of the sovereign will but supplement it with material of their own choosing. In so doing, the successful constructors approach the task of the founders. Their determination of constitutional meaning can only be suggested by the sovereign will but cannot be required by it.

The individuals who engage in constructions are also partial in the sense that they do not fully represent the whole. Constructions emerge precisely where there was no agreement over the terms of constitutional governance. The later formulation of such meaning operates in a context where the whole cannot be represented and is not consulted. Instead, constructions reach out to the minority in a less compelling way. The views of the minority are not fully represented in the construction, and those who advocate the construction do not fully open themselves to the whole. Rather than suspending the operation of the government and seeking the full consideration of the people as a whole on the disputed question, the advocates of construction cobble together a settlement within the confines of the current governing structure. Sufficient support is sought to stabilize constitutional meaning, but insufficient efforts are made to reach out to the community as a whole and to pursue independent deliberations on future constitutional rules.

Finally, constructions are partial in that they are not fully authoritative. Without the full weight of popular sovereignty behind them, constructions cannot claim an authority equivalent to the constitutional text itself. As a result, the construction cannot claim a legally binding force. Instead, the authoritativeness of the construction is maintained only by the continuing efforts of political actors themselves. The construction has insufficient authority to be imposed from above, though it may have sufficient authority to claim the continuing commitment of political agents. As the authors of the construction, political actors may change it themselves. It does not possess an independent authority derived from the people at large with which to bind future political actors who do not choose to adhere to it voluntarily. Constructions are like custom in that they exist only through and by virtue of the continuing adherence to them by political actors. As a result, the partial sovereign is always active—there is no law, only consistency.[156] Thus, although government officials are legally bound by the terms of the Constitution, they are only contingently constrained by the terms of constitutional constructions.

The idea of potential sovereignty indicates the basis for constitutional authority, as well as a particular method of interpreting the document. Potential sovereignty emphasizes the democratic foundation of the Constitution and provides a mechanism for understanding what is required by consensual government in the context of a durable constitutional text. Rather than being a deviation from democratic government, the creation of a binding constitution realizes democratic values in the context of representative government. By distinguishing between the source of political authority and the government, popular sovereignty establishes the basis for enforcing limits on government action. By asserting the popular nature of governmental authority, it gives the citizenry itself control over both the powers and limits of government. A jurisprudence of originalism helps secure this democratic structure by enforcing the popular will against the agents of the people. In doing so, it emphasizes yet another separation of political functions, but one that exists in hierarchical relation to the government as a whole. As a final check against abusive government, the people have separated the basis of political authority from the bearer of political powers. Originalism ensures that no branch of government dismantles that final democratic safeguard on the liberties of the people.

6. The Nature and Limits of Originalist Jurisprudence

We have examined what I believe to be the appropriate justifications for a judicial review employing original intent under the federal Constitution. These arguments indicate that there is a positive case to be made for originalism, that it is not simply the default position after other interpretive methods have been rejected for various failings. Yet the most persuasive justifications have only been implicit in existing originalist theory. With these more fully articulated justifications in hand, then, it is easier to see the appropriate responses to various remaining criticisms. Moreover, these justifications indicate the correct form that an originalist jurisprudence should take, and thus they provide some basis for clarifying the theory and settling some disputes and misconceptions within the originalist camp itself. My primary concern is to apply the lessons already learned to a variety of remaining problems. These further demonstrations also point out the ultimate limitations of originalism, however. Although they do not suggest the need for a different interpretive approach to be applied by the courts, these limitations do provide an opening for a broader and more complete constitutional theory, the implications of which we shall then consider.

Of What Is and What Should Never Be

Originalism has been plagued with a vast swarm of indictments against it. Perhaps the energy and desperation of the continuing effort to bury it are indicative of the strength and vitality of the idea. At the very least, this persistence reveals a lingering uneasiness with dismissing originalism as an interpretive method, despite general dissatisfaction with the current set of responses (or nonresponses, as the case may be) its proponents offer to criticisms. Its defenders have not always put forth a persuasive case for their theory and on key points have not bothered to make elaborated arguments at all. Moreover, there remains a difficulty in identifying a consistent theory of originalism. The result has been that critics have often satisfied themselves with attacking the least plausible aspects of some theories of originalism, allowing stronger theories to survive with minimal damage even as the critic departs, convinced of the method's failure. The appropriate response to such difficulties is not, however, to drive some beleaguered originalists out of the fold. There remains room for intramural disputes. Nonetheless, in the interest of avoiding confusion and of actually grappling with important counterarguments, originalists should be careful to clarify their own positions and to specify the direction the theory should go. I shall address both tasks, seeking to respond to some of the more prominent indictments against originalism while at the same time staking out its most plausible version for future debate and development.

ORIGINALISM AND THE "INTENTIONAL FALLACY"

The identification of originalism with "intentionalism" creates unfortunate associations with a largely discredited school of literary theory. Such association has led to certain confusions and widespread assumptions about the nature of originalism that feed skepticism of its value but that can easily be avoided.

The intentionalist school of literary criticism contended that the meaning and value of a work of literature depended on the intentions of its author. One difficulty with this approach is the paucity of historical evidence of authorial intent. As a consequence, in order to understand a text the critic had to project himself into the author's mind and realize his hidden, mental state. The response of the New Critics of the 1930s and 1940s was to discount the intentions of the author as generally unknowable and always irrelevant in order to focus exclusively on the text itself. The work of literature became an independent artifact given meaning through the application of various critical conventions, which often valorized ambiguity. Those critics who attempted to look past the artifact into its origins committed the "intentional fallacy."[1]

In this form, the difficulties with intentionalism become more familiar to the legal profession. The rejection of the theory in literature was prefigured by its rejection in the law. Oliver Wendell Holmes's classic discussion of contracts and the necessity of avoiding investigations into the subjective intent of the contracting parties, in favor of examining the text itself in light of appropriate legal conventions, responded to the same problem. The parties to the contract involved in a legal dispute are obviously unreliable witnesses to their original intentions when entering the contract. At the same time, there is unlikely to be any external evidence, other than the text of the contract itself, as to what their subjective intentions were in contracting together. Thus, Holmes reasonably concluded that the judge should not attempt to re-create the unknown mental states of the authors by pursuing intentions but should simply construe the available contract as written—an artifact to be interpreted through legal conventions.[2]

Such theories of interpretation began as pragmatic responses to situations of limited information that nonetheless required a response. The enterprise of literary criticism could not very well stop with the absence of evidence of authorial intent, nor could judges refuse to enforce the terms of a contract because there was no reliable external evidence of the meaning of the contract's requirements. Given that the limitations and unreliability of such evidence are so great, an effort to rely upon it would itself lead to flights of critical or judicial fancy. The prescriptions of early British judges inveighing against efforts to seek "private intent" outside the bounds of the "public" statutory text itself in the context of minimal or nonexistent records of legislative deliberations can be understood in the same way.[3]

Originalism in the context of constitutional interpretation can be distinguished from these practices in two primary ways. First, unlike these instances, the exercise of the power of judicial review is unnecessary in the absence of reliable evidence of intent, and the consequences of the unjustified use of that power are much more severe than in these classic cases. Unlike literary criticism, contractual relations, or even statutory law, constitutionalism does not depend upon authoritative interpretation. Of course, the adoption of the written Constitution did entail the practice of judicial review, but it did so only in the context of identifiable meaning. Unlike the case of the disputing contracting parties, the people have other means of recourse than repairing to the courts. Thus, there can be no imperative to act in the absence of information in the case of judicial review.

More fundamentally, reliance on original intent in constitutional adjudication is not faced with such evidentiary problems. Although the historical record is hardly perfect, there is little reason for concluding that it is generally radically deficient.[4] Unlike private contracts and literary works, the constitutional debates were extensive, public, and documented. The goal of originalism is not to reimagine the fleeting thoughts in the mind of some private individual at the time of the founding. It is rather to examine the articulated elaborations of textual meaning with which the Constitution was defended and upon which the ratifiers relied in reaching their judgment as to the desirability of the document. Given the availability of substantial historical material on the intentions behind the text, as well as a proper understanding of the nature of textual meaning itself, there can be little justification for adopting a general rule against the introduction of authorial intentions in the case of the Constitution or for accusing advocates of originalism of an effort to engage in the legal equivalent of mind reading.

Such arguments do take on some critical bite, however, in considering efforts to update constitutional meaning in line with the narrow intentions of the founders. Such a concern can be recognized in attempts to engage in historical counterfactuals in order to imagine what the founders would decide if they were somehow faced with the present case. Thus, for example, some originalists might contend that the appropriate method for determining whether abortions are constitutionally protected would be to determine what James Madison would think if faced with Jane Roe—or electronic listening devices, or airplanes, or computer software, as the case may be. Such comments can be accepted as a metaphorical way of expressing the correct goal of understanding textual intent, or even of the legal method of analogizing between like cases. If taken literally, as an expression of the correct methodology for ascertaining that intent, however, they can lead to difficulties. The goal of originalism is not to imagine the subjective intent of members of the ratifying convention but to seek evidence of the objective intent that informs the meaning of the text.

ORIGINALISM IS NOT ANTHROPOMORPHISM

The anthropomorphic error has its origins in hermeneutical theory, influenced by the German Romantics. As with the intentionalist approach, these hermeneutical theories called for the inventive reimagining of the collective *geist* of a prior age. Periods in history could be conceptualized not simply as collections of interacting individuals but as organic entities with identifiable wills of their own. Such views were soon discounted in hermeneutical theory, which continued to recognize the importance of contextualizing a given work but no longer perceived that context as a unified whole capable of independent expression and historic existence.[5]

The criticism of the idea of a "group mind" was imported into legal theory by way of the Realists, who were reacting against all formal theories of interpretation.[6] In this argument, attempts to interpret statutes, primarily, in light of the intentions of the drafting legislature incorrectly inferred the existence of some collective mind that could hold an intent independently of the various legislators themselves. Facile references to the "intent of the legislature" mistook an organization for an individual, and thereby judges attributed psychological states to an entity that did not exist, or at least did not exist in the psychological, cognitive sense required to possess intentions.

The limited effect of such criticisms is evident. Indeed no credible originalist holds that a group mind exists and that the judge's task is to discover the intent contained in that mind. Rather, originalism refers to the intentions of the various individuals who composed the ratifying convention and the degree of agreement that they expressed over the meaning of constitutional terms. As individuals, the founders were capable of agreeing to a common text with a commonly understood meaning, and it is this meaning that the originalist hopes to uncover. Even if the criticism carries little intrinsic force, it does suggest two other, potentially more persuasive difficulties with originalism. First, there are problems associated with the hard contextualism of certain modern theories of language and history. Legislatures may not have group minds, but historical periods may share a collective discourse that is difficult or impossible to access from the outside but that fundamentally structures the meaning of individual actions and statements. The modern plausibility of such theories gives continuing implicit credence to this Realist characterization of originalism, but the ultimate failure of even such modern theories has already been demonstrated. The second continuing implication of the anthropomorphic error is the modern "summing" problem of determining how to aggregate the disparate intentions of numerous individuals into a doctrine that can then be applied, and this problem is addressed below.

ORIGINALISM IS NOT INTERPRETIVISM

Although largely abandoned now, throughout the late 1970s and early 1980s a debate raged as to whether originalism simply was interpretivism, with all other methods relegated to noninterpretive judicial review. The dispute is less intense now, but the very nature of my proffered justifications for originalism may suggest that I hope to revive this categorization. I do not.[7] Relatively little in the way of argumentative clarity is gained by the categorization, and something of substance may in fact be lost. Thus, it is worthwhile to clarify the point that although originalism is the appropriate mode of judicial interpretation of the Constitution, it is not the only possible method available.

Thomas Grey introduced the distinction between interpretive and noninterpretive judicial review in 1975, making explicit a long-held distinction in twentieth-century debates over judicial review. The distinction enjoyed some prominence through the early 1980s. Although not strictly limited to originalism, a purely interpretive approach was said to limit itself to what could be found within the "four corners" of the text of the Constitution. "Interpretation" was taken to include both a pure textualist approach, relying on the semantic meaning of constitutional language, and an originalist approach. Various methods that employed natural law, contemporary morality, or fundamental rights philosophy were seen as drawing from outside the text and thus were not truly interpreting the text itself but supplementing it with external principles in order to reach judicial decisions.[8]

Ronald Dworkin largely put an end to this distinction in arguing that so-called noninterpretive methods were actually particular forms of interpretive argument. The argument proceeds on two points. First, both approaches to judicial review seek to understand its practice as it has developed and the nature of the fundamental law that authorizes and limits the government; thus, both attempt to interpret "the Constitution," properly understood. Second, both approaches are fundamentally rooted in the text and are merely seeking plausible ways in which to contextualize that text in order to determine its proper meaning.[9] In both respects, Dworkin is drawing upon modern understandings of the nature of language and correctly points out their implications for understanding texts. In doing so, he shifts the focus from whether to interpret the Constitution to defining what "the Constitution" is and how best to interpret it.

This basis for rejecting Grey's distinction is consistent with the method of analysis pursued in this book. A critical question for the originalist is how to determine the appropriate context for judicial interpretation. In philosophy and literary theory, as well as in legal theory, there have been numerous efforts to determine the relationship between text and context and the appropriate stance the interpreter should take toward them. My burden is to demonstrate that given a common goal of interpreting the constitutional text, one method understands that task better and is more likely to lead to correct results. Some putative methods of interpretation—for example, extreme forms of deconstruction—should not properly be regarded as a method of interpretation at all but as of a form of analysis, more akin to Charles Beard's *An Economic Interpretation of the Constitution of the United States* than *Corwin and Peltason's Understanding the Constitution*. Given such exclusions, however, a broad range of interpretive practices remains.[10] But within this set of available interpretive methods, some are preferable to others. Among the grounds for preferring some methods is that they are better able to realize the purpose of interpretation itself. We cannot get very far simply by excluding some approaches to the Constitution as noninterpretive. Thus, as Dworkin himself has done, we must ask after both the nature of the Constitution and the nature of interpretation in order to discover the best interpretive method for this text. There are various ways to contextualize the Constitution. But the original intentions are the context most appropriate to our constitutional project.

ORIGINALISM IS NOT CLAUSE-BOUND

Just as John Ely was a major figure in labeling originalism "interpretivism," he was also instrumental in condemning it as "clause-bound." Ely argued that the "standard form" of originalism approached the Constitution "essentially as self-contained units and interpreted on the basis of their language, with whatever help the legislative history can provide, without significant injection of content from outside the provision."[11] Thus, the text is divided into clauses, with each clause carrying its own semantic and historical meaning, but essentially separated from the remaining document, which is viewed as largely incidental from the perspective of the case at hand. As Ely develops it, the argument actually has two senses. In the first, clause-bound interpretivism can be understood as positing that each part of the document must be understood independently of the others and that cases can be categorized so as to fall under particular controlling clauses. In the second form of the argument, however, Ely goes further and contends that the difficulty with clause-bound interpretivism is not that it excludes other parts of the text but that it excludes relevant external sources of information that could shed light on a particular clause. Thus, originalism fails because it does not take into account both the internal relations within the text and the relation between a given "open textured" clause and the philosophical context outside the "four corners" of the document.

These are really separate claims, the latter unrelated to whether originalism is narrowly focused on individual clauses or whether it ranges over the entire text. As William Harris's typology helpfully makes clear, Ely's first complaint focuses on the distinction between a positivist and a structuralist approach to the Constitution; the second indictment turns on the immanence or transcendence of constitutional meaning—that is, whether it is contained, or immanent within, the text or melds with a larger source of meaning external to, or transcendent of, the text.[12] The first claim is the focus here.[13] There can be little doubt that a great deal of adjudication and traditional constitutional commentary in fact follows this format.[14] Interpretation can largely be understood as the effort to translate textual details into even more detailed judicial doctrines. Nonetheless, the clauses themselves taken in isolation are not the only source of information for the formulation of judicial doctrine and are certainly not the only source of information for originalism. There is no principled reason why originalism cannot take into account the intent of the founders as embodied in their choices of ordering the constitutional text, dividing powers among different branches and forms of government, and relating powers, duties, and rights. The real difficulty is with the level of historical evidence that is needed to give meaning to structural aspects of the Constitution, and to this degree structurally based interpretation is not theoretically different from clause-bound interpretation. Therefore, originalists object not to the simultaneous examination of the Ninth, Fourteenth, First, Third, Fourth, and Fifth Amendments but to a conclusion drawn from them that there is a judicially enforceable right to privacy formed from their composite that exceeds the historically more limited text. In contrast, the use of the Fourth, Fifth, Sixth, Seventh, and Eighth Amendments may be of use to the originalist in determining the meaning of the Fifth or Fourteenth's due process guarantees. Structural information can be used to provide greater specificity in the text, not to build more abstract theories that then override the existing textual particulars.[15]

ORIGINALISM, CONSERVATISM, AND JUDICIAL RESTRAINT

Originalism has been associated with judicial restraint in the modern context. Moreover, it has been linked with the contemporary conservative political views of the New Right. Neither identification is wholly accurate. Refounding originalist theory on more defensible justificatory arguments provides the basis for understanding why it cannot be so easily connected to either stance; rather, it must be understood as a separate doctrine. As such, originalism can neither be advanced nor defeated with simple arguments for or against judicial passivism or political conservatism but must be debated on its own terms.

The identification of originalism with conservative politics has, no doubt, become prevalent because so many of its modern defenders are also identifiable conservatives.[16] This easy identification has developed in part because of a failure of imagination as to what a truly "conservative" judicial policy might be, despite the existence of various academic exemplars. A truly conservative approach to judicial interpretation would focus not on a relatively neutral methodology such as originalism but would embrace a more explicitly substantive vision of constitutional meaning that brought it into line with conservative policy making. Three such methods have in fact been critically discussed: Richard Epstein's libertarian fundamental rights theory, Richard Posner's law-and-economics-inspired pragmatism, and Hadley Arkes's natural law philosophy.[17] Even if libertarianism is segmented as a separate political and judicial movement, there can be little doubt that such staunch originalist conservatives as Robert Bork and Antonin Scalia share a great deal with such anti-originalist conservatives as Richard Posner and Harry Jaffa. Nonetheless, the latter are harsh critics of originalism, advocate different interpretive methodologies, and reach radically different adjudicative results. Thus, for example, where Bork would overturn *Roe v. Wade* and return control over abortion to the states, other conservatives would supplant *Roe* with a decision extending constitutional protection to the fetus and bar the performance of abortions in any state.[18] Ultimately, both in their advocacy of judicial restraint and in their adoption of a theoretically neutral interpretive device, originalists have not committed themselves to a conservative policy program and could, in principle, reach results that are actually antagonistic to that program.

Perhaps more distressing is the connection between originalism and a form of judicial restraint I call "judicial passivism." A judge can be restrained either by adhering to existing doctrine and refusing to overturn precedent or by construing the judicial role such that the courts rarely strike down legislation.[19] By judicial passivism, I refer only to the second form of restraint. A passive Court may be willing to overturn its own precedent, but it would be unwilling to intervene actively in the political process and strike down a large number of laws or executive actions. Although some originalists have made efforts to make peace with existing case law, the clear implication of originalism as it has been primarily argued is that a number of precedents would have to be overturned.[20] It is less clear, given the originalist emphasis on judicial passivism, whether a number of laws would be struck down as inconsistent with original intent. Originalism is only contingently associated with judicial passivism.

Many originalists have advanced justifications for the method that have relied on claims about the value of judicial restraint, including the benefits of democratic majoritarianism and the limited policy-making capacity of the courts. Those claims are implausible, both in general and especially as unique justifications for originalist jurisprudence. The justifications developed in this book do not rely on the benefits of judicial restraint but defend originalism directly. The judiciary is not a problem to be worked into American constitutionalism but an integral component of that enterprise, and it is positively authorized to take action under it. In that context, judicial passivism is appropriate at the limits of interpretive knowledge but is distinctly inappropriate when the constitutional law is available to be interpreted and applied. Whether the judiciary should intervene in a particular case is a function of the government action under consideration and the particulars of the historical evidence that is applicable to it. As the primary interpreter of constitutional law, the judiciary's role requires that it do neither more nor less than fully enforce that law. To fail to do so would in fact undermine the justifications for judicial review and for originalism itself just as surely as inappropriate interpretation and interventionism would. Uniform passivism in the face of violations of the interpretable Constitution would also destabilize the meaning of the text and contradict the expressed intent of the sovereign people.

THE PROBLEM OF PRECEDENT

If originalism is distinguished from passivism, and if for the sake of argument it is assumed that at least some of the existing Court doctrine cannot be reconciled with the intent of the ratifiers,[21] there remains a problem of how originalism should handle the existence of those precedents. Full consideration of this problem would be outside the scope of this book, but a tentative indication of how originalists should think about precedent can be offered.[22]

First, respect for precedent is primarily a pragmatic concern. Precedent helps ensure that the judiciary follows known rules, does not make arbitrary decisions, preserves stability in the law, and is not forced constantly to reconsider the same issues but can move on to new concerns.[23] None of these benefits is trivial, but many can be reached by other mechanisms. Notably, correct interpretation of the constitutional text itself would achieve many of these same goals. Assuming significant portions of the present constitutional law cannot be reconciled with the original intent, then two difficulties emerge: the fact that the use of precedent is one of the tools of legal interpretation itself, and the transition to correct interpretation.

Judges should not assume their own infallibility. The process of translating the constitutional text into more specific, judicially applicable constitutional rules requires more than a copy of the Constitution and a word processor. Even given the body of historical evidence that is necessary to determine textual meaning, courts must also rely on existing judicial doctrines to provide guidance as to how that evidence is to be explored and how conclusions are to be formulated as doctrine. Simply beginning consideration of each case de novo, as if a body of prior consideration did not exist, strains the bounds of even judicial hubris. Thus, as a mechanism for focusing issues, weighing evidence, and formulating questions, precedent cannot and should not be abandoned by an originalist judge but should be used as an interpretive tool along with others.

The potentially more difficult problem is making the transition from nonoriginalist law to originalist law, assuming that important parts of the current law are in fact bad and in need of serious revision.[24] At this point, Alexander Bickel's prudential wisdom is in order. The Court largely has control over its own agenda and moreover has a number of ways of settling particular disputes without having to issue major declarations on substantive constitutional law.[25] An originalist Court need not seek to overturn the existing corpus of constitutional law overnight, or even over a decade. Reconsideration and modification of existing precedent can take place over a series of cases over a period of years without unduly damaging either the judiciary or the structure of constitutional law. Indeed, the Court's own eventual abandonment of *Plessy*'s constitutional protection for de jure segregation in *Brown*, which struck at over half a century of settled and deeply embedded political practice, was presaged by a number of more limited decisions undermining the basis for both existing judicial doctrine on and the constitutional practice of segregation.[26] The gradual reconsideration of existing case law preserves the benefits of precedent by securing some stability and predictability in law and by ensuring that the Court takes advantage of continuing criticism and debate on the validity of its interpretive movement.

Such a gradual return to correct interpretation not only serves the internal values of the judiciary but also allows time for political accommodation to the shift. To the extent that other government institutions are constrained not by the correct interpretation of the Constitution but by the judicial pronouncement of constitutional meaning, it makes little sense to imagine that they could sharply reorder their behavior to account for rapid changes in judicial doctrine. The reliance of others on prior judicial decisions, even those made in error, must be taken into account; yet it can be, by a clear signaling of the Court's intentions. In this regard, the signaling must indicate both the substantive direction of future constitutional law and the proper interpretive approach that will guide the Court. In doing so, the judiciary would not only provide a mechanism by which other institutions could predict the ultimate goal of judicial action and therefore shift policies to meet it, but it would also indicate the seriousness of the judiciary's commitment to that change. Part of the cognitive dissonance created by its ringing vindication of the right to be free from segregation, followed by the uncertain trumpet call of "all deliberate speed," was that the Court had not successfully signaled the ultimate interpretive method it would adopt or the end point it would reach in its earlier segregation decisions.[27] *Brown*, therefore, appeared as a sudden and immediate threat to southern institutions instead of as the natural conclusion to a process already begun. Consequently, the judiciary and the states had to engage in the ground-clearing and political restructuring necessary for desegregation after the decision, rather than before.

In order to begin such a process of gradually moving toward correctly grounded doctrine, an originalist judiciary would have to begin immediately to shift the logic of those doctrines. Primarily this means that an originalist judiciary would halt the extension of a current line of cases that had been guided by nonoriginalist interpretive methods and would begin to apply the logic of an originalist interpretation. To take a recent example, in striking down the federal criminalization of guns near public schools, the Court struck at the very margins of modern commerce clause legislation.[28] By indicating that the commerce clause actually does place limits on federal action, the Court signaled the need for reconsideration of doctrine and political practice in this area. But by striking down a law that was clearly so marginal to the commerce power, the Court did not pose an imminent threat to the existence of, say, the federal regulation of manufacturing, which would have been far more trau-matic to the stability of law and of governmental and economic institutions.[29]

The extreme fear of originalism's relationship to precedent comes not only from political disagreement with the likely results but also from an inadequate constitutional theory.[30] Many originalists and their critics operate with an implicit assumption of judicial supremacy. The result is that shifts in judicial interpretation of the Constitution are taken to be equivalent to shifts in the Constitution itself, or more immediately to shifts in political practice under the Constitution. This is obviously true to a degree. As the preceding exam-ple indicates, at least for the time being, the federal government can no longer regulate firearms in public schools. Nonetheless, the constitutional rules that can be discovered by interpretation must be supplemented by practices built through constitutional construction. This realm remains open, regardless of judicial interpretation, and existing constructions would be critical to the determination of how the nation would operate with an originalist judiciary. The key to the Constitution is not only the law but also politics.

Judicial interpretation of the Constitution takes place against a back-ground of politically constructed constitutional meaning. A significant por-tion of what we understand the Constitution to mean has been determined outside the judicial context. Perhaps more tellingly, political actors settle many "constitutional" issues without recourse to explicit legal reasoning at all. From almost the moment the Constitution was proposed by the Philadelphia Con-vention, political actors have had to settle ambiguities or gaps in its text in order to constitute a working government. Early government officials had to fill in the details of textual provisions by adopting their own practices. The decision of the First Congress to allow presidents to remove executive branch officials without congressional involvement, George Washington's determi-nation to limit the Senate to a ratification role rather than an advisory role in treaty making, and Thomas Jefferson's acquisition of the Louisiana Territory created a settled constitutional meaning where the text was unclear. Later offi-cials have decided issues ranging from whether states could secede from the union, to the extent to which police could employ wiretaps, and the means by which Congress would control the executive bureaucracy. Judges act within a web of assumptions and practices about what the Constitution means and how the American government works, and that web is woven by innumerable individuals, movements, and institutions both inside and outside the gov-ernment itself.[31]

The faulty assumption of judicial supremacy leads in turn to the flawed conclusion that there must always be an interpretive answer to every constitu-tional problem. Thus, for example, Gregory Bassham is driven to construct an

originalist theory designed to ensure "that all (or nearly all) constitutional provisions will *have* an original intent, either actual or constructed."[32] The recognition of the existence of constructions, however, provides an avenue for filling
gaps in interpretable constitutional meaning. The Constitution does not always
speak through the judiciary and does not always speak with one voice. Recognizing the limits of interpretation, and therefore the limits of the courts, makes
clear that the entire edifice of modern government practice need not be struck
down by an originalist Court, *even if it rests on questionable originalist foundations.* A constitutional theory respecting the role of both interpretation and
construction in fact assumes the existence of practices that cannot be justified
in originalist terms, for constructions necessarily operate where interpretations
cannot go. Thus, an originalist judiciary, as sketched here, would not strike
down every government action that cannot be justified in originalist terms but
only those that are inconsistent with known constitutional requirements. The
distinction is significant. The founders may not have intended the civil service
system and the partial insulation of executive branch officials from presidential
oversight, but they did not preclude it either. The judiciary need only ask
whether such arrangements are consistent with the constitutional design, not
whether they are necessary to it.

The existence of constitutional constructions not only points to the limits
of judicial interpretation but also helps account for why some items would
remain "off the agenda" even if not kept there by the courts.[33] On one level,
simply because the judiciary adopts an originalist method, it does not follow
that the Court is therefore bound to reopen such issues as the constitutionality of legal tender.[34] The presumption that it would overlooks the distinct
nature of the judiciary. Although the courts have some control over whether
to decide a given case on constitutional grounds, and therefore whether to prevent certain items from entering its agenda, it more significantly cannot initiate its own cases and therefore does not have complete autonomy in putting
items on its agenda. There are two implications of this for present purposes.
First, it emphasizes that an originalist judiciary is not the same as an originalist legislature. Legislatures are active institutions, which means that they are
looking for problems to solve and indeed that they define what constitutes a
"problem." The judiciary, on the other hand, is a dispute-resolving institution;
it must wait for problems to be defined elsewhere and brought to it. Thus, even
if legal tender laws are contrary to originalist constitutional requirements, the
Court cannot reach out on its own initiative to strike them down.[35] This leads
to the second point, that constitutional constructions help define what counts
as a current constitutional dispute. Constructions, like interpretation, define
what is "off the agenda," both for the courts and others. Even if the correct orig-

inalist interpretation would question the legality of legal tender laws, this would not itself make such laws the subject of serious controversy. Even if the bench were filled with originalist judges, it is exceedingly unlikely that there would be a host of litigants queuing up to have legal tender overthrown.[36] Not every constitutional error must be, or can be, corrected by the courts.

A second aspect of the implications of construction for this question deals not with the prior judicial expansion of political power but with the prior judicial extension of rights. In an originalist America, would not the government engage in flogging and branding of criminals, forced sterilization, white supremacy, electronic eavesdropping, silencing of evolutionary teachings, and so on?[37] Although it may be true that an originalist judiciary would no longer stand ready to prevent such things, it would not impose them, either. Such positive government action requires decisions by political representatives, not by judges, and thus the charge really turns on the willingness of legislatures to issue appropriations for branding irons. Although some of these practices were finally halted by judicial action, many were not.[38] More critically, the question is not how these practices originally died, but how they are now prevented from being revived. The mere fact that such a list can be evoked to such political effect is indicative of the universal opprobrium that is attached to its contents now. It is the continuing vitality of the political construction of the equal protection clause that ensures that white supremacy is not on the legislative agenda. The critical constitutional questions of today are not those of the 1950s but those that operate on the edge of those earlier settlements—such as whether and when affirmative action is appropriate and whether special schools or classrooms for adolescent girls or black males are permissible efforts to enhance their educational progress. If originalism has no authoritative response to such issues as these, then the question becomes whether it is preferable for a judiciary motivated by other methods to intervene and prevent political resolution of these issues.[39] The same response available to judicial activists who assert that the evil days of *Dred Scott* and *Lochner* are ancient history is available to originalists who recognize the reality of constitutional constructions. Those days are gone, not because of the adoption of correct interpretive methods but because of the adoption of new constitutional constructions.[40] Moreover, they will remain gone only to the extent that those constructions remain stable. Such events as the fall of the Berlin Wall, the abolition of the Interstate Commerce Commission, and the rise of Richard Epstein should serve as convincing proof that what were once unthinkable ideas condemned to the dustbin of history can become vital political movements. The adoption of appropriate interpretive standards can only do so much. The rest is politics, and always has been.[41]

Ultimately, however, the emphasis on precedent is a bit of a distraction. Critics of originalism are perhaps less concerned about the fate of earlier achievements in American politics than they are with the possibility of future social change. For many people raised in the heady days of the Warren Court, the judiciary holds the promise of political victories not yet recognized. In this vision, an unfettered Court is valuable for what it might do in the future, whether in advancing homosexual rights, prohibiting capital punishment, mandating more extensive social services, or aiding some other cause not yet imagined. Admittedly, originalist jurisprudence has little to offer those who hope to achieve social change through judicial fiat. Such progressive optimism must be tempered with a historically informed skepticism. The Court's willingness to advance politically unpopular goals was a short-lived anomaly in the nation's history. More often, the Court has facilitated popular evils through constitutional error. The federal judiciary's complicity in the turn-of-the-century's system of racial oppression should serve as a warning of the political possibilities once an unwavering focus on the Constitution's terms and purposes is lost. An originalist judiciary is unlikely to be a threat to the present constitutional consensus, but it will also be unlikely to form the vanguard of future social change.

ORIGINALISM IS NOT THE END OF HISTORY

The discussion of the problem of precedent provides the basis for briefly clarifying a point that has been subject to some confusion and misrepresentation. Foes of originalism sometimes assert, and its friends sometimes pretend, that the adoption of this interpretive method can be regarded as the equivalent of reducing difficult constitutional questions to mechanical ease. Not only are all constitutional issues essentially legal issues, but all legal issues can be resolved by the application of the correct judicial template. As a critique of originalism, at least in its plausible forms, the argument is vacuous.

There can be substantial disagreements both within originalism and over the nature of the theory. More significantly for present purposes, there can be disagreement within a single theory over correct interpretations. In arguing for originalism as a "neutral" mechanism, an "objective" standard, or as pointing to a "fixed and stable" text, originalists should not be misunderstood to mean that there cannot therefore be disagreements among sincere and competent originalist judges. Ultimately, there should be answers to such disagreements, even if the correct answer is that the constitutional meaning is indeterminate, but the availability of ultimate answers does not prevent the existence of disputes in the process of reaching those answers. Originalism should not promise to put an end to dissenting opinions and overruled lower courts, but it does argue that the appropriate disputes within interpretation should be over the evidence of intent, not over the best form of democracy or the existence and substance of natural law.[42]

Further, originalism should not be regarded as a form of "mechanical jurisprudence," crassly understood.[43] It remains an open question whether there ever were judges who believed in or attempted to practice such a mechanical art, but the charge of simpleminded formalism has always resonated with opponents of originalism. In a more generous sense, mechanical jurisprudence can be understood to refer to any formal method of interpretation, that is, one that is not guided by a prior substantive vision of correct outcomes. In this sense, originalism must mount a defense of a kind of formalism. In the more common, rhetorical sense, originalism must deny that it believes in or advocates a mechanical jurisprudence. As should be evident by now, there is no simple template that a judge can apply to reach interpretive answers. Originalist jurisprudence requires careful judgment, as to the definition of the issue at hand, of the relevant evidence, of the weight and meaning of the evidence, of the formulation of judicial doctrine, of the disposition of the case, and so forth. Such judgments can never be wholly avoidable or beyond controversy. But they can be subjected to criticism on their own terms, and they can be evaluated in a relatively specifiable and objective context.

Finally, the adoption of originalism would not put an end to constitutional controversy. Even if the constitutional law were stabilized by an originalist interpretation, constitutional politics would not come to an end. As long as aspects of the constitutional text are indeterminate, constitutional constructions will continue to be necessary to create and govern political practice. Outside the context of legal interpretation, constitutional disputes will remain and continue to be conducted in heated terms and with critical results for the life of the nation. The adoption of originalism should not be understood as putting an end to constitutional debate and ushering in an era of consensus and expedient politics. Originalism would have an effect on the course of those debates, but it would not replace them.

ORIGINALISM IS NOT EXTRATEXTUAL

The concern with extratextual interpretive methods is of two radically different kinds, though they share common assumptions. The "pure textualist" criticizes originalism for departing from the constitutional text that is alone the authoritative law in order to replace it with an entirely different one contained in various historical sources. The second concern approaches from the opposite direction and contends that since even originalism has abandoned a pure textualist approach, then the text is dead and everything is permitted. In this context, critics of originalism may argue that its proponents are in the same boat as the other noninterpretivists and therefore have no principled basis for objecting to the importation of external sources of meaning.

There are relatively few strict textualists left, given modern understandings of the nature of language and the belief in the emptiness of the phrase "plain meaning" and the indispensability of linguistic context. The criticism has been deployed by more than traditional textualists, however. Those who regard the Constitution as a "public document" share with the textualists the belief that it exists as an independent text that can be lifted and read on its face. Although more sophisticated exponents of this view may not believe in the possibility of a true plain-meaning interpretation, they nonetheless agree that originalists are extratextual and seek to smuggle something from outside the document and enforce it in the stead of the text itself.

Although it has modern defenders, this view has a long lineage and was perhaps most ably stated by Frederick Douglass, who argued that slavery could only be regarded as constitutional "by disregarding the plain and common sense reading of the instrument itself; by showing that the Constitution does not mean what it says, and says what it does not mean; by assuming that the written Constitution is to be interpreted in the light of a secret and unwritten understanding of its framers."[44] Douglass himself had once been an originalist, along with the Garrisonians, and on that basis had denounced the Constitution as a pact with the devil that should be rejected. Douglass's conversion took him to a different abolitionist camp, where they took the text as they found it, including ambiguities that could render the document not merely perfectible but already perfect.[45] Originalism was a "mean, contemptible, underhand method" of interpreting the Constitution, not simply because it led to undesirable substantive results but more fundamentally because it was extratextual and thus imported meaning into the text in an "underhanded" fashion in order to reach those results.[46] In this reading, no political effort was necessary to change the nature of the Union and abolish slavery. It could be done immediately, in the courts and by legalistic means.[47] In this formulation, the textualist critique retains support from academic commentators.

Originalism can escape from the twin horns of this dilemma by recognizing the correct relationship between intent and the text. Far from abandoning the text in favor of an external authority or from opening the door to a search for preferred context within which to read the document, originalism seeks to make evident what is already contained within it. The linguistic foundations for this claim have already been laid, for there is a unique relationship between the text and the context of authorial intent. If the idea of an "autonomous" text is seen as resting on false premises, then both claims—that originalism is extratextual and that all contexts are permitted—collapse.

A text cannot be taken as autonomous. At the very least, we cannot accept the idea that marks on a piece of paper constitute a meaningful text if we take the marks as being autonomous of an author. An author must always be implied, if he is not already known. In either case, whether the author is implied or actual, he comes with the text. He is included and inseparable from textual meaning. If this is so, then the claim that the original intentions of the author are extratextual rests on a confusion about the nature of a text. Of course, there may be difficulty in identifying who the author is, or more relevantly, what the authorial intent is; but originalism provides an answer as to where to look. The notion of the Constitution as a "public" document in which "we" are the authors leads back to originalism as well. Either "we" are the governing people, and therefore represented in the political action being examined by the court, or "we" are the sovereign people, in which case the best evidence of intentions is embodied in the originalist text. Similarly, the identification between original intent and written text indicates a distinction between that context and all others. The intentions are not extratextual in any meaningful way, and thus it is a mistake in category to include them with the various other contexts in which the document might be examined, such as contemporary moral theory. To the extent that one wishes to interpret the document, those other contexts are simply secondary mechanisms, or supplementary evidence, for discovering the intent of the authors.

This discussion can be clarified further, as can the nature of originalist interpretation, by noting the different ways in which we commonly refer to "meaning" and "intent" and by identifying which is actually embodied in the text. We can distinguish between three common forms of "meaning": literal meaning, reader's meaning, and speaker's meaning.[48] Focus on the reader's meaning ("What does this mean to me?") is inconsistent with the interpretive enterprise itself. Literal meaning (the "plain meaning") can only be regarded as an interpretive halfway house to the discovery of the speaker's meaning ("What did the speaker mean by this?"). Literal meaning does not exist in some natural state in the text but must be developed through the use of a host of linguistic and social conventions. Concluding the interpretive effort with the application of those conventions may in fact be highly misleading, as for example when the speaker uses nonstandard conventions to express his meaning or violates existing conventions altogether.[49]

In attempting to understand the speaker's meaning in a text, however, we can distinguish between different kinds of intentions that the speaker might have possessed. Primarily, we can distinguish between an intent to do some-thing and an intent in doing something.[50] The former is also called motiva-tion; the latter is the intent proper. The motivations of a writer are in fact extratextual. They do not appear on the face of the text itself; moreover, they exist prior to the text and possess only a contingent relationship to it as it is eventually formed. On the other side, the same can be said for expectations about the effect of the text. An expectation, in and of itself, is derived from the text and as a prediction about its effects in the future is only contingently related to the text. Unlike intentions proper, or even motivations, the author has no special authority relative to expectations about effects. An example may clarify such contingent relationships, for assuming that Charles Beard is correct, the founders can be understood as motivated by their private finan-cial interests not only to write a new federal constitution but to include par-ticular kinds of provisions in its terms.[51] Beard's account, therefore, provides a motivation, purpose, or intention for both a text and specific textual clauses within the eventual text, such as the federal power to tax. Obviously, those motivations existed even prior to the gathering in Philadelphia and certainly had to be formed before the text was written (and thus existed outside and in-dependently of the text, even if the text had never actually been written). Fur-ther, they were not directly expressed in the text since there is no direct textual reference to using taxes to repay the revolutionary debts held by its drafters. More important, those motivations are only contingently related to the text, for Beard in fact was wrong. The same text exists, with the same meaning, even if the founders are now understood to have possessed completely different motivations from those that Beard posited, or even from each other.

The second form of intention does not bear this contingent relationship to textual meaning but is a necessary feature of the text itself. In meaning x, the text must be understood as "embodying a particular intention in x-ing."[52] The text is literally incomprehensible without recognition of these illocu-tionary intentions, which express the action that is captured in the text. If I say, "Jane is smiling," I am expressing a description of Jane. If the listener, in interpreting the text, does not grasp that act of description, then he cannot understand the text itself. I may have had myriad motivations in making the statement, but no particular motivation is necessary for the text to have its meaning. The intention conveyed in making the utterance is distinct from the intention for making the utterance and is ultimately more fundamental to the act of communication. In fact, "A knowledge of the writer's intentions in writ-ing . . . is not merely relevant to, but is actually *equivalent* to, a knowledge of what he writes."[53] Although the text itself is one source of that knowledge, it is obviously not the only one available. Therefore, historical material is "not merely relevant to" but required by the search for textual meaning.

It is this necessary relationship between textual meaning and authorial intent that distinguishes the use of historical material from the use of other extratextual material and gives rise to three primary implications. First, originalism cannot properly be understood as drawing from a grab bag of external information in order to divert textual meaning in a particular direction. Rather, originalism draws upon sources of information that are in a sense required by the constitutional text itself. What particular pieces of evidence are usefully available to illuminate textual intent is an open question, but the fact that textual meaning depends upon intentions that such evidence could illuminate is not. Second, originalism cannot properly be understood to deal with the "secret and unwritten" intentions of the founders. To the extent that the text is accepted, the intentions expressed in that text are accepted as well. Given that those intentions are in the text itself, they are neither secret nor unwritten. They may, however, be unclear. It is to correct this lack of clarity that additional evidence of meaning is sought, not to amend secret meanings to the previously existing text. Finally, originalism should not be concerned with the motivations and purposes of the text. Like other pieces of information, evidence of founding motivations is relevant to textual meaning only to the extent that it sheds light on the intentions embodied in the text. Evidence of motivations is just a tool for reaching textual intentions, not direct evidence of those intentions themselves. Bearing only a contingent relationship to textual meaning, motivations must be handled with care by the interpreter to discover whether they were eventually embodied in the text and also how.

ORIGINALISM IS NOT SELF-REFUTING

It has been widely argued that originalism is actually self-refuting. The argument relies almost entirely on the work of H. Jefferson Powell in a 1985 law review article.[54] In brief, Powell undertook a historical investigation of the founding period and the methods of legal interpretation employed and advocated at the time. He concluded that, consistent with the legal conventions of the time, the founders did not intend that the written Constitution be interpreted to mean what they themselves thought it meant. Instead, the founders hoped that the text would "endure for the ages" and, in order for it to do so, they intended that it be interpreted by later generations in light of the latter's own situation, beliefs, and morality. The "interpretive intent" of the founders, therefore, was that subsequent interpreters ignore the "substantive intent" of the founders. For a consistent originalist to adhere to the intent of the founders, he must ironically abandon an originalist method. Although some versions of originalism are potentially vulnerable to this form of criticism, the version advocated here is not. Originalism, properly developed, is neither self-refuting nor subject to this form of attack.

The first difficulty with the argument is that it is in all likelihood historically inaccurate.[55] Powell's primary device for arguing for the inessential quality of intent is to contend that although canons of legal interpretation dominant in America and Britain directed judges to look for the intent of the document in question, they did so in only a special sense. Specifically, the public intent of the document was to be found not in the external evidence of the historical origins of the text but in the words of the document itself. Indeed, in Powell's gloss on the distinction, "the 'intent' or 'intention' of a document could denote either the meaning that the drafters wished to communicate or the meaning the reader was warranted in deriving from the text." Upon further investigation, Powell concludes that "the 'intent' of the maker of a legal document and the 'intent' of the document itself were one and the same; 'intent' did not depend upon the subjective purposes of the author."[56] Although the judicial pursuit of this textualist meaning was constrained by common law rules, it did not lead back to the private, internal, or subjective motivations of the author. We can lay aside the theoretical question as to whether this is a coherent way of expressing the nature of authorial intent, since the concern is not whether this is philosophically correct but whether it is what was believed at the time. Unfortunately for Powell, it was not.

There is no reason to develop the detailed case against the accuracy of Powell's reconstruction of the interpretive understandings of the time. That has been done sufficiently and in detail elsewhere. It is enough simply to note that Powell's interpretation is anachronistic, reading common law injunctions in light of current views of language. The Lockean conception of language dominant during the period did not make the sharp distinction between subjective intent and the meaning of the text.[57] Words were not taken as autonomous but were recognized to be a potential source of miscommunication. The intent of the author and the intent of the document were seen as interchangeable at the time, and it made no sense to try to distinguish between the two. Due to the difficulties of language, both judges and legal authors were deeply concerned that legal documents be written and read with great care, since a reader's misinterpretation of the author's intent was always a risk. In a context of minimal documentation of the origins of texts, the words in the text themselves were usually the only reliable indicator of authorial intent, again suggesting care in reading and writing and appreciation of the purposes expressed in the text itself. The founders' concern with avoiding the instability of British constitutionalism is likewise inconsistent with Powell's thesis that the founders were relatively accepting of the fluidity of texts over time in the hands of judicial interpreters. The founders were primarily concerned about the "intent of the document itself," but they did not imagine that the document was distinct from the author in the fashion that Powell suggests.

Although the failure of the historical case to establish a contradiction between the founders' interpretive and substantive intent is sufficient to defeat the threat of self-refutation, some clarification of the nature of originalism can be gained by examining the theoretical point further. Even if it were correct that the founders did not have an originalist interpretive intent, it would not defeat an appropriately conceived originalist theory. Originalism neither depends on the interpretive intent of the founders nor employs that intent.[58] It can be noted immediately, especially given the preceding discussion, that there are various forms of "intent" and that not all of them can be regarded as embodied in the text. The interpretive intentions of the founders are among those thoughts that did not "make it" into the Constitution as drafted and ratified.

The proper exclusion of interpretive intent can be seen at several points. First, the justifications offered here do not draw upon any conception of how the founders intended that the text be interpreted. In fact, any justification depending on their interpretive intentions is either circular or parasitic on other justifications (such as a pragmatic goal of restraining judges). Second, examination of the justifications that have been offered suggests that a search for interpretive intentions is misguided. Grounding originalism in the nature of a written text and a theory of popular sovereignty supplies an independent basis for it, regardless of the interpretive intentions of the founders. Originalism is the appropriate method of interpretation because it provides stability in the law in the sense that it enforces the will of the law and because it provides an avenue for the expression of popular sovereignty. Both justifications direct the courts to the substantive meaning of the constitutional text as it is litigated, and thus the interpretive intent is never involved.

Authorial intent is meaningful only to the extent that it is embodied in the text. Although it is easy to imagine an amendment directing the Court to adopt some specific interpretive method, and thus converting an interpretive intent into a substantive directive, no such clause exists in the Constitution.[59] Although there was a widespread understanding that the judiciary would exercise a power of constitutional review at the time of the founding, that power was a function of the political theory that pervaded the period and motivated the founding; it was not embodied specifically in the text.[60] Instead, the Court initiated a construction of its own powers in a republican government at a relatively early date, and that construction, being consistent with agreed-upon political principles, was accepted at the time and has remained compelling since. Having instituted the practice of judicial review as a construction, the appropriate interpretive method to adopt is yet another construction that must be consistent with the discoverable text but that cannot be regarded as clearly contained in it.

Finally, numerous commentators have contended that the choice of an interpretive method is a political one and cannot simply be derived from the text itself. As a challenge to the continuing legitimacy of the practice of judicial review, this contention cannot go unnoticed. The adoption of an originalist methodology is not politically neutral but is firmly grounded in a compelling political theory that explains the nature of constitutionalism in the United States (see chapter 5). Moreover, though couched in the formal terms of philosophical analysis of the nature of interpretation, my earlier arguments are embedded in a normative vision of constitutionalism as well (see chapters 3 and 4). Constitutional theory cannot be reduced to semantics, but the latter is a necessary part of analyzing the nature of American constitutionalism. The appropriateness of an originalist jurisprudence is a matter of constitutional theory, not of constitutional interpretation.

CONCEPTS, CONCEPTIONS, AND LEVELS OF GENERALITY

Both originalists and their critics have struggled with the question of the relevant level of generality at which intentions should be understood. At least initially, one can imagine intentions ranging from the very narrow and specific to the very broad and abstract. At the most narrow, it is possible that in framing the prohibition on "cruel and unusual punishment" the founders only intended to prohibit a specifiable and finite list of activities. At the most broad, they may have intended simply to exclude those activities that are, or may be regarded to be, shocking, grotesque, or barbaric. In the latter case, there is no finite list that could have been drawn up and substituted for the textual clause; the prohibition is inherently open. Cutting along somewhat different lines, the intent may be regarded as prohibiting those actions "that really are" cruel and unusual, regardless of what any particular set of individuals thinks those might be. In this case, the list of prohibited punishments is not open, but neither is it determined by the opinion of the founders. Although unable to provide conclusive results for any particular case, a theory of originalism should indicate how to proceed in understanding the level of generality in the founders' intentions.

There are essentially two ways of casting this problem. One is normative, and the other is semantic. In the normative approach, intentions should be read at the level of generality that results in the best judicial decisions now. Since the ultimate purpose of interpreting the constitutional text is to provide good answers to current political problems, when faced with an essentially arbitrary choice among levels of generality the interpreter should choose the one that is normatively the best. Ronald Dworkin has been the primary exponent of this view, and it fits with his overall conception of judicial interpretation.[61] Since, in Dworkin's view, legal interpretation deals with hard cases by appealing beyond the law in question to political principles that can supplement the law itself and fill in gaps in meaning, then consultation with the abstract intentions of the founders provides the framework for interpreting meaning generally and clarifies such vague textual clauses as "cruel and unusual."[62]

As applied here, Dworkin distinguishes between the "concepts" and the "conceptions" of the founders. The founders' concept of the cruel and unusual language was to prevent cruel punishments. Their particular conception of what that means might have barred public burnings but might have allowed floggings. Conceptions are particulars related to the general concept, but there may be numerous overlapping and nonoverlapping sets of conceptions consistent with a given concept. If we now believe that floggings, as well as burnings, are cruel punishments, then Dworkin would argue that a prohibition on flogging is the only way to construe the clause consistently with the intent of the framers and our own sense of the "best" meaning of the phrase. Only the concepts of abstract textual phrases are constitutionalized, not the conceptions of them held by the founders (or anyone else other than the current interpreter). Dworkin's classic example of a father directing his child to be "fair" gives the theory even greater significance. The father directs the child to be "fair" (the concept) while believing that being fair requires particular unspecified actions (the conception). The child, however, determines that being fair requires doing something in contradiction to his father's beliefs. The interpreter does not simply supplement the founders' conceptions but ignores them as irrelevant and replaces them with his own.[63]

A somewhat different approach is primarily dependent on the philosophy of language rather than on normative theory.[64] In this argument, language is understood to convey meaning about the world by referring directly to external objects, in accord with a causal theory of reference.[65] For example, in referring to "Nixon" I intend to refer to a particular individual. I may be understood to mean by that name an individual meeting a certain description (man elected president in 1968), an individual meeting a substantial portion of a cluster of descriptions (man elected president, man forced to resign as president, author of *The Real War*), or an individual identified through a causal or historical chain of consistent identifications leading to a baptism of the individual with that name.[66] Of most relevance here is the fact that the descriptive theories of reference rely on beliefs about the individual, whereas the causal theory resorts to the true essence of the individual in question. If my description of Nixon is wrong, then the subject of my reference becomes uncertain. In the causal theory, on the other hand, the reference is determined by the essence and thus is always certain. I could be wrong in referring to "Nixon" as the "man elected as president in 1964," but in the descriptive theory I could never be wrong about my reference, since my "Nixon" is defined by the 1964 election. The causal theory avoids converting factual errors into semantic ones and thereby opens the possibility that we could be wrong in our use of language. If combined with a moral realism that assumes that not merely individuals and natural objects, but also moral concepts, have identifiable essences, then it becomes possible to argue that in prohibiting "cruel and unusual" punishments, the founders meant those acts that really are "cruel and unusual" and not merely the ones that they would use to describe the phrase "cruel and unusual." In this case, we should bar flogging not because it would be the best thing to do but because it is what the words of the text require.[67]

Although neither of these theories is persuasive, they do point to the need to clarify originalist theory in this regard. Dworkin's argument can be dealt with briefly. His initial claim was that in using broad phrases like "equal protection" and "cruel," the founders necessarily intended to constitutionalize concepts of equality and cruelty since the text is not specific.[68] The difficulty with this claim is apparent once it is noted that the text does not have meaning independent of intentions, and therefore the founders could well have used "broad" terms to convey relatively narrow thoughts. Few people, for example, believe that the founders literally meant that Congress could pass "no law" infringing speech, yet in order to recognize this it must be admitted that the absolutist phrase meant something more narrow to the authors who wrote it. Once this initial plausibility is removed, then the issue reduces to the historical one of whether the founders had something more specific in mind than equality and cruelty in writing the constitutional text. Dworkin provides no evidence for his assertions about historical intent, and evidence on both specific textual clauses and broader understandings of constitutionalism militate against the concept thesis.[69]

In response to such criticisms, Dworkin later claimed that he regards both the concept and conception as being "intentions." The founders did not choose one or the other but necessarily possessed both since one cannot have a conception without also having a concept upon which it is based. The choice between them when they come into conflict is a normative, not a historical, one. Given his larger interpretive theory, the Constitution has to be read in its "best light," which in turn requires the rejection of bad conceptions in favor of better ones.[70] Dworkin is no doubt right that in order to have conceptions of fairness, we must also have a concept of what it is to be fair. It does not follow, however, that both were constitutionalized, nor does it remove the issue from one of historical evidence to normative debate. Dworkin's conclusion again only follows if one accepts his assumption that the text is intrinsically vague and thus open to normative consideration. As should now be clear, this is not the case. If I tell my son to "play fair" at basketball, by which I mean to refrain from knocking down his opponents and stealing the ball, which he is otherwise wont to do, it is not true that my phrase is inherently vague or operating at two levels of specificity. It is, in context, both specific and motivated by a broader theory of fairness. If my son nonetheless knocks down his opponent, who had previously pushed him, he is not acting on an alternative conception of fairness within my intended concept, but is in fact violating my instructions. It is a historical question as to whether I intended for him to use his own judgment in being fair or intended something more specific.[71]

In order to answer the semantic critique of originalism, it is unnecessary to demonstrate that either the causal theory of reference or moral realism is incorrect. It is enough to be reminded that they are inappropriately applied in the context of judicial interpretation of the Constitution. It is important to note that the semantic theory of reference is just that, semantic. Yet semantics is ultimately of limited use in interpreting specific texts. The role of semantics is to analyze the nature of language in the abstract; however, actual communication occurs not at the level of abstract language but at the level of specific, intended utterances. In the latter case, the question of whether a term is meant to be used in accord with its conventional sense is a specific one and turns on the intentions of the speaker.[72] A classic example in the literature can make this clear. Under the descriptivist theory, we take "tiger" to mean "a large carnivorous quadrupedal feline, tawny yellow in color with blackish transverse stripes and white belly." The causal counterexample is of an as yet undiscovered "creature which, though having all the external appearance of tigers, differs from them internally enough that we should say that it not the same kind of thing. We can imagine it without knowing anything about this internal structure."[73] Even laying aside specific complaints that a descriptivist theory could take this kind of example into account, the distinction is without significance for interpreting an utterance. Suppose I yelled, "Look out for the tiger," as a creature crouched behind you. It would be possible to interpret the meaning of the warning regardless of whether the creature was a true tiger or had a different internal structure. Moreover, I may have even known that the creature behind you was not a true tiger at the time of my warning, and yet it would not affect the interpretation. We could contend that I was mistaken in my use of the language, but we could not say that my warning actually "meant" to take notice of the true tiger the next time you visited a zoo. The case is simplified because the referent was proximate; I could have pointed and made my meaning clear (and in effect baptized the creature as a "tiger"). Nonetheless, the point is general—the meaning of specific uses of language depends on the speaker's intentions, not on semantic conventions.[74]

If the meaning of constitutional referents turns on the meaning that the founders intended, and not simply on the correct semantic meaning of the words, then we are returned to the historical question of their intended reference.[75] Regardless of whether such moral terms as "cruel" have real, substantive content apart from conventional beliefs, and even apart from whether the founders believed that moral terms have real, substantive content, the textual meaning of those terms nonetheless depends on what the founders thought the terms meant in using them.[76] The semantic realists have amassed no more evidence than Dworkin to demonstrate that the founders intended for terms such as "cruel" to be substantively empty. Unlike the argument from semantics, however, the originalist must be guided by the intentions of the founders on a case-by-case basis. Thus, it may be possible that in particular instances, the authors of constitutional language intended to refer to the "correct" meaning of a term, rather than to any specifically considered meaning. To borrow an example,[77] we can assume a statute was passed in 1945 that stated in its entirety that "toxic substances must be handled with due care." The expert definition of both "toxic" and "due care" have changed subsequently, and the question arises as to whether substances newly recognized as toxic must be disposed of with the care considered due in 1945. With intentions as our guide, it becomes evident that the legislators intended the terms "toxic" and "due care" to be defined in accord with the best available scientific standards, and therefore the new definitions, unknown and unimagined by the 1945 legislators, should appropriately be applied.[78] It is, of course, possible that the legislators had faith in neither scientific opinion nor judges, or that lobbyists had convinced the legislators that 1945-era scrubbers were a good way to handle waste. As a result, legislators may have actually intended that the toxic substances of 1945 alone be disposed of in accord with 1945 standards. In such cases, the correct interpretation would be both unfortunate and clear, just as it would be if the legislators had detailed the requirements for due care just to ensure that scientific technocrats would not later abuse their discretion and abandon the scrubbers. In fact, it is possible that the legislature meant substances that were toxic to the spirit, like pornography. It would be no more justifiable for judges to transform a misguided environmental statute into a more environmentally advantageous one simply because it was on the books and conveniently semantically vague than it would be to transform an antipornography statute into a waste disposal statute.[79]

What these responses indicate for originalism is that the search for intention must be guided by the historical evidence itself. The level of generality at which terms were defined is not an a priori theoretical question but a contextualized historical one. In some instances, the founders may have used terms quite expansively, and at other times seemingly broad terms were conceptualized at a relatively narrow level. Dworkin is quite right to point out that the founders may have held both general and specific ideas about given terms. Whether in drafting and ratifying the text, the founders intended to convey the one or the other is a distinct question. Therefore, just as Dworkin was misguided in subsuming specific conceptions under a broad concept, originalists would be equally misguided in simply dismissing the possibility that the founders intended to constitutionalize broader concepts. Originalists cannot limit their own interpretive efforts to creating lists of narrow examples of a term used in the Constitution.[80] In establishing general rules for determining what government actions are authorized or proscribed, the founders could readily have looked beyond a limited list. As a result, the founders themselves could be wrong in their assessment as to the correct application of the rule that they had established. In looking for intentions about levels of generality, the interpreter should not be misled into incorporating expectations instead of intentions into the text. Similarly, different levels of generality render the Constitution applicable in different situations. Whether the Constitution has interpretable meaning in a given context depends on the applicability of the intentions embedded in the text but does not depend on whether the founders themselves envisioned such an application.[81] The Constitution should not be stretched in order to force legal answers from it, but neither should it be unduly shrunk by neglecting the nature of intended meanings. The intended forest should not be lost among the detailed trees.[82]

COLLECTIVE INTENTIONS ARE MEANINGFUL

Before considering the difficulties in summing the intentions of the founders, it is worthwhile to deal with a different attack on the meaningfulness of collective intentions.[83] This critique has developed from the rational choice literature and contends that regardless of how intent is determined, it is necessarily meaningless, and therefore interpretation is a pointless exercise disguising judicial policy making. Such criticisms are rarely addressed in constitutional theory, and yet they have gained substantial influence in the public law literature more generally. Despite this influence, the application of rational choice theory to the immediate concerns of originalism has not been developed in any depth and, as currently conceived, does not present insuperable problems to originalist theory.

The argument has been most forcefully stated in the recent celebrated work of empirical public law, Jeffrey Segal and Harold Spaeth's *The Supreme Court and the Attitudinal Model.* In the section "The Meaninglessness of the Legal Model," Segal and Spaeth assure us that "it is well established, via mathematical proofs, that every method of social or collective choice . . . violates at least one principle required for reasonable and fair decision making." The result of these mathematical proofs is that "intent and interpretivism" are "without objective meaning" and produce "arbitrary" results.[84] The problem that so condemns democratic decision making was first identified by the economist Kenneth Arrow in a different context in the 1950s and rests on the demonstration that given certain assumptions, voting mechanisms cannot produce consistent results.[85] Among other potential difficulties, the vote may "cycle" between several equally preferable possibilities, so that the actual result is arbitrary from the perspective of the collective will.

The reason for this can be briefly described. We can begin by assuming three voters, each given an equal vote, who are faced with three policy options. Each voter ranks the policy options from one to three, but each ranks them differently.[86] The voters vote in a majority-rule system. Each supports his favored outcome, voting his first choice before all others and his second choice before his third. Although each pairing of policy options produces a winner between the pair, any other pairing also produces a winner. Thus, with two votes for each winner, A beats B, B beats C, but C also beats A. There is no single stable preference among the three options; thus there cannot be said to be a collective intent to favor any of the three options, even if one is actually passed and becomes law. Depending on the pairing of alternatives, any of these three policies could be enacted into law. Although this is a special case, the result can be generalized.[87] The analysis can be applied to any voting situation, including the voting of justices on doctrines in a case.[88] There is no guarantee of cycles for any given vote, but they are always a potential, and until voter preferences are revealed, they are unpredictable. Any vote could be subject to cycles and thereby be without meaning.[89]

There are several difficulties with drawing such sweeping conclusions from such formal models. They can be approached by questioning whether Arrow's conditions really are just minimal conditions of fairness and by questioning whether social choice theory can be appropriately applied to issues of constitutional intent. Although Arrow's initial conditions are described as normative, the putative inescapability of the cycling problem is actually an empirical issue. As an empirical matter, both the underlying assumptions of the model and its predicted consequences are rarely met.[90]

If cycles rarely occur, then this problem hardly merits a general rejection of efforts to locate the meaning that does exist in the vast majority of cases. Although cycle situations do sometimes occur, it is not at all clear that they present a genuine problem in real life.[91] There are a number of possible explanations for this divergence between formal theory and political reality. Cycles emerge only with the presence of certain distributions of voter preferences. It is possible that such distributions are rare. Notably, so-called "single peaked" distributions on a single dimension avoid the problem entirely. Such distributions are single peaked because if the preferences of voters are aggregated, a single alternative will be the unique social choice, drawn graphically as a single peaked curve. Such distributions most commonly exist on a single political dimension—that is, if voters agree about the question, even they disagree about the answer. For example, if a policy can be defined along a standard left-right political spectrum, then it exists on a single dimension, and voters can agree that policy x is conservative, z is liberal, and y is moderate. The preference distribution would be single peaked if voters ranked their choices along that dimension so that conservatives regard liberal policies as less desirable than moderate policies, for example.[92] It is also possible that political structures are designed to reduce problems to a single dimension or to constrain the number of options available at any given time, creating a "structurally induced equilibrium."[93] For example, parties and committees operate so as to restrict the choices that actually emerge on the floor of a legislature and are subject to a vote. Less concrete institutions, such as parliamentary procedures or political norms, can achieve the same effect.[94]

Moreover, introducing an element of temporality and social interaction serves to undercut the applicability of social choice models. "Social choice" and the "aggregation of individual preferences" may not be the most appropriate way to conceptualize or justify democratic procedures. Such models operate on the assumption that preferences are independent and given. In a real political environment, however, individual preferences are endogenous over time.[95] A voter does not simply appear in the voting booth with a set of hard-wired preferences, as if one were born to vote Republican. Argument and deliberation, recommendations and authority, party commitments and personal relations can affect the formation of preferences. Over the course of debate, a voter's preference profile may change. Since the entire point of deliberation is to change voters' minds, successful deliberation could result in the coalescing of preferences. Similarly, deliberation could affect how political problems are perceived in the first place. Policy dimensions cannot be regarded as natural givens but are constructed by political agents through debate.[96] Thus, the policy space and the distribution of individual preferences are not simple data but are themselves interpretive objects.[97] A rhetoric of preferences may be less descriptive than one of intentions. Rather than relying on such misleading formal models of democratic decision making and its predictions as to the relative "meaningfulness" of those decisions, political deliberations may be better understood through the contextualized process of interpretation.

Not only is the descriptive utility of rational choice theories open to question, but the normative persuasiveness of its "minimal conditions" and disfavored outcomes is also dubious. Many of Arrow's assumptions are undoubtedly desirable, such as his exclusion of "dictators" or single individuals who can always determine the outcome regardless of the preferences of others. Other normative assumptions are less obviously plausible. Expectations that groups of individuals adhere to the same standards of rationality against which individuals are judged, such as the transitivity of preferences, may suffer from a tendency to inappropriately anthropomorphize societies, whose decisions may be quite comprehensible, even if not "rational."

More immediately, the actual existence of cycles would not necessarily indicate the meaninglessness of ultimate decisions. The existence of a cycle merely indicates that there is not a unique outcome to a social decision, given the existing set of preferences. The lack of uniqueness of an outcome, however, does not necessarily make it "arbitrary" and certainly does not make it "meaningless." Any actual outcome is arbitrary only from the perspective of a social choice literature concerned with predicting results, given full information about preferences. From the perspective of those engaged in the process, however, the results are both the product of legitimate decision-making procedures and consistent with the desires of the voters. The fact that a different outcome could have emerged given the same set of actors but a different deliberative dynamic is neither surprising nor particularly disconcerting to individuals who approach politics from an interpretive perspective. The more problematic possibility is that the existence of a cycling situation opens a space for political manipulation. The significance of such manipulation in general, and specifically in the context of constitutional ratification, is not weighty, however, and is observable and manageable within an interpretive context.[98]

Finally, the difficulties associated with Arrow's theorem are far less serious for constitutional interpretation than has been suggested by its proponents.

Despite suggestions to the contrary, formal models cannot readily be applied to the ratification context. The evident existence of constitutional debates, changed opinions, the formation of factions, and efforts to define the relevant framework for debate and voting act to complicate the application of any such model. The additional facts that ratification took place under a "closed rule"— that is, the ratification conventions considered and approved a complete constitutional text without being faced with additional amendments—and that successful ratification required substantial support suggest the likelihood that the preferences for the Constitution were relatively stable. In any case, the fact that a different Constitution could have been drafted and ratified does not undermine the legitimacy of the one that was, rendering it an "arbitrary" outcome. The text that was adopted may be quite comprehensible in its own terms regardless of whether it was a unique outcome of the conventions.[99]

The very applicability of social choice models to questions of constitutional intentions is misguided. Constitutional intentions are ultimately not analogous to social choice preferences. From an interpretive perspective, the founders were not simply voting their preferences (what they would have liked to see in the text). They were also expressing their understanding of what was in the text they were constituting. The founders were in both a policy, or social choice, setting and in an interpretive situation. The interpretive dimension of both the formation of constitutional intent and adjudication falls outside the scope of social choice models. The application of such models to constitutional interpretation misunderstands the nature and limits of both formal theory and the interpretive enterprise.[100] In contrast to the standard demonstration of social choice models, the resultant constitutional text is not the only source of information we have as to the policy preferences of its drafters. Extensive records of constitutional debates certainly expose the preferences that motivated the drafting of the Constitution. More significantly, however, these debates provide evidence of the intentions that are embedded in the text, not just the preferences that motivated the approval of the text. Although those motivations could have resulted in multiple possible texts, those intentions could only be embedded in that single text. As an expression of intent, the Constitution is a unique document. In deliberating on how they understood the text they were approving, the ratifiers were not faced with a task of choosing among various options but of expressing the meaning of the text. It is of course possible that there was no agreement as to the meaning of various parts of the text, but there seems to be little theoretical or empirical reason to take the general stance that all such texts are intrinsically meaningless.[101] Despite the formal extravagance of such theories, they do not provide reasons to conclude out-of-hand that constitutional meaning was nonexistent or indeterminate.

In fact, it is not clear that they add anything significantly new to the old debate over the problem of summing intentions.

THE PROBLEM OF SUMMING

The problem of summing is a relatively practical problem within the confines of originalism itself. In order to convert it from an academic theory into a working model for adjudication, recommendations will have to be made as to how judges are to determine the authoritative "intent of the founders," given various individual statements contained in the historic record. Ultimately, this is largely a pragmatic issue to be worked out by the practitioners of originalism themselves in the context of specific legal issues rather than a question for normative theory. Nonetheless, in the way of a prolegomenon to practice, a few issues can be clarified, especially as they bear on whether originalism is even possible and how the justification for it affects that practice.

Perhaps the first point to note is the problematic character of labeling the difficulty of discovering intentions in a group as a "summing problem," or some similar variation on a theme of aggregating "intention votes." The implications of such language can be seen in the preceding discussions. As one commentator has noted, originalism can be conceived of as "a kind of multiple choice examination to be administered to the framers, in which all the questions look like this: 'Constitutional provision X covers fact-pattern Y. True or false?' "[102] Interpreters are reduced to playing a counterfactual game of imagining how the founders would have responded to particular facts. Further, intentions are reduced to the most basic level of narrow conceptions, even if those conceptions are only counterfactual ones. Rather than attempting to interpret the founders' understanding of cruel punishments, such an originalist creates a list of possible punishments by asking, "How many delegates disapproved of ritual mutilation?" Finally, a rhetoric of aggregating intention votes feeds a belief in the relevance of social choice theories to efforts at constitutional interpretation.[103]

Such approaches to originalist interpretation are misguided and should not be reintroduced as a method of aggregating collective intentions. Approaching textual clauses as if they were in fact a checklist of particular examples structures the investigation so as to discourage a recognition of constitutional principles that may in fact be embodied in the text.[104] Such an approach may be justified as less likely to encourage judicial discretion, but it is actually likely to encourage it. Attempting to create a collective biography of the convention delegates is an extraordinarily difficult task, yet one to which narrow conceptualists become committed as they search for an adequate number of intention votes.[105]

Although such biographical data may largely be available for such facts as the occupation and financial holdings of delegates, evidence is likely to be wholly lacking as to a delegate's opinion of thumbscrews. Such an originalist would be pushed either to relying on a narrow sample of delegates who did express such an opinion and then extrapolating their intention votes to the others, or to turning to ever more exotic sources of information to suggest a likely voting pattern. Both responses are unwarranted and prone to error. Additional alternatives of using a "delegation theory" of intent or excluding facts for which the intention votes cannot be found fare no better. A delegation theory incorrectly assumes a legislative model for constitutional deliberation. Although there were particularly prominent and active ratifiers, there were no officially recognized or authoritative "sponsors" of constitutional language who can be assumed to speak for the other delegates in articulating the meaning of the text. The exclusion of facts creates indeterminacy through the use of a flawed method. Discovering that there were few explicit intention votes barring thumbscrews would be unpersuasive in establishing that the founders really did not regard thumbscrews as cruel and did not intend to prohibit them with the adopted constitutional language. Such a method would lead to underenforcing constitutional requirements by unnecessarily misinterpreting the founders' intent.

Richard Kay has offered one of the few explicit responses to the summing problem. Consistent with my discussions of language theory, Kay holds that the text cannot properly be said to have any meaning at all unless there was a shared intention to animate it. He therefore recognizes the possibility that the text could be adopted without any identifiable meaning, if in fact there were radical disagreements among the founders as to the meaning of the text in question. In response, Kay argues that in order to be binding, the text must contain an intention held by a sufficient majority of the founders to constitute an "authoritative lawmaker." In this reading, a handful of idiosyncratic founders could be excluded but major disagreements among the founders would vitiate an authoritative intention on that subject.[106]

This account is quite powerful, though it must be qualified. Responding to such approaches, Gregory Bassham has made the important point that ratification and interpretation requirements are distinct. The requirements for supermajority support for textual ratification were to ensure both constitutional stability and a general working agreement over governing principles; the summing problem is directed toward ensuring that the founders' intentions, not the interpreter's, are enforced.[107] Having made this point, however, Bassham takes an unfortunate turn by developing supplementary rules that ensure that the judge can always specify a constitutional meaning, even when the original intent is indeterminate.[108]

Such an error flows from the assumption of judicial supremacy and a flawed understanding of the nature of textual meaning. As Kay notes, it is impossible to have "intentionless meaning." But supplementary rules designed to overcome actual indeterminacies in the text so that judges can make a positive interpretation in every case, therefore, misunderstand the limitations of interpretation. Bassham's additional concerns can be met in two ways. First, we must be careful to distinguish the ontological claim from the epistemological one. Although the text is ontologically equivalent to the intentions of the founders, and therefore meaning cannot exist without agreement among them, our ability to discover that level of agreement may be limited. As Bassham notes, the goal of originalism is to discover the founders' intentions, not to reratify the Constitution. But the prior and actual existence of agreement on textual meaning is necessary for intentions to be discoverable. If we were to discover fundamental disagreement among the founders over meaning, then we must admit that this undercuts the determinacy of the text. We cannot simply initiate steps to avoid that disagreement, unless positive evidence can be found to demonstrate the idiosyncratic nature of the dissenters.[109] Bassham is correct to note that a small number of delegates cannot hold the others hostage by refusing to accept the majority's interpretation, but he reaches that conclusion for the wrong reason. In his theory, disagreement can simply be discarded in the interest of creating a determinate textual meaning. On the contrary, evidence of genuine disagreement over meaning by a sizable minority could prevent the effective ratification of the amendment in regard to that area of controversy, but such original understandings must be sincerely held. A minority of protext founders cannot hold the majority hostage simply by declaring their belief that the federal power to raise taxes actually means that the federal government must ask the states for donations. Though such cases are unlikely to be so evident (or particularly common), an interpreter should be wary of insincerely held declarations of "intent" designed purely for the consumption of later interpreters, just as he should discount other post hoc statements of intent in which the speaker has an interest in a particular outcome.

The distinction between ontological and epistemological requirements also emphasizes that the belief that the founders held the general understanding of textual language can only be presumptive. Linguistic conventions provide a mechanism for approaching textual meaning but do not themselves determine that meaning. A survey of conventional understandings of the time period would be insufficient to establish the intent held by the founders. An additional effort would be necessary to ensure that the founders did not express contraventions of or qualifications to those conventional meanings.

Finally, it should be emphasized that the process of summing intentions is neither the mechanical one of adding up statements of intent nor an uncontroversial one that can be carefully confined by a proliferation of interpretive rules. The summing of intentions is one of the critical stages in the process of interpretation. It requires an educated judgment by the interpreter as to where the weight of the evidence lies and to whether disagreements were relatively contained (or irrelevant to the case at hand) or whether they broke loose and undermined the determinacy of the textual meaning itself. Given agreement on a common enterprise, such disagreements among originalists are manageable. Such interpretive judgments are subject to criticism, defense, and evaluation, but they cannot be scaled, measured, or reduced to certain demonstration. Originalist interpretation can hope to be objective in that it relies on external, demonstrable historical evidence and intersubjective standards of evaluation, but it should neither pretend to uphold nor be criticized for failing to meet standards of proof that eliminate the significance and role of an interpreter making an argument.

The Limits of Originalism and Interpretation

The final criticism of originalism to be addressed actually points the way toward going beyond originalism itself and indicating how it serves as a prelude for a larger constitutional theory; thus, it deserves separate consideration. The so-called "dead hand" problem, also known as the intergenerational or living constitution problem, has been a major stumbling point for originalism, a fact that indeed is neither surprising nor excessively distressing. The problem cannot be fully overcome by any constitutional theory, originalist or otherwise. In grappling with the difficulty, however, we can clarify the nature and limitation of originalism and begin to suggest how it must be incorporated into a larger constitutional theory.

Such a theory must build upon the strengths and justifications for originalism, which are rooted in the very nature of American constitutionalism. Without this foundation, the proper operation of our constitutional system would make little sense. Confining our analysis to any interpretive method makes just as little sense. Constitutional practice cannot be fully understood in terms of judicial interpretation. This is not simply because the Court has not always been a faithful constitutional interpreter but because interpretive theory does not describe all the Constitution. One advantage of originalism is that it fits within this larger constitutional theory. The foundations of originalism do not themselves describe the operation of the whole, but they do indicate why the interpretive part is incomplete in and of itself and how it might be supplemented with something more. That something more is constitutional construction.

The final type of argument to be considered is the so-called dead hand problem, a difficulty that has always been prominently put forth by critics of originalism and that forms a vexing dilemma for any theory of constitutional interpretation. Nonetheless, there are responses available to originalism that cannot eliminate the problem but that can help alleviate its burden.

Briefly stated, the problem holds that originalism cannot be adopted as a method of constitutional interpretation because it renders the Constitution unduly rigid and burdens the present generation with the outmoded opinions of a previous generation. The argument can proceed on either a pragmatic or a theoretical level, although both are normative. The pragmatic argument holds that the constitutional amendment process has proven far too difficult than either the founders assumed or the practical requirements of government can allow. The result has been a necessary accommodation in the interpretation of the text, giving it a flexibility that adherence to the original intent would not have permitted. The overall effect is to allow government to respond to social changes in beneficial ways while giving the nation greater stability by maintaining the "civic religion" that has grown up around the untrammeled constitutional text.

The more theoretical argument does not rely on the putative benefits of the government's violation of the originalist text but argues that a constitution dependent on the intentions of the founders would be illegitimate. Building on a theory of self-government, this reading holds that each generation is entitled to a government of its own making. Yet the current generation obviously did not write the originalist Constitution. Government by the consent of the governed must be based on a "living constitution," not one that restricts the popular will like a "dead hand from the past."[110]

Originalist theorists have not yet provided a sufficient response to such objections, partly because of the problematic reasons that have been advanced for adherence to originalism itself. These traditional justifications have not supplied the theoretical groundwork necessary to address the problem. Partly because of this inadequacy, originalists have failed to see the connection between their interpretive method and a larger constitutional theory, one that I outline here under the name of constitutional construction. These new foundations provide a better starting point for approaching the problem of a living constitution by demonstrating that originalism need not hold the untenable position of denouncing it.[111] Rather, originalism may claim the enviable position of being particularly well suited to reconciling judicial interpretation with it. Some limitations of the dead hand argument as currently put forth must first be considered, and then I shall suggest the manner in which the theory developed here minimizes the burdens of that argument.

An initial difficulty with the dead hand argument is raised by the problem of how we are to make the Constitution "live" in this fluid sense. One option, favored since the Warren era, is the judicial exploitation of the text's "vague" phrases to alter inherited meaning. Although some textual clauses are relatively clear on their face, others employ broad phrases or sweeping ideas that have a less obvious meaning. The Constitution is made to "grow" by providing these broad terms with meaning drawn from contemporary sensibilities. Thus, Ronald Dworkin, for example, advocates enforcing the text's commitment to "equality" by interpreting it in light of our current best conceptions of what equality might require.[112] With this strategy, judicial interpretations of the text retain at least a veneer of plausibility, since the Court avoids easy refutation by its reliance on vague textual hooks. Yet such interpretive maneuvers are fundamentally flawed. Although some textual phrases may in fact be indeterminate, indeterminacy is not simply a function of broad language. Such phrases as "equality," "due process," or "cruel and unusual" are no more inherently substantively empty than are such phrases as "reasonable," "crimes and misdemeanors," or "cases and controversies." Specificity arises from the determinacy with which a phrase was used, not from its semantic narrowness. A living constitutionalism that relies on the superficial broadness of textual language is either mistaken or disingenuous.

A second possibility for realizing the goal of a living constitution, as used here, is the abandonment of interpretation. At various points in our history, this response has been advocated as an explicit strategy. In the *Lochner* era, many reformers concluded that the fundamental flaw was in the document itself, not in the Court, and the solution would have to be found in moving beyond "the Constitution," traditionally understood. In the immediate afterglow of the Warren era, scholars were explicit about the need to lay aside interpretive results in order to pursue justice more directly.[113] But this approach raises difficult issues of legitimacy. When the question is put so directly, the full force of Bickel's countermajoritarian difficulty can be felt. The justifications for an active judiciary advancing its own favored ideas of constitutional design are exceedingly weak. Certainly the Court has been unwilling to rely on them. It has instead generally tempered its own rhetoric of interpretive flexibility with references to broad concepts actually intended by the founders in writing such a text.[114] As James A. Gardner has noted,

> Any lawyer knows that he or she cannot respond in court to an argument based on the original understanding of the Constitution by claiming that the concept of original intent is incoherent. The only effective response is to offer an alternative and more persuasive vision of the original understanding; the use of originalist vocabulary is simply obligatory for participants in the legal system.[115]

If the burden is placed on advocates of a living constitution to explain why and how it should be implemented, then it becomes clear that originalist interpretive commitments have not been abandoned, even if they are not firmly held. The dead hand argument has proven to be more of a convenient weapon against originalists than the basis for a positive argument for judicial review. As many of the early advocates of living constitutionalism recognized, the easiest avenue to such constitutional fluidity is for the judiciary simply to get out of the way. Living constitutionalism is most readily justified in the absence of judicial review. Such a result, however, is not consistent with either our inherited constitutional design or the desires of contemporary scholars.

The difficulty of justifying living constitutionalism in a straightforward manner has resulted in a number of inconsistencies within the dead hand argument. One such problem arises with the breadth of the application of the idea of a living constitution. Consistent application of this principle would require more adjustments in textual meaning than advocates of the approach normally suggest or are willing to defend. The Constitution is not generally regarded as flexible in all its parts for the good reason that such flexibility is contrary to the nature of constitutionalism and to the obvious intentions embedded in the text.

The logical conclusion of the dead hand argument is that the Constitution should provide no constraints on current actions other than those that we place upon ourselves. Depending on the theory, such contemporary constraints can come from either democratic action or substantive judicial theorizing, but in either case government should be free from unjustified restrictions. Every exercise of judicial review, however, places restraints on current government officials, so the justification for such restrictions must ultimately be found in contemporary constitutional theory; but this is drastically underdetermined relative to the continuing restrictiveness of the constitutional text. Such apparently functional adjustments to perceived modern governmental failings as Pres. Harry Truman's steel mill seizure, the legislative veto, the Gramm-Rudman-Hollings Act, and state-imposed term limits have been struck down by the modern Court.[116] Contemporary theorizing is notoriously inadequate for addressing such structural concerns, especially those that are grounded in textual commitments that are still taken to be fairly clear and specific.[117] But if living constitutionalism is applied consistently, and the entire document is reduced to a transcription of current institutional practices, except for those few areas of activism advocated by favored modern theorists, then the written Constitution ceases to be even a symbol of American government. The text would become a mere historical artifact. In order to retain its own legitimacy and plausibility, living constitutionalism must operate against a background of textual requirements largely accepted from the dead past. That background, however, can be neither questioned nor defended within the context of the theory.

A second inconsistency with the dead hand argument as currently applied is that it cannot account for the continued weight that intentions are given in judicial and scholarly interpretations. No advocate of living constitutionalism seems willing to embrace the complete rejection of intentions from constitutional interpretation, yet such a rejection would appear to be required by the theory. Whether in its pragmatic or its theoretical guise, living constitutionalism hinges the legitimacy of judicial review and constitutional law on its consistency with present desires and needs. Determining present desires and needs, however, requires no reference to past intentions of either the founders or of judges. Nonetheless, the forms of legal interpretation continue to require that such past judgments be "weighed" against more contemporary concerns. The theory makes clear that the weight of those past intentions, as intentions, should be zero and thus should be ignored entirely. Our continuing commitment to interpretation, however, has required introducing inconsistencies into the application of that theory.

The inconsistency becomes more acute when more recent constitutional amendments or more specific constitutional language is considered. If the intentions of prior generations are irrelevant to the determination of contemporary political necessities, then even recent amendments should be subjected to the same (lack of) respect to originalist meanings as the main text, and yet such judicial behavior would seem strikingly incorrect. One can imagine a constitutional amendment passed thirty years before a judicial decision, or one passed in the prior year. Within three decades, there will be substantial change in both society in general and the membership of the mature political population. Most current political actors would have had no hand in the passage of the offensive amendment but would feel the burden of the almost-dead hand of their fathers.[118] In the second case, the nation may well have been in the grip of an intense, but relatively short-lived, desire to alter the Constitution—perhaps to impose term limits on national legis-lators. Subsequent events may well calm the nation, and the deliberate judg-ment of the people and prominent opinion leaders may then regard the amendment as the embarrassing consequence of a nation not in its right mind. Under such circumstances, present political actors would be living under their own version of the dead hand problem. Their current desires, and perhaps their current well-considered judgment, are at odds with those expressed by a public that seems a distant and unpleasant memory.[119] Yet under either circumstance, revisionist alterations of the textual evidence of the still-fresh intentions would seem deeply inappropriate, even though required by a consistent theory of a living constitution.

Varying the specificity of the text serves the theory no better. The Consti-tution requires that the president be a natural-born citizen and at least thirty-five years old.[120] As some commentators have pointed out, the apparent specificity of this textual language depends on the interpretive method adopted.[121] If we adopt different conventions about age or native birth, then the text could seem relatively broad and indeterminate. Moreover, it seems evident that the drafters of this language possessed broad concepts that drove their particular conceptions, and those concepts may now suggest that polit-ical loyalty and maturity can be ensured by means other than nativism and age requirements. Living constitutionalism is all about the selection of an interpretive method, and yet it accepts some narrowing conventions about the text that impose restraints on present majorities. We can imagine a pop-ulation that regarded native birth to be a radically outmoded vision of citi-zenship and therefore would happily elect as president an individual who was born on other shores. Nonetheless, legal interpretation is unlikely to read ambiguity into this textual requirement but would instead continue to impose the dead hand of the past on this cosmopolitan populace.

In such circumstances, the Court would be compromising its commit-ment to living constitutionalism in the face of relatively obvious authorial intentions. From the perspective of the dead hand argument, however, any such compromise is illegitimate. The dilemma for the judiciary is created by its institutional commitment to interpretation, which requires the discovery of meaning in the text, and its theoretical commitment to the dead hand argu-ment, which requires a disregard for the discoverable meaning of the text. Putting examples of relatively obvious intent before the Court clarifies the nature of the dilemma and the institutionally appropriate response to it. There is no principled distinction between those examples, however, and the types of clauses to which the dead hand argument is usually applied. The only dif-ference between the cases is the relative difficulty of discovering intent. A continuing commitment to written constitutionalism is in necessary conflict with the idea of a living constitution, at least as generally imagined.[122]

Driving the dead hand problem is the conviction that the Article 5 amendment procedures have become an insurmountable obstacle to change. Without this assumption, it becomes much more difficult to maintain the argument that the people are implicitly opposed to the current constitutional provisions and need the judiciary to write their current opinions into constitutional law. If the Constitution can be amended, then the putative lack of tacit consent in the text as written becomes untenable in the face of its continuation. Despite the critical importance of this link in the chain of logic in living constitutionalism, there has been no serious effort to examine it, which would also be outside the scope of this book. The important point for an originalist to note, however, is that this claim is at best unproven and rests on no more than the assertion of critics. Until a more substantial argument or evidence is marshaled to demonstrate this assertion, the dead hand argument cannot be taken as conclusive or even particularly compelling.

The usual process in making the critique is simply to announce the effective "death" of Article 5. More adventurously, some critics have supported this contention by noting that "of more than nine thousand constitutional amendments that have been introduced in Congress, only twenty-six have been adopted—fifteen since the close of the eighteenth century."[123] The mere recitation of such numbers tells us little about the viability of Article 5, however. Such proposal counting fails to consider the number of proposals that go into a single amendment, for example. The ten amendments constituting the Bill of Rights were themselves culled from hundreds of proposals from numerous sources, most of which expressed the same concerns. Further, such a ratio takes no account of the independent effect of nontextual changes in doctrine. It cannot be doubted that judicial activism itself can sap the strength of a movement to amend the Constitution and thus has done its own part to kill Article 5.

The fundamental threshold question remains: How many amendments would have to be passed for Article 5 to be considered viable? Critics have not provided even a hint of a standard for evaluating such ratios. Yet the lopsided quality of the numbers does not itself reflect the failure of the amendment process. It may even represent the procedure's success. For example, numerous antiflag-burning amendments have been introduced in Congress since the Court determined that flag burning was protected under the First Amendment.[124] Very few constitutional scholars would regard it as a failure of the amendment process that such proposals have not, to this writing, succeeded. The exclusion of such amendments can be defended on both substantive and procedural grounds. Few theorists would find flag burning to be worthy of government regulation, let alone constitutional prohibition. Further, despite the uproar at the time of the decisions, it is doubtful that the people's considered judgment regards flag burning as a point of constitutional significance. As aspects of a sudden burst of popular passion, the amendment proposals were not prime candidates for constitutional inclusion on proceduralist terms. If those assumptions are correct, then Article 5's ability to prevent such proposals from becoming additions to the Constitution should be counted as evidence of its living success, not of its failure and death.

As is so often the case, advocates of the living constitution weight the scales toward constitutional change, without noting the role of the Constitution as a mechanism for preventing change. Article 5 serves both functions—allowing constitutional adjustment, but preventing intemperate change. Critics of the amendment procedure need to support the substantive argument that constitutional provisions should be changed in accord with the wishes of lesser majorities. In other words, such critics must make the positive case for reducing the protections of political minorities by making constitutional change over their objections easier to accomplish.

A more extreme question must also be asked. If it is true that Article 5 renders constitutional change too difficult, then why should we retain our fidelity to the text at all? If Article 5 procedures are flawed, why is living constitutionalism the necessary recourse?[125] Perhaps the more appropriate alternative is the abandonment of the text entirely. Although the Constitution is formally relatively difficult to change in its individual parts, it is much easier to change in its entirety. If later generations had actually been committed to a different constitutional system that did not rely on a written text, an originalist interpretation, or a variety of outdated clauses, then they could easily have abandoned the existing Constitution, just as we could now.

This process of constitutional revolution is as simple as the founding itself.[126] Indeed, the current fear of a constitutional convention derives from this fact. In contrast to Article 5's supermajorities in Congress and among the states, the only requirement for changing the constitutional system is a good proposal and some authoritative expression of acceptance. A bare majority of the nation could readily abandon the existing text through referendum, for example, although the success of the constitutional experiment undertaken with such an act is hardly ensured. The key point is that while amending the Constitution is difficult, changing the Constitution is not. If, in fact, written constitutionalism is as burdensome as the living constitutionalists contend, then it could have easily been swept aside, even while retaining many of the substantive commitments contained in the existing text. More significantly from the normative perspective, if originalism is as burdensome as it is argued, then it may be swept aside. Originalism is merely the implication of being governed by a written text. Without the text, originalism would make no sense. Moreover, those interpretive implications of a written text could be explicitly countermanded in a new text. If some future generation wished to be free of the text and its implications, as living constitutionalists contend that the present generation already wishes, then it could be, and it would not need the approval of Congress or the state legislatures to achieve that freedom.

Such problems and inconsistencies with the dead hand argument help mitigate its impact, but the problem remains a real one. Nonetheless, an appropriately developed originalist theory can be largely reconciled with the need to account for a multigenerational constitution. In approaching this issue, however, it is worthwhile to reframe the problem. The dead hand argument posits the existence of current majorities unduly restricted by the actions of prior majorities, but it does not make clear the alternative mechanisms by which present majorities can be represented. Specifically, as a critique of originalism, the dead hand argument suggests the question, "If not the founders' intentions, then whose?" Originalism provides that current majorities can only be restricted by the demonstrable intentions of prior supermajorities, which could in fact be overturned. In practice, however, the proponents of the dead hand argument do not employ it as a critique of originalist judicial activism but as a critique of relative judicial restraint. The living constitutionalists of the post-*Brown* generation expect the judiciary to be active in striking down legislation that is contrary to contemporary constitutional theory. Regardless of whether constitutional strictures are applied by originalist judges or by activist living-constitutionalist judges, current political actors are bound without their consent. The underlying problem of political theory that the dead hand problem seeks to bring forward is not unique to an originalist jurisprudence. Judicial review and constitutionalism necessarily imply that current majorities will be constrained by standards fixed outside their own deliberation. The real issue revolves around what those standards will be and who will determine them. Those problems are universal to American constitutional theory.[127]

Originalism can be justified on a fairly robust theory of democratic lawmaking (see chapter 5). On such a basis, originalism not only is responsive to the problem represented by the dead hand objection, but it can also claim some relative advantages in meeting its key assumptions. Compared to other theories, originalism offers a comparatively generous accommodation to consensual government. Although the dead hand label rhetorically biases the argument against historically oriented methods such as originalism, the logic of the argument goes against any interpretive method that looks outside the desires of current majorities. A more neutral phrasing of the argument would therefore focus on an "external" hand reaching in from any direction to intervene in current democratic politics rather than a specifically dead hand reaching from the past. In this context, the hand rests lightly on originalist theory.

Originalism accommodates this criticism because it can be grounded in a larger democratic theory that can account for both a respect for consensual government and a system of judicial review operating as a result of that form of government. It is important to note that this is not a variation on the judicial restraint argument proposed by some originalists to address this objection. Judicial restraint per se provides inadequate justification for an originalist method and does not match the nature of the Constitution as written. Grounding originalism in a theory of popular sovereignty does both, however, and in doing so explains how judicial review is both consistent with and enhances democratic governance. Such an argument demonstrates that originalism does not simply and arbitrarily impose the political preferences of the dead on the living; it recognizes the continuing nature of sovereignty and conserves the mechanism for its expression in the present. By interpreting the Constitution and enforcing constitutional law in accord with original intentions, this approach may not be acting in the name of living governmental majorities, but it does act in the name of the living potentiality of the sovereign people.

The assertion of the dead hand problem has been portrayed as a knockdown argument against originalism not only because of mistaken assumptions about that theory but also because of mistaken assumptions about the judiciary and constitutional theory. Like the countermajoritarian problem itself, the need for flexible interpretation in order to secure a living constitutionalism appears particularly acute since it is the unelected judiciary that construes the document and sets the degree of looseness in the restraints. This fear of an overly restrictive constitution, however, emerges from an unconsidered acceptance of judicial supremacy. If the judiciary alone is responsible for constitutional meaning, then whatever flexibility it finds in the document is ipso facto the amount of flexibility that exists in the constitutional system overall. This assumption is mistaken.

A more complete constitutional theory should take into account how the political construction of constitutional meaning supplements the judicial interpretation of the requirements of the text. By demonstrating that the alternatives are not a stark choice between legal interpretation and a political free-for-all, construction alleviates the pressure on the judiciary to provide and account for all the flexibility that might exist in the Constitution. If it is admitted that constitutional interpretation, at least with an originalist methodology, encounters indeterminacies in textual meaning, then the recognition of constitutional constructions can indicate how constitutional meaning is shaped so as to accommodate contemporary political needs and desires. Such indeterminacies need not be resolved by the judiciary in order to update constitutional meaning but can be constructed by the political branches themselves. Again, it is worthwhile to emphasize that this path does not return to the familiar originalist response from a thesis of judicial restraint. Although the idea of restraint in the face of interpretive indeterminacies leaves space for constructions, the operation of the two theories is different. For restraint-oriented originalists, as for other judicial supremacists, the actions of the political branches in the absence of legally imposed limitations cannot be explained in constitutional terms at all; rather, they operate outside the Constitution, in a realm of pure politics governed by unprincipled self-interest and fluctuating interest groups. Our historical experience with constitutional politics suggests that this account leaves out an important component of American political and constitutional practice. The Jacksonian reconceptualization of federalism, the Progressive transformation of the goals of government, the postwar growth of presidential war powers, and legislative expansion of civil rights are mere examples of the political interplay of principles and interests in the reconstruction of constitutional meaning and institutional practices. The Federalist Congress was first to struggle with the question of how executive officials were to be removed, the Jeffersonians had to determine whether and how the federal government could acquire new territories, and the precise contours of federalism and the separation of powers have been continually configured and reconfigured.[128] Government officials other than judges struggle with the duties and limits of their offices and the aspirations of the country. Politics is not only constrained externally by the judiciary but also internally by the political operation of constitutional understandings.

In this context, the alternatives are not between a living constitutionalism sustained by a flexible interpretive method and an inflexible constitutionalism imposed by an interpretive method emphasizing the past. Rather, the choice is between two forms of living constitutionalism: one imposed by the judiciary on the political branches, and one created and sustained by electoral politics itself. The approach offered here is similar to the types of arguments offered by living constitutionalists who emphasize the broad and vague terms of the inherited constitutional text. Unlike those approaches, however, originalism takes the text seriously. It does not rely on such a naive theory of textual meaning that insists that superficially broad terms are therefore inherently vague terms. Upon examination, however, some of the language of the Constitution may in fact turn out to be indeterminate, especially in the context of the contemporary applications that interest us. In such instances, interpretation can shed no further light on constitutional meaning, and historically inherited restraints on current majorities do not exist. The primary role of the judiciary in articulating constitutional meaning must also be questioned, however, when the broadness of textual terms actually implies textual indeterminacy. An important contribution of originalism is that it highlights the indeterminacies in the text as well as illuminating and enforcing its known requirements. In doing so, originalism points out the space for future constitutional development, without asserting judicial supremacy in determining the shape of that development.

Given that valuable indeterminacies remain within originalist interpretation and that those interpretive spaces are filled by political deliberation, the force of the dead hand is lessened. As long as determinate answers in legal interpretation remain, however, the constitutional deliberation of the past will continue to impinge on the politics of the present; thus, originalism can only mitigate the problem and not avoid it entirely. Having made that admission, however, a properly developed originalism can claim a more positive position as well. Originalism recognizes and encourages a form of constitutional politics that gives full meaning to the notion of a living Constitution.

First, originalism encourages constitutional politics through the recognition of textual indeterminacies. Although many methods of interpretation recognize the possibility of a textual vagueness, the response of most such methods is to develop the necessary supplementary rules to eliminate such uncertainties. Of course, Dworkin does so by refusing to recognize the very possibility of indeterminacy by simply incorporating political principles into his interpretive approach so that vague textual meanings become broad concepts to be filled in by the judicial elaboration of the underlying political principles. Dworkin's stated surprise at the continuing controversy this approach has generated is understandable, for though alternative approaches recognize that there may be gaps in the "law" they do not recognize that there may be gaps in the judicial articulation of that law.[129] Bassham contends that a "judge must often leap beyond the evidence" in order always to provide a determinate answer, and he struggles to provide a method that would authorize if not produce such answers.[130] He is perhaps more explicit about his task than others, but this explicitness is largely a function of his working with traditional originalist theory and trying to move from that position to one more within the theoretical mainstream. Since non-originalist approaches to interpretation are not anchored in the actual intent of the founders (and thus in the finite understandings of historical individuals), they are free to extrapolate on their initial foundations and draw possibilities into their interpretive web.

Linked to a flexible source of meaning, non-originalist methods provide flexible interpretations. The judiciary will always have an answer.

The value of indeterminacy is that it allows for political thought and action on constitutional principles. The "forum of principle" is expanded beyond the narrow confines of a legal elite and enters into a more general arena of popular participation, electoral accountability, and institutional flexibility. Rather than drawing all constitutional conflicts into the judicial sphere for an imposed resolution, some are allowed to remain outside constitutional law to be settled by political discussion and compromise. By refusing to create legal answers where none exists, an originalist judiciary focuses attention on the existence of constitutional politics and shifts responsibility for constitutional deliberation back onto political actors. In this sense, originalism fosters a living constitutionalism. Moreover, by refusing to resolve an issue judicially, an originalist Court emphasizes that government action is taking place at the margins of the Constitution. In such cases, the government is not acting in strict conformity with the known sovereign will but is itself acting in the place of the sovereign, constructing a new norm on which to act. By calling attention to this fact, the judiciary puts the citizenry on call as to the basis for government action and allows them to make their own decision as to the future limits of government authority.[131] The originalist judiciary refuses to place itself in the role of the sovereign by refusing to create constitutional law where constitutional meaning does not exist. Constitutional deliberation thus is not confined to either the long-dead past or the closeted chambers of the judiciary but is encouraged and allowed to proliferate and develop among those people who will be most affected by its results.

The Constitution is not radically indeterminate, however, and the judiciary is both capable of and obliged to deliver legal answers where proper interpretation does yield results. It is in these instances that the dead hand argument has its greatest force, for it is here that the constitutional deliberation of the founders is brought to bear on the government actors of the present. Nonetheless, even here a properly conceived originalism can be seen as fostering a living constitutionalism. It is precisely where the Constitution is most binding that the sovereign people are called upon to reconsider the continuing desirability of its constraints. By superseding that process, and therefore by eliminating the opportunity for a general deliberation on constitutional principles, the judiciary contributes to the maintenance of the Constitution as a cultural icon and historical artifact but subverts its existence as a living tool of governance.[132] The asserted impossibility of constitutional amendment becomes a self-fulfilling prophecy. Just as political participation in constitutional constructions becomes unnecessary if the judiciary leaps beyond interpretation to provide authoritative answers, so too do efforts at constitutional creation become unnecessary if the judiciary preempts popular deliberation by revising constitutional meaning on its own.[133] By insisting on the possibility that the Constitution can restrict current popular will, originalism also insists that the Constitution is mutable. The possibility of constitutional change is retained because something is left outside the existing Constitution.[134] If the Constitution becomes perfectible through judicial interpretation, however, constitutional change becomes unnecessary because nothing is excluded from its present terms.

Of course, in that case it is the judiciary that controls the pace of adjustment. Ironically, it is judicial activism that becomes the deeply conservative position, for it is judicial activists who fear the possibility of nonlegal efforts at constitutional revision. Sacrificing original constitutional meaning preserves the constitutional text, but to do so in this way also serves to preserve judicial power over the text. By stabilizing textual meaning, originalism also accepts the risk of the judiciary's loss of control over ultimate constitutional meaning—that is, it accepts the risk of constitutional creation. Madison himself expressed this conservatism in arguing against Jefferson's proposal to resolve disputes over constitutional meaning by popular convention. Though Madison hastily admitted that "the people are the only legitimate fountain of power," he rushed on to emphasize that Jefferson's proposal only "*seems* strictly consonant to the republican theory."[135] Although Madison had particular objections to Jefferson's specific proposal and its ability to resolve all types of constitutional violations, his primary point rested on a fear of popular participation in the constitutional operations of the government. The new government would be more secure if a popular "veneration" of it was encouraged through the pretense that there were no defects in the Constitution as written; "the reason of man" could be kept "timid and cautious" in the face of community prejudice. Instead of embracing the value of popular deliberation on the fundamental principles of governance, Madison emphasized the "danger of disturbing the public tranquility" and contended that the constitutional "experiments are of too ticklish a nature to be unnecessarily multiplied." It was fear of the people that led Madison to recommend that the public "passions ought to be controlled and regulated by the government" through the device of restricting rational deliberation on constitutionalism to government elites.[136] In the context of judicial review, the popular will can be regulated and managed by the careful fine-tuning of constitutional meaning by the firm and only partially visible hand of the judicial elite.[137] By returning control over constitutional meaning to the people, originalism recovers the popular possibilities of living constitutionalism.

BEYOND INTERPRETATION

Constitutional interpretation cannot be the end of constitutional theory. If the very effort to supply a justification for judicial review and the legal interpretation of the Constitution suggests that there are limits to that interpretation, then it also provides the starting point for analyzing what lies beyond those limits. Although the arguments for originalism considered here are primarily designed to explore the nature of judicial interpretation and to justify an originalist approach, the examination of such arguments indicates that originalism is limited in its capacities. Rather than being a flaw in its program or an opportunity to call for a simple judicial restraint, the margins of originalism should be built upon to understand the Constitution as a whole, not just as it is interpreted through the courts.

The basis for this further development of constitutional theory is evident in a number of points in the argument for originalism. Perhaps the most important is the initial step of recognizing that the law has limits. As an effort to discover the meaning of the Constitution as a judicially enforceable law, interpretation cannot proceed beyond the gaps that are inherent in that law itself. Although there are legal tools available to help clarify constitutional meaning at the borders of these gaps, the space between discoverable meaning and legal text will necessarily remain. In part this is the natural result of writing law to address future political concerns. Regardless of the skill of the lawmaker, the future is unpredictable. The specific requirements of future government action will always be uncertain. As a result, any effort to formulate rules to empower or constrain government as it addresses a new range of issues will necessarily fall short. Even though general principles can be provided and specific rules formulated, there will ultimately emerge discrepancies between the law as it was written and the facts the law is called upon to address. The difficulty is increased by the limitations of language itself. As the founders themselves recognized, language is an imperfect vehicle. Though care is taken to be clear, new situations will expose the uncertainties that exist at the margins of the terms used and perhaps at the margins of the ideas that the words were intended to express. The tension between the need to convey meaning clearly and the need to speak broadly enough to encompass future events ensures that the body of law will always include the existence of hard cases with no determinate answers.

If legal theory suggests that there will be gaps in the law, and therefore in its interpretation, hermeneutics suggests that those gaps are likely to widen over time. Some radical versions of hermeneutic theory would contend that we are so estranged from the past that it cannot be accessed, or at least that it cannot be translated into the present. Yet such theories rely on misconceived notions of the nature of language, history, and historical knowledge. Nonetheless, if such theories overstate the case, taking such arguments seriously points out the kernel of truth from which they grew. The past is different from the present in important ways. The founders were not primarily concerned with our political disputes, or even with disputes that are closely analogous; they had their own problems with which to contend. In writing a constitution to endure over time, they did not set out to confine themselves to those immediate problems, but their conception of politics and constitutionalism was naturally defined by their own experiences and historical context. Both their text and, more important, their explanation of it were laid out within a particular historical situation. Interpreting their intentions will always require bridging the distance between their situation and our own. It is possible to span that distance. But as time passes and the problems to be resolved grow more distant, that path becomes more uncertain and the cracks in the initial material grow wider. In time, we find ourselves increasingly operating at the margins of constitutional meaning, where interpretation is less likely to provide clear answers. Judicial review should become less relevant to our political life over time, not more.

Although a number of implications of the writtenness of the Constitution indicate the appropriateness of an originalist interpretive method, there are limits both to the implications of textualism and to originalism. Various philosophical and literary approaches to understanding historical texts assert in their strongest form that an interpreter cannot discover the intent of a written document. The distance between interpreter and writer is said to be too great, and the medium of writing too inadequate, to allow such faithful application of constitutional intent. Such strong conclusions were found to rest on flawed foundations. Nevertheless, in a weaker form, such arguments do shed light on how texts are perceived in the world. As has been long recognized, written words cannot speak for themselves. Not only do they require an interpreter to convey their meaning—as indeed the spoken word does—but they cannot react and correct errors in interpretation. Thus, the text can be perceived as autonomous of the intentions of the individuals who wrote it, and those perceptions can have real effects even if they cannot be regarded as proper interpretations.

In the realm of constitutionalism, the autonomy of the text has political repercussions. As a basic element of America's "civil religion," the Constitution has often been used as a banner for a variety of political movements. It has been invoked as authority for actions both diverse and contradictory, and, as a written text available for public use, such appropriations are to be expected. As new political principles, problems, and interests emerge and gain influence, the durable text of the Constitution can be used as a catalyst to spur further insights into the nature of American politics and the principles that have guided or ought to guide it. Even if such new conceptions of constitutional meaning are grounded on an incorrect interpretation, a misreading of the Constitution, they nonetheless may gather force and have consequences as real and significant as those of the constitutional law derived from proper interpretation. These consequences of the public Constitution suggest another element to constitutionalism, a political element to be added to the legal element invoked by interpretation.

The particular difficulties of originalist adjudication likewise point beyond interpretation to other methods of constitutional elaboration. If originalism is theoretically possible, and in fact required to ground the practice of judicial review, it remains practically difficult. As critics have pointed out, the record of the founders' intent is less extensive and clear than might be desired. Although the broad outlines of the constitutional meaning may be reasonably clear, interpretation of the text often falls short of providing clear guidance in making the fine distinctions required to settle contemporary disputes. Moreover, at least in some instances, modern problems may be capable of resolution under the structure of the existing Constitution but still address issues of little or no concern to the founders. In such cases, the founders could reasonably be said to have no intent relevant to a given question, and thus constitutional law has no determinate answer to provide. The settlement of such issues requires guidance from outside the text, supplementing interpretation to correct for its limitations.

By emphasizing the original contexts within which constitutional meaning was formulated, originalism keeps such indeterminacies in the foreground. Hans-Georg Gadamer was right to suggest that the reader brings something to the text in order to flesh it out and render it concrete in a new context. The error of radical hermeneutic theory lies in assuming that nothing substantial or distinctive remains of the original text. The two texts coexist, but not in the "fusion" of a melting pot that assimilates diverse elements into a seamless new alloy. Rather, the result is a patchwork as new elements are added to the persistent fragments of the original text. The changing context of the political world calls forth something more than the interpretation of the text. In its political environment, the Constitution supports not only what its text requires but also much that it merely suggests or allows. Whereas the unelected denizens of the federal judiciary are primarily responsible for what the text requires—the legal constitution—other members of the federal government are perhaps more concerned with what the text suggests—the political constitution. The latter element requires a process of construction to add to the text to realize its suggested meaning.

Similarly, exploration of a theory of popular sovereignty and its promise of higher lawmaking provides a grounding for judicial review and constitutionalism as a whole, and yet it also suggests the limitations of written constitutionalism. Sovereignty requires an active sovereign to provide a determining will in the political realm. Although it is possible for the people to instruct, empower, and constrain their government agents through the written rules contained in the constitutional text, that text by itself can only go so far. As the arguments for a living constitutionalism attest, the absence of the popular sovereign from the realm of practical, daily politics invites its overthrow and effective replacement with a "government by judiciary," or some other claimant to the empty throne. A theory of popular sovereignty may provide the justification for judicial review, but it also provides a caution. Political power flows from a political will, and a will that is always mediated through agents and dusted with age will gradually lose its persuasiveness and authority. The originalist grounding for judicial review, therefore, directs our attention to the ways in which the Constitution unfolds and is reshaped in order to respond to political needs. As the embodied voice of the founders grows more faint and less relevant, the active voice of a lesser sovereignty extends the logic and applications of the original constitutional design.

The theory of sovereignty is not simply a theory of power; it is primarily one of democratic, participatory political authority. If the full presence of the sovereign people required for constitutional creation is rarely brought to bear, the reflection of that sovereignty is often found in political life. The extension of the constitutional project is not simply an exercise in philosophy but is the task of conflicting political participants drawing upon the authority of political principles and the power of political institutions and interests. If such creative forces cannot simply be let loose to undermine the restraints placed on government during periods of more complete deliberation, they are critical to the operation of government. Such continuing, active, and widespread consideration of fundamental political norms is essential to animating the bare constitutional framework created by the founders. Originalism emphasizes a theory of popular sovereignty and therefore a theory of higher lawmaking, not just of government action or restrictions on daily politics. In doing so, originalism carves out a role for judicial review, but it also suggests a constitutional politics that lies outside the scope of interpretive theory and its narrow focus on the work of the Court. In emphasizing the interpretable nature of the written Constitution, originalism also draws attention to the constitutional practice that does not rely on interpretation and that has developed alongside the text. In justifying their own existence, interpretation and originalism also suggest the existence of something outside themselves.

Conclusion:
Interpretation and the
Constitution as Law

If the Court has corrupted us by seducing us into looking to it rather than to the Constitution, it can also play a role in reversing some of that damage. It can recognize the limitations of its own role in the constitutional system and admit that constitutional meaning and constitutional law do not form identical sets. To do so would not require an abandonment of the judiciary's status as a constitutional guardian, but it does require that the Court rededicate itself to its function as the interpreter of the law. By degrees, the interpretive efforts of the Court would again make clear the nature and limits of the law. Perhaps this example would encourage the rest of us to take up our own task of looking beyond the courts in order to see how the Constitution actually governs.

Given a legitimate method of constitutional interpretation, the Court has a role to play in elaborating constitutional meaning. Without such a method, however, its responsibilities collapse into those of other political institutions. On such a level playing field, the Court is at a distinct disadvantage, with little to claim for itself except its lack of accountability and its distance from the citizenry upon whom it acts. In order to justify its unique status as a final authority on constitutional meaning, the judiciary needs a theory of interpretation that suits its talents and indicates the importance of the institution of judicial review within a system of separated powers.

There are, in fact, several possible methods of interpretation that could potentially serve such a purpose. The guiding aim of constitutional theory, at least for the past thirty years, has been to provide such an interpretive method that could direct the courts in their work and justify the continuing practice of judicial review. The continuation of that debate for such a lengthy period, which itself follows earlier periods of such debate, is indicative of the general dissatisfaction with the available options. Although many interpretive approaches address the central issues of judicial authority and the nature of the Constitution, none has emerged as fully persuasive. Frustration with the search for an adequate method, combined with a concern over the practice of judicial review in recent American politics, has led to the emergence of various voices calling for the abandonment of the quest entirely or at least for its redefinition. Such frustrations are expressed in the empirical public law literature and its avoidance of any effort to justify judicial behavior, the Critical Legal Studies movement and its call for the abandonment of meaningless theory in favor of willful action, and a reinvigorated pragmatism and its recommendation of a foundationless incrementalism for judicial policy making. Somewhat more subtly, these frustrations are also expressed by the constitutional "dialogues" literature that has placed the Court within the context of a continuing debate among multiple political actors over constitutional meaning. In each case, constitutional interpretation is either abandoned entirely or disconnected from the special problematic of judicial review. It is assumed that the judiciary can simply exercise power over elected officials, relying entirely on a political tradition of deference to judicial rulings and a popular willingness to accept judges as yet another layer of government technocrats.

Such despair offers little hope of constitutional legitimacy but promises the substitution of "good government" in its stead. Constitutional interpretation may not be possible, such critics assert, but judicial policy making is within reach. I have argued here that although various theories of constitutional interpretation are insufficient, a theory of original intent does provide authority for the judicial veto of legislation and executive actions. The development of such an originalist justification for judicial review, however, also suggests the boundaries of the judiciary's unique relationship with the Constitution. Although other political institutions may engage in constitutional interpretation, the legal assumptions of that enterprise create a comparative advantage for the courts, and the assigned task of the judiciary requires that it take action on its interpretations. Proper interpretation has its limitations, however, and the defense of originalist jurisprudence suggests both the nature of those limits and the means of overcoming them. A theory of constitutional interpretation must be supplemented by an understanding of constitutional construction.

The necessity of a supplement must not exclude the reality of the interpretive core of constitutional meaning. Constitutionalism both authorizes political action and attempts to constrain it. If those constraints are to be made real, there must be a means of enforcing those limits outside politics. Of course, the ultimate source of limits is rooted in politics. Whether grounded in contemporary liberal theory or in the understandings of the framers of the federal Constitution, any conception of the limits of legitimate political behavior will develop from a larger political theory. Arguments in favor of unfettered majoritarianism or individual rights, the divine right of kings or republican popular rule, do not emerge unencumbered from the natural order of the world but are the products of contestable political thinking. Moreover, the establishment of those limits and the creation of mechanisms for their enforcement require not only political thinking but also difficult political action. The results will reflect a political settlement of the first order. Having established such first-order constitutional rules, however, their enforcement can be distinguished from the everyday, second-order politics that occurs within them. It is this internal politics that is bounded by the Constitution and for which institutions such as judicial review are established as constraints. A theory of legal constitutionalism must assume the possibility of the separation of the two realms. For the separation to be sustainable, however, it must be possible to interpret the first-order rules of the Constitution. If the constitutional text is a law that emerges from the constitutional politics of the people, it is a law that must be enforced against the encroachment of administrators and politicians chosen to conduct the people's business. The possibility of the interpretation of that fundamental law separates the judiciary from the normal realm of politics and authorizes it to regulate the conduct of government.

Originalism provides an account of how legal constitutionalism is to operate. By drafting a written text to serve as a constitution for the federal government, the founders chose to create external rules to restrain political actors. In contrast to the British tradition of unwritten constitutionalism, the American experiment legalized constitutional procedures by codifying them in a written text. In doing so, the founders implied a full legal framework for enforcing constitutional norms, including the institution of judicial review. As the branch charged with interpreting the laws, the judiciary is well positioned to serve as a formal mechanism for applying the fundamental law. The creation of a written text to serve as a constitution was meaningful only if such a text represented a modification of the British practice. The legalization of constitutional principles was such a modification, is implied by the introduction of a text, and is consistent with later practice under the Constitution.

The implications of introducing the device of a written constitution into the British tradition of constitutionalism require an originalist approach to interpreting the document. Thus, the form of constitutionalism developed in the United States uniquely authorizes originalism. Other forms of constitutionalism are possible, as the British case indicates, and various substantive principles can be accommodated within a single form, as the variety of written constitutions adopted by the American states and other nations indicates. But the structure of a written constitution suggests as complementary features the practice of judicial review and the interpretive method of originalism. The distinctiveness of written texts can be located in their relative specificity of principle, their capacity to act as legal instruments, and their invocation of an originalist intent. In each instance, such characteristics require the adoption of originalist methods of interpretation.

The Constitution represents more than an effort to carve out an island of stability in the stream of history. It is also an expression of the revolutionary basis of popular government. The extensive territories and administration of the modern nation-state would not be possible if the people actually governed themselves. Self-government has proven an elusive dream in modern history. Nonetheless, the possibility and promise of self-government can be secured by the ranking of political tasks. The historical state is inconsistent with self-government, but only if the popular sovereign need be constantly active. Although the people cannot rule at all times, they can deliberate on the fundamental questions of politics, defining the type of nation they wish to create. Popular sovereignty insists that government authority is only a conditional trust. Government officials cannot be allowed to believe that their title is a function of their own actions, that by their own efforts they have garnered personal authority over others. Constitutionalism depends on the separation of power and authority. Those who are allowed to wield power have no authority of their own but possess only the authority of their office. Although their ability to influence events may rise and fall, their license to exercise that influence is constant. The popular sovereign alone retains the right to define the extent of that license.

Self-government in this regard requires the limitation of government. The Constitution serves as a reminder of the reality of popular rule. Its maintenance as a governing text prevents government officials from taking into their own hands the constitutive power of defining the extent and nature of their own powers. It also preserves that power in the hands of the people at large. The Constitution did not arise from the earth or drop from the skies but was written by real men at a specific time. It expresses their agreement on the nature of a government that they commonly created. At that moment of founding, a people created itself and designated its instrument for serving the public good. With deliberation and care, individuals consented to become a citizenry, choosing to live under "this Constitution" and no other. The grandeur of American constitutionalism is that we might make that choice again. We can only do so, however, if the Constitution is preserved intact. If the choices that we have made can be undone, if the laws can be remade by those selected to administer them, then the possibility of self-government has been removed. The right to determine the form of government under which we will live would be reduced to the partisan struggle for office. Originalism sustains the authority of the Constitution over government by insisting that it is a law made by men, not by politicians. The primary obligation of government is to uphold that law until it is changed by the heirs of those who made it. Our inheritance from the founders is not just a law, but the power to make law. The judicial adoption of originalism ensures that we do not squander that inheritance.

One feature of the law is that it is not self-effectuating, which is both an asset and a liability. It is an asset because it allows for the separation of the formation of law from its application. Legislators need not focus on the particular case but can view a problem from a more general perspective. Without the prospect of a particular application before them, lawmakers are less likely to be influenced by specific prejudices against a set of individuals or a particular interest. Although the law may still be specifically harmful to whole classes of people, the legislature is distanced from the effects of the law and is less likely to be drawn into the partisanship inherent in particular applications. Likewise, those who must face particular situations are provided the guidance of a more general rule. Although the judge or executive may become entangled in the momentary interests at stake in a particular dispute, the previously existing laws provide a broader perspective on the purposes and needs of government and serve as a hedge against transitory enthusiasms. The law could only effect its own realization in the world if the power of legislation and execution were combined in one body, capable of both determining standards and executing judgment. Such an active sovereign could realize its will, but its will would most likely be blinkered and narrow.

The inability of the law to enforce its own terms, however, requires a reliance on agents. This dependence raises the question of trust, for although the law may be carefully and wisely formulated it must still be applied in order to gain significance. That the law can only control those wielding political power by right, but not by act, means that there is a constant threat that those charged with enforcing the law will also violate it, sacrificing right for power. The rule of law in fact as well as in right requires the deliberate fidelity of those who apply the law to those who make it, or at least to the terms of the law that the legislators have made. Originalism is the interpretive method associated with such fidelity to the law of the Constitution. The Constitution cannot require its own correct application; it is dependent on the adoption of correct interpretive principles by the executors of the sovereign will. The mere fact of such constitutional dependence on government fidelity does not mean that government agents are free agents. The law does not cease to exist or become a blank slate because it exists without natural effect. The law's executor is not autonomous just because the lawmaker is absent.

Its lack of self-enforcement is not the only limitation of the law. The law is not omnipotent. It can neither enforce its own terms nor account for everything that might affect it. It necessarily exists within a context that is itself only partially shaped by the law. The law must survive in a world that is not entirely of its own making and that it does not have the capacity to control fully. For example, the law is the product of the legislative will. Just as the law cannot act for itself, it cannot will itself into existence. The political will that creates law is at least partially independent of the law it creates. Rousseau and other republican theorists emphasized this feature of the law through discussions of virtue and corruption. The republic could only be free under the law if the citizenry possessed adequate virtue, both as lawmakers and as subjects. The law can only be as good as the underlying society that creates it and gives it force. Recognizing that the Constitution is broader than the Constitution as law also allows us to realize that constitutional law cannot provide everything that is necessary for its own existence. The legal constitution has contributed to constitutionalism. It has helped maintain the limits of government, and it has been used to create and strengthen the popular sovereign. Nonetheless, although constitutional rules have been responsive to the need to bolster the reality of popular government, the legal constitution cannot and has not itself ensured that reality. There may be a constitutional need to support the existence of the popular sovereign, but that does not mean that all of those supports are specified and required by the law. The maintenance of a republican form of government is a political task as well as a legal one. The courts are not the only instruments of constitutional development.

To the extent that the courts are concerned with interpreting the law, they must adopt a jurisprudence of original intent, not because it is the only available method of interpretation, but because it is the best. Originalism is most capable of realizing the goals internal to the interpretive project itself and of actualizing the obligations of democratic constitutionalism. The abandonment of originalism risks the abandonment of those projects as well, and it ensures the corruption and inadequacy of our pursuit of them. Of course, some alternatives to originalism are not interpretive methods at all, properly understood, but are the rejection of the interpretive project itself. Other alternatives, however, do maintain the judicial role of interpretation, but do so badly. The non-originalist Court may be seeking the correct goal, but it would be guided by the wrong map. Each step it takes threatens to lead it off the correct path and into a wilderness of judicial control over constitutional meaning. The Court thus gradually draws the Constitution into a world of its own making, spinning out a new political universe to replace the one initiated by the founders. Such a descent into judicial solecism obscures the original purpose of the courts and flattens the richness of the Constitution. The Court's creation cannot match the vitality and authority of the original, not because its vision is poorer but because it is more limited. The discipline of originalism promises to protect the Court from itself, and in so doing, to protect us from the Court.

Notes

1. CONSTITUTIONAL INTERPRETATION

1. See also Mark A. Graber, "Why Interpret? Political Justification and American Constitutionalism," *Review of Politics* 56 (1994): 415; Howard Gillman, *The Constitution Besieged* (Durham, NC: Duke University Press, 1993); Michael J. Klarman, "Antifidelity," *Southern California Law Review* 70 (1997): 381; Rogers M. Smith, "The Inherent Deceptiveness of Constitutional Discourse: A Diagnosis and Prescription," in *Integrity and Conscience: NOMOS XL,* ed. Ian Shapiro and Will Kymlicka (New York: New York University Press, 1998).

2. Ronald Dworkin, *Law's Empire* (Cambridge: Harvard University Press, 1986), and "Symposium: Fidelity in Constitutional Theory," *Fordham Law Review* 65 (1997).

3. Francis Lieber used these same terms in the early nineteenth century to distinguish between different forms of construing the Constitution. Although the distinction drawn here is similar, it cannot be wholly reduced to Lieber's. Like Lieber, I conclude that interpretation is "the discovery and representation of the true meaning of any signs, used to convey ideas," and that true meaning is "that meaning which those who used [the signs] were desirous of expressing" (*Legal and Political Hermeneutics* [Boston: Charles C. Little and James Brown, 1839], 17, and see also 66, 86, 102). His "construction," however, is really traditional equity jurisprudence. He is concerned with resolving textual contradictions and the application of the text to unforeseen situations, and he pursues such constructions in the context of textually intended principles. My concept of construction applies more broadly to instances when the text cannot be fairly said to have a discoverable meaning. Cf. Lieber, 57–58, 124–126; but see also 139–140. Similarly, and more recently, Chester Antieau has contrasted construction and interpretation but defines both more narrowly than I do here; see his *Constitutional Construction* (New York: Oceana, 1982).

4. The distinction can be made normative by arguing that the logical tendencies of the approaches are matched by moral and political duties that the judiciary should follow. Thus, it could be normatively argued that the courts should not engage in constructions. At this juncture, I do not develop that argument, though I do contend that courts behave in a more "legalistic" fashion when engaging in interpretation. Whether and when courts must behave legalistically is a question requiring a more extended answer than can be provided here.

5. William F. Harris II, *The Interpretable Constitution* (Baltimore: Johns Hopkins University Press, 1993), 118, 1 n.2 (emphasis omitted). Harris's phrasing is useful here, but his understanding of constitutional elaboration is quite different.

6. I use "standards" and "rules" here interchangeably. The rulelike quality of constitutional law can embrace both legal "rules" and binding legal "principles." See also E. Philip Soper, "Legal Theory and the Obligation of a Judge: The Hart/Dworkin Dispute," *Michigan Law Review* 75 (1977): 479–484. For a discussion that does rely on distinguishing the two, see Duncan Kennedy, "Form and Substance in Private Law Adjudication," *Harvard Law Review* 89 (1976): 1685.

7. Marbury v. Madison, 5 U.S. (1 Cranch) 137, 177 (1803).

8. Interpretations are essentially constantive and can be judged to be either correct or incorrect. As will be elaborated, constructions are more appropriately understood as performative. On this distinction, see J. L. Austin, *How to Do Things with Words* (Cambridge: Harvard University Press, 1975).

9. The distinction was first advanced in Thomas Grey, "Do We Have an Unwritten Constitution?" *Stanford Law Review* 27 (1975): 710–714, and was taken up by several others. The distinction is criticized in Ronald Dworkin, *A Matter of Principle* (Cambridge: Harvard University Press, 1985), 34–38. The categorization offered here between interpretation and construction does not seek to reopen this debate. For an argument that originalism should not be understood as interpretation simply, see chapter 6. Further, the interpretation/construction categorization does not map onto the interpretation/noninterpretation distinction. The interpretation/noninterpretation debate simply seeks to locate the proper source for judicial pronouncements. The concern here, however, is with the degree of determinacy and the nature of the answers that different methods of construing meaning can provide different institutions in order to create a multitiered elaboration of constitutional meaning. In interpretation, any method will suffer constraints imposed by textual details, historic origins of the text, overall constitutional structure, and so on, all of which are incorporated into legal interpretation regardless of the larger methodology adopted. In construction, on the other hand, the political branches are free to develop normative theories independently of such constraints. The interpretation/construction distinction emphasizes the essential connection between Walter Murphy's several and separate questions of "what," "who," and "how" to interpret; the interpretation/noninterpretation debate accepts their separation and revolves around the "what" question. Cf. Murphy, "Who Shall Interpret? The Quest for the Ultimate Constitutional Interpreter," *Review of Politics* 48 (1986): 401.

10. Purposefully, relatively little information is provided in this example. The literal meaning of the text leaves a rather large gap to be filled by construction. Additional information beyond the conventions of the English language would allow the interpreter to exclude more possibilities and further specify the command's meaning. Perhaps in the social context of the sentence, only poodles are available for sale. Perhaps it occurs in a conversation about whether to purchase one of the neighbor's puppies. The general availability of such narrowing information does not affect the point made, however.

11. Michael Perry has made a similar distinction, labeling constructions as "specifications" or "constitutive choices" (*The Constitution in the Courts* [New York: Oxford University Press, 1994], 75–76). As Perry argues, such decisions are essentially nondeductive, requiring an exercise in judgment. Nonetheless, constructions and specifications can be distinguished in several ways. First, Perry is almost exclusively concerned with Court rulings, yet the judiciary is not the primary site for such judgments. Second, he erases the boundaries between the relatively narrow judgments made by the Court and those made by political actors engaging in constructions. The judicial function need not be mechanical in order to be limited and rulebound, yet Perry seems to embrace just such a mechanical model to justify his move beyond originalist interpretation. Third, specifications and constructions should be distinguished in that specifications suggest a choice between discrete alternatives, whereas constructions build constitutional meaning from the raw material of politics instead of choosing from a menu contained in the text. Indeed, Perry's own example of whether prohibiting the use of wine at Mass is a violation of the nondiscrimination

requirement of free exercise indicates both the relatively narrow range of interpretive judgment and how the development of legal rules can frame the decision. Thus, Perry's judicial focus skews his argument toward a legalistic model. Finally, constructions cut across, and not just along, Perry's distinction between indeterminacy of meaning and of meaning in context. Specification is limited to indeterminacy of a legal directive in the context of an application. Construction, on the other hand, also addresses indeterminacies in discovering the directive itself. The consideration of nonjudicial actors who must take positive action would have clarified the breadth of such decisions. Compare my example of a directive to purchase a dog with Perry's example of an ordinance governing automobiles, which he frames as a deductive application (75).

12. James Madison noted such difficulties. Even where there were clear distinctions between natural facts, the human mind may not be able to specify them accurately. Moreover, "Obscurity arises as well from the object itself as from the organ by which it is contemplated," especially when social facts are considered. See Alexander Hamilton, James Madison, and John Jay, *The Federalist Papers*, ed. Clinton Rossiter (New York: Mentor, 1961), No. 37, 228.

13. W. B. Gallie, "Essentially Contested Concepts," *Philosophy and the Historical Understanding* (New York: Schocken Books, 1964), 157–191.

14. U.S. Constitution, art. 4, § 4. See also Charles O. Lerche Jr. "Congressional Interpretation of the Guarantee of a Republican Form of Government During Reconstruction," *Journal of Southern History* 15 (1949): 192, and David F. Epstein, *The Political Theory of* The Federalist (Chicago: University of Chicago Press, 1984), 120–123.

15. I am here concerned with genuine legal gaps, not "jurisdictional gaps" created when no court is designated to resolve a given legal question. It is possible for there to be constitutional interpretation where the judiciary has no jurisdiction, such as in impeachments. In the constitutional context, however, jurisdictional gaps are a good indication of the additional existence of legal gaps. See Joseph Raz, *The Authority of Law* (New York: Oxford University Press, 1979), 70.

16. Cf. "Contrary to much popular imagining, there are no gaps when the law is silent. In such cases closure rules, which are analytic truths rather than positive legal rules, come into operation and prevent the occurrence of gaps" (ibid., 77 [footnotes omitted]).

17. Thomas Aquinas indicates that the positive law may be derived from the natural law by either "conclusion from premises," such as proscription on murder from a proscription on doing harm, or by "determination of certain generalities," such as moving to a particularly shaped house from the general form of a house. The former have the force of the natural law. The latter "have no other force than that of human law" (*The Political Ideas of St. Thomas Aquinas*, ed. Dino Bigongiari [New York: Hafner Press, 1953], 58–59). The first case is unduly restrictive of the whole of interpretation, but the second does indicate one basis for construction. Aquinas does not fully account for the limitations that the general form may place on the determination of specifics (the ways in which interpretation can constrain construction) or the manner in which particular determinations may be advocated as the best or even correct expression of the general form (the ways in which constructions are exclusionary).

18. Donald S. Lutz, *Popular Consent and Popular Control* (Baton Rouge: Louisiana State University Press, 1980), 65–66 (emphasis in original).

19. In the case of gaps in the law, "The question of which of the possibilities within the frame of the law to be applied is the 'right' one is not a question of cognition directed

toward positive law—we are not faced here by a problem of legal theory but of legal politics. . . . One cannot obtain by interpretation the only correct statute from the constitution" (Hans Kelsen, *Pure Theory of Law* [Berkeley: University of California Press, 1970], 353). Constitutional "conventions" serve a similar function in the British context. Powers may be legally available to the government, but convention may dictate that it is constitutionally inappropriate to use them. See, for example, In the Matter of Section 6 of The Judicature Act, 1 R.C.S. 753 (1981).

20. For ease of discussion, I present these instances as if there were hard lines between interpretively discovered rules of the constitutional law and the constructively created rules of the statutory law, as if the Court simply marked a clear boundary between the permissible and the impermissible. This is one case in which constructions arise, but not the only case. Instead of finding that the text protects x but not y, an interpreter could simply find that the text clearly protects x but is unclear about y. In the instance of "hard cases" with no right answer, constructions are the means by which we provide an answer (what is "due process"?). In the context of cases with a right answer, constructions may provide the means to supplement that answer (having determined that we may prohibit obscene speech, should we prohibit it?).

21. Zurcher v. Stanford Daily, 436 U.S. 547, 559 (1978).

22. Ibid., 567.

23. Act of Oct. 13, 1980, P.L. 96-440, Title I, Part A, § 101, 94 Stat. 1879. See also Louis Fisher, *Constitutional Dialogues* (Princeton: Princeton University Press, 1988), 255–257.

24. Olmstead v. United States, 277 U.S. 438, 466, 465 (1928).

25. See Louis Fisher, "Congress and the Fourth Amendment," *Georgia Law Review* 21 (1986): 124–138. The Court eventually reentered the field with its opinion in *Katz,* though this did not end the interbranch dialogue on how far and under what circumstances protections against wiretaps should extend.

26. Goldman v. Weinberger, 475 U.S. 503 (1986).

27. Act of Dec. 4, 1987, P.L. 100-180, Div. A, Title V, § 508(a)(2), 101 Stat. 1086.

28. Edward S. Corwin, "Constitution v. Constitutional Theory: The Question of the States v. the Nation," *Corwin on the Constitution,* ed. Richard Loss, 3 vols. (New York: Cornell University Press, 1981–1988), 2:186.

29. It should be emphasized that I make no empirical claim as to how much of the Court's historical practice has consisted of "interpretation," as opposed to "construction." Undoubtedly, the Court has engaged in many constructive efforts to render the indeterminate constitutional text determinate in order to decide particular cases. The Court's normative commitments, however, are to interpretation.

30. Bruce Ackerman becomes mired in confusions precisely where he tries to replicate judicial efforts at discovering applicable doctrines in such political events as the New Deal. Ultimately, his preservationist Court is unmoored by its efforts to derive a generalized right to privacy sufficient to constitutionalize a right to abortion from a political movement determined to impose national regulations and qualifications on the use and possession of private property. See his *We the People* (Cambridge: Harvard University Press, 1991). See also Michael J. Klarman, "Constitutional Fact/Constitutional Fiction: A Critique of Bruce Ackerman's Theory of Constitutional Moments," *Stanford Law Review* 44 (1992): 788–790.

31. U.S. Constitution, art. 5, art. 7. In formalizing the process of amendment, the Constitution also domesticates it. As a result, constitutional creation remains a process of mere *amendment* to an existing and stable text, not the replacement of one constitution with

another. Constitutional creation, therefore, remains on the same spectrum of constitutional elaboration with interpretation and construction. The process of replacing the constitutional text with a new constitution may be called "constitutional revolution" and is illustrated by the adoption of the Constitution and the abandonment of the Articles of Confederation. See also Harris, *Interpretable Constitution,* 186–187.

32. Lieber labels these "extravagant constructions," which carry "the effect of the text beyond its true limits" and abandon "the spirit of the law" (*Legal and Political Hermeneutics,* 81). This problem may also be compared to the debate over the possibility of "unconstitutional" constitutional amendments, or unconstitutional creations, which conflict excessively with the spirit of the existing document even as they create new text. On "unconstitutional" amendments, see Harris, *Interpretable Constitution,* 164–208; Sanford Levinson, *Constitutional Faith* (Princeton: Princeton University Press, 1988), 149–154; Laurence Tribe, *Constitutional Choices* (Cambridge: Harvard University Press, 1985), 21–28; and Walter Dellinger, "The Legitimacy of Constitutional Change: Rethinking the Amendment Process," *Harvard Law Review* 97 (1983): 386.

33. U.S. Constitution, art. 4, § 3. Even if such unconstitutional constructions are justiciable, and yet cannot as a practical matter be overturned by the courts, it may be best for the judiciary to withhold its imprimatur from such hidden creations and strive to limit the constitutional damage by resisting efforts to repeat or to build upon such actions in the future. See also Sotirios Barber, *On What the Constitution Means* (Baltimore: Johns Hopkins University Press, 1984), 153–154.

34. This is essentially Ackerman's proposal.

35. Stephen Griffin has argued that the creation of a "legalized Constitution" creates a tension between two forms of constitutional understanding. The Court pursues a narrowing, though unstable, understanding of the Constitution as law through legal mechanisms of interpretation. A second, political constitution remains irreducible to and undisciplined by those interpretive rules, however (*American Constitutionalism* [Princeton: Princeton University Press, 1996], 13–18, 152–158).

36. Ronald Dworkin is an exception, since his method is supposed to produce answers in even the "hard cases" that appear to have no legally authoritative answer. Whether his project is successful, or whether he stays within the confines of "interpretation," is an open question (see *Taking Rights Seriously* [Cambridge: Harvard University Press, 1978]).

37. The Supreme Court can be seen as acting similarly in establishing judicial review as a part of the judicial function delegated to the courts, or in developing the exclusionary rule as a judicial mechanism for enforcing the search-and-seizure requirements of the Fourth Amendment.

38. E.g., In the Matter of Section 6 of The Judicature Act, 1 R.C.S. 753 (1981).

39. See also Philip Bobbitt, *Constitutional Fate* (New York: Oxford University Press, 1982), and Robert F. Nagel, *Constitutional Cultures* (Berkeley: University of California Press, 1989). Cass Sunstein is making such a distinction, though without accepting my view of its constitutional significance, when he finds that the "silencing effect" of pornography on women is real but provides insufficient guidance for judicial interpretation: "The silencing effect is an important part of the political argument against pornography; but it probably should not be part of the First Amendment debate" (*The Partial Constitution* [Cambridge: Harvard University Press, 1994], 395 n.14). Sunstein is probably right that such arguments should not influence clause-bound interpretation but is mistaken in thinking that the debate over the regulation of pornography can be separated from a debate over constitutional meaning.

40. For more specific consideration of constructions, see also Keith E. Whittington, *Constitutional Construction* (Cambridge: Harvard University Press, 1999).

41. As will be discussed, the idea of a "single" interpretive method is only relative. Originalism does not require the abandonment of such traditional interpretive resources as precedent, textual structure, and so on. It merely organizes those resources by prioritizing the search for intent. Cf. Griffin, *American Constitutionalism,* 143–152, and Bobbitt, *Constitutional Fate,* 3–119.

2. THE DILEMMAS OF CONTEMPORARY CONSTITUTIONAL THEORY

1. Martin Shapiro, "Fathers and Sons: The Court, the Commentators, and the Search for Values," in *The Burger Court,* ed. Vincent Blasi (New Haven: Yale University Press, 1983), 220, and Laura Kalman, *The Strange Career of Legal Liberalism* (New Haven: Yale University Press, 1996).

2. Even those scholars who have attacked judicial activism generally, such as Robert Bork, have done so through the mechanism of an interpretive theory. See, e.g., Robert Bork, *The Tempting of America* (New York: Free Press, 1990). Cf. Walter Berns, "Judicial Review and the Rights and Laws of Nature," in *The Supreme Court Review, 1982,* ed. Philip B. Kurland, Gerhard Casper, and Dennis J. Hutchinson (Chicago: University of Chicago Press, 1983), 50.

3. G. Edward White, "From Sociological Jurisprudence to Realism: Jurisprudence and Social Change in Early Twentieth-Century America," *Virginia Law Review* 58 (1972): 999, and Paul W. Kahn, *Legitimacy and History* (New Haven: Yale University Press, 1992), 97–133. See, e.g., Lochner v. New York, 198 U.S. 45, 75 (1906).

4. Roscoe Pound, "Liberty of Contract," *Yale Law Journal* 18 (1909): 467 (emphasis in original).

5. Karl Llewellyn, "The Constitution as an Institution," *Columbia Law Review* 34 (1934): 31, and "Some Realism About Realism—Responding to Dean Pound," *Harvard Law Review* 44 (1931): 1236.

6. Thomas Reed Powell, "The Logic and Rhetoric of Constitutional Law," *Journal of Philosophy, Psychology and Scientific Methods* 15 (1918): 646.

7. G. Edward White, "The Evolution of Reasoned Elaboration: Jurisprudential Criticism and Social Change," *Virginia Law Review* 59 (1973): 279. See also Kahn, *Legitimacy and History,* 134–147.

8. Erwin Griswold, "Foreword: Of Time and Attitudes—Professor Hart and Judge Arnold," *Harvard Law Review* 74 (1960): 85, 94.

9. Herbert Wechsler, "Toward Neutral Principles of Constitutional Law," *Harvard Law Review* 73 (1959): 15, 19.

10. Alexander M. Bickel, *The Least Dangerous Branch* (Indianapolis: Bobbs-Merrill, 1962), 3, 16.

11. Ibid., 58, 68, 64. Bickel denounced the Realists as not only unrealistic in their abandonment of the role of principled deliberation but also as inadequate in their failure to establish the legitimacy of judicial review. If judicial pronouncements were merely a reflection of personal whim and power, then "their authority over us is totally intolerable and totally irreconcilable with the theory and practice of political democracy" (80).

12. Alexander M. Bickel, *The Supreme Court and the Idea of Progress* (New York: Harper

and Row, 1970), and Robert K. Faulkner, "Bickel's Constitution: The Problem of Moderate Liberalism," *American Political Science Review* 72 (1978): 925.

13. See, e.g., Gerald Gunther, "The Subtle Vices of the 'Passive Virtues'—A Comment on Principle and Expediency in Judicial Review," *Columbia Law Review* 64 (1964): 1, and Skelly Wright, "Professor Bickel, the Scholarly Tradition, and the Supreme Court," *Harvard Law Review* 84 (1971): 769.

14. Hans Linde, "Judges, Critics, and the Realist Tradition," *Yale Law Journal* 82 (1972): 255. But see also Barry Friedman, "The History of the Countermajoritarian Difficulty, Part One: The Road to Judicial Supremacy," *New York University Law Review* 73 (1998): 333.

15. I do not consider here Bruce Ackerman's "dualist democracy," which makes a distinctive argument far more consistent with the larger theory presented here than with the "democratic" theorists considered in this section.

16. Before the institution was firmly established, however, some commentators did exclude judicial review as inconsistent with republican government. See, e.g., Eakin v. Raub, 12 Serg. & Rawle 330, 344 (Pa. 1825); "Brutus," in *The Anti-Federalist,* ed. Herbert J. Storing (Chicago: University of Chicago Press, 1985), 163–166, 183–187.

17. See, e.g., James Bradley Thayer, "The Origin and Scope of the American Doctrine of Constitutional Law," *Harvard Law Review* 7 (1893): 129; Learned Hand, *The Bill of Rights* (Cambridge: Harvard University Press, 1958); and Bork, *Tempting,* 139–141.

18. For a theory that does inventory the charges against the undemocratic practice of federal representative bodies, see Jesse Choper, *Judicial Review and the National Political Process* (Chicago: University of Chicago Press, 1980), 4–59. See also Mark A. Graber, "The Non-Majoritarian Difficulty: Legislative Deference to the Judiciary," *Studies in American Political Development* 7 (1993): 35.

19. John Hart Ely, *Democracy and Distrust* (Cambridge: Harvard University Press, 1980), 74 (emphasis in original).

20. Ibid., 59. Ely lampoons reasoned adjudication as "We like Rawls, you like Nozick. We win, 6–3," although he does accept that reasoning can clarify the implications of moral assumptions (58).

21. Ibid., 80–87.

22. Ibid., 75, 88–101, 123.

23. Ibid., 101–104.

24. U.S. Constitution, art. 1, § 9; Amend. 8.

25. U.S. Constitution, art. 1, § 8.

26. In noting the "clear" requirements of the text to secure certain substantive rights, I am not suggesting that those rights are somehow known in some preinterpretive manner but merely that any reasonable interpretive method would indicate the existence of such rights in the text and thus their complete dismissal would be unwarranted. How those rights are to be construed once recognized is a further task of more refined interpretive argument.

27. On the general problems of reading such progressive paths into historical events, see Herbert Butterfield, *The Whig Interpretation of History* (New York: Norton, 1965).

28. See also Laurence Tribe, *Constitutional Choices* (Cambridge: Harvard University Press, 1985), 9–20; Mark Tushnet, "Darkness on the Edge of Town: The Contributions of John Hart Ely to Constitutional Theory," *Yale Law Journal* 89 (1980): 1037; and Paul Brest, "The Substance of Process," *Ohio State Law Journal* 42 (1980): 131.

29. See, e.g., Frank Michelman, "Foreword: Traces of Self-Government," *Harvard Law*

Review 100 (1986): 4, and "Law's Republic," *Yale Law Journal* 97 (1988): 1493; Suzanna Sherry, "Civic Virtue and the Feminine Voice in Constitutional Adjudication," *Virginia Law Review* 72 (1986): 543.

30. Cass Sunstein, *The Partial Constitution* (Cambridge: Harvard University Press, 1993). Republicanism, or at least Sunstein's version of it, has the advantage of decentering the courts in constitutional theory. Although I am obviously sympathetic to this instinct, the legal republican variations of it are half-hearted at best. See Kathryn Abrams, "Law's Republicanism," *Yale Law Journal* 97 (1988): 1591, and Paul Brest, "Further Beyond the Republican Revival: Toward Radical Republicanism," *Yale Law Journal* 97 (1988): 1623.

31. Sunstein, *Partial Constitution,* 24–37, 133–134, 156–161.

32. Ibid., 98–104, 134–136.

33. Ibid., 162–194. See also Michelman, "Law's Republic," and William H. Riker and Barry Weingast, "Constitutional Regulation of Legislative Choice: The Political Consequences of Judicial Deference to Legislatures," *Virginia Law Review* 74 (1988): 373.

34. Although legal republicanism as a theory of constitutional interpretation and judicial review may be flawed, the historical concept of republicanism may be quite beneficial in understanding particular aspects of the constitutional text.

35. On the history of republican thought, see J. G. A. Pocock, *The Machiavellian Moment* (Princeton: Princeton University Press, 1975); Bernard Bailyn, *The Ideological Origins of the American Revolution* (Cambridge: Harvard University Press, 1967); Gordon Wood, *The Creation of the American Republic, 1776–1787* (New York: Norton, 1969); Robert E. Shalhope, "Republicanism and Early American Historiography," *William and Mary Quarterly* 39 (1982): 334; and Daniel T. Rodgers, "Republicanism: The Career of a Concept," *Journal of American History* 79 (1992): 11.

36. Initial discussions of the history of republicanism emphasized the break from republican thought that the Constitution represented; see, e.g., Wood, *Creation,* 519–564. Although subsequent work has continued to find traces of republicanism in American thought long after the founding era, few scholars argue that the Constitution exclusively reflects republican ideals. For pure republican interpretations, see Pocock, *Moment,* 506–552, and Russell L. Hanson, *The Democratic Imagination in America* (Princeton: Princeton University Press, 1985), 54–91. Cf. Forrest McDonald, *Novus Ordo Seclorum* (Lawrence: University Press of Kansas, 1985), and Isaac Kramnick, "The 'Great National Discussion': The Discourse of Politics in 1787," *William and Mary Quarterly* 45 (1988): 3. Cass Sunstein was more cognizant of this limitation in an earlier article; see "Beyond the Republican Revival," *Yale Law Journal* 97 (1988): 1558, 1561.

37. Sunstein, *Partial,* 123–161. Sunstein is properly hesitant about authorizing the courts to engage in this aspect of the republican project, yet it seems clear that certain aspects of it would require judicial intervention either to advance the cause or to resist it in the name of other concerns.

38. For a discussion of community building, and exclusion, in American politics, see Rogers M. Smith, *Civic Ideals* (New Haven: Yale University Press, 1997).

39. See, e.g., S. M. Shumer, "Machiavelli: Republican Politics and Its Corruption," *Political Theory* 7 (1979): 5.

40. See also Richard H. Fallon Jr., "What Is Republicanism, and Is It Worth Reviving?" *Harvard Law Review* 102 (1989): 1730–1733.

41. See, e.g., Laurence H. Tribe and Michael C. Dorf, *On Reading the Constitution* (Cambridge: Harvard University Press, 1991); David A. J. Richards, *Toleration and the Constitution*

(New York: Oxford University Press, 1986); Rogers M. Smith, *Liberalism and American Constitutional Law* (Cambridge: Harvard University Press, 1985); and Stephen Macedo, *The New Right v. the Constitution* (Washington, DC: Cato Institute, 1987).

42. Ronald Dworkin, *Taking Rights Seriously* (Cambridge: Harvard University Press, 1978), 133. Dworkin's later work emphasized the nature of an interpretive community rather than his liberal neutralism and rights foundationalism, although the substantive change is minimal; see *Law's Empire* (Cambridge: Harvard University Press, 1986). Most recently, Dworkin has claimed that his vision of rights is required by a commitment to "democracy" (*Freedom's Law* [Cambridge: Harvard University Press, 1996], 2–38).

43. Dworkin, *Taking Rights,* 138 (emphasis in original). However, Dworkin is ultimately vague about defining the "objectivity of moral principle" and from where moral principles come (*Law's Empire,* 78–84).

44. Dworkin, *A Matter of Principle* (Cambridge: Harvard University Press, 1985), 18–28.

45. Ibid., 67–68, 188–193, 293–303; Dworkin, *Taking Rights,* 199, 240–258.

46. Richard A. Epstein, *Takings* (Cambridge: Harvard University Press, 1985), 30, 31.

47. Ibid., 4–15, 331–340.

48. The basis of these values is problematic, however, and contributes to the imbalance of rights theorizing. See also Stanley C. Brubaker, "Conserving the Constitution," *American Bar Foundation Research Journal* 1987 (1987): 274–276; William A. Galston, "Defending Liberalism," *American Political Science Review* 76 (1983): 621; and Ian Shapiro, "Gross Concepts in Political Argument," *Political Theory* 17 (1989): 51.

49. See, e.g., Bork, *Tempting,* 199–219; Paul Brest, "The Fundamental Rights Controversy: The Essential Contradictions of Normative Constitutional Scholarship," *Yale Law Journal* 90 (1981): 1063; and Lief H. Carter, *Contemporary Constitutional Lawmaking* (New York: Pergamon, 1985), 104–127.

50. Owen Fiss, "Foreword: The Forms of Justice," *Harvard Law Review* 93 (1979): 10.

51. See, e.g., Sotirios A. Barber, *On What the Constitution Means* (Baltimore: Johns Hopkins University Press, 1986), and *The Constitution of Judicial Power* (Baltimore: Johns Hopkins University Press, 1993); Michael J. Perry, *Morality, Politics, and Law* (New York: Oxford University Press, 1988); Graham Walker, *Moral Foundations of Constitutional Thought* (Princeton: Princeton University Press, 1990); Hadley Arkes, *Beyond the Constitution* (Princeton: Princeton University Press, 1990); and Michael S. Moore, "A Natural Law Theory of Interpretation," *Southern California Law Review* 58 (1985): 277.

52. Arkes, *Beyond,* 13.

53. Ibid., 21, 5, 29.

54. Ibid., 27 (emphasis omitted).

55. In contrast, Dworkinian moralism operates only at the margins of an unclear text. See E. Philip Soper, "Legal Theory and the Obligation of a Judge: The Hart/Dworkin Dispute," *Michigan Law Review* 75 (1977): 517–518.

56. Ibid., 38. See also Thomas Aquinas, *The Political Ideas of St. Thomas Aquinas,* ed. Dino Bigongiari (New York: Hafner Press, 1953), 67–70.

57. Walker, *Moral Foundations,* 62–63 n.127. This point is not limited to natural law theories, however. See also Mark A. Graber, "Why Interpret? Political Justification and American Constitutionalism," *Review of Politics* 56 (1994): 430, and Mark V. Tushnet, "The Hardest Question in Constitutional Law," *Minnesota Law Review* 81 (1996): 1.

58. Stanley Brubaker appeals to epistemological skepticism to sustain a version of judicial restraint ("Reconsidering Dworkin's Case for Judicial Activism," *Journal of Politics* 46

[1984]: 512–517). In response, Walker contends that epistemological skepticism and onto-logical confidence must be held in "tension," not resolved in favor of the former; other-wise, the skepticism becomes absolute and the ontological confidence becomes groundless. Thus, judges should recognize their own fallibility while continuing to look for moral truth (Walker, *Moral Foundations*, 160–161). Although this may be a reasonable theological, and even political, recommendation, the tension becomes too much in the legal context where the judge is armed with the force of the state but is ultimately unac-countable to correction.

59. See also Jeremy Waldron, "A Right-Based Critique of Constitutional Rights," *Oxford Journal of Legal Studies* 13 (1993): 18. Positive law may be based on the natural law and derive its meaning from it. The immediate source for judicial interpretation, however, is the legally encoded aspects of the natural law, which provide a more determinate source for judicial exploration and obviate the need to consider the reality and validity of the natural law. See also Jules L. Coleman, "Legal Duty and Moral Argument," *Social Theory and Practice* 5 (1980): 391–392, 404, and "Negative and Positive Positivism," *Journal of Legal Studies* 11 (1982): 146–152; Soper, "Legal Theory," 512–514.

60. See, e.g., Jeffrey A. Segal and Harold J. Spaeth, *The Supreme Court and the Attitudi-nal Model* (New York: Cambridge University Press, 1993).

61. See, e.g., Roberto Unger, "The Critical Legal Studies Movement," *Harvard Law Review* 96 (1983): 561; Mark V. Tushnet, *Red, White, and Blue* (Cambridge: Harvard University Press, 1988); and David Kairys, ed. *The Politics of Law* (New York: Pantheon, 1990). For an exchange on the nature of the antitheoretical position, see Douglas Laycock, Mark V. Tush-net, and Lino Graglia, "Colloquy: Does Constitutional Theory Matter?" *Texas Law Review* 65 (1987): 766–798.

62. See, e.g., Richard A. Posner, *The Problems of Jurisprudence* (Cambridge: Harvard Uni-versity Press, 1990); and Philip Bobbitt, *Constitutional Fate* (New York: Oxford University Press, 1982), and *Constitutional Interpretation* (Cambridge: Basil Blackwell, 1991).

63. Richard Posner, "What Has Pragmatism to Offer Law?" in *Pragmatism in Law and Society,* ed. Michael Brint and William Weaver (Boulder, CO: Westview Press, 1991), 35–36.

64. Martin Shapiro, "Recent Developments in Political Jurisprudence," *Western Political Quarterly* 36 (1983): 544, and "The Supreme Court: From Warren to Burger," in *The New American Political System,* ed. Anthony King (Washington, DC: American Enterprise Insti-tute, 1978), 179.

65. Shapiro, "Recent Developments," 543, and "Fathers and Sons," 237, 238.

66. Catherine Wells, "Situated Decisionmaking," and Martha Minow and Elizabeth V. Spelman, "In Context," both in Brint and Weaver, eds. *Pragmatism,* 275 and 266.

67. Bobbitt, *Fate,* 181–249, and *Interpretation,* 6–10, 111–186.

68. Moreover, even on a descriptive level the behaviorist literature provides little basis for exploring the relative proportion of politics and legal interpretation. The dominance of politics is an unexamined first principle rather than a defended analytical result. See also Rogers M. Smith, "The Inherent Deceptiveness of Constitutional Discourse: A Diag-nosis and Prescription," in *Integrity and Conscience: NOMOS XL,* ed. Ian Shapiro and Will Kymlicka (New York: New York University Press, 1998).

69. Martin Shapiro, *Law and Politics in the Supreme Court* (New York: Free Press, 1964), 22. His response is to Griswold, "Foreword," 85.

70. See, e.g., Earl Maltz, *Rethinking Constitutional Law* (Lawrence: University Press of Kansas, 1994), 1–18; H. W. Perry, *Deciding to Decide* (Cambridge: Harvard University Press,

1991); and Ronald Kahn, *The Supreme Court and Constitutional Theory, 1953–1993* (Lawrence: University Press of Kansas, 1994).

71. See, e.g., Bruce Ackerman, *Reconstructing American Law* (Cambridge: Harvard University Press, 1984).

72. Donald Horowitz, *The Courts and Social Policy* (Washington, DC: Brookings Institution, 1977); Gerald Rosenberg, *The Hollow Hope* (Chicago: University of Chicago Press, 1991); and Paul Weiler, "Two Models of Judicial Decision Making," *Canadian Bar Review* 46 (1968): 406.

73. The pragmatic dependence on the success of the critical case is made evident in Posner's critique of Bork's originalism. Posner denies that the pragmatist judge is "lawless," because he is "mindful of the systemic consequences of judicial lawlessness." Thus, the pragmatist must maintain enough interpretation to sustain the belief in the rule of law. How often the judge departs from interpretation in order to "do justice" in a particular case depends on judgments of long-term utility, which in turn presumably depend on judgments as to the stability of the political system and the intensity of the judicial desire to act contrary to the law in any given case. Where Posner may find the utilitarian trade-off worthwhile in striking down economic regulation, others may calculate that the system could tolerate upholding restrictions on free speech. Moreover, Posner assumes interpretive indeterminacy in order to make room for his policy judgments; "The social consequences of alternative interpretations are decisive; to the consistent originalist, they are irrelevant." How one is to delimit the set of "alternative" interpretations is not specified. Presumably, the originalist judge either finds an indeterminate result (with a set of multiple, equally plausible interpretations) or a determinate one. If pragmatism is limited to the former case, then Posner prefers judges to impose their policy-driven construction of constitutional meaning on the political branches. If he includes the latter case, then Posner's judge would actually reject the correct interpretation in order to impose an incorrect interpretation of the law that would lead to judicially preferred results. Discussion of "alternatives" in that context is simply disingenuous. See Posner, "Bork and Beethoven," *Stanford Law Review* 42 (1990): 1380. See also William F. Harris: "The central idea is that the systematic interpretability of the Constitution is essential to its bindingness as fundamental law. The converse is that ad hoc interpretations or the random taking up of convenient interpretive techniques fundamentally undermines the constitutional order. . . . The point is that an unsystematic and ungrounded interpretive strategy denies the only kind of constitutive meaning that could be authoritative in the way that political meaning at this fundamental level must be" (*The Interpretable Constitution* [Baltimore: Johns Hopkins University Press, 1993], 6 [emphasis omitted]).

74. See, e.g., Lynn A. Baker, " 'Just Do It': Pragmatism and Progressive Social Change," in Brint and Weaver, eds., *Pragmatism*, 99.

75. Thomas C. Grey, "What Good Is Legal Pragmatism?" in ibid., 26.

76. There remain certain problems with the formulation of the countermajoritarian dilemma itself, notably the fact that every exercise of judicial review does not contradict the will of any identifiable political majority. See, e.g., Graber, "The Non-Majoritarian Difficulty"; Maltz, *Rethinking*, 46–49; and Friedman, "Countermajoritarian," 343–356.

77. For overviews of the originalist debate, see Daniel A. Farber, "The Originalism Debate: A Guide to the Perplexed," *Ohio State Law Journal* 49 (1989): 1085; Gregory Bassham, *Original Intent and the Constitution* (Lanham, MD: Rowman and Littlefield, 1992); Scott Douglas Gerber, *To Secure These Rights* (New York: New York University Press,

1995), 1–15; and John Arthur, *Words That Bind* (Boulder, CO: Westview Press, 1995), 7–43. Although originalism as an interpretive method can be applied by nonjudicial institutions and originalist methods can be used in statutory interpretation as well, my concern here is limited to judicial interpretation of the Constitution.

78. Bork, *Tempting*, 144.

79. The results of this qualification can be counterintuitive. For example, the same phrase "due process of law" appears in both the Fifth and Fourteenth Amendments, drafted and ratified nearly a century apart, and could have different meanings in each instance.

80. Alexander Hamilton, James Madison, and John Jay, *The Federalist Papers,* ed. Clinton Rossiter (New York: New American Library, 1961), No. 10, 82. The sovereign people in convention are like the king in council: "These filters to the monarch's authority are so much organs of himself that he only acts as monarch in acting through them" (Bertrand de Jouvenel, *Sovereignty* [Chicago: University of Chicago Press, 1963], 207). The Philadelphia Convention was in the same situation as the Continental Congress, of which John Rutledge observed that "we have no coercive or legislative Authority." It was the ratification conventions that possessed such sovereign legislative authority and thus gave legal force to the Constitution (quoted in Wood, *Creation,* 317).

81. At some risk of confusion, I use the phrase "public understandings," despite the fact that some scholars have used it to expand the authoritative founders beyond the scope of the convention delegates. Cf. Bork, *Tempting,* 144; Henry Monaghan, "Stare Decisis and Constitutional Adjudication," *Columbia University Law Review* 88 (1988): 725. For discussion, see Bassham, *Original Intent,* 56–65.

82. Thayer, "Origin and Scope," 144, 151. Rather than a "clear mistake" rule, perhaps an originalist Court should adopt something more closely approaching a "preponderance of the evidence" rule to strike down laws on originalist grounds. The contingent relationship between originalism and judicial restraint has been increasingly noted by recent commentators, e.g., Michael J. Perry, *The Constitution in the Courts* (New York: Oxford University Press, 1994), 54–55, 81–82, and Maltz, *Rethinking,* 18–20.

83. Lino Graglia, "How the Constitution Disappeared," *Commentary* 81 (1986): 22.

84. The problem is raised in somewhat different forms in Brest, "Fundamental Rights," 1091–1092, and in Dworkin, *Matter of Principle,* 48–50, and *Taking Rights,* 134–136.

85. Griswold v. Connecticut, 381 U.S. 479, 484 (1965).

86. It should be noted that this objection does not apply against Justice Goldberg's concurrence, which relied on the Ninth Amendment's reservation of unenumerated rights rather than on the penumbras of enumerated rights. See Griswold v. Connecticut, 381 U.S. 479, 486 (1965).

87. Bork, *Tempting,* 98–100, 148–150; Robert Bork, "Address at the University of San Diego Law School," in *The Great Debate* (Washington, DC: Federalist Society, 1986), 47–49; Gary McDowell, *Curbing the Courts* (Baton Rouge: Louisiana State University Press, 1988), 109–113; and Raoul Berger, *Government by Judiciary* (Cambridge: Harvard University Press, 1977), 166–192.

88. Although few such writers regard themselves as articulating a version of originalism, their historical orientation has occasionally led to their being grouped with originalists for some purposes. See, e.g., Maltz, *Rethinking,* 50–73.

89. See, e.g., Bickel, *Least Dangerous,* 25–43, 82; Dworkin, *Taking Rights,* 138–147, 240–258, and *Law's Empire,* 176–275; Harry H. Wellington, *Interpreting the Constitution* (New Haven: Yale University Press, 1990), 77–95; and Fiss, "Foreword," 1–29.

90. Maltz, *Rethinking*, 74–107; Graglia, "Constitution," 26, and "Do Judges Have a Policy-Making Role in the American System of Government?" *Harvard Journal of Law and Public Policy* 17 (1994): 125–126; Bork, "San Diego," 45; Robert Bork, *Tradition and Morality in Constitutional Law* (Washington, DC: American Enterprise Institute, 1984), 7; Frank Easterbrook, "The Influence of Judicial Review on Constitutional Theory," in *A Workable Government?* ed. Marshall Burke (New York: Norton, 1987), 182, 185–186; and Lillian R. BeVier, "Judicial Restraint: An Argument from Institutional Design," *Harvard Journal of Law and Public Policy* 17 (1994): 7.

91. Michael Perry has explicitly granted this type of criticism and modified his opinion to accommodate it, although it is an open question as to how successfully his more recent theories avoid these types of problems; see *The Constitution, the Courts, and Human Rights* (New Haven: Yale University Press, 1982), 91–145.

92. Ely, *Democracy*, 56–70.

93. Sunstein, *Partial*, 159.

94. Bork, "San Diego," 45.

95. Bork, *Tradition*, 10–11.

96. McDowell, *Curbing*, 27–28; Berger, *Government*, 363–366. A subsidiary benefit of placing greater constraints on judges is the reduction of uncertainty as to legal outcomes and the legal environment within which individual plans are made; see Thomas Sowell, *Knowledge and Decisions* (New York: Basic Books, 1980), 294–296, and Richard S. Kay, "Adherence to the Original Intentions in Constitutional Adjudication: Three Objections and Responses," *Northwestern University Law Review* 82 (1988): 289–292.

97. In a different context, see also, H. L. A. Hart, "American Jurisprudence Through English Eyes: The Nightmare and the Noble Dream," *Essays in Jurisprudence and Philosophy* (New York: Oxford University Press, 1983), 130–132.

98. Edwin Meese, "Address before the D.C. Chapter of the Federalist Society Lawyers Division," in *Great Debate*, 39.

99. Easterbrook, "Influence," 185–186; Bork, "San Diego," 52; Graglia, "Constitution," 19, "Policy-Making," 119–120, 123–127, and " 'Interpreting' the Constitution: Posner on Bork," *Stanford Law Review* 44 (1992): 1020; Raoul Berger, "New Theories of 'Interpretation': The Activist Flight from the Constitution," *Ohio State Law Journal* 47 (1986): 8–12.

100. Kent Greenawalt, *Law and Objectivity* (New York: Oxford University Press, 1992), 38–39.

101. H. L. A. Hart, "Positivism and the Separation of Law and Morals," in *Essays*, 71, and *The Concept of Law* (New York: Oxford University Press, 1961), 124. "The purely cognitive interpretation by jurisprudence is therefore unable to fill alleged gaps in the law. The filling of a so-called gap in the law is a law-creating function that can only be performed by a law-applying organ; and the function of creating law is not performed by jurisprudence interpreting law. Jurisprudential interpretation can do no more than exhibit all possible meanings of a legal norm." Urging a single "correct" interpretation "does not render a function of legal science, but of legal politics" (Hans Kelsen, *Pure Theory of Law* [Berkeley: University of California Press, 1970], 355, 356 [footnote omitted]). See also Francis Lieber, *Legal and Political Hermeneutics* (Boston: Charles C. Little and James Brown, 1839), 25–35.

102. Dworkin, *Takings Rights*, 1–130, and *Law's Empire*, 176–275.

103. Coleman, "Legal Duty," 388, and Soper, "Legal Theory," 488–491, 496–498.

104. Unfortunately, Dworkin has absorbed many of the most promising labels for this approach, rendering any descriptive label seeking to identify a third approach ambiguous.

105. C. L. Ten, "The Soundest Theory of Law," *Mind* 88 (1979): 532, and see also 529–530.

106. Such a critical morality could be either external or internal. A judge could reject parts of a legal tradition because they do not comport with what the best law would be, or he could reject parts because they do not comport with the "best traditions" of the legal community. In either case, the determination is made on the basis of normative judgments as to the value of the law rather than on interpretive judgments as to the consistency, weight, or intended consequence of the law.

107. Rolf E. Sartorius, *Individual Conduct and Social Norms* (Encino, CA: Dickenson University Press, 1975), 196. Sartorius concludes that "the degree of systematic, authoritative control which exists in even the hardest of hard cases is thus on my view so great that it is incorrect to speak of judicial creativity as *at any point* becoming discretionary," thus replicating Dworkin's results without invoking normative judicial judgments (197 [emphasis in original]).

108. Soper, "Legal Theory," 485.

109. Ibid., 488 (footnote omitted).

110. See also Andrew Altman, *Critical Legal Studies* (Princeton: Princeton University Press, 1990), 31-56, and Coleman, "Positivism." Hart later qualified his initial statements to recognize the existence of limiting devices but maintained that judges must ultimately legislate (*Essays*, 6–7).

111. In part, originalism can recognize this space by limiting itself to constitutional theory rather than legal theory more generally. In the context of judicial review, the final resolution of an individual dispute through judicial legislation takes on a more ominous air than in the context of normal litigation. Rather than leap into the breach to create a judicial result to dispose of a case, the judiciary should recognize the contingent nature of constitutional cases and the possibility of principled deliberation elsewhere.

112. Robert Bork, "Neutral Principles and Some First Amendment Problems," *Indiana Law Journal* 47 (1971): 1–7, *Tempting*, 146, 171, 177–178, and *Tradition*, 46; Graglia, "Constitution," 24, "Policy-Making," 129, and "'Interpreting,'" 1026–1027; Henry Monaghan, "Our Perfect Constitution," *New York University Law Review* 56 (1981): 371–372; and William H. Rehnquist, "The Notion of a Living Constitution," *Texas Law Review* 54 (1976): 702–706. Although favoring judicial activism, Maltz accepts Bork's grounding of originalism in neutral principles (*Rethinking*, 49, 74).

113. Graglia, for example, directly favors judicial restraint, arguing that democracy under originalism is enhanced because the Court would rarely, if ever, strike down laws. He supports such a conclusion by endorsing Marshall's broad reading of the commerce and necessary and proper clauses, which would allow Congress wide latitude in making national public policy. Graglia gives no indication as to how such interpretations are grounded in originalist methodology rather than in his clear normative desire for judicial restraint. In any case, he is clear in favoring current majoritarianism over the neutral application of a fundamental law (see "'Interpreting,'" 1026–1028).

114. These issues are considered further in chapter 6.

115. Bork, "San Diego," 45, and *Tempting*, 256–257; Meese, "Address," 36–39; Rehnquist, "Notion," 703–706.

116. Bork, "Neutral Principles," 6, and *Tempting*, 265.

117. Hamilton et al., *Federalist Papers*, No. 1, 33. See also Richards, *Toleration*, 3–64, and Kahn, *Legitimacy*, 9–31.

118. Berger, *Government by Judiciary*, 351–362, and *Congress*, 198–284; Bork, *Tempting*,

145–149, 173–175; Easterbrook, "Influence," 175–179; Graglia, "Constitution," 20; McDowell, *Curbing,* 29; Rehnquist, "Notion," 696; and Monaghan, "Perfect," 366.

3. THE AUTHORITY OF ORIGINALISM

1. See, e.g., Lino Graglia, "How the Constitution Disappeared," *Commentary* 81 (1986): 20; Gary McDowell, *Curbing the Court* (Baton Rouge: Louisiana State University Press, 1988), 27–28; and Robert Bork, *The Tempting of America* (New York: Free Press, 1990), 146–147.

2. Larry Simon, "The Authority of the Framers of the Constitution: Can Originalist Interpretation Be Justified?" *California Law Review* 73 (1984): 1487.

3. Ibid.; Michael Perry, "The Authority of the Text, Tradition, and Reason," *Southern California Law Review* 58 (1985): 586; Larry Simon, "The Authority of the Constitution and Its Meaning," *Southern California Law Review* 58 (1985): 612; Cass Sunstein, *The Partial Constitution* (Cambridge: Harvard University Press, 1993), 95–99; David Lyons, "Constitutional Interpretation and Original Meaning," *Moral Aspects of Legal Theory* (New York: Cambridge University Press, 1993), 141–154; Sotirios Barber, *The Constitution of Judicial Review* (Baltimore: Johns Hopkins University Press, 1993), 118–119.

4. See, e.g., Hayden White, *The Content of the Form* (Baltimore: Johns Hopkins University Press, 1987), and Fernand Braudel, *On History* (Chicago: University of Chicago Press, 1980).

5. Consider Stanley Fish's example of arranging a list of names in such a way as to invoke a poetic interpretation of what would otherwise have been appropriately read as a simple list (*Is There a Text in This Class?* [Cambridge: Harvard University Press, 1980], 322–337), or Jonathan Culler's journalism-cum-poetry, *Structuralist Poetics* (Ithaca, NY: Cornell University Press, 1975), 161.

6. Constitutional interpretation is a social practice. Like all social practices, it occurs within a context of other practices that makes it meaningful. Though some variation in a given practice is tolerable, too much variation renders it unrecognizable, in effect creating a new practice. Thus, we are familiar with the rules of football and are comfortable recognizing several variations of the game as examples of the game of football, despite their differences. The nature of the activity makes some modes of playing inappropriate. That is, one may still play with the football, but one may not appropriately call what one is doing playing football. Some uses of the ball are in fact "intrinsic" and "definitional"; by shaping a round leather ball into an oblong one, we call forth some practices and rule out others. This analysis is shaped by Ludwig Wittgenstein, *Philosophical Investigations* (New York: Macmillan, 1958), §66, 564. For a similar metaphor, see Michael Perry, "Why Constitutional Theory Matters to Constitutional Practice (and Vice Versa)," in *Legal Hermeneutics,* ed. Gregory Leyh (Berkeley: University of California Press, 1992), 244. Though, to extend the metaphor, in this chapter I indicate that the Constitution is more like a game-specific football than Perry's roundball, appropriate for many games. Oblong balls, like our written Constitution, set greater constraints on what can be done with them.

7. Sunstein, *Partial,* 93. Similarly, "One presupposes, as jurist, that one ought to conduct oneself as the historically first constitution prescribes. That is the basic norm" (Hans Kelsen, "The Function of a Constitution," in *Essays on Kelsen,* ed. Richard Tur and William Twining [New York: Oxford University Press, 1986], 114). Although constitutional theorists

may question the continuing value of a written constitution, the judiciary must assume the authority of the Constitution and justify its own actions on that assumption.

8. On the concept of "interpretive intention," and its use to criticize originalism on "originalist" grounds, see Paul Brest, "The Misconceived Quest for the Original Understanding," *Boston University Law Review* 60 (1980): 204, 215–216; H. Jefferson Powell, "The Original Understanding of Original Intent," *Harvard Law Review* 98 (1985): 885; and Paul Finkelman, "The Constitution and the Intentions of the Framers: The Limits of Historical Analysis," *University of Pittsburgh Law Review* 50 (1989): 349. Cf. Charles Lofgren, "The Original Understanding of Original Intent?" *Constitutional Commentary* 5 (1988): 77; Raoul Berger, "The Founders' Views—According to Jefferson Powell," *Texas Law Review* 67 (1989): 1033, and " 'Original Intention' in Historical Perspective," *George Washington Law Review* 54 (1986): 296; Michael Perry, *The Constitution in the Courts* (New York: Oxford University Press, 1994), 50.

9. This is in contrast to interpreting the text of the Constitution itself, when the words of the founders carry weight because of who they are (the authors), not because their ideas were necessarily good. It should also be noted that the arguments for adopting a written constitution may not always be good ones but that once such a constitution is adopted, the arguments explain what to do with it.

10. "It is not a positive norm, posited by a real act of will, but a norm presupposed in juristic thinking" (Kelsen, "The Function of a Constitution," 115). See also Jules L. Coleman, "Legal Duty and Moral Argument," *Social Theory and Practice* 5 (1980): 388; E. Philip Soper, "Legal Theory and the Obligation of a Judge: The Hart/Dworkin Dispute," *Michigan Law Review* 75 (1977): 488–491, 496–498; and Richard S. Kay, "Preconstitutional Rules," *Ohio State Law Journal* 42 (1981): 189–190. That the judicial task would be different in a legal regime based on coin-tossing, for example, does not change the fact that inherent judicial duties arise from the legal system itself rather than from specific legal directives within that system.

11. Benjamin F. Wright Jr., "The Early History of Written Constitutions in America," in *Essays in History and Political Theory in Honor of Charles Howard McIlwain*, ed. Carl Wittke (Cambridge: Harvard University Press, 1936), 344. See also Robert N. Clinton, "Original Understanding, Legal Realism, and the Interpretation of 'This Constitution,' " *Iowa Law Review* 72 (1987): 1186–1197.

12. Quoted in James Wilson, "Lectures on Law," *The Works of James Wilson*, ed. Robert Green McCloskey, 2 vols. (Cambridge: Harvard University Press, 1967), 1:310. See also Gordon Wood, *The Creation of the American Republic, 1776–1787* (New York: Norton, 1969), 260–262; Charles McIlwain, *Constitutionalism: Ancient and Modern* (Ithaca, NY: Cornell University Press, 1947), 3. John Phillip Reid has noted that there was a tension in British constitutional thought between the old doctrine of limiting custom and the new of parliamentary sovereignty. It was partially this tension that drove the split between the British and the Americans. See, generally, Reid, *Constitutional History of the American Revolution*, 4 vols. (Madison: University of Wisconsin Press, 1987–1993), vol. 3. The split was exacerbated by the overlap of the division between new and old constitutions with one between British and imperial constitutions, in which the colonies continued to assert old principles of limited parliamentary authority. See Jack P. Greene, *Peripheries and Center* (Athens: University of Georgia Press, 1986).

13. By the 1760s, British constitutionalism had been sufficiently challenged that a member of Parliament could write, "I believe principles have less to do than we suppose. The

Critics were made after the poems. The Rules of architecture after ye houses, Grammar after language and governments go *per hookum & crookum* & then we demonstrate it *per hookum.* There is not that argument or practice so bad that you may not have precedents for it" (quoted in Greene, *Peripheries,* 65).

14. This was in particular the line taken by James Otis, perhaps the premier defender of the unwritten law of the British constitution and nature during the revolutionary period. See James Otis, "A Vindication of the British Colonies," and "The Rights of the British Colonies Asserted and Proved," in *Pamphlets of the American Revolution,* ed. Bernard Bailyn (Cambridge: Harvard University Press, 1965), 1:554–579, 419–482. For an analysis of Otis, see Wood, *Creation,* 262–265, and Bernard Bailyn, *The Ideological Origins of the American Revolution* (Cambridge: Harvard University Press, 1967), 176–181. Otis's defense of unwritten constitutions was extreme even for its time, and even those who shared certain of his assumptions about natural law sought to embody them in a fixed text after the Revolution. See Reid, *Constitutional History,* 3:5, and Gary Jacobsohn, *The Supreme Court and the Decline of Constitutional Aspiration* (Totowa, NJ: Rowman and Littlefield, 1986).

15. J. G. A. Pocock, *The Ancient Constitution and the Feudal Law* (New York: Cambridge University Press, 1987), 36.

16. Reid, *Constitutional History,* 2:147–149.

17. The postrevolutionary shift in American attitudes ran across all aspects of the common law. See Morton Horwitz, *The Transformation of American Law, 1780–1860* (Cambridge: Harvard University Press, 1977), 1–30. This concern expanded and intensified over the next several decades. See Richard Ellis, *The Jeffersonian Crisis* (New York: Norton, 1974).

18. Samuel Adams, *The Writings of Samuel Adams,* ed. Harry Cushing, 4 vols. (New York: G. P. Putnam's Sons, 1904–1908), 3:262; see also "In all Free States the Constitution is fixed," ibid., 1:184. Similarly Edmund Randolph wrote that a written constitution would be a "standing ark" and a "perpetual standard" that would remain regardless of "revolutions of time, of human opinion, and of government" (*History of Virginia,* ed. Arthur Shaffer [Charlottesville: University Press of Virginia, 1970], 253, 255). Both men recognized that the fixed principles could only be effective given an appropriate interpretive method (Adams, *Writings,* 3:262; Randolph, *Virginia,* 253).

19. Benjamin Franklin, *The Papers of Benjamin Franklin,* ed. William Willcox, 33 vols. to date (New Haven: Yale University Press, 1959–), 21:110–111. Similarly, the earl of Abingdon observed at the time of the Revolution, "There is nothing so much talked of, and yet nothing so little understood, as the *English Constitution.* Every man quotes it, and upon every occasion too: but few know where to find it" (quoted in Reid, *Constitutional History,* 2:4).

20. One problem for the Americans was that the external foundations of the charters were weak in that the British did not accept them as binding. The certainty of the text was subsumed in the uncertainty of parliamentary practice. As a result, in the decade leading up to the Revolution, American writers complained that their constitutions were subject "to a *perpetual mutability*" (quoted in Greene, *Peripheries,* 54 [emphasis in original]). A colonial governor of Massachusetts wrote, "I consider Government not to be a Right but a trust, and that the Royal Grants of Jurisdiction in America either to private persons or Corporations are no more than temporary provisions untill the Parliament that is the whole Legislature, shall settle the Government. . . . Surely this is the law now, whatever it was before the [Glorious] Revolution" of 1688. The final qualification emphasizes the changing constitutional conception in Britain toward parliamentary sovereignty, which undermined the traditional constitutionalism upon which the Americans relied (quoted

in Edmund S. Morgan and Helen M. Morgan, *The Stamp Act Crisis* [Chapel Hill: University of North Carolina Press, 1953], 12).

21. Wright, "Early History," 346. Long after the Revolution, Rhode Island continued to rely on its charter in this fashion, though with some difficulty. See James Varnum, "The Case of Trevett against Weeden" (Providence, RI: John Carter, 1787), Early American Imprint Series, 1st Series, Charles Evans' American Bibliography no. 20825 (New York: Readex Microprint, 1985); Sylvia Snowiss, *Judicial Review and the Law of the Constitution* (New Haven: Yale University Press, 1990), 20–22, 29–30; and William Crosskey, *Politics and the Constitution in the History of the United States*, 3 vols. (Chicago: University of Chicago Press, 1953–1980), 2:965–968. As written governing devices for the colonies, royal charters were supplemented by politically autonomous covenants. See Donald S. Lutz, *The Origins of American Constitutionalism* (Baton Rouge: Louisiana State University Press, 1988), 23–49, and Andrew C. McLaughlin, *The Foundations of American Constitutionalism* (New York: New York University Press, 1932), 3–62.

22. Bailyn, *Origins*, 189–192; Reid, *Constitutional History*, 2:137, 142; Wood, *Creation*, 269.

23. Lutz, *Origins*, 63 (emphasis in original). The break was more in form than in substance, however. See, e.g., James R. Stoner Jr., "The Idiom of Common Law in the Formation of Judicial Power," in *The Supreme Court and American Constitutionalism*, ed. Bradford P. Wilson and Ken Masugi (Lanham, MD: Rowman and Littlefield, 1998), 49–61.

24. See, e.g., Eakin v. Raub, 12 Serg. & Rawle 354 (Pa. 1825).

25. VanHorne's Lessee v. Dorrance, 2 U.S. (2 Dall.) 307, 308 (1795).

26. Joseph Story, *Commentaries on the Constitution of the United States* (Durham: Carolina Academic Press, 1987), § 193. Alexander Hamilton also feared that "the influence of some strong interest, or passion, or prejudice" could obscure the unwritten law of moral and political reasoning (Alexander Hamilton, James Madison, and John Jay, *The Federalist Papers*, ed. Clinton Rossiter [New York: Mentor, 1961], No. 31, 194). See also John Locke, "Second Treatise," in *Two Treatises of Government*, ed. Peter Laslett (New York: Cambridge University Press, 1988), § 124. A similar understanding can be seen as motivating the writing of the Canadian Constitution. See, e.g., Roy Romanow, John Whyte, and Howard Leeson, *Canada . . . Notwithstanding* (New York: Caswell/Methuen, 1984); Barry Strayer, *The Canadian Constitution and the Courts* (Toronto: Butterworths, 1983); and Ian Greene, *The Charter of Rights* (Toronto: James Lorimer and Company, 1989).

27. British parliamentary supremacy suggested a dual conflict with American constitutionalism, both in form and in theoretical substance. Not only was the common law evolutionary by design, but parliamentarianism was active power in theoretical aim, undercutting the goal of limited government. In contrast, the Americans were "defending a static, customary, prescriptive constitutionalism against a dynamic constitutionalism of will, power, and command" (Reid, *Constitutional History*, 4:5). Ultimately, form and substance were linked.

28. See Melvin Aron Eisenberg, *The Nature of the Common Law* (Cambridge: Harvard University Press, 1988).

29. Thomas Cooley, *A Treatise on the Constitutional Limitations* (Boston: Little, Brown, and Company, 1868), 55, 54 (emphasis in original). See also John Randolph Tucker, *The Constitution of the United States*, 2 vols. (Chicago: Callaghan and Company, 1899), 1:180, 350–351; Thomas Jefferson, *Memoir, Correspondence, and Miscellanies, from the Papers of Thomas Jefferson*, ed. Thomas Jefferson Randolph, 4 vols. (Boston: Gray and Bowen, 1830), 4:3; Raoul Berger, *Government by Judiciary* (Cambridge: Harvard University Press, 1977), 252, 291, 366.

30. At the level of interpretation, the example of the meandering history of judicial free-speech doctrines indicates the limits of constitutional isolation from contemporary politics; cf. Schenck v. United States, 249 U.S. 47 (1919); Dennis v. United States, 341 U.S. 494 (1951); and Brandenburg v. Ohio, 395 U.S. 444 (1969). Even at the level of the constitutional text, the rigorous amendment process has not prevented the inclusion of momentarily popular, but later regretted, amendments, e.g., U.S. Constitution, Amends. 18, 21, and 22.

31. The contention of this argument is that a fixed text is a necessary, not a sufficient, condition for judicial review. The argument that the adoption of a written constitution sufficiently departed from the British practice to justify judicial veto over legislation was not even uniformly accepted in the United States. See Eakin v. Raub, 12 Serg. & Rawle 354 (Pa. 1825). Moreover, written constitutions have been adopted elsewhere without providing for or allowing judicial review. See Graglia, "Constitution," 20, and Wood, *Creation,* 292. The unwritten text of the common law can affect the judicial approach to legislation, as statutory law can draw upon common law terms and conventions in expressing the legislature's meaning and statutes can be written to be placed in the context of the existing common law such that the latter is intended to control the former, but in neither instance does the common law provide an independent authority for judicial review of legislation.

32. Cf. Ronald Dworkin, *Taking Rights Seriously* (Cambridge: Harvard University Press, 1978), 14–130, and Perry, *Constitution in the Courts.*

33. Dr. Bonham's Case, 8 Co. 114 (C.P. 1610). Cf. William Blackstone, *Commentaries on the Laws of England,* 4 vols. (Chicago: University of Chicago Press, 1979), 1:91; Snowiss, *Judicial Review,* 13–16; F. W. Maitland, *The Constitutional History of England* (New York: Cambridge University Press, 1941), 301.

34. Wood, *Creation,* 292–293.

35. Ibid., 293; Tucker, *Constitution* 1:350–351; Bork, *Tempting,* 147; James Iredell, *Life and Correspondence of James Iredell,* ed. Griffith J. McRee, 2 vols. (New York: D. Appleton and Company, 1857–1858), 2:172–173; William Rawle, *A View of the Constitution of the United States of America* (Philadelphia: H. C. Carey and I. Lea, 1825), 266; and Wilson, *Works,* 1:329. A similar thinking has led to the expansion of the Canadian constitution in written form. See Romanow, Whyte, and Leeson, *Canada;* Strayer, *Canadian;* Greene, *Charter;* Patrick Monahan, *Politics and the Constitution* (Toronto: Carswell, 1987); and Jennifer Smith, "The Origins of Judicial Review in Canada," *Canadian Journal of Political Science* 16 (1983): 115. The 1982 constitution provides for both judicial review and a mechanism for legislatively overriding the judicial interpretation of constitutional provisions, providing the limitations of a written constitution in the context of legislative supremacy (Constitution Act, 1982, Part 1, § 33; Part 7, § 52). Similarly, the early French republics explicitly undercut the implications of adopting a written constitution by specifically prohibiting judicial review in order to secure legislative supremacy and established a constitutional court only in the postwar period in order to check the legislature. See Alec Stone, *The Birth of Judicial Politics in France* (New York: Oxford University Press, 1992), and John Bell, *French Constitutional Law* (New York: Oxford University Press, 1992).

36. Iredell, *Life,* 174, 173.

37. Hamilton et al., *Federalist Papers,* No. 78, 465. The anti-Federalist charged that the grant of equity jurisdiction would allow the Court to appeal to the "reasoning spirit of [the Constitution], without being confined to the words or letter" (Herbert Storing, ed., *The Anti-Federalist* [Chicago: University of Chicago Press, 1985], 164). Hamilton carefully hedged his position in response, noting that, to preserve the written constitution, the courts

were authorized "to declare all acts contrary to the manifest tenor of the Constitution void," but interpreting the equity clause narrowly. Given the purpose and context of his argument, Hamilton's choice of adjectives to modify the Constitution's "tenor" cannot be ignored (No. 78, 466; No. 80, 480; No. 81, 482). In any case, Hamilton represented to opponents that the Court would be constricted to judgments that could spark no serious disagreement. Thus, for example, he doubted a free-press guarantee could be drafted with enough specificity to be judicially enforceable (No. 84, 514). Sotirios Barber's contention (*Constitution,* 50–51) that Hamilton (No. 81, 482) immediately undercuts this restriction by drawing out the power of judicial review from "the general theory of a limited Constitution" ignores the different standards at work in applying the Constitution as part of judicial interpretation and justifying the role and methodology of such interpretation, though such a distinction is a centerpiece of Barber's own attack on originalism.

38. Marbury v. Madison, 5 U. S. (1 Cranch) 177 (1803); see also Spencer Roane in Kamper v. Hawkins, 1 Va. Cases 38 (1793). The metaphor serves to bolster judicial authority by denying the rationality of alternative readings of the terms at issue, thus allowing the Court to posit controversial interpretations without admitting their controversial nature. On the rhetoric of judicial opinions, see James Boyd White, "Judicial Criticism," in *Interpreting Law and Literature,* ed. Sanford Levinson and Steven Mailloux (Evanston, IL: Northwestern University Press, 1988), 393–410.

39. In the three pages of Marshall's opinion in which he lays out his core argument for judicial review, he refers to the specifically written nature of the U.S. Constitution no less than eight times, including describing the reduction of constitutions to writing as "the greatest improvement on political institutions" (Marbury v. Madison, 5 U.S. [1 Cranch] 177–179 [1803]).

40. This is not to contend that premises that do not gain a consensus are therefore a product of pure will rather than reason but that several premises may be rationally justifiable and thus the choice of a single starting point would require an act of will. British judges could rationally defend several different axioms for their decisions, but it could appear willful to select one over the others. For somewhat divergent discussions of will and reason in such contexts, see Owen Fiss, "The Varieties of Positivism," *Yale Law Journal* 90 (1981): 1007, and Paul W. Kahn, *Legitimacy and History* (New Haven: Yale University Press, 1992). Cf. Bork, *Tempting,* 177, and his *Tradition and Morality in Constitutional Law* (Washington, DC: American Enterprise Institute, 1984).

41. Frank Easterbrook, "The Influence of Judicial Review on Constitutional Theory," in *A Workable Government?* ed. Marshall Burke (New York: Norton, 1987), 176–177. The argument maps onto Sanford Levinson's "protestant" view of the Constitution, though it is part of my argument that the adoption of a written constitution requires such a perspective. See Sanford Levinson, " 'The Constitution' in American Civil Religion," in *The Supreme Court Review, 1979,* ed. Philip Kurland and Gerhard Casper (Chicago: University of Chicago Press, 1980), 123.

42. Kamper v. Hawkins, 1 Va. Cases 38, 78 (1793) (emphasis in original).

43. Ibid. See also Marbury v. Madison, 5 U.S. (1 Cranch) 176–177 (1803), and VanHorne's Lessee v. Dorrance, 2 U.S. (2 Dall.) 308 (1795). The explicitness of the judiciary's starting point is linked to the need for the public justification that marks the liberal rule of law, in contrast to vertical commands. The major premise of the Court's syllogism is both public and publicly accountable. See Stephen Macedo, *Liberal Virtues* (New York: Oxford University Press, 1991), 40–50.

44. U.S. Constitution, art. 6. It may be the case that the modern public would accept (and arguably has accepted) the legitimacy of a judiciary straying over the contemporary moral landscape regardless of textual foundations. See, e.g., Alan Hyde, "The Concept of Legitimation in the Sociology of Law," *Wisconsin Law Review* 63 (1983): 379, and Jan G. Deutsch, "Neutrality, Legitimacy, and the Supreme Court: Some Intersections Between Law and Political Science," *Stanford Law Review* 20 (1968): 169. I am concerned here, however, with interpretive authority, given the logic of a political decision to adopt a written text, not the sociological legitimacy of what governing styles the public might empirically accept. After all, mere popular acceptance of questionable government actions is hardly the standard of constitutionality we would wish to accept. On this distinction, see also Ken Kress, "Legal Indeterminacy and Legitimacy," in Leyh, ed., *Legal Hermeneutics*, 203.

45. The Constitution may be more than a piece of legislation, but it is also legislation. Stephen Griffin has suggested that the Constitution is not strictly analogous to any other type of legal text. Although this is true, the Constitution as law is legislation, even if it also transcends the legislative analogy. Cf. Stephen Griffin, *American Constitutionalism* (Princeton: Princeton University Press, 1996), 13–14, 145–148.

46. Of course, mere tradition may be accepted and reflected in practice, but it cannot be "ratified" without specific embodiment in a written document. Embodying inherited custom renders it explicit and subject to conscious consideration and endorsement.

47. The common law finesses the problem of an unwritten law by distinguishing between the sources of law and the law itself as contained in official legal documents, such as judicial opinions, and more significantly by denying the existence of law*making*, emphasizing that the judicially articulated common law is the faithful representation of existing social custom (Eisenberg, *Common Law*, 10–11, 33). See also John C. Gray, *The Nature and Sources of the Law* (New York: Columbia University Press, 1909).

48. Bailyn, *Origins*, 182–183. Note that directed and deliberate consideration of a specific text is at the core of the logic of a written constitution. Without a specific text to consider, the people cannot express their will in a clear and limited manner and cannot deliberate on a specific proposal. Compare the rather vague expressions of popular will permitted by Bruce Ackerman's higher lawmaking (*We the People* (Cambridge: Harvard University Press, 1991).

49. Thomas Aquinas, *The Political Ideas of St. Thomas Aquinas*, ed. Dino Bigongiari (New York: Hafner Press, 1953), 10.

50. Thomas Paine, *The Rights of Man* (New York: Viking Penguin, 1984), 186.

51. "What is a Constitution? It is an act of extraordinary legislation." See Eakin v. Raub, 12 Serg. & Rawle 330, 347 (Pa. 1825); see also Kamper v. Hawkins, 1 Va. Cases 20, 36 (1793); VanHorne's Lessee v. Dorrance, 2 U.S. (2 Dall.) 303, 305 (1795); Whittington v. Polk, 1 Harris & Johnson 242 (Md. 1802); Wood, *Creation*, 281; Tucker, *Constitution*, 1:351; and Berger, *Government by Judiciary*, 252.

52. Aquinas, *Ideas*, 8. "The enactment of a law, like the giving of an order, *is* a deliberate datable act" (H. L. A. Hart, *The Concept of Law* [New York: Oxford University Press, 1961], 44 [emphasis in original]). Customary social rules may well be followed outside of governmental law, but the involvement of the coercive power of the state requires authoritative/authored law. Cf. Friedrich A. Hayek, *Law, Legislation and Liberty*, 3 vols. (Chicago: University of Chicago Press, 1973–1979), 1:72–93.

53. This is not to assert that the law of the sovereign people is not modeled after the law of a higher sovereign still, only that the written text embodies any such law to the extent

that it is legally relevant (i.e., judicially enforceable). Part of the point of a written constitution was to affirm and declare natural law principles so as to be clear, and one of the audiences to which such clarity was directed is the judiciary. See Bailyn, *Origins,* 187; Jacobsohn, *Supreme Court,* 57–94. This later constitutionalism included a marked shift in the phrasing of textual provisions from a hortatory "should" to an obligatory "will," the latter providing further ground for judicial enforcement of such legal, as opposed to moral or political, limits. See Donald S. Lutz, "The United States Constitution as an Incomplete Text," *Annals of the American Association of Political and Social Science* 496 (1988): 23.

54. Samuel Freeman has objected to this form of argument, noting that a fundamental law is not like ordinary legislation and thus it is a contingent fact that the judiciary serves as the final interpreter of the Constitution. A separate constitutional court could equally perform the task, as is the case in Germany, which indicates that the justification for judicial review, and by implication the appropriate interpretive method, cannot be derived from separation of powers, rule of law, or judicial function arguments. See his "Constitutional Democracy and the Legitimacy of Judicial Review," *Law and Philosophy* 9 (1990–1991): 358–359. The argument has several difficulties. First, the exercise of constitutional review by a distinct institution requires a positive creation of such a body and the delegation of such a power; otherwise, the power falls to the judiciary by implication as the natural organ for that function. Thus, Germany had to be explicit in creating a constitutional court, and France had to be explicit in barring judicial review; both acted to block the natural effects of the adoption of a written constitution. Second, regardless of the body exercising the function, the interpretation of the U.S. Constitution as law is a judicial function. The federal Constitution makes provision for only one specifically interpretive institution, and thus the task falls on it. Designating a special constitutional court would only be dividing the judicial jurisdiction, similar to the division of civil and criminal courts, not denying the judicial aspect of that function. Third, by ignoring constructions, Freeman overlooks the relation between statute and constitution. He makes much of the fact that the Constitution is composed of "exceptional rules that constitute the three powers of government and assign them their ordinary powers," and thus the judiciary is setting itself above the other powers by claiming the right to interpret such constitutive rules. But constitutive rules may be contained in statutes and applied by the courts, such as those creating the lower federal courts or the various executive departments and independent regulatory agencies, which suggests that the distinction between ordinary law and fundamental law is not so sharp. The Constitution operating as law is simply legal in a rather conventional sense, even if occupying a superior place in the legal hierarchy. Of course, this is qualified by the additional aspects of the Constitution that are not legal but purely political. John Marshall was not wrong in seeing the Constitution as law but only in implying that the Constitution was nothing but law.

55. Philip Kurland, *Watergate and the Constitution* (Chicago: University of Chicago Press, 1978), 7.

56. Iredell, *Life,* 146; VanHorne's Lessee v. Dorrance, 2 U.S. (2 Dall.) 303, 308 (1795); Whittington v. Polk, 1 Harris & Johnson 242, 244 (Md. 1802); Kamper v. Hawkins, 1 Va. Cases 20, 36, 49, 59, 78 (1793).

57. "The executive and judicial powers are drawn from the same source, and are now animated by the same principles, and are now directed to the same ends, with the legislative authority: they who execute, and they who administer the laws, are so much the servants, . . . of the people, as those who make them" (Wilson, *Works,* 1:293); see also Edward

Corwin, *The "Higher Law" Background of the Constitution* (Ithaca, NY: Cornell University Press, 1955), 89.

58. "Certainly all those who framed written constitutions contemplate them as forming the fundamental and paramount law of the nation, and, consequently, . . . an act of the legislature, repugnant to the constitution, is void. This theory is essentially attached to a written constitution" (Marbury v. Madison, 5 U.S. [1 Cranch] 177 [1803]); see also Commonwealth v. Caton et al., 4 Call. 8 (Va. 1782); Iredell, *Life* 2:172–173, 148; and Wood, *Creation,* 266.

59. It should be emphasized that the judiciary is *applying* the *principles* of the text to new circumstances. Such an application is not necessarily a mechanical operation of reading off the result from the "plain meaning" of the text or the practices of the framers. In realizing the text in its application, it is the original principle that must remain true to the founders and unchanging for the judiciary to avoid overstepping its role and transforming the terms of the constitutional charter, but gray areas will always remain.

60. "Statutory interpretation involves a blend of emphases upon original intention and historical context, and a full recognition of the unprincipled, and imperfect, nature of an enactment produced by compromise" (Henry Monaghan, "Our Perfect Constitution," *New York University Law Review* 56 [1981]: 392–393). "Indeed, it would be difficult to say what interpretation of the law means if not to determine the intent of the lawmaker" (Graglia, "Constitution," 19). See also Joseph Raz, "Intention in Interpretation," in *The Autonomy of Law,* ed. Robert P. George (New York: Oxford University Press, 1996), 250–259. Again, this scheme of interpretation gains its meaning and significance from the contrast to the system rejected by the adoption of a written constitution. The British constitutional system not only leads to a different understanding of the constitution itself but also suggests a different approach to statutory law since such law is constitutive of the constitution in that system. See A. V. Dicey, *Introduction to the Study of the Law of the Constitution,* 8th ed. (New York: Macmillan, 1915), 402–409, and McIlwain, *Constitutionalism,* 132.

61. Sunstein, *Partial,* 40–61.

62. Dworkin, *Taking Rights,* 14–130. Dworkin has recently invited just such an experiment: see his *Freedom's Law* (Cambridge: Harvard University Press, 1996), 37.

63. See also Carl Auerbach, "A Revival of Some Ancient Learning: A Critique of Eisenberg's *The Nature of the Common Law,*" *Minnesota Law Review* 75 (1991): 539.

64. Hamilton et al., *Federalist Papers,* No. 1, 33; No. 37, 224–226; No. 38, 237; No. 41, 255–256; No. 49, 315; see also Kahn, *Legitimacy,* 9–23.

65. James Madison, *The Writings of James Madison,* ed. Gaillard Hunt, 9 vols. (New York: G. P. Putnam's Sons, 1900–1910), 9:191.

66. Thus, Locke wrote, "Words in their primary or immediate Signification, stand for nothing, but the *Ideas* in the Mind of him that uses them. . . . That then which Words are the Marks of, are the *Ideas* of the Speaker: Nor can any one apply them, as Marks, immediately to any thing else, but the *Ideas,* that he himself hath: For this would be to make them Signs of his own Conceptions, and yet apply them to other *Ideas*" (*An Essay Concerning Human Understanding,* ed. Peter Nidditch [New York: Oxford University Press, 1975], bk. 3, ch. 2, § 2); see also bk. 3, chaps. 1–3, 9–10. Locke recognized that there could be miscommunication between speakers, and therefore they should use words carefully and strive to be clear. He did not, however, recognize that words once used could change their meaning to something other than the speaker's meaning as time passed and contexts changed.

67. See also Clinton, "Original Understanding," 1190–1193, and Gregory Bassham, *Original Intent and the Constitution* (Lanham, MD: Rowman and Littlefield, 1992), 80.

68. Tucker, *Constitution,* 1:365, 180; see also Iredell's similar metaphor of "the deliberate voice of the people" (*Life* 2:146); Kamper v. Hawkins, 1 Va. Cases 20, 88 (1793). "The first and fundamental rule in the interpretation of all instruments is, to construe them according to the sense of the terms, and of the intention of the parties" (Story, *Commentaries,* § 181). "The true rule therefore seems to be no other than that which is applied in all cases of impartial and correct exposition; which is to deduce the meaning from its known intention and the entire text" (Rawle, *View,* 28). Story, however, does not provide very specific guidance in locating that intent (*Commentaries,* § 181).

69. Wittgenstein, *Investigations,* § 293. Without a known referent even a "private language" is unreliable, as there is no way to ensure the consistency of references over time. As a result, a purely private language ceases to be a system of language at all but becomes a series of unrelated notations. For the idea that communication, and thus intentionality, underlies even semantic analyses of language, which traditionally avoided grounding language on this function, see P. F. Strawson, *Logico-Linguistic Papers* (London: Methuen, 1971), 171–189. On the limited scope of semantics, see Kent Bach, *Thought and Reference* (New York: Oxford University Press, 1987), 4–6.

70. Paul Grice, *Studies in the Way of Words* (Cambridge: Harvard University Press, 1989), 117–137, 213–223, 283–303; P. F. Strawson, "Intention and Convention in Speech Acts," *Philosophical Review* 73 (1964): 439; and Kent Bach and Robert M. Harnish, *Linguistic Communication and Speech Acts* (Cambridge: MIT Press, 1979), 4–10.

71. Wittgenstein, *Investigations,* § 337.

72. Story, *Commentaries,* § 181, 183.

73. Gerald Graff, "'Keep off the Grass,' 'Drop Dead,' and Other Indeterminacies: A Response to Sanford Levinson," *Texas Law Review* 60 (1982): 410.

74. Nathaniel Chipman, *Principles of Government* (Burlington, VT: Edward Smith, 1833), 254; see also "The Constitution is a written instrument. As such its meaning does not alter. That which it meant when adopted it means now. . . . 'It is not only the same in words, it is the same in meaning'" (South Carolina v. United States, 199 U.S. 448-449 [1905]).

75. Marshall pursued such a strategy in accepting the Second National Bank, noting that the political branches had repeatedly and deliberately interpreted the Constitution to allow the incorporation of a bank, and the Court could find no prohibition of such an instrument, concluding that it was within the range of the indeterminate language of the Constitution (McCulloch v. Maryland, 17 U.S. [4 Wheat] 316 [1819]; see also Frederick Schauer, "An Essay on Constitutional Language," in Levinson and Mailloux, eds., *Interpreting Law and Literature,* 150, and Andrew Jackson, "Veto Message," *A Compilation of the Messages and Papers of the Presidents,* ed. James D. Richardson, 20 vols. (New York: Bureau of National Literature, 1897–1914), 3:1144–1147. Originalist jurisprudence cannot rely exclusively on a negative approach, however. Constraining the federal government to its enumerated powers may require a positive definition of those powers as well as a negative constricting of their outer boundaries. Marshall's example in *McCulloch* is a cautionary tale, demonstrating both the utility of the negative approach and its danger if incautiously applied.

76. Graff, "Keep Off," 411. "But it is precisely this embedding of an understanding of political texts in institutional modes of action that distinguishes *legal* interpretation from the interpretation of literature, from political philosophy, and from constitutional criticism"

(Robert Cover, "Violence and the Word," *Yale Law Journal* 95 [1986]: 1617 [emphasis in original]); Madison, *Writings,* 9:191.

77. Ludwig Wittgenstein, *On Certainty,* ed. G. E. M. Anscombe and G. H. von Wright (New York: Harper and Row, 1972), § 110, 115.

78. Graff, "Keep Off," 408, 411; Robert Bork, "Address at the University of San Diego Law School," in *The Great Debate: Interpreting our Written Constitution* (Washington, DC: Federalist Society, 1986), 45; and Thomas Sowell, *Knowledge and Decisions* (New York: Basic Books, 1980), 291–294.

79. Madison, *Writings,* 5:273.

80. Cf. Blackstone, *Commentaries,* 1:158–159; Prohibitions del Roy, Mich. 5 Jacobi, 7 Co. 64–65 (C.P. 1609).

81. "It is a plainly written document, not in Hebrew or Greek, but in English. . . . It is not even like the British Constitution. . . . The American Constitution is a written instrument full and complete in itself," and "I am only in reason and in conscience bound to learn the intentions of those who framed the Constitution *in the Constitution itself* " (both in Frederick Douglass, *The Life and Writings of Frederick Douglass,* ed. Philp Foner, 5 vols. [New York: International Publishers, 1950–1975] 2:468 and 2:157 [emphasis in original]).

82. Paine, *Rights,* 187.

83. Quoted in Sanford Levinson, *Constitutional Faith* (Princeton: Princeton University Press, 1988), 30.

84. "To begin with, writing renders the text autonomous with respect to the intention of the author. What the text signifies no longer coincides with what the author meant; henceforth, textual meaning and psychological meaning have different destinies" (Paul Ricoeur, *Hermeneutics and the Human Sciences,* ed. John Thompson [New York: Cambridge University Press, 1981], 139). Though Ricoeur's idea of "distanciation," that the text distances itself from the author's meaning by surviving the author's original context, is useful for this purpose, this section is concerned with a specific form of distanciation, the use of the Constitution as a rallying point for political action. The larger implications of Ricoeur's work are dealt with later.

85. Thomas Jefferson, *The Papers of Thomas Jefferson,* ed. Julian Boyd, 27 vols. to date (Princeton: Princeton University Press, 1950–), 14:660. See also Randolph, *Virginia,* 255; Thomas Jefferson, *The Writings of Thomas Jefferson,* ed. Paul Leicester Ford, 10 vols. (New York: G. P. Putnam's Sons, 1892–1899), 8:159–160, and 10:302. Cf. "I do not consider the judiciary as the champions of the people, or of the Constitution, bound to sound the alarm, and to excite an opposition to the legislature"(Kamper v. Hawkins, 1 Va. Cases 20, 30 [1793]).

86. Jefferson, *Papers,* 14:660.

87. For analyses of the use of texts and key words as political symbols, see Daniel T. Rodgers, *Contested Truths* (New York: Basic Books, 1987), and J. David Greenstone, "Political Culture and American Political Development: Liberty, Union, and the Liberal Bipolarity," *Studies in American Political Development* 1 (1986): 1. On the political shaping of Jefferson's own constituting text, see Pauline Maier, *American Scripture* (New York: Knopf, 1997).

88. Madison, *Writings,* 5:273; see also Hamilton et al., *Federalist Papers,* No. 10.

89. Paine, *Rights,* 187.

90. Graglia, "Constitution," 23–24; Commonwealth v. Caton et al., 4 Call. 5, 18 (Va. 1782).

91. Madison, *Writings,* 5:273. See also Hamilton et al., *Federalist Papers,* No. 84, 514; William F. Harris II, *The Interpretable Constitution* (Baltimore: Johns Hopkins University

Press, 1993); and Samuel Freeman, "Original Meaning, Democratic Interpretation, and the Constitution," *Philosophy and Public Affairs* 21 (1992): 11–17.

92. Eakin v. Raub, 12 Serg. & Rawle 330, 354 (Pa. 1825).

93. As Levinson observes, a protestant view of the Constitution not only commits one to focusing on the central text but also multiplies the number of legitimate interpreters, though the two positions do not logically necessitate one another. The multiplication of interpreters fractures interpretive agreement, as Levinson argues, and also multiplies interpretive strategies. See Levinson, *Constitutional Faith,* 9–53, and "Civil Religion." See also Douglass, *Life,* 2:407–424, 467–480, and 4:392–403. To this degree, the early arguments for an independent judiciary not only emphasized the need for impartial judges protected from the people but also for judges with specialized training and time to study the law. In the constitutional context, this concern readily maps onto the originalist desire for judges who can reconstruct the historical intentions. See, e.g., Hamilton et al., *Federalist Papers,* No. 78, 471.

94. More aspirational-minded theorists place little stress on the question of whether the goals they perceive in the text were conceived of by the framers or are even consistent with the framers' intentions. The aspirational argument assumes that the nation, or at least its ideological elite, makes moral progress over time, pursuing some constitutionally embodied ideal. Such a belief in progress lays relatively little stress on and leaves little room for concern with the moral ideals of preceding generations. Michael Perry, for example, explicitly identifies the aspirationalist text with a non-originalist conception (*Morality, Politics, and Law* [New York: Oxford University Press, 1988]); see also his "Authority"; Sotirios Barber, *On What the Constitution Means* (Baltimore: Johns Hopkins University Press, 1984); and David A. J. Richards, *Toleration and the Constitution* (New York: Oxford University Press, 1986). Strangely, Sunstein urges a historical interpretive method in order to constrain judges, but history is only to be binding as long as it would "improve the operation of constitutional democracy" (*Partial,* 120–121). These arguments should be distinguished from Jacobsohn, who finds an authoritative and rather different aspirationalism in the founders' intent distinct from contemporary aspirations imposed on the founders' document.

95. Thomas Grey, "The Constitution as Scripture," *Stanford Law Review* 37 (1984): 1. "One must respond to the incessant prophetic call of the text—one must recall and heed the aspirations the text symbolizes—and thereby create and give always-provisional, always-reformable meanings to the text" (Perry, "Authority," 560). See also Richards, *Toleration,* 100–101, 286.

96. For the purposes of this view, the Preamble so overshadows the document that Levinson takes Chief Justice Warren Burger's call to teach the Constitution's "principles" to be a reference to the Preamble only (see *Constitutional Faith,* 12).

97. William Brennan, "Address to the Text and Teaching Symposium at Georgetown University," in *Great Debate,* 11. Abraham Lincoln melded the Constitution with the Declaration of Independence and gave both a similarly aspirational reading, claiming that the founders "meant to declare the *right,* so that the *enforcement* of it might follow as fast as circumstances should permit. They set up a standard maxim for free society, which could be familiar to all, and revered by all; constantly looking to, constantly laboring for, and even though never perfectly attained, constantly approximated, and thereby constantly spreading and deepening its influence. . . . The assertion that 'all men are created equal' . . . was placed in the Declaration of Independence, not for [the founders' use], but for future use" (*Abraham Lincoln: His Speeches and Writings,* ed. Roy Basler [New York: Da Capo, 1990], 361).

98. "The realization of the text in the lives of the people . . . reveals much that is hidden in the text. . . . [The text's unanticipated consequences] endow the people with a greater capacity to comprehend the significance of their constitution" (Anne Norton, "Transubstantiation: The Dialectic of Constitutional Authority," *University of Chicago Law Review* 55 [1988]: 464).

99. Ibid.

100. Madison, *Writings*, 5:271–272.

101. Norton, "Transubstantiation," 465, 466–467; Drucilla Cornell, "From the Lighthouse: The Promise of Redemption and the Possibility of Legal Interpretation," in Leyh, ed., *Legal Hermeneutics*, 154–155, 170.

102. Brennan, "Address," 18; see also Harris, *Interpretable*, 113–119; and Perry, "Constitutional Theory," 246.

103. Brennan, "Address," 25.

104. Barber, *What the Constitution Means*, 60, and Harris, *Interpretable*, 118, 161.

105. Brest, "Quest," 225.

106. For example, see the work of John Rawls in political philosophy: *A Theory of Justice* (Cambridge: Harvard University Press, 1971), "Justice as Fairness: Political Not Metaphysical," *Philosophy and Public Affairs* 14 (1985): 223, and "Kantian Constructivism in Moral Theory," *Journal of Philosophy* 77 (1980): 515. See also Cornell, "Lighthouse," 159–161; Richards, *Toleration;* Susan Moller Okin, *Justice, Gender, and the Family* (New York: Basic Books, 1989), 97–109; and Richard Parker, "The Jurisprudential Uses of John Rawls," in *Constitutionalism: NOMOS XX*, ed. J. R. Pennock and J. W. Chapman (New York: New York University Press, 1979), 269–295.

107. Brest, "Quest," 226–227.

108. Barber, *What the Constitution Means*, 59–60.

109. Levinson concludes his book with an invitation for each citizen to sign his own name to the Constitution, individually ratifying it (a suggestion significantly at odds with the founders' method of ratification), but advises that the original document is unworthy of "esteem" unless supplemented by a host of additional, external texts (see *Constitutional Faith*, 185–186).

110. See, e.g., Sanford Levinson, "Law as Literature," *Texas Law Review* 60 (1982): 373; Gary Peller, "The Metaphysics of American Law," *California Law Review* 73 (1985): 1151; Allan Hutchinson, "From Cultural Construction to Historical Deconstruction," *Yale Law Journal* 94 (1984): 209; Joseph William Singer, "The Player and the Cards: Nihilism and Legal Theory," *Yale Law Journal* 94 (1984): 1; Thomas Heller, "Structuralism and Critique," *Stanford Law Review* 36 (1984): 127; and see, generally, Christopher Norris, *Deconstruction and the Interests of Theory* (Norman: University of Oklahoma Press, 1989), 126–155.

111. See, e.g., Stanley Fish, *Doing What Comes Naturally* (Durham, NC: Duke University Press, 1989); James Boyd White, "Law as Language: Reading Law and Reading Literature," *Texas Law Review* 60 (1982): 415; and David Couzens Hoy, "Interpreting the Law: Hermeneutical and Poststructuralist Perspectives," *Southern California Law Review* 58 (1985): 135.

112. At the extreme is Roberto Unger's work, known for its minimal citation; but unacknowledged traces are pervasive in other, more rigorously footnoted scholars. For Unger, see especially "The Critical Legal Studies Movement," *Harvard Law Review* 96 (1983): 561; *Knowledge and Politics* (New York: Free Press, 1975); *Politics*, 3 vols. (New York: Cambridge University Press, 1987). See also Hayden White, *Metahistory* (Baltimore: Johns Hopkins University Press, 1973), 433.

113. Ferdinand de Saussure, *Course in General Linguistics* (La Salle, IL: Open Court, 1986). For good introductions to structuralism, see Terence Hawkes, *Structuralism and Semiotics* (Berkeley: University of California Press, 1977); Culler, *Structuralist Poetics;* Fredric Jameson, *The Prison-House of Language* (Princeton: Princeton University Press, 1972); and Jacques Ehrmann, ed., *Structuralism* (New York: Anchor, 1970).

114. Within a given language, key sounds are recognized as meaningful despite the wide range of ways actual speakers may vocalize those sounds, primarily by "hearing" unfamiliar sounds as expected, meaningful sounds.

115. We know what "hot" is primarily by opposing it to "cold," "warm" in opposition to "hot" or "cold," and so on. Note that the positive content of the concept is fairly empty; we identify meaning by excluding possible meanings.

116. For example, a storyteller may not be aware of the deep structures underlying myths that on their surface seem to be unrelated and fantastic, but a careful anthropologist may be able to uncover these structures and extract more significant meanings from them. Similarly, an analyst may understand the structural features of an analysan's dreams, or of an economic system's actions, where the involved "agents" may have no awareness at all.

117. Thus, Michel Foucault pursued an "archeology" rather than a history, denoting the unlayering of successive "systems of simultaneity" rather than the unraveling of vertical relations through time (*The Order of Things* [New York: Vintage, 1973], xxiii); see also his *Archeology of Knowledge* (New York: Pantheon, 1972).

118. Foucault, *Order of Things,* xiv.

119. Michel Foucault, "What Is an Author?" in *Language, Counter-Memory, Practice,* ed. Donald Bouchard (Ithaca, NY: Cornell University Press, 1977), 113. "For him, for us too, it is the language which speaks, not the author; to write is, through a prerequisite impersonality . . . to reach that point where only language acts, 'performs,' and not 'me' " (Roland Barthes, "The Death of the Author," in *Modern Criticism and Theory,* ed. David Lodge [New York: Longman, 1988], 168).

120. Barthes, "Death," 168; Roland Barthes, "From Work to Text," in *Textual Strategies,* ed. Josué V. Harari (Ithaca, NY: Cornell University Press, 1979), 73. The adoption of the word "text" is meant to convey the existence of an autonomous entity subject to the examination of the reader rather than the positive creation, or "work," of an author.

121. Thus, the title of Jameson's book on structuralism, *The Prison-House of Language.*

122. Foucault uses the example of a mythical taxonomy to note the "stark impossibility of thinking *that,*" though the impossibility of thinking in the alien structure's terms is not for lack of "precise meaning and demonstrable content" (*Order of Things,* xv).

123. "We are not, therefore, claiming to show how men think in myths, but rather how the myths think themselves out in men and without men's knowledge" (Claude Levi-Strauss, "Overture to *le Cru et le cuit,*" in Ehrmann, ed., *Structuralism,* 46).

124. Terence Ball, "Constitutional Interpretation and Conceptual Change," in Leyh, ed., *Legal Hermeneutics,* 135.

125. Claude Levi-Strauss, *The Savage Mind* (Chicago: University of Chicago Press, 1966), 257.

126. Useful introductions to poststructuralist thought include Christopher Norris, *Deconstruction* (New York: Routledge, 1991); Jonathan Culler, *On Deconstruction* (Ithaca, NY: Cornell University Press, 1982); and Harari, ed., *Textual Strategies.* Poststructuralism cannot be readily distinguished from structuralism, given that most identified structuralists eventually moved to claim the poststructuralist label with no sharp break in their work.

See Culler, *On Deconstruction,* 25. Others, such as Michel Foucault, denounced the structuralist label in the first place; see, e.g., *Order of Things,* xiv, and *Archeology of Knowledge,* 15, 204. For Foucault's problematic relationship to structuralism, see Hubert Dreyfus and Paul Rabinow, *Michel Foucault: Beyond Hermeneutics and Structuralism* (Chicago: University of Chicago Press, 1983). For an example of a legal theorist assimilating Foucault's work to structuralism, see Heller, "Structuralism."

127. Culler, *Poetics,* 14–15.

128. This project of breaking down rigid oppositions is most fully exemplified in the works of Jacques Derrida; see esp. *Of Grammatology* (Baltimore: Johns Hopkins University Press, 1976), *Disseminations* (Chicago: University of Chicago Press, 1981), *Margins of Philosophy* (Chicago: University of Chicago Press, 1982), and *Writing and Difference* (Chicago: University of Chicago Press, 1978).

129. Derrida, "Différance," in *Margins,* 3–27.

130. Deconstructive interpretations often take the form, therefore, of pursuing etymologies of words in order to place a text into a variety of strange conventions and to demonstrate the new meanings thus generated by the very forms of language and processes of reading. See, e.g., J. Hillis Miller, "The Critic as Host," in *Modern Criticism and Theory,* 278–285. "The text expresses its own aporia" (Miller, *Theory now and then* [Durham, NC: Duke University Press, 1991], 108).

131. Indeed, the text becomes like a machine, endlessly generating new meanings without the active involvement of the author, and perhaps even a machine capable of manipulating and "creating" the author himself against his will. See Paul de Man, "The Purloined Ribbon," *Glyph* 1 (1977): 41, 44–45, and "Political Allegory in Rousseau," *Critical Inquiry* 2 (1976): 668, 671; Derrida, *Margins,* 316.

132. Jacques Derrida, *Positions* (Chicago: University of Chicago Press, 1981), 26 (emphasis in original). "The text is a tissue of quotations drawn from the innumerable centres of culture" (Barthes, "Death of the Author," 170). The end of "linear writing" will make this even clearer, as computer access to vast data banks of information allows readers routinely to draw upon decontextualized "sound bites" (Derrida, *Grammatology,* 86, 332 n.35).

133. Derrida, *Grammatology,* 11–12, 17, 20, 40–45.

134. Barthes, "Death of the Author," 171.

135. Derrida, *Writing and Difference,* 292.

136. For useful introductions, see Susan Suleiman and Inge Crosman, eds., *The Reader in the Text* (Princeton: Princeton University Press, 1980); Jane Tompkins, ed., *Reader-Response Criticism* (Baltimore: Johns Hopkins University Press, 1980); Elizabeth Freund, *The Return of the Reader* (New York: Routledge, 1987); and the related Robert Holub, *Reception Theory* (New York: Routledge, 1984). Reader-response theory has been brought into legal interpretation primarily through the influence of Stanley Fish, who assimilates poststructuralism to reader-response in *Doing What Comes Naturally,* 37–67.

137. Interpretation of a text becomes a form of self-discovery. See, e.g., Wolfgang Iser, "The Reading Process: A Phenomenological Approach," 68, and Norman Holland, "Unity Identity Text Self," both in Tompkins, ed., *Reader-Response Criticism,* 118–133.

138. Robert Crosman, "Do Readers Make Meaning?" in Suleiman and Crosman, eds., *Reader in the Text,* 154.

139. Susan Suleiman, "Introduction: Varieties of Audience-Oriented Criticism," in ibid., 3–45.

140. Fish, *Is There a Text,* 268–292.

141. "Intention like anything else is an interpretive fact; that is, it must be construed " (Fish, *Doing What Comes Naturally,* 100); see also his "Play of Surfaces: Theory and the Law," in Leyh, ed., *Legal Hermeneutics,* 300. For Fish, one result of this is that all viable interpretations are equally concerned with authorial intent, only that the author and reader both are functions of their potentially quite distant interpretive communities (see *Doing What Comes Naturally,* 98–100, 116–118, 296, 315–467 passim).

142. "No recourse to the foundation document—the Constitution—being genuinely possible. . . . They are simply *different* Constitutions. There are as many plausible readings of the United States Constitution as there are versions of *Hamlet*" (Levinson, "Law as Literature," 391); see also Paul Brest, "The Fundamental Rights Controversy: The Essential Contradictions of Normative Constitutional Scholarship," *Yale Law Journal* 90 (1981): 1063; and Fish, *Doing What Comes Naturally,* 330.

143. Simon, "Authority of Constitution," 620; see also, Mark V. Tushnet, "Following the Rules Laid Down: A Critique of Interpretivism and Neutral Principles," *Harvard Law Review* 96 (1983): 802, 818–819; and Brest, "Misconceived Quest." But Fish would deny that there is any truly "external" perspective.

144. Ronald Dworkin, *Law's Empire* (Cambridge: Harvard University Press, 1986), 52–53, 349–350, 360.

145. Harold Bloom, *The Anxiety of Influence* (New York: Oxford University Press, 1973), and *A Map of Misreading* (New York: Oxford University Press, 1975). Bloom's works contain echoes of the "strong judge" in Karl Llewellyn, *The Bramble Bush* (New York: Oceana, 1960), and Jerome Frank, *Law and the Modern Mind* (Gloucester, MA: Peter Smith, 1970).

146. Hermeneutics comes in many forms, some of which fully accept the determinacy of the text and the authority of authorial intent. See, e.g., E. D. Hirsch Jr., *The Validity of Interpretation* (New Haven: Yale University Press, 1967). This section focuses largely on a more recent branch of hermeneutics that denies this possibility, developed by Martin Heidegger and primarily represented by Hans-Georg Gadamer; Michael Ermarth, "The Transformation of Hermeneutics: 19th Century Ancients and 20th Century Moderns," *Monist* 64 (1981): 175; and Martin Heidegger, *Being and Time* (New York: Harper and Row, 1962), esp. § 32.

147. Ricoeur, *Hermeneutics,* 154, 160–161, 216–218; the written text is fundamentally different from spoken dialogue, however, precisely in its indeterminacy as a result of the absence of an author or original context. Thus, the oral dialogue is a model that not only represents the hermeneutic ideal but also the fallen state of the written text. See Hans-Georg Gadamer, *Truth and Method* (New York: Continuum, 1975), 390–395, and "Text and Interpretation," in *Dialogue and Deconstruction,* ed. Diane Michelfelder and Richard Palmer (Albany: State University of New York Press, 1989), 34. Cf. Fish, *Doing What Comes Naturally,* 37–44, who denies any greater determinacy for spoken discourse.

148. For "distanciation," see Ricoeur, *Hermeneutics,* 132–144.

149. Gadamer, *Truth and Method,* 276–277.

150. Ibid., 293, 297.

151. Ibid., 296.

152. Gadamer posits that individuals exist within "horizons" of pregiven experiences, a background of thoughts and actions. The more distant individuals are from one another in terms of historical experience, the less overlap will exist between their horizons, requiring greater positive effort to forge links between them. Individuals separated by time do not share horizons at all, but an interpretive tradition can offer a link between horizons, allowing a reader to extend his own sufficiently to accomplish a "fusion" of horizons consistent

with neither the author's nor the reader's original horizon of meaning (*Truth and Methods*, 163–167, 246–247, 261–262, 292–309.

153. Ibid., 162, and Ricoeur, *Hermeneutics*, 91, 139.

154. Ultimately, this fusion of the author's project with the reader's application suggests that any interpretation, regardless of specific interpretive method, yields an equally "originalist" meaning, for all interpretations are equally marked by and divergent from authorial intentions. See David Couzens Hoy, "The Hermeneutical Critique of the Originalism/Non-originalism Distinction," *Northern Kentucky Law Review* 15 (1988): 479.

155. For a discussion of the difference between application and appropriation, see David Couzens Hoy, *The Critical Circle* (Berkeley: University of California Press, 1982), 89–90, and on objectivity of interpretation within tradition, 50; see also "Interpreting the Law."

156. Gadamer, *Truth and Method*, 207.

157. For a useful review of a part of this movement, see John Toews, "Intellectual History After the Linguistic Turn: The Autonomy of Meaning and the Irreducibility of Experience," *American Historical Review* 92 (1987): 879.

158. H. White, *Metahistory*, 430, and *Tropics of Discourse* (Baltimore: Johns Hopkins University Press, 1978), 43, 47.

159. For an example of a critique based on practical difficulties for originalist interpretations but that does not call into question the ideal of accurate historical knowledge, see James Hutson, "The Creation of the Constitution: The Integrity of the Documentary Record," *Texas Law Review* 65 (1986): 1.

160. H. White, *Tropics*, 84.

161. Any given historical "fact" can support a multitude of interpretations, and this plurality of conflicting meanings can be reduced to a determinate unit only through the imposed will of the interpreter. Since the various possible interpretations are equally likely, the ultimate judgment as to which is to be adopted can only be a matter of individual preference and will instead of rational choice. See H. White, *Metahistory*, 7, and *Tropics*, 47, 61, 94.

162. Roland Barthes, "The Discourse of History," *Comparative Criticism* 3 (1981): 16. "But in general there has been a reluctance to consider historical narratives as what they most manifestly are: verbal fictions, the contents of which are as much *invented as found*" (H. White, *Tropics*, 82 [emphasis in original]). See also Louis O. Mink, "History and Fiction as Modes of Comprehension," *New Literary History* 1 (1970): 541.

163. Hoy, *Critical Circle*, 49; H. White, *Content of Form*, 80; Gadamer, *Truth and Method*, 97–99; Dominick LaCapra, *Rethinking Intellectual History* (Ithaca, NY: Cornell University Press, 1983), 37–38; John Keane, "More Theses on the Philosophy of History," in *Meaning and Context*, ed. James Tully (Princeton: Princeton University Press, 1988), 204–217.

164. "The best grounds for choosing one [historical] perspective on history rather than another are ultimately aesthetic or moral rather than epistemological" (H. White, *Metahistory*, xii); see also Robert Gordon, "Historicism in Legal Scholarship," *Yale Law Journal* 90 (1981): 1017.

4. A DEFENSE OF ORIGINALISM

1. Lino Graglia, "How the Constitution Disappeared," *Commentary* 81 (1986): 23–24. See also Samuel Freeman, "Original Meaning, Democratic Interpretation, and the Constitution," *Philosophy and Public Affairs* 21 (1992): 7, 8, 14–17, 25–27, 37.

2. For examples of judicial restraint grounded on forms of skepticism, see Stanley Brubaker, "Reconsidering Dworkin's Case for Judicial Activism," *Journal of Politics* 46 (1984): 503, and Robert Bork, *Tradition and Morality in Constitutional Law* (Washington, DC: American Enterprise Institute, 1984). For examples of activist critiques, see Sotirios Barber, "Epistemological Skepticism, Hobbesian Natural Right and Judicial Self-Restraint," *Review of Politics* 8 (1986): 374, and Ronald Dworkin, *Taking Rights Seriously* (Cambridge: Harvard University Press, 1978), 131–149.

3. Cf. Michael Perry, *The Constitution in the Courts* (New York: Oxford University Press, 1994).

4. The term-limits movement is indicative of such political activism and reform based on a non-originalist understanding of textual principles. Originalism has traditionally ignored the possibility of principled political action, unnecessarily weakening its ability to explain the relationship between the judiciary and other political actors. See, e.g., Justice Clarence Thomas's dissent in U.S. Term Limits v. Thornton, 131 L.Ed. 2d 881, 926 (1995).

5. To the extent that he sought to pursue his antislavery aims through legislation, Lincoln's aspirationalism can be seen to fit this model. As noted, Gary Jacobsohn's moral reading of the Constitution is largely consistent with originalism.

6. U.S. Constitution, art. 2, § 1; Edward Corwin, *The President* (New York: New York University Press, 1984).

7. Compare James Madison, *The Writings of James Madison,* ed. Gaillard Hunt, 9 vols. (New York: Putnam, 1900–1910), 5:271–272, with Drucilla Cornell, "From the Lighthouse: The Promise of Redemption and the Possibility of Legal Interpretation," in *Legal Hermeneutics,* ed. Gregory Leyh (Berkeley: University of California Press, 1992).

8. If constitutional guarantees encouraged the judicial development of a general right to privacy, their parsimoniousness also sparked and justified a conservative reaction paring it back and a sprawling modern state that routinely encroaches on personal privacy to an extent unimaginable at the founding.

9. If Lincoln's example is accepted as the purest case of the aspirationalist text in action, then the fact that the transformative potential of the Declaration's phrasing (not primarily the Constitution's) lay dormant for so long, not to emerge until adopted by particular political actors in a political struggle and pressed into the service of a preexisting agenda, calls into question the general claim that written constitutions by their very nature are particularly transformative and aspirational. Justice William Brennan's quixotic acceptance of the Eighth Amendment as an aspirationalist text that has transformed the nation to the extent that capital punishment is no longer valid suggests that such transformations may most often be imposed from above. See his "Address to the Text and Teaching Symposium at Georgetown University," in *The Great Debate* (Washington, DC: Federalist Society, 1986), 24–25.

10. See, e.g., William F. Harris II, *The Interpretable Constitution* (Baltimore: Johns Hopkins University Press, 1992); Anne Norton, "Transubstantiation: The Dialectic of Constitutional Authority," *University of Chicago Law Review* 72 (1986): 1237; and Michael Perry, *Morality, Politics and Law* (New York: Oxford University Press, 1988). For a related discussion of promises, see Paul de Man, "Political Allegory in Rousseau," *Critical Inquiry* 2 (1976): 668.

11. Madison, *Writings,* 5:272. Though some of the founders clearly hoped that a bill of rights would help protect against a momentary passionate majority, this was hardly the appeal to a Rousseauean "true sovereign" that current theorists such as Harris and Norton

depend upon. See Herbert Storing, *What the Anti-Federalists Were For* (Chicago: University of Chicago Press, 1981), 64–70. There is reason to believe that the inadequacy of the judicial check on determined national majorities has been borne out. See, e.g., Robert Dahl, "Decision-Making in a Democracy: The Supreme Court as National Policy-Maker," *Journal of Public Law* 6 (1957): 279; William Lasser, *The Limits of Judicial Power* (Chapel Hill: University of North Carolina Press, 1988); and Mark A. Graber, "The Non-Majoritarian Difficulty: Legislative Deference to the Judiciary," *Studies in American Political Development* 7 (1993): 35–73.

12. Gordon Wood, *The Creation of the American Republic, 1776–1787* (New York: Norton, 1969); Storing, *Anti-Federalists;* Sheldon Wolin, *The Presence of the Past* (Baltimore: Johns Hopkins University Press, 1989); Hannah Arendt, *On Revolution* (New York: Viking Penguin, 1965); Forrest McDonald, *Novus Ordo Seclorum* (Lawrence: University Press of Kansas, 1985); and David Epstein, *The Political Theory of* The Federalist (Chicago: University of Chicago Press, 1984). Compare Jean-Jacques Rousseau, *On the Social Contract* (New York: St. Martin's Press, 1978) and "Discourse on the Origin and Foundations of Inequality," in *The First and Second Discourses* (New York: St. Martin's Press, 1964), with Thomas Hobbes, *Leviathan* (New York: Viking Penguin, 1968), chaps. xiv, xvii, xviii, xxi; John Locke, "Second Treatise of Government," in *Two Treatises of Government* (New York: Cambridge University Press, 1988), chaps. ii, vii, viii; and Alexander Hamilton, James Madison, and John Jay, *The Federalist Papers,* ed. Clinton Rossiter (New York: Mentor, 1961), No. 51.

13. Brennan, "Address," 17, 15.

14. On the circularity of judicial disputes, compare, e.g., Employment Division, Department of Human Resources of Oregon v. Smith, 485 U.S. 660 (1988), and Reynolds v. U.S., 98 U.S. 145 (1879); Butchers' Benevolent Association v. Crescent City Livestock Landing & Slaughterhouse Co., 83 U.S. (16 Wall.) 36 (1873); West Coast Hotel Co. v. Parrish, 300 U.S. 379 (1937); and Dolan v. City of Tigard, 114 S.Ct. 2309 (1994). On the false evolution of doctrine, compare, e.g., Schenck v. U.S., 249 U.S. 47 (1919), Dennis v. U.S., 341 U.S. 494 (1951); and Brandenburg v. Ohio, 395 U.S. 444 (1969).

15. Frederick Schauer, "An Essay on Constitutional Language," in *Interpreting Law and Literature,* ed. Sanford Levinson and Steven Mailloux (Evanston, IL: Northwestern University Press, 1988), 142–146. Though this tendency is conceivably avoidable, the variation in types of provisions in the constitutional text leads aspirationalists to edit it in order to reconstruct a moral text. See, e.g., David A. J. Richards, *Toleration and the Constitution* (New York: Oxford University Press, 1986), 49–52. Cf. "Address of the Convention, March 1780," in Oscar and Mary Handlin, eds., *The Popular Sources of Authority* (Cambridge: Harvard University Press, 1966), 434.

16. See, e.g., Donald Horowitz, *The Courts and Social Policy* (Washington, DC: Brookings Institution, 1977). Ronald Dworkin is a leading advocate of accepting such principled absolutism as the very purpose of the judiciary, but in the constitutional realm this often downplays the potential conflict of rights and the possibility that even principles may be subject to compromise. See Dworkin, *Taking Rights, Law's Empire* (Cambridge: Harvard University Press, 1986), and *A Matter of Principle* (Cambridge: Harvard University Press, 1985).

17. Welcome exceptions to this pattern are now emerging, including Sotirios Barber and Stephen Griffin.

18. U.S. Constitution, art. 2, § 1; Amend. 14; Amend. 22; art. 2, § 2; art. 5. See also William Eskridge and Sanford Levinson, eds., *Constitutional Stupidities, Constitutional Tragedies* (New York: New York University Press, 1998).

19. Sotirios Barber, *On What the Constitution Means* (Baltimore: Johns Hopkins University Press, 1984), 156, 197–201.

20. An exception is Freeman, "Original Meaning," who states explicitly that the Court could not overrule such unjust aspects of the text as the apportionment of senators on the basis of geography (state representation). Having made the concession, however, it becomes difficult to determine what alternative interpretive framework is actually guiding the courts in order to provide this backstop to distinguish "unreasonable" but codified requirements from constitutional norms that are unreasonable but insufficiently embedded to demand judicial respect (35). The divergence of the (historically intended) subjective meaning of the text and a posited "objective" meaning represented by some version of a Rawlsian original position indicates that the Constitution simply is a subjective text. There is no principled mechanism for distinguishing presidential age limits and the due process clause in grounding the authority of the document and developing an interpretive method. To the question of why historical intentions are followed in the one case but not the other, aspirationalists can reply only that in the latter the text itself is sufficiently unclear that the judge can "get away with it" but that in the former the judicial manipulation of meaning would be too obvious to ignore. See Freeman, "Constitutional Democracy and the Legitimacy of Judicial Review," *Law and Philosophy* 9 (1990–1991): 361.

21. See also Owen Fiss, "Foreword: The Forms of Justice," *Harvard Law Review* 93 (1979): 38. Compare Cass Sunstein's assertion that each judicial ruling requires independent consent from the citizenry (*The Partial Constitution* [Cambridge: Harvard University Press, 1993], 100).

22. U.S. Constitution, art. 1, § 9; Amend. 3; Amend. 7; art. 4, § 2. Note further the incongruity of a "promissory" constitution requiring a formal amendment (Amend. 13) in order to overturn this last clause, which presumably would be naturally eliminated by the aspirational nature of the text being realized over time.

23. John Rawls, *A Theory of Justice* (Cambridge: Harvard University Press, 1971), 253, and Immanuel Kant, *Groundwork of the Metaphysics of Morals* (New York: Harper and Row, 1964). This Kantian tradition can also be rendered as more broadly Continental to take into account similar themes in Rousseau and others who have also served as inspirations for recent constitutional applications.

24. See also Henry Monaghan, "Our Perfect Constitution," *New York University Law Review* 56 (1981): 356–358.

25. For the reducito ad absurdum of this mold, see Charles Larmore, *Patterns of Moral Complexity* (New York: Cambridge University Press, 1987): "A liberal political system need not feel obliged to reason with fanatics; it must simply take the necessary precautions to guard against them" (60).

26. Hamilton et al., *Federalist Papers,* No. 1, 33; No. 37, 224–226; No. 38, 237; No. 41, 255–256; No. 49, 315. See also Mark A. Graber, "Our (Im)perfect Constitution," *Review of Politics* 51 (1989): 86.

27. John Hart Ely, *Democracy and Distrust* (Cambridge: Harvard University Press, 1980), 58.

28. Cass Sunstein criticizes Ely on the similar grounds that the theory of democracy is underdetermined and cannot specify what form of democracy a judge should impose on the populace. Unfortunately, Sunstein's own republican-based, mild aspirationalism is similarly undetermined (*Partial*, 104–108, 121–123). Freeman recognizes this dilemma and restricts the Court to striking down only laws that are outside the bounds of a set of rea-

sonable norms, but then this makes the actual constitutional text, which is more specific than that in several instances, difficult to explain ("Original Meaning," 26).

29. Such aspirationalists mirror the radical abolitionist attack on the Constitution as a whole, in contrast to antislavery judges such as Story and Shaw, who sought to distinguish between their judicial duties and their political goals. See Robert Cover, *Justice Accused* (New Haven: Yale University Press, 1975).

30. For a critique of the Kantian foundations of Rawls, see Michael Sandel, *Liberalism and the Limits of Justice* (New York: Cambridge University Press, 1982).

31. See, e.g., Rogers Smith, *Liberalism and American Constitutional Law* (Cambridge: Harvard University Press, 1985), and Barber, *What the Constitution Means.* Stephen Macedo may also fit this group, though he more often cites neo-Kantians than neo-Lockeans; see his *Liberal Virtues* (New York: Oxford University Press, 1991).

32. Smith, *Liberalism,* 40–45, 222–223; John Dunn, *The Political Thought of John Locke* (New York: Cambridge University Press, 1969), and *Political Obligation in Its Historical Context* (New York: Cambridge University Press, 1980), 29–52.

33. Locke, "Second Treatise," § 149, 168, 176, 207–209, 223–226, 230.

34. One must still be careful not to fall into the trap of regarding the constitutional text as a piece of political theory, however. The document will reflect different political perspectives and thus contain contradictory aspects that might be irrational within other contexts but reasonable for a political document in which compromises are necessary but create interpretive difficulties. Cf. Barber, *What the Constitution Means,* 155–156.

35. Smith, *Liberalism,* 223; Julian Franklin, *John Locke and the Theory of Sovereignty* (New York: Cambridge University Press, 1978).

36. It seems clearly inadequate simultaneously to emphasize the normative need for rational deliberation and to constrain the debate to elite, and unaccountable, institutions. It is preferable to reconstruct and understand politics than to abandon it. Cf. H. Jefferson Powell, *The Moral Tradition of American Constitutionalism* (Durham, NC: Duke University Press, 1993), 49, and Perry, *Constitution in the Courts,* 106–110. In a recent essay, Ronald Dworkin begins with the claim that there "is a particular way of reading and enforcing a political constitution, which I call the *moral* reading." Despite this reference to the "political constitution," Dworkin begins his next paragraph with the assertion that the "moral reading therefore brings political morality into the heart of constitutional law." By not distinguishing between the political and legal dimensions of the Constitution, he is led from a reasonable premise to a faulty conclusion; see *Freedom's Law* (Cambridge: Harvard University Press, 1996), 2. James Gardner points out the risk of political error in that the representative branches of government may not always represent the people's considered judgments. Given the high standard of certainty he sets before the Court could act on its perception of the people's current constitutional will, it is uncertain how significant the concession is in practice; see "The Positivist Foundations of Originalism: An Account and Critique," *Boston University Law Review* 71 (1991): 34–44.

37. Paul Brest, "The Misconceived Quest for the Original Understanding," *Boston University Law Review* 60 (1980): 225.

38. Consider, for example, the more variegated nature of "consent" within a living community provided by more situated theories, such as Hanna Pitkin, "Obligation and Consent—I," *American Political Science Review* 59 (1965): 990, and "Obligation and Consent—II," *American Political Science Review* 60 (1966): 39, and Pitkin, *Wittgenstein and Justice* (Berkeley: University of California Press, 1972), 193–219; Michael Walzer, *Obligations*

(Cambridge: Harvard University Press, 1970), ix–xvi, and *Spheres of Justice* (New York: Basic Books, 1983); Sandel, *Liberalism*, 107–114, 175–183; Dworkin, *Law's Empire*, 195–216; Hans-Georg Gadamer, *Truth and Method* (New York: Continuum, 1975), 271–281; Nancy Hirschmann, *Rethinking Obligation* (Ithaca, NY: Cornell University Press, 1992); Michael Oakeshott, *Rationalism in Politics and Other Essays* (Indianapolis: Liberty Fund, 1991); and Edmund S. Morgan, *Inventing the People* (New York: Norton, 1988), 199–208. Such theories suggest not only that political commitments develop within and for less than ideal contexts but also that such commitments do not form an undifferentiated whole, allowing the possibility for institutionally differentiated obligations, even in relation to the same textual object.

39. Cooper v. Aaron, 358 U.S. 1, 17 (1958); Baker v. Carr, 369 U.S. 186, 211 (1962); Powell v. McCormack, 395 U.S. 486, 549 (1969); U.S. v. Nixon, 418 U.S. 683, 704 (1974).

40. An originalist judiciary contributes to this process by ensuring that the written Constitution reflects the people's most considered judgments until they are authoritatively amended. Cf. Paul Dimond, *The Supreme Court and Judicial Choice* (Ann Arbor: University of Michigan Press, 1989).

41. On the judicial interpretation of political compromises generally, see Frank Easterbrook, "Foreword: The Court and the Economic System," *Harvard Law Review* 98 (1984): 4.

42. See, generally, Monaghan, "Perfect."

43. Moreover, legal interpretation involves rather different considerations from literary criticism. Theories of indeterminacy have thrived in disciplines that particularly value interpretive pluralism, but legal interpretation is motivated by different concerns. Legal writing presupposes an institutional context in which coercion and violence follow from textual exegesis. Under such circumstances, textual indeterminacy is both less desirable and less compelling.

44. William Nelson, "History and Neutrality in Constitutional Adjudication," *Virginia Law Review* 72 (1986): 1237. Hayden White's arguments for historical indeterminacy, for example, rest on an examination of writers of unusually sweeping "histories" such as Hegel, Marx, Michelet, and Ranke. His thesis becomes increasingly less plausible as more narrow historical questions are considered. See Maurice Mandelbaum, "The Presuppositions of *Metahistory*," *History and Theory* 19 (1980): 41–42, and Eugene Golub, "The Irony of Nihilism," *Theory and History* 19 (1980): 60–61.

45. See, e.g., Easterbrook, "Foreword." The hermeneutical assumption that writing is less contextualized than speech is open to gradations; some writing is more contextualized than others in order to convey intent to the expected, remote reader. Legal writing suggests the characteristics of a "speech act" rather than a mere instance of a *langue*. Cf. Paul Ricoeur, *Hermeneutics and the Human Sciences* (New York: Cambridge University Press, 1981), 139–144. There remains a problem of studied ambiguity as political actors attempt to avoid decision, creating a text potentially absent of intent; see Graber, "Non-Majoritarian"; cf. Easterbrook, "Foreword." Similar objections are addressed below, though it is notable that such situations suggest the need for an open recognition of the limits of interpretation.

46. See, e.g., John Searle, "The World Turned Upside Down," *New York Review of Books* (27 October 1983): 74. Such arguments are more telling in relation to hermeneutics than poststructuralist theories, for the latter ultimately see writing as a useful stand-in for language more generally; however, their misrepresentation of writing undercuts the remainder of their demonstration. On the enhanced capacity of writing and writing-like speech, see Walter Ong, *Orality and Literacy* (New York: Routledge, 1982), and Basil Bernstein, *The-*

oretical Studies Towards a Sociology of Language, vol. 1, *Class, Codes and Control* (New York: Routledge, 1971).

47. Stanley Fish, *Is There a Text in This Class?* (Cambridge: Harvard University Press, 1980), 136, 148, 174, 268.

48. A particularly startling example of this can be found in Levinson's seminal article in which he grants all the rejoinders to his key claims in a footnote but without apparently recognizing the effect these concessions should have on his main text; see "Law as Literature," *Texas Law Review* 60 (1982): 373, 382 n.33.

49. Derrida, for example, has no difficulty making normal references to textual meaning and authorial intent, including his own; see *Of Grammatology* (Baltimore: Johns Hopkins University Press, 1976), 39, 70, 158, 243. Harold Bloom's necessary "misreadings" nonetheless suggest recognizably correct readings, even if such readings are indications of weak poets or the silencing of the poet within ourselves; see *The Anxiety of Influence* (New York: Oxford University Press, 1973), 5, 25, 30, 57, 65, 95. Ultimately, deconstruction cannot deny the determinacy of intentional textual meanings but "*suspends* that view for its own specific purpose of seeing what happens," in order to go beyond a mere "doubling commentary" (Christopher Norris, *Deconstruction* [New York: Routledge, 1991], 128). But such a "doubling commentary" is the very nature of legal interpretation, the substitution of a complex legal code for a general constitutional text. Recognizing that deconstructive pyrotechnics only follow from a willful decision to suspend normal interpretive assumptions, poststructuralists must provide the authority for a judge to make such a choice.

50. Historical hermeneutics has also retreated from its strongest claims, admitting certain critical distinctions between history and fiction. See, e.g., Hayden White, *Tropics of Discourse* (Baltimore: Johns Hopkins University Press, 1978), 23, 121, and *The Content of the Form,* 54. None of this leads to the conclusion that there are no interpretive disagreements, only that such disagreements are of a relatively familiar kind, in which judgments are made in accord with available evidence and such judgments are subject to rational evaluation and comparison.

51. Michel Foucault, *The Order of Things* (New York: Vintage, 1973), xv. By conbrast, the actual classification schemes offered by Marshall Sahlins are eminently comprehensible, even if they are relatively exotic. As Sahlins demonstrates, cultural texts may not be transparent, but with appropriate attention to context they can be understood; see *How "Natives" Think* (Chicago: University of Chicago, 1995), 158–164.

52. See, e.g., Ferdinand de Saussure, *Course in General Linguistics* (La Salle, IL: Open Court, 1986), 114–115.

53. John Holloway, "Language, Realism, Subjectivity, Objectivity," in *Reconstructing Literature,* ed. Laurence Lerner (Totowa, NJ: Barnes and Noble, 1983), 73, and Cedric Watts, "Bottom's Children: the Fallacies of Structuralist, Post-Structuralist and Deconstructionist Literary Theory," in Lerner, ed., *Reconstructing Literature,* 23.

54. On "mind," see Richard Rorty, *Philosophy and the Mirror of Nature* (Princeton: Princeton University Press, 1979), chap. 2. Compare "sheep" vs. "mutton" (Saussure, *Course,* 114).

55. Jurgen Habermas, *On the Logic of the Social Sciences* (Cambridge: MIT Press, 1988), 174. For Habermas's more recent formulation, taking into fuller account the mediating aspect of language, see "What Is Universal Pragmatics?" *Communication and the Evolution of Society* (Boston: Beacon Press, 1979), 1–68. For other accounts mediating material reality and socially constructed consciousness, see Karl-Otto Apel, "The Problem of Philosophical Foundations in Light of a Transcendental Pragmatics of Language," in *After Philosophy,*

ed. Kenneth Baynes, James Bohman, and Thomas McCarthy (Cambridge: MIT Press, 1987), 250–290; Ludwig Wittgenstein, *Philosophical Investigations* (New York: Macmillan, 1958); John Searle, *Intentionality* (New York: Cambridge University Press, 1983); James Harris, *Against Relativism* (La Salle, IL: Open Court, 1992); George Lakoff and Mark Johnson, *Metaphors We Live By* (Chicago: University of Chicago Press, 1980); Donald Davidson, "A Coherence Theory of Truth and Knowledge," in *Truth and Interpretation,* ed. Ernest Le-Pore (New York: Basil Blackwell, 1986), 307–319, and Oscar Handlin, *Truth in History* (Cambridge: Harvard University Press, 1979), 133, 180–181.

56. Donald Davidson, *Inquiries into Truth and Interpretation* (New York: Oxford University Press, 1984), 125–139, 183–198, and Harris, *Against Relativism,* 78–122.

57. Stanley Fish, *Doing What Comes Naturally* (Durham, NC: Duke University Press, 1989); Steven Knapp and Walter Benn Michaels, "Against Theory," *Critical Inquiry* 8 (1982): 723, "A Reply to Our Critics," *Critical Inquiry* 9 (1983): 790, and "Reply to George Wilson," *Critical Inquiry* 19 (1992): 186.

58. "The distinction between text and context is impossible to maintain and cannot be the basis of demarcating alternative theories with their attendant consequences" (Fish, *Doing What Comes Naturally,* 330). "Since, in our view, everyone engaged in a genuine interpretive controversy is *already* trying to find out what the author intended, there is no point in *recommending* that interpreters look for the author's intention" (Knapp and Michaels, "Reply to George Wilson," 187 [emphasis in original]).

59. Davidson distinguishes between a "prior theory" with which we approach a text, and a "passing theory," which must be constructed in order to understand each individual text. E. D. Hirsch develops a similar idea as a "corrigible schemata." In either case, interpretation is not purely conventional but must respond creatively to each new text in order to grasp its specific intent. See Davidson, *Inquiries,* 265–280, and "A Nice Derangement of Epitaphs," in LePore, ed., *Truth and Interpretation,* 433–446; E. D. Hirsch, *The Aims of Interpretation* (Chicago: University of Chicago Press, 1976), 30–35. See also Thomas Kent, "Interpretation and Triangulation: A Davidsonian Critique of Reader-Oriented Literary Theory," in *Literary Theory after Davidson,* ed. Reed Way Dasenbrock (University Park: Pennsylvania State University Press, 1993), 37–58, and Dasenbrock, "Do We Write the Text We Read?" in Dasenbrock, ed., *Literary Theory after Davidson,* 18–36; Thomas Greene, *The Vulnerable Text* (New York: Columbia University Press, 1986), 159–174. On the variegated nature of background beliefs, see Searle, *Intentionality,* 141–159, and Harris, *Against Relativism,* 27–50, 123–172.

60. The following account is, in varying degrees, drawn from Hirsch, *Aims,* and *Validity in Interpretation* (New Haven: Yale University Press, 1967); P. D. Juhl, *Interpretation* (Princeton: Princeton University Press, 1980); Emilio Betti, "Hermeneutics as the General Methodology of the *Geisteswissenschaften,*" in *Contemporary Hermeneutics,* ed. Josef Bleicher (New York: Routledge, 1980), 51–94; Gary Iseminger, "An Intentional Demonstration?" in *Intention and Interpretation,* ed. Gary Iseminger (Philadelphia: Temple University Press, 1992); Knapp and Michaels, "Against Theory," "Reply to George Wilson," "A Reply to Our Critics," "Against Theory 2: Hermeneutics and Deconstruction," *Critical Inquiry* 14 (1987): 49, and "Intention, Identity, and the Constitution: A Response to David Hoy," in Leyh, ed., *Legal Hermeneutics,* 187–199; Walter Benn Michaels, "The Fate of the Constitution," *Texas Law Review* 61 (1982): 765, "Response to Perry and Simon," *Southern California Law Review* 58 (1985): 673, and "Against Formalism: The Autonomous Text in Legal and Literary Interpretation," *Poetics Today* 1 (1979): 23. It should be noted at the outset that the argument for

the identity of the text and its original meaning is an ontological claim, not simply a normative contention that the text should be read as if it meant what was originally intended. The latter is Hirsch's claim, but he is wrong in asserting that the text can have determinate meaning only if it is read as having its intended meaning (as Fish demonstrates), and his claims for authorial ownership are compelling only in some institutional contexts (though law is one).

61. Knapp and Michaels, "Against Theory," 727.

62. In Gricean language, the marks would shift from being non-natural to natural signs. As the former, we can interpret them for an agent's meaningful communication. As the latter, we can only explain them in order to create meaning ourselves out of the natural order. See Paul Grice, *Studies in the Ways of Words* (Cambridge: Harvard University Press, 1989), 213–223.

63. Always assuming, of course, that there is no Author who communicates to us through such natural objects as waves and stars.

64. Iseminger, "Intentional," 88–89; George Dickie makes a similar point, using a more conventional example of a computer generating random character sequences to point to the "semantic autonomy" of texts ("Meaning and Intention," *Genre* 1 [1968]: 183).

65. Knapp and Michaels, "Against Theory 2," 57.

66. Iseminger, "Intentional," 90. Deconstructionists revel in precisely this variety of convention-generated meaning; see, e.g., J. Hillis Miller, "The Critic as Host," in *Modern Criticism and Theory,* ed. David Lodge (New York: Longman, 1988), 278–285.

67. In a British case, uttering "let him have it" resulted in a policeman being shot, rather, than as the utterer later maintained he intended, the shooter surrendering the gun to the officer. The utterance is conventionally ambiguous, but it is clearly of significance what the correct interpretation is, and that is what the utterer actually intended. M. J. Trow, *Let Him Have It, Chris* (London: Grafton, 1992).

68. This is not to say that the shouter could not be held responsible for the effects of his actions. Though he may not have intended to trigger such a linguistic convention, he certainly accidentally did and thus his intentional action had unforeseen, though foreseeable, consequences for which he may be held responsible. Similarly, shooting a gun in the air in celebration may result in a death from the falling bullet, but we would easily distinguish between the action's intent, or celebratory meaning, and its effect. See also chapter 6 on the distinction between motive and meaning.

69. In his recent work, Perry correctly sees the text as communication, but he does not carry the analysis far enough and continues to imagine the possibility that "communication" can exist in which the authors do not seek to control textual meaning (*Constitution in the Courts,* 50, 30–37). David Lyons, on the other hand, thinks interpretation can be separated from communication. For him, the law has a different function from "those of literature and personal communications," and therefore he finds literary theories of interpretation implausible in the context of "an authoritative public text" that is coercive and thus "requires justification." The concern is misplaced, however. Not only is originalism deeply connected with a concern for justification, but to identify legal "interpretation" with legal justification is to erase the reality of interpretation and the written law. A judge primarily concerned with justifying the effects of governmental action, as opposed to applying the law, would make no reference to existing law at all but would refer directly to the benefits of a given governmental action. Such judicial action would not be interpretive (concerned with what the law is) but legislative (concerned with what the law should be);

see Lyons, *Moral Aspects of Legal Theory* (New York: Cambridge University Press, 1993), 145–146.

70. While adhering to this argument, Knapp and Michaels nonetheless conclude a recent essay with the admonition that a judge, finding that the framers meant different things by "equal," "would have to decide which of the texts produced by the framers counted as the Fourteenth Amendment" ("Intention, Identity, and the Constitution," 199 n.15). As written, this claim is confusing. Either all the alleged "framers" are not actually framers (and thus the judge must discover which framers "count," and thus which text counts), or all the framers count and the text is legally meaningless, entitling the judge to do nothing. For example, some southern statements as to the amendment's meaning may be discounted as not representing the majority that authored the amendment (as the anti-Federalists would be relative to the original document), which may even include nearly all southerners if the amendment is seen as a wartime northern imposition upon the South and not a properly ratified amendment at all. See, e.g., Bruce Ackerman, "The Storrs Lectures: Discovering the Constitution," *Yale Law Journal* 93 (1984): 1065–1069, and "Constitutional Politics/Constitutional Law," *Yale Law Journal* 99 (1989): 500–507.

71. Thus, Oliver Wendell Holmes thought contracts should be interpreted as if from a "normal speaker" in recognition of the fact that contracts between "two adversaries" could be voided simply by the bad will of one party in offering unverifiable evidence of an abnormal intent. Nonetheless, he recognized that "we let in evidence of intention not to help out what theory recognizes as uncertainty of speech, and to read what the writer meant into what he has tried but failed to say, but, recognizing that he has spoken with theoretic certainty, we inquire what he meant in order to find out what he said" (*Collected Legal Papers,* ed. Harold J. Laski [Gloucester, MA: Peter Smith, 1952], 205). Similarly, an originalist constitutional interpretation should exclude private expressions of meaning that contradict public expressions, not simply because of issues of verifiability and sincerity but because the Constitution is a public document, ratified by the people. Though Holmes may be justified in laying down strong conventions to avoid difficult judgments about intent in a multitude of poorly documented commercial contracts, such interpretive limitations would be unwarranted in dealing with the Constitution. See also Michaels, "Against Formalism."

72. This problem blurs the boundary between motive and intent. The student's motive was to pass the test, convey knowledge to the teacher, use a verb in pluperfect form, and so on, but his intent in the utterance was the expression of the passage in the foreign language in the correct form. See also Francis Lieber, *Legal and Constitutional Hermeneutics* (Boston: Charles C. Little and James Brown, 1839), 22.

73. Note that as with all explanations, this one may or may not be correct. That is, the author may not simply be rephrasing his original text in order to convey the same intent but be replacing the text with another in order to express a new intent. The author is not privileged in interpreting the original text, as the author too may be wrong, whether by forgetfulness or deceitfulness. Contrast this case with the student from the first case, who may protest his grade by proclaiming that the correct translation was "what I meant!" or the case of the persecuted Jesuit who denied that he was a priest, only later to amend that he meant "a priest of Apollo." See Anthony Grafton, "The Soul's Entrepreneurs," *New York Review of Books* (3 March 1994): 36. Cf. John Keane, "More Theses on the Philosophy of History," in *Meaning and Context,* ed. James Tully (Princeton: Princeton University Press, 1988), 206–207, and Schauer, "Essay," 140.

74. The power of the dialogues is that when the Athenians protest, "That's not what I meant, Socrates; you twist my words," we know that indeed that is exactly what they meant and Socrates has exposed the roots of their words. The Athenians wilt in the face of Socrates' assault, not because he has twisted their words to contradict their intent but because he has shown that the intent embedded in their words contradicts their motives or other intentions. Cf. Stanley Cavell, *Must We Mean What We Say?* (New York: Cambridge University Press, 1976), 39–40.

75. Cavell correctly notes that learning the implications of words is part of learning a language, but it does not follow that every use of those words conveys all those implications. As deconstructionists note, the implications of words can often be contradictory. As I shall argue, the speaker's intent singles out some of those diverse implications over others. Under Cavell's reading, for example, the word "paranoid" is necessarily theory-laden and carries the full implications of its surrounding theory, and yet the word has been co-opted by normal speakers who use it with much more limited intentions, with little if any communicative difficulty. See ibid., 11–12.

76. "There's glory for you!"

   "I don't know what you mean by 'glory,'" Alice said.

   Humpty Dumpty smiled contemptuously. "Of course you don't—till I tell you. I meant 'There's a nice knock-down argument for you!'"

   "But 'glory' doesn't mean 'a nice knock-down argument,'" Alice objected.

   "When *I* use a word," Humpty Dumpty said, in rather a scornful tone, "it means just what I choose it to mean—neither more nor less."

   "The question is," said Alice," whether you *can* make words mean so many different things."

   "The question is," said Humpty Dumpty, "which is to be master—that's all."
(Lewis Carroll, *Alice in Wonderland and Other Favorites* [New York: Washington Square Press, 1960], 190). Avoiding charges of Humpty-Dumptyism is a recurrent exercise in the intentionalist literature.

77. Ironically, Wittgenstein could now say "bububu" and mean "if it doesn't rain I shall go for a walk," just as Humpty Dumpty could now use "glory" to mean "there's a nice knock-down argument." Since signifiers are arbitrary, they can be changed with a relative degree of freedom, but such changes must be discoverable. Similarly, mathematical and logical operations routinely begin by defining terms in accord with individual intent ("Let x be the price of apples"). As long as this momentary convention is consistently followed, or explicitly amended, textual meaning clearly follows intent (Wittgenstein, *Philosophical Investigations*, 18).

78. Saussure, *Course*, 118 (emphasis in original).

79. The binary logic used by computers operates in this manner. "Computer language" is completely defined in terms of on and not-on, but such a system would remain meaningless without external references provided and defined by the computer programmer. See also Holloway, "Language," 75–76.

80. Richard Ellis, *Against Deconstruction* (Princeton: Princeton University Press, 1989), 46–50; E. D. Hirsch, "Derrida's Axioms," *London Review of Books* (21 July–3 August 1983), 17; and Eric Wanner and Lila Gleitman, eds., *Language Acquisition* (New York: Cambridge University Press, 1982).

81. Fish, *Doing What Comes Naturally*, 317–321, and Ricoeur, *Hermeneutics*, 216–218.

82. Ricoeur, *Hermeneutics*, 154, 160–161.

83. Hirsch, "Derrida's Axioms"; Searle, "World Turned Upside Down"; Ellis, *Against Deconstruction*, 6–7, and Watts, "Bottom's Children," 29.

84. Derrida, *Grammatology*, 65, and *Margins of Philosophy* (Chicago: University of Chicago Press, 1982), 13. In fact, Derrida accuses structuralism of surreptitiously importing a positive element, presumably intent, in order to fix the play of references (*Writing and Difference* [Chicago: University of Chicago Press, 1978] 24–26). For Derrida, presence can be found only in the cry of a baby, which is infinite in its expression and meaning since it is undifferentiated linguistically and expresses a conceptually undifferentiated desire and thus does not refer to anything outside itself (*Grammatology*, 247–248).

85. Derrida, *Grammatology*, 158–159, and Fish, *Doing What Comes Naturally*, 44–47. Fish incorrectly finds this element, which is consistent with his own theory, to be the whole of Derrida's claim, ignoring the latter's debt to structuralist linguistics.

86. The later Wittgenstein is a prominent example. See Richard Ellis, "Wittgensteinian Thinking in the Theory of Criticism," *New Literary History* 12 (1981): 437, and *Against Deconstruction*. Even Madison, 200 years ago, recognized that words were a "cloudy medium" for communicating ideas, hardly capable of providing unmediated access to the origins of texts, and yet he still relied upon a written constitution. See Hamilton et al., *Federalist Papers*, No. 37, 229.

87. "In a kind of autonomous overassemblage of meanings, . . . speaking frightens me because, by never saying enough, I also say too much"(Derrida, *Writing and Difference*, 9). "The instituted trace cannot be thought without thinking the retention of difference within a structure of reference where difference appears *as such* and thus permits a certain liberty of variations among the full terms" (Derrida, *Grammatology*, 46–47).

88. Deconstructionists differ somewhat as to whether such traces actually alternate among innumerable conventions, as Culler and Fish would have it, or simultaneously reflect them all, as Miller and sometimes Derrida suggest. The former method implies a greater stability of meaning, but both are equally flawed.

89. The word "fire," for instance, takes on different meanings in different situations, and the deconstructionist would take all these meanings as simultaneously controlling rather than recognizing that a single word, though having only one potentially complex meaning at a time, may be used to express multiple meanings at different times. It is an empirical difficulty to discover whether someone meant "Shoot!" or "Run!" when yelling "Fire!" in a theater, but the mere fact that the exclamation is often used to mean either one does not logically prevent it from meaning only one in this case. The presence of an actual fire in the back row is not an extraneous fact in interpreting the statement.

90. Davidson, "A Nice Derangement," and *Inquiries*, 265–280; Knapp and Michaels, "Against Theory 2"; and P. F. Strawson, "Intention and Convention in Speech Acts," *Philosophical Review* 73 (1964): 439.

91. John Searle, "Reiterating the Differences: A Reply to Derrida," *Glyph* 1 (1977): 198.

92. Further, the suspension of meaning, as potential meanings are examined and intertextual references are taken into account, is at most an analytical concept, not a temporal one, as deconstructionists suggest. Meaning is not actually deferred and the reader frozen in *aporia*, for the context establishes these references simultaneously, both positively including some meanings and negatively excluding others. See Ellis, *Against Deconstruction*, 55–56.

93. Gadamer, *Truth and Method*, 99, 148, 200–207, 296, 340–344, 374, 390–395; Cf. Hoy's defense of Gadamer in David Couzens Hoy, *The Critical Circle* (Berkeley: University of California Press, 1982), 50, 68–72.

94. Davidson, "Nice Derangement," and *Inquiries*, 265–280; Hirsch, *Aims*, 32–34; Greene, *Text*, 168–172.

95. Roy Bhaskar, *The Possibility of Naturalism* (Atlantic Highlands, NJ: Humanities Press, 1979), 200. See also Hirsch, *Validity*, 245–264; Cf. Gadamer, *Truth and Method*, 17, 97–99, 148, 161–167, 268–269, 296–306. Though Gadamer clearly does not intend this result, his philosophical assumptions undercut his interpretive hope. If historical texts are known only through interpretive traditions, as Gadamer contends, then what is known is the tradition, not the text. There is no place within such a system for a genuine dialogue with the author but only with the tradition. To the extent that Gadamer retains his assumptions, he is forced either to admit all interpreters into the ranks of "originalists" as they are all products of the same ongoing interpretive context, or to abandon claims to be locating any particular intent at all. In either case, the expected "fusion" gives way to one side or the other; and Gadamer, like other strong contextualists, has no theoretical base for distinguishing between different forms of interpretive evidence. For the former option, see David Couzens Hoy, "The Hermeneutical Critique of the Originalism/Non-originalism Distinction," *Northern Kentucky Law Review* 15 (1988): 479; for the risk of the latter, see the exchange between Gadamer and Derrida in Diane Michelfelder and Richard Palmer, eds., *Dialogue and Deconstruction* (Albany: State University of New York Press, 1989), 21–57, 103–113.

96. Of course, the intent must still be discovered. But again, this is an epistemological problem, not an ontological one. Gadamer is concerned with both, and his confusion on the latter problem leads to difficulties with the former.

97. See, e.g., Wolfgang Iser, "The Reading Process: A Phenomenological Approach," in *Reader-Response Criticism*, ed. Jane Tompkins (Baltimore: Johns Hopkins University Press, 1980), 50.

98. See, e.g., the application of the Fourth Amendment's search and seizure clause to wiretapping. Olmstead v. United States, 277 U.S. 438 (1928), esp. Butler's dissent.

99. See, e.g., the increased interpretation of the Bill of Rights in the twentieth century, the end of interpretation of the fugitive-slave clause, or the reduced significance of interpretation of clauses dealing with governance of territories.

100. By "consistent," I mean good-faith efforts employing the same interpretive standards. Such interpretations may "contradict" in that some interpretations may correct others, but such interpretive fluctuations do not affect the fixity of textual meaning. Further, there is no necessity that textual meaning be simple or unitary; thus a full interpretation may include numerous qualifiers, multilayered meanings, deliberate ambiguities, and so on. Cf. Morton J. Horwitz, "Foreword: The Constitution of Change: Legal Fundamentality Without Fundamentalism," *Harvard Law Review* 107 (1993): 30.

101. Hirsch, *Validity*, and "Meaning and Significance Reinterpreted," *Critical Inquiry* 11 (1984): 202. While correctly revising his earlier understanding of meaning to take into account instantiations of general meanings, in his later article Hirsch understates the degree to which Gadamer goes beyond such instantiations to posit a general meaning that changes through the process of instantiation.

102. Cf. Gadamer, *Truth and Method*, 390.

103. It is important to recognize that Gadamer is not concerned with a Popperian trial-and-error approach to a stable truth but sees a new truth at work in each application.

104. This is a crude metaphor for the purpose of providing a spatial model. I do not mean to imply that an art critic influenced by Gadamer would actually advocate taking brush

and paint to the Old Masters, but see James Beck, with Michael Daly, *Art Restoration* (London: J. Murray, 1993). Thomas Greene has illustrated the Gadamerian approach to editing texts through the practice of "modernizing" punctuation and spelling, a process that cuts modern readers off from the text by glossing over how it differs from us (*Text,* 159–168). It should be noted that a more moderate reading of Gadamer could indicate not that every painting, or text, is completely obscured and fragmented and in need of radical reworking but that many are plagued with only modest smudges in need of touching up. In fact, I am quite sympathetic to this more moderate reading, which does not have the strong anti-originalist implications as those arguments with which I am concerned here.

105. Of course, as noted, there are always certain background assumptions at work even at this level. One needs certain background information to identify any image as an image of anything at all, with a need to be reconstructed. A jigsaw puzzle is just a pile of paper without a prior understanding of the concept of a puzzle. Nonetheless, such basic assumptions operate at a different level from the more complex information necessary for such a computer, as the example conveys. One can recognize the fragments, but it takes a computer to fill in the image. The notion of an interpretive "tradition" can easily flatten out these distinctions.

106. This might be contrasted with a statute that merely required that the land be maintained in its pristine condition, which might require the eventual exclusion of foot traffic. Note that in either case, the appropriate environmental standard of "natural" or "pristine" would have to be defined in nineteenth-century terms. The twenty-first-century reading may be wrong, not only because it excludes nonvehicles but also because it requires an excessive degree of noninterference in order to qualify as a "natural" park.

107. And in part, such concerns derive from the strong contextualism of the idea of incommensurable conventions. Such considerations have been sufficiently discussed. For a similar response to historiographical theories of indeterminacy, see Mark Bevir, "The Errors of Linguistic Contextualism," *History and Theory* 31 (1992): 276.

108. H. White, *Tropics of Discourse,* 27–50, esp. 41–50.

109. See, e.g., Louis Mink, "The Autonomy of Historical Understanding," *History and Theory* 5 (1966): 24, and "Philosophical Analysis and Historical Understanding," *Review of Metaphysics* 21 (1968): 667; Quentin Skinner, "Meaning and Understanding in the History of Ideas," in Tully, ed., *Meaning and Context,* 29–67; R. G. Collingwood, *The Idea of History* (New York: Oxford University Press, 1956); C. Behan McCullagh, "Can Our Understanding of Old Texts Be Objective?" *History and Theory* 30 (1991): 302; and Golub, "Irony," 56–57.

110. "That dilemma rests on the disjunction that thought is either pure immediacy, in which case it is inextricably involved in the flow of consciousness, or pure mediation, in which case it is utterly detached from that flow. Actually it is both immediacy and mediation" (Collingwood, *Idea,* 300).

111. Similarly, life is experienced as possessing temporal hierarchies. We do not simply live moment by moment but divide time into self-contained units with recognizable, if indistinct, boundaries and goal-oriented significance. See David Carr, "Narrative and the Real World: An Argument for Continuity," *History and Theory* 25 (1986): 117, and "Review Essay: *Temps et Récit.* Tome I. By Paul Ricoeur," *History and Theory* 23 (1984): 357; Maurice Mandelbaum, "A Note on History as Narrative," *History and Theory* 6 (1967): 413.

112. Among these external referents are not simply actions themselves but also their significance and relations. See, e.g., William Dray, *On History and Philosophers of History* (New York: E. J. Brill, 1989), 131–163, and Searle, *Intentionality,* 112–140. The point is that mean-

ing is part of reality, not an element imposed from above by the observer. This does not require that the historian simply report the interpretations suggested by the participants; meaning is a real category and as such is subject to evaluation and judgment.

113. H. White, *Content of the Form*, 1–25.

114. Mandelbaum, "Note," 43–44.

115. For the purposes of constitutional interpretation, the founders' intentions are controlling. For other purposes, the meanings recognized by the participants may not be the only or even the most significant meaning, though the intentions of human agents are critical to understanding actions.

116. Donald Davidson, *Essays on Actions and Events* (New York: Oxford University Press, 1980), 3, and Searle, *Intentionality*, 112–140.

117. Searle, *Intentionality*, 79–111.

118. This distinction does not exclude the possibility of analyzing the unintended effects of intended human actions, but such accounts would seriously misrepresent reality if they did not include the intentions of those actions and distinguished between intentional action and intended consequences and those unintended effects. See also Collingwood, "Idea," 213.

119. See, e.g., Skinner, "Meaning and Understanding," "Motives, Intentions and the Interpretation of Texts," and " 'Social Meaning' and the Explanation of Social Action," in Tully, ed., *Meaning and Context*, 29–96, and "Hermeneutics and the Role of History," *New Literary History* 7 (1975): 209; Dunn, *Political Obligation*, 13–28, 81–111; J. G. A. Pocock, *Politics, Language and Time* (Chicago: University of Chicago Press, 1989), 3–41, and *Virtue, Commerce, and History* (New York: Cambridge University Press, 1985), 1–34; Peter Janssen, "Political Thought as Traditionary Action: The Critical Response to Skinner and Pocock," *History and Theory* 24 (1985): 115.

120. Handlin, *Truth*, 406.

121. Bevir, "Errors," 278–294. Speech-act theory originated with J. L. Austin, *How to Do Things with Words* (Cambridge: Harvard University Press, 1975). For a version relying on convention, see John Searle, *Speech Acts* (New York: Cambridge University Press, 1969); contrast Searle to Strawson, "Intention and Convention in Speech Acts."

122. John Gunnell, "Interpretation and the History of Political Theory: Apology and Epistemology," *American Political Science Review* 76 (1982): 326–327. "I simply cannot conceive of constructing an analysis of any issue in contemporary political theory around the affirmation or negation of anything which Locke says about political matters" (Dunn, *Political Thought of Locke*, x).

123. In fact, Pocock and especially Skinner have distanced themselves to some degree from their earlier strong contextualism; see Janssen, "Political Thought," 115. Compare Pocock, *Politics, Language and Time*, 3–41, with *Virtue, Commerce and History*, 1–34. Compare Skinner, "Conventions and the Understanding of Speech Acts," *Philosophical Quarterly* 20 (1970): 118, with "Analysis of Political Thought and Action," and "A Reply to My Critics," in Tully, ed., *Meaning and Context*, 106, 276. These moves are insufficient, however. Even Skinner, though abandoning claims that the context autonomously produces meaning, still holds the view that meaning requires conventions to be communicable (as an ontological, not an epistemological claim). This critique should be distinguished from Keith Graham's contention that an utterance may fit multiple conventions and thus exceed its intended meaning. Such claims make the same error as the indeterminacy theories already considered and like them flow from an excessively conventionalist notion of language. See Graham, "How

Do Illocutionary Descriptions Explain?" in Tully, ed., *Meaning and Context,* 152–153. Modification of speech-act historiography to fit with the originalist theories previously outlined also addresses the difficulty of taking into account the external effects of an utterance, which is an appropriate subject for historical study but is usually institutionally excluded from judicial constitutional interpretation. See Ian Shapiro, "Realism in the Study of Ideas," *History of Political Thought* 3 (1982): 535–578.

5. POPULAR SOVEREIGNTY AND ORIGINALISM

1. Cass Sunstein, *The Partial Constitution* (Cambridge: Harvard University Press, 1993), 100. Sunstein is arguing explicitly about "obedience to the Court," but his argument makes clear that his real target is the "decision to be bound by the Constitution itself" (100).

2. Paul Brest, "The Misconceived Quest for Original Understanding," *Boston University Law Review* 60 (1980): 226. An evaluation of Brest's statements is complicated somewhat by his acceptance of the then-common distinction between originalist interpretive and non-originalist, and therefore noninterpretive, methods of judicial decision making. Regardless of labels, however, it seems evident that Brest would demand that judicial practice be externally justified, relative to the Constitution. More recently, see "Symposium: Fidelity in Constitutional Theory," *Fordham Law Review* 65 (1997).

3. Stanley C. Brubaker has argued for a purely "internal perspective" because "we do not question whether the Constitution has authority, but inquire into the basis of that assumed authority in order to understand more clearly the Constitution's meaning." I am not so confident that such an examination can be so contained. His own subsequent arguments tend to indicate the positive value of maintaining constitutional authority. See his "Conserving the Constitution," *American Bar Foundation Research Journal* 1987 (1987): 274.

4. Alexander Hamilton, James Madison, and John Jay, *The Federalist Papers,* ed. Clinton Rossiter (New York: New American Library, 1961), No. 1, 33.

5. Marbury v. Madison, 5 U.S. (1 Cranch) 137, 176–177 (1803). See also Sylvia Snowiss, *Judicial Review and the Law of the Constitution* (New Haven: Yale University Press, 1990), and Robert N. Clinton, Marbury v. Madison *and Judicial Review* (Lawrence: University Press of Kansas, 1989).

6. Hamilton et al., *Federalist Papers,* No. 78, 467.

7. Robert H. Bork, "Neutral Principles and Some First Amendment Problems," *Indiana Law Journal* 47 (1971): 2, 3. See also Raoul Berger, *Death Penalties* (Cambridge: Harvard University Press, 1982), 66, and Henry P. Monaghan, "Our Perfect Constitution," *New York University Law Review* 56 (1981): 366. This also underlies originalist "rule of law" arguments that judges should be constrained to applying rules formulated legislatively/democratically. See, e.g., Lino A. Graglia, "Do Judges Have a Policy-Making Role in the American System of Government?" *Harvard Journal of Law and Public Policy* 17 (1994): 119, and Richard S. Kay, "Adherence to the Original Intentions in Constitutional Adjudication: Three Objections and Responses," *Northwestern University Law Review* 82 (1988): 288–292.

8. This is a specifically "originalist theory of popular sovereignty" in that I do not attempt to develop here a fully articulated and defended theory of popular sovereignty. Rather, the theory is to serve the narrow purpose of establishing the basis for judicial review based on an originalist interpretation of the Constitution, and in order to justify that position, it is sufficient to sketch out a somewhat more limited theory.

9. For the emergence of modern sovereignty, see F. H. Hinsley, *Sovereignty* (New York: Cambridge University Press, 1986), 99–101, 120–125; Quentin Skinner, *The Foundations of Modern Political Thought*, 2 vols. (New York: Cambridge University Press, 1978), 2:284–302; Nicholas Greenwood Onuf, "Sovereignty: Outline of a Conceptual History," *Alternatives* 16 (1991): 425; Harold J. Laski, *The Foundations of Sovereignty and Other Essays* (Rahway, NJ: Harcourt, Brace and Company, 1921), 1–29; and William John Antholis, "Liberal Democratic Theory and the Transformation of Sovereignty" (Ph.D. diss., Yale University, 1993), 44–107.

10. Jean Bodin, *Six Books of the Commonwealth*, ed. and trans. M. J. Tooley (London: Basil Blackwell, 1955), 7.

11. Ibid., 8, 18–19, 25.

12. Ibid., 109–127. Antholis argues that the "perpetual" aspect of sovereignty was critical to Bodin, for the bond between subject and sovereign was irrevocable. Although there is a "timeless logic of command and obedience" at work in Bodin, the actual maintenance of sovereign power is a constant effort and thus "perpetuity" is composed of discrete moments of power politics; cf. Antholis, "Liberal," 66–71.

13. Bodin, *Six Books*, 8, 5. See also Stephen Holmes, *Passions and Constraint* (Chicago: University of Chicago Press, 1995), 100–133.

14. "All the other attributes and rights of sovereignty are included in this power of making and unmaking law, so that strictly speaking this is the unique attribute of sovereign power" (Bodin, *Six Books*, 44).

15. Ibid., 197.

16. Ibid., 18–19; Onuf, "Sovereignty," 430; Bertrand de Jouvenel, *Sovereignty* (Chicago: University of Chicago Press, 1963), 29; Charles McIlwain, *Constitutionalism and the Changing World* (New York: Macmillan, 1939), 26–31. Cf. Laski, *Foundations*, 210.

17. Bodin, *Six Books*, 43, 130–131.

18. "For the prince cannot tie his own hands in this respect, nor take from his subjects the means of redress, supplication, and petition, notwithstanding the fact that all rules governing appeals and jurisdictions are matters of positive law, which we have shown does not bind the prince. . . . Were it otherwise, and the prince could acquit his subjects or his vassals from the obligation to submit their causes to him in the last instance, he would make of them sovereigns equal with himself" (ibid., 45, 46; see also 89–90). This point was particularly important in the medieval French context, in which courts were used both to check the king and to provide a hierarchy of king over lower feudal lords, as the decisions of the latter had to be submitted to the king's court. See Julian H. Franklin, *Jean Bodin and the Rise of Absolutist Theory* (New York: Cambridge University Press, 1973), 2, 21, 106.

19. Bodin, *Six Books*, 27–32, 89–90. See also Holmes, *Passions*, 103–120; McIlwain, *Constitutionalism*, 26; J. U. Lewis, "Jean Bodin's 'Logic of Sovereignty,' " *Political Studies* 16 (1968): 206; and J. H. Burns, "Sovereignty and Constitutional Law in Bodin," *Political Studies* 7 (1959): 174.

20. Thomas Hobbes, *De Cive or The Citizen* (New York: Appleton-Century-Crofts, 1949), 10, and Hobbes, *Leviathan* (New York: Viking Penguin, 1968), 82.

21. Cf. Antholis, "Liberal," 96.

22. Hobbes, *Leviathan*, 118–120, 134, 151–152, 183–186.

23. Ibid., 228 (emphasis omitted).

24. "This more than Consent, or Concord; it is a reall Unitie of them all, in one and the same Person" (ibid., 227).

25. Ibid., 217, 220.

26. Ibid., 228–229, 232–233. "A social system based on hedonism entails a political author-ity that can resist being used by particular interests as best suits them—an authority whose laws will be ukases from on high, not emanations of the social conflict" (de Jouvenel, *Sov-ereignty*, 243). The subject does not participate in the sovereignty as an active part of the governmental process but by embracing the universe of meaning that is the common-wealth. The individual authors the sovereign decision by accepting the "common Rule of Good and Evill" that the sovereign establishes (Hobbes, *Leviathan*, 120); see also William F. Harris II, *The Interpretable Constitution* (Baltimore: Johns Hopkins University Press, 1993), 46–96.

27. Hobbes, *Leviathan*, 186–190, 223–228; Carl Schmitt, *Political Theology* (Cambridge: MIT Press, 1985), 32–34. The operation of the Leviathan is comparable to a ouija board. The players are united only in their engagement in a common enterprise. The resulting message is intended by none and yet authored by all. The game is fertile in that the single common-ality, acceptance of the device, produces more, the messages resulting from the device.

28. Hobbes, *Leviathan*, 221, 242–243.

29. Ibid., 238–242.

30. Ibid., 120, 202, 232, 274, 285, 365, 381, 405.

31. Ibid., 236, 368, 372.

32. Antholis, "Liberal," 119; Ruth W. Grant, *John Locke's Liberalism* (Chicago: University of Chicago Press, 1987), 77.

33. Skinner, *Foundations*, 2:119–122; Julian H. Franklin, *John Locke and the Theory of Sov-ereignty* (New York: Cambridge University Press, 1978), 1–2; and Otto von Gierke, *The Development of Political Theory* (New York: Norton, 1939), 143–144. The theory of popular sovereignty was fully developed by Johannes Althusius in the early seventeenth century, combining Bodin's concept of sovereignty with the monarchomachi's theory of govern-ment agency and right of resistance. See Althusius, *The Politics of Johannes Althusius* (Boston: Beacon Press, 1964).

34. Franklin, *Locke*, 1–52; Margaret Atwood Judson, "Henry Parker and the Theory of Parliamentary Sovereignty," in *Essays in History and Political Theory in Honor of Charles Howard McIlwain*, ed. Carl Wittke (Cambridge: Harvard University Press, 1936), 138–167; Richard Ashcraft, *Revolutionary Politics and Locke's* Two Treatises of Government (Prince-ton: Princeton University Press, 1986), esp. 286–337; and Edmund S. Morgan, *Inventing the People* (New York: Norton, 1988), 55–121.

35. John Locke, *Two Treatises of Government*, ed. Peter Laslett (New York: Cambridge University Press, 1988), § 6, 176, and *An Essay Concerning Human Understanding*, ed. Peter H. Nidditch (New York: Oxford University Press, 1975), bk. 3, ch.9, §23, and 4, 19, 4.

36. Locke, *Two Treatises*, § 77, 124–126.

37. Of course, a trust is both empowering and limiting. See John Dunn, *Rethinking Mod-ern Political Theory* (New York: Cambridge University Press, 1985), 34–54.

38. Locke, *Two Treatises*, § 3, 27, 31–33, 46–50, 65, 78, 83. For a particularly strong view of the power of the political community in Locke, see Willmoore Kendall, *John Locke and the Doctrine of Majority-Rule* (Urbana: University of Illinois Press, 1965).

39. Bodin, *Six Books*, 43, 44, 45, 47, and Locke, *Two Treatises*, § 129, 146, 132, 242, 134. See also Grant, *Locke's Liberalism*, 78, and Antholis, "Rejecting Eternity: The Revolt Against Sovereignty," paper presented at annual meeting of the American Political Science Associ-ation, New York City, September 1–4, 1994, 33–34.

40. Locke, *Two Treatises,* § 98 (emphasis in original).

41. Ibid., § 132–134, 243.

42. Ibid., § 150. Locke does add the significant qualification of the delegation's duration, while the sovereign community extends infinitely into the future (§ 132, 121). Cf. Bodin, *Six Books,* 25; political power is limited only by natural law and the limits of obedience (28–32); Hobbes, *Leviathan,* 215, 223–224, 268–272, 298; Locke, *Two Treatises,* § 135, 223–225.

43. Locke, *Two Treatises,* § 150, 159; see, generally, Franklin, *Locke.*

44. "And thus the *Community* may be said in this respect to be *always the Supream Power,* but not as considered under any Form of Government, because this Power of the People can never take place till the Government be dissolved" (Locke, *Two Treatises,* § 149; see also 243). See also Ashcraft, *Revolutionary,* 286–337; Grant, *Locke's Liberalism,* 78; and Antholis, "Democratic Theory," 129–131. The inherited Whig view is represented by William Blackstone: "The power and jurisdiction of parliament . . . is so transcendent and absolute, that it cannot be confined, either for causes or persons, within any bounds . . . this being the place where that absolute despotic power, which must in all governments reside somewhere, is entrusted by the constitution of these kingdoms. . . . So long therefore as the English constitution lasts, we may venture to affirm, that the power of parliament is absolute and without control" (*Commentaries on the Laws of England,* [Chicago: University of Chicago Press, 1979], 1:156, 157).

45. Montesquieu, *The Spirit of the Laws,* trans. and ed. Anne M. Cohler et al. (New York: Cambridge University Press, 1989), 10, 18.

46. Ibid., 4–7.

47. Locke, *Two Treatises,* § 56–63.

48. Montesquieu, *Spirit,* 8 (emphasis omitted).

49. Ibid., 10.

50. Ibid., 22–23, 35. Montesquieu emphasizes that virtue is a function of feeling, not reason. This allows him to extend it to all parts of society, as everyone is capable of feeling even if some are less open to reason. It also poses a risk, however, for it recognizes that reason can lead to a separation of self-interest from the general interest (42–43).

51. Ibid., 156–166.

52. "In many writers [of the constitutionalist school] the theoretical acceptance of popular sovereignty only produces a crop of political maxims, in lieu of any real juristic interpretation" (Otto von Gierke, *Natural Law and the Theory of Society,* 2 vols. (New York: Cambridge University Press, 1934), 1:153). See also idem, *Political Theory,* 168.

53. Jean-Jacques Rousseau, *The First and Second Discourses* (New York: St. Martin's Press, 1964), 107–111, 116, 128, 151, and *On the Social Contract* (New York: St. Martin's Press, 1978), 46–47, 53, 56. See also Bertrand de Jouvenel, "Rousseau's Theory of the Forms of Government," in *Hobbes and Rousseau,* ed. Maurice Cranston and Richard S. Peters (Garden City, NY: Anchor Books, 1972), 484–497.

54. Rousseau, *Social Contract,* 53–54 (emphasis in original). The process may not be so "instant," however; Rousseau explains that a "legislator" may be necessary to found the republic in the first place—that is, to create a people out of a multitude (67–70). See also Judith N. Shklar, *Men and Citizens* (New York: Cambridge University Press, 1969), 160–161.

55. Rousseau, *Social Contract,* 59, 66, 78–79, 84–87.

56. Ibid., 109–112, 78–80. "If my private will had prevailed [in the voting], I would have done something other than what I wanted. It is then that I would not have been free. This presupposes, it is true, that all the characteristics of the general will are still in the majority.

When they cease to be, there is no longer any freedom regardless of the side one takes" (111). See also Rousseau's distinction between the sovereign general will and the corrupt "will of all" (61). Contrast this conception of voting with Hobbes and Locke, who represent it as a mechanical process in which the "body" of the legislature follows the greater "weight" of the majority. The minority is pulled along in that model, not embraced within. See Locke, *Two Treatises*, § 96, and Hobbes, *Leviathan*, 242–243, 276–277.

57. This element of assertion over opposition, both internal and external, indicates one reason why Rousseau speaks in terms of a sovereign will as opposed to a moral rule, natural law, or mere consent. See also Shklar, *Men*, 184–197; John Plamenatz, "Ce Qui Ne Signifie Autre Chose Sinon Qu'on Le Forcera D'être Libre," in Cranston and Peters, eds., *Hobbes and Rousseau*, 321–323, 330–331; and Jacques Derrida, *Of Grammatology* (Baltimore: Johns Hopkins University Press, 1976), 297–302. Cf. Schmitt, *Political Theology*, 48–49, and Patrick Riley, *Will and Political Legitimacy* (Cambridge: Harvard University Press, 1982), 98–124.

58. Rousseau, *Social Contract*, 106, 96, 100–103, 59–64, 82, 108–109.

59. As will become evident, there are similarities between my arguments in this chapter and those of Bruce Ackerman. Ackerman has been criticized for his quite limited effort to ground his theory of "dualist democracy" in the founding, which he discusses primarily through consideration of a few passages in *The Federalist Papers*. Such a critique is misguided, however—certainly for my work, and I think for Ackerman's. Those aspects of the *Federalist* are of interest for their ability to illustrate a dualist theory and to demonstrate that dualism is not foreign to the American tradition. The grounding of the theory is in the normative value of consensual government, not in its traditionalist roots in the authority of Madison. Ackerman is misguided if he is pursuing a purely interpretive approach to our constitutional tradition but would be correct in arguing for a "connected" normative theory. See Ackerman, *We the People* (Cambridge: Harvard University Press, 1991), 165–199, 295–314. Cf. Suzanna Sherry, "The Ghost of Liberalism Past," *Harvard Law Review* 105 (1992): 926–928, and Holmes, *Passions*, 304 n.80.

60. In 1774 James Wilson introduced his pamphlet on parliamentary authority over colonial taxation with the claim that "he entered upon them with a view and expectation of being able to trace some constitutional line between those cases in which we ought, and those in which we ought not, to acknowledge the power of parliament over us. In the prosecution of his inquiries, he became fully convinced that such a line does not exist; and that there can be no medium between acknowledging and denying that power in *all* cases" ("Considerations on the Nature and Extent of the Legislative Authority of the British Parliament," *Works of James Wilson*, ed. Robert Green McCloskey, 2 vols. [Cambridge: Harvard University Press, 1967], 2:721). See also Bernard Bailyn, *The Ideological Origins of the American Revolution* (Cambridge: Harvard University Press, 1967); 198–229; Jack P. Greene, *Peripheries and Center* (Athens: University of Georgia Press, 1986), 203–205; and John Philip Reid, *Constitutional History of the American Revolution*, 4 vols. (Madison: University of Wisconsin Press, 1987–1993), 3:75–76.

61. See, e.g., Wilson, *Works*, 1:174, 186, 293, 300; Hamilton et al., *Federalist Papers*, No. 78, 465–472; and Marbury v. Madison, 5 U.S. (1 Cranch) 137 (1803). See also Gordon S. Wood, *The Creation of the American Republic, 1776–1778* (New York: Norton, 1969), 446–449, 456; Edmund S. Morgan, *Inventing the People* (New York: Norton, 1988), 260–261; and Donald S. Lutz, *Popular Consent and Popular Control* (Baton Rouge: Louisiana State University Press, 1980), 38, 98.

62. Ashcraft, *Revolutionary,* 286–337; Franklin, *Locke;* Morgan, *Inventing,* 55–121; and Lutz, *Popular Consent,* 72.

63. Thomas Jefferson, "Notes on the State of Virginia," in *The Writings of Thomas Jefferson,* ed. H. A. Washington, 9 vols. (New York: John C. Riker, 1857), 8:363–367, 371–372. See also Merrill D. Peterson, "Thomas Jefferson, the Founders, and Constitutional Change," in *The American Founding,* ed. J. Jackson Barlow, Leonard W. Levy, and Ken Masugi (New York: Greenwood Press, 1988), 275–293, and Hannah Arendt, *On Revolution* (New York: Viking Penguin, 1965), 234–235.

64. Hamilton et al., *Federalist Papers,* No. 10, 81, 82; No. 39, 241; No. 49, 313–314, 315, and Michael Lienesch, *New Order of the Ages* (Princeton: Princeton University Press, 1988), 134. Thus, Madison discussed previous state exercises in constitution making not as acts of popular politics but as tentative experiments attempting to establish the best and therefore last constitution (*Federalist Papers,* No. 47, 307). See also James Madison, *The Writings of James Madison,* ed. Gaillard Hunt, 9 vols. (New York: G. P. Putnam's Sons, 1900–1910), 5:271–272, and *The Papers of James Madison,* ed. Charles Hobson and Robert Rutland, 18 vols. to date (Charlottesville: University Press of Virginia, 1962–), 13:18–26. This larger theoretical goal did not prevent Publius from tactically admitting imperfection in the document. Despite current imperfections, which might suggest the need for and possibility of future change, Publius emphasized that the text was the best possible—current imperfections were to be taken as another sign of the uniqueness of the founding, for even it could not achieve perfection but could only come as close as humanly possible. See David F. Epstein, *The Political Theory of* The Federalist (Chicago: University of Chicago Press, 1984), 19–23.

65. Hamilton et al., *Federalist Papers,* No. 39, 245; No. 49, 314, 315. Similarly, Hamilton did not hesitate to refer to the various American governments as sovereign (see, e.g., No. 9, 76; No. 81, 487). Cf. Madison, *Writings,* 6:348–349. Madison's emphatic placement of the power of constitutional interpretation in the government and not in the people was particularly instructive not only in light of Rousseau's comments on periodic conventions to check government but also of Bishop Hoadly's widely reported remark that "whoever hath an absolute authority to interpret any written or spoken laws, it is he who is truly the lawgiver, to all intents and purposes, and not that person who first wrote or spoke them" (*The Works of Benjamin Hoadly,* 3 vols. (London: W. Boyer and J. Nichols, 1773), 2:404.

66. Lutz, *Popular Consent,* 41; Antholis, "Democratic Theory," 315–318; Lienesch, *New Order,* 138–183; Sheldon Wolin, *The Presence of the Past* (Baltimore: Johns Hopkins University Press, 1989), 82–99; and Joshua Miller, "The Ghostly Body Politic: *The Federalist Papers* and Popular Sovereignty," *Political Theory* 16 (1988): 99.

67. McCulloch v. Maryland, 17 U.S. (4 Wheat.) 316, 415 (1819). Contrast earlier Federalists, who expected the Constitution to "stand the test of ages" because of the correctness of its principles, not the looseness of its restrictions. See Lienesch, *New Order,* 135.

68. Antholis, "Democratic Theory," 20–21, and Onuf, "Sovereignty."

69. Rousseau, *Social Contract,* 102, and A. V. Dicey, *Introduction to the Study of the Law of the Constitution* (London: Macmillan, 1915), 145.

70. Wilson, *Works,* 1:77–78, 2:770; Antholis, "Democratic Theory," 320–322; and Garry Wills, "James Wilson's New Meaning for Sovereignty," in *Conceptual Change and the Constitution,* ed. J. G. A. Pocock and Terence Ball (Lawrence: University Press of Kansas, 1988), 99–106.

71. In arguing for the popular ratification of a new state constitution, Thomas Tucker contended that it should be constructed "on the firm and proper foundation of the express consent of the people" (quoted in Wood, *Creation*, 281). Although not literally from the state of nature, the popular creation of constitutions opens government authority to question and holds government officials responsible to the deliberate consideration of the people, which has always been the goal of the theories of popular sovereignty.

72. As I have throughout this book, I limit myself here to consideration of the American federal Constitution. Other constitutions could be analyzed in similar terms but would require more particular consideration. Donald Lutz has demonstrated that there is an inverse relationship between constitutional amendability and interpretive flexibility. If constitution making is removed as an option, then judicial revision tends to become the substitute. See Lutz, "Toward a Theory of Constitutional Amendment," in *Responding to Imperfection*, ed. Sanford Levinson (Princeton: Princeton University Press, 1995).

73. I should emphasize that my concern is specifically with the authority of and correct interpretive approach to the Constitution. My consideration of consensual government, therefore, occurs within that context. It may be possible that the notion of tacit consent retains some usefulness in political theory more broadly, even though it is not a useful concept for approaching constitutional authority.

74. This is the approach of the democratic theorists considered in chapter 2, although they differ among themselves as to how those voting mechanisms are to be maintained. See, e.g., John Ely, *Democracy and Distrust* (Cambridge: Harvard University Press, 1980); James Gardner, "The Positivist Foundations of Originalism: An Account and Critique," *Boston University Law Review* 71 (1991): 1; and Sunstein, *Partial*. It is also adopted by others, however, including neopragmatists.

75. Although underlying most current rights-foundationalist theories, the work of Samuel Freeman is an exemplary case of this style of argument; see "Original Meaning, Democratic Interpretation, and the Constitution," *Philosophy and Public Affairs* 21 (1992): 3, and "Constitutional Democracy and the Legitimacy of Judicial Review," *Law and Philosophy* 9 (1990–1991): 327.

76. Tacit consent can also be used to interpret specifically political but antigovernment activities as nonetheless accepting government authority; thus, the continued residence of a cell of revolutionaries could be taken as implying tacit consent, even as the revolutionaries actively and consciously rejected government authority. See, e.g., John P. Plamenatz, *Consent, Freedom and Political Obligation* (New York: Oxford University Press, 1968), 6–8.

77. See, e.g., Gardner, "Foundations," 15–20. Tacit consent was the basis for British legislative sovereignty; Reid, *Revolution*, 3:108–110. See also Paul W. Kahn, *Legitimacy and History* (New Haven: Yale University Press, 1992), 177.

78. Declining voter turnout could, therefore, be taken as a problem for tacit constitutional authority, since by opting out of the political system, nonvoters are no longer engaging in an activity that demonstrates their acceptance of its results. On the other hand, refusal to vote could be taken as the ultimate sign of acquiescence, since a desire for change would motivate a citizen to go to the polls, whereas agreement with the present system provides little rationale for expending the resources involved in actually voting.

79. Plamenatz, *Consent*, 170–171.

80. See also A. John Simmons, *On the Edge of Anarchy* (Princeton: Princeton University Press, 1993), 218–224, and Harry Beran, *The Consent Theory of Political Obligation* (New York: Croom Helm, 1987), 71–77. Moreover, elections fail to accommodate the need to sep-

arate a policy preference from a constitutional will. In the context of an immediate policy dispute, partisans may ignore constitutional restrictions that they would otherwise support. Deliberate constitutional change requires a separation between policy making and constitution making, which can be achieved through temporal distance or by the physical separation of the two kinds of political power. See, e.g., Jon Elster, *Ulysses and the Sirens* (New York: Cambridge University Press, 1984), 95.

81. Such authority can be either implicit or explicit. In the former, some issues are simply removed from the constitutional domain and regarded as matters of policy; see, e.g., Lino Graglia, " 'Interpreting' the Constitution: Posner on Bork," *Stanford Law Review* 44 (1992): 1026–1028. In the latter, the Constitution is accepted as confining, but its meaning may be changed to accommodate current preferences; see, e.g., Gardner, "Foundations," 40–45.

82. I purposely leave out such constitutional features as bicameralism and separation of powers. Although such elements of gridlock can prevent the immediate gratification of the popular will, I do not think that they can be regarded as serious impediments to the expression of the more durable popular will meant to be captured in constitutional meaning.

83. Moreover, government policy making breeds a partisan division inconsistent with the requirements of authoritative sovereignty. The point is not simply that individuals disagree about policy but that such disagreements are ultimately concluded, not removed, with a policy outcome. Decision procedures, such as majority voting, are designed in a policy context to impose a resolution on a conflict over the objections of dissenters. Policy disputes, therefore, involve factions that are persistent, even if defeated. See also Epstein, *Political Theory,* 133–136, 195–196, and Ackerman, *We the People,* 184, 191–192, 236–240, 255, 262–263.

84. Frankfurter's characterization of the Constitution as "not a document but a stream of history" eliminates that distance, reducing the Constitution to a purely descriptive component of reflecting whatever government officials actually do. Quoted in Sanford Levinson, *Constitutional Faith* (Princeton: Princeton University Press, 1988), 33. See also Harris, *Interpretable,* 76–78.

85. Freeman, "Original Meaning," 35.

86. The point extends to rights-oriented theories as well (see chap. 2). Amy Gutmann has contended that in cases where the Constitution is specific, and contrary to the preferred theory of justice, "the argument from tradition holds sway against judicial" activism in the interest of the preferred theory. Gutmann, like others, does not indicate why "tradition" in this sense has any moral value. A theory of popular sovereignty indicates why the text is to be obeyed, even when it contradicts current theories of justice. This is not simply a function of a judicial habit of deference to the text but of the positive value of popular sovereignty to defining the powers and limits of government. See Gutmann, "How Liberal Is Democracy?" in *Liberalism Reconsidered,* ed. Douglas MacLean and Claudia Mills (Totowa, NJ: Rowman and Allanheld, 1983), 45.

87. "But the opinions of a majority cannot be known, but in an Assembly of the whole society; and no *part* of the society has a right to decide upon a measure which equally affects the *whole,* without a consultation with the whole, to hear their arguments and objections. . . . I mean the *opinions* of the *whole society,* formed on the *information* and *debates* of the *whole society.* These opinions can be formed no where but in a Convention of the *whole State,* or of their *Representatives*" (Noah Webster, *A Collection of Essays and Fugitiv Writings* [Boston: I. Thomas and E. T. Andrews, 1790], 56 [emphasis in original]; see also

74). Webster thought the state legislature could achieve this as well as a special convention, but his point about the need for assemblies is general. See also Benjamin Barber, *The Conquest of Politics* (Princeton: Princeton University Press, 1988), esp. 193–211.

88. Such Newtonian mechanical metaphors have been out of favor for most of this century. A Darwinian organic metaphor has been preferred, not incidentally because it buries consent in the constitutional roots while giving current officials control over the living growth of government. One can recognize that constitutional government develops over time, however, while still requiring consent before alien organisms are grafted to the original.

89. Elster, *Ulysses,* 94, 95. Elster does not emphasize the capacity for positive willing, as I do. His first convention is truly accidental, in that it could not readily create the conditions for its own emergence. For simplicity, I lay aside the later textual amendments, which were of course also expressions of consent.

90. McCulloch v. Maryland, 17 U.S. (4 Wheaton) 316, 401 (1819). The New Deal Court completed the reversal, effectively abandoning nonrights-based limits on congressional power. See also Howard Gillman, "The Collapse of Constitutional Originalism and the Rise of the Notion of the 'Living Constitution' in the Course of American State-Building," *Studies in American Political Development* 11 (1997): 191. Compared to the later Court, however, Marshall required a relatively strong means-end nexus in construing federal implied powers.

91. McCulloch, 405.

92. Ackerman, *We the People,* 264. Ackerman's error in this regard is that he is too accommodating to governmental sovereignty. When challenged by the Constitution, his government officials need not point to it but only to their electoral mandates—an ambiguous instrument always at hand. On the need for public justification for authority, see also Stephen Macedo, *Liberal Virtues* (New York: Oxford University Press, 1991), 39–78.

93. Although misconstruing its significance, Jacques Derrida is correct to emphasize that writing implies the absence of the author. The idea of law is meaningful only if the legislator is not currently present to apply his own will without mediation. See Derrida, *Grammatology,* 40–41, 110–112, 142, and *Writing and Difference* (Chicago: University of Chicago Press, 1978), 11–14.

94. See, e.g., Gardner, "Consent, Legitimacy and Elections: Implementing Popular Sovereignty Under the Lockean Constitution," *University of Pittsburgh Law Review* 52 (1990): 214–219.

95. "Just as the private will acts incessantly against the general will, so the government makes a continual effort against sovereignty . . . when the prince no longer administers the State in accordance with the laws and usurps the sovereign power. Then a remarkable change takes place, which is that not the government but the State shrinks. I mean that the large State dissolves and another is formed within it that is composed solely of the members of government and is no longer anything for the rest of the people except its master and tyrant" (Rousseau, *Social Contract,* 96, 97–98). See also de Jouvenel, "Rousseau's Theory."

96. See, e.g., "The Court has acted as a continuing constitutional convention, so to speak" (Arthur S. Miller, *Social Change and Fundamental Law* [Westport, CT: Greenwood Press, 1979], 349).

97. Webster, *Essays,* 54.

98. The power of constitutional amendment is a modification of this separation. Two observations should be made about this qualification. First, it is precisely that—a qualification on the power of sovereignty. The amendment process is not a resurrection of the

original sovereign power of creation but is only the exercise of a subsidiary power of amendment. The amendment power is exercised by virtue of the Constitution and therefore is limited by the original sovereign authority. The fully sovereign people could replace the entire Constitution, but the Article 5 procedures provide only a mechanism for modifying that basic structure. See Harris, *Interpretable*, 164–208. Second, Article 5 nonetheless carefully divides the power of amendment between the general and state governments. The effect is not only to ensure consensus but also to maintain a distinction between regular government and the sovereign power. No government can amend the Constitution, although it does allow thirty-nine governments (the general plus thirty-eight states) acting separately but in concert to do so. Bruce Ackerman's dualism is faulty in part because it erases this distinction, consolidating the amendment power within the hands of the same government agents who will administer policy under it. Ackerman labels this the "nationalization" of sovereignty; Rousseau would have called it the shrinking of sovereignty. See Ackerman, *We the People*, 266–294.

99. See, more generally, Wayne D. Moore, *Constitutional Rights and Powers of the People* (Princeton: Princeton University Press, 1996).

100. For Ackerman to designate the "Court to represent the *absent* People" is somewhat problematic for this reason (*We the People*, 264 [emphasis in original]). The "people" are not truly absent if they are represented, whether by a judge, a legislature, or a convention. The necessity for interpretation emerges when the *people* are not represented and only an expression of their *will* remains. Clarity on this point is necessary to maintain the paramount authority of the Constitution itself over all government agents. It is a short step from the claim that the Court represents the people to the claim that the Court is a continuing constitutional convention.

101. James Wilson, *Works,* 2:770.

102. See also Arendt, *On Revolution,* 157. "The American revolutionary insistence on the distinction between a republic and a democracy or majority rule hinges on the radical separation of law and power, with clearly recognized different origins, different legitimations, and different spheres of application" (166). See also Morgan, *Inventing,* 84–87.

103. This aspect of political life is captured in the fear of a child asking his parents, "What did you do during the revolution?" One can pick one's own "revolution," yet the embarrassment comes not from being on the wrong side but from not participating in a formative event of the society. Similarly, Woodstock evokes nostalgia in millions of people of a given age not because they love mud and Jimi Hendrix but because they must participate, even if only retroactively, in a defining moment of their generation. As Montesquieu observed, we *want* to be part of the sovereign. See also Epstein, *Political Theory,* 16; Arendt, *On Revolution,* 115–140, 253; and Ackerman, *We the People,* 236–240.

104. Thus, Sen. Arthur Vandenburg told Harry Truman that he would need to "scare the hell out of the American people" in order to win foreign aid appropriations for a political faction in Greece, diminishing the significance of claims of national security and the reality of popular deliberation. See Garry Wills, "The New Revolutionaries," *New York Review of Books* (10 August 1995): 54. See also Jeffrey K. Tulis, *The Rhetorical Presidency* (Princeton: Princeton University Press, 1987), 161–204.

105. Cf. Ackerman, *We the People,* 292, 310–311.

106. This is not to say that nothing can be done to enhance the influence of reason in public deliberations. The adoption of the convention device is an example of such an effort. But the judgment of the people cannot be measured against some external standard of

truth, found wanting, and then *laid aside as not legally binding.* The possibility of criticism and persuasion, however, is always open.

107. Don Herzog, "Democratic Credentials," *Ethics* 104 (1994): 469.

108. See also Wilson, *Works,* 2:771; Joseph de Maistre, "Study on Sovereignty," *The Works of Joseph de Maistre,* ed. Jack Lively (New York: Schocken Books, 1971), 103–108, and also idem, "Essay on the Generative Principle of Political Constitutions," 157. Herzog's point is more powerful when made against single-layer democrats. For such democrats, constraints on representative officials are equivalent to restraints on democracy itself. If democracy is held to be the primary political value, then it is difficult to justify any restraints on government by this method, although Amy Gutmann has made an interesting argument for the derivation of many liberal rights from democratic commitments (see "How Liberal," 27–36). Popular sovereignty need not attempt that derivation, however. The sovereign can constrain government for any reason, whether drawing from democratic, republican, liberal, or socialist theory. Judicial review and constitutional authority are grounded on democratic values, but the constraints imposed on government are substantive and independent of the value of democracy itself. The democratic decision has been made that "certain values are too important, or certain tools too dangerous, to be subject to the current control of the politicians" (Elster, *Ulysses,* 90). Like liberals, an advocate of popular sovereignty recognizes that "loss in the authoritative control of a representative assembly over legislation" is not equivalent to a reduction in democracy. The relevant choice is not between the judiciary and the legislature, but between the judiciary and the "people" deliberating on the Constitution (Gutmann, "How Liberal," 38–40, 43–44).

109. Robert Cover, "Violence and the Word," *Yale Law Journal* 95 (1986): 1601. Cover has also usefully analyzed the choice of judges to enforce an unjust law in the context of slavery; see *Justice Accused* (New Haven: Yale University Press, 1975).

110. Recall that the point of consideration is the basis of constitutional authority, not correct interpretive method. I put the issue in such stark terms because they highlight the basis of the disagreement. The disagreement here is not over the correct interpretation of given constitutional terms but over who should set the meaning of the fundamental law. Herzog, for example, explicitly rejects the idea that the people should set the meaning of the law and therefore implicitly accepts that judges may act against the known will of even the current sovereign people (see "Credentials," 470–472).

111. See also Jeremy Waldron, "A Right-Based Critique of Constitutional Rights," *Oxford Journal of Legal Studies* 13 (1993): 18.

112. For related, though somewhat different, arguments to this effect, see William N. Nelson, *On Justifying Democracy* (Boston: Routledge and Kegan Paul, 1980), 94–130.

113. Lon Fuller, *The Morality of Law* (New Haven: Yale University Press, 1969), 46–49, and Friedrich A. Hayek, *Law, Legislation and Liberty,* 3 vols. (Chicago: University of Chicago Press, 1973–1979), 1:72–144.

114. Hamilton et al., *Federalist Papers,* No. 49, 314–317, and Epstein, *Political Theory,* 133–136. Ultimately, as FDR realized, partisan action is much easier if government officials can simply act in the present rather than deliberate on and legislate for the future. See William E. Leuchtenburg, *The Supreme Court Reborn* (New York: Oxford University Press, 1995), 82–162.

115. Morgan, *Inventing,* 14–15, 91, 152; Kahn, *Legitimacy,* 52, 58–59, 177, 218; and Harris, *Interpretable,* 92.

116. Harris's excellent discussion of popular sovereignty and representation is the starting point for much of this section; see Harris, *Interpretable,* 46–113.

117. Morgan points out that the idea of popular sovereignty can never be made literally true. Various subsets of the population will always be excluded from the electorate; and as Rousseau noted, reliance on elections themselves stretches the meaning of self-governance. It is not deviations from the literal that undermine the legitimacy of the system, but deviations from the accepted abstraction. See Morgan, *Inventing,* 119, 152.

118. In fact, American representatives have substantial incentives to "represent" all their constituents. See, e.g., R. Douglas Arnold, *The Logic of Congressional Action* (New Haven: Yale University Press, 1990), 3–146; Bruce Cain, John Ferejohn, and Morris Fiorina, *The Personal Vote* (Cambridge: Harvard University Press, 1987), 27–117; and Richard F. Fenno Jr., *The Making of a Senator* (Washington, DC: CQ Press, 1989), 131–133.

119. See, e.g., George Lakoff and Mark Johnson, *Metaphors We Live By* (Chicago: University of Chicago Press, 1980); Raymond W. Gibbs Jr., "Process and Products in Making Sense of Tropes," in *Metaphor and Thought,* ed. Andrew Ortony (New York: Cambridge University Press, 1993), 252–276; and George Lakoff, "The Contemporary Theory of Metaphor," in Ortony, *Metaphor and Thought,* 202–251. For a suggestive discussion of the relation of metaphor to politics, see Lawrence C. Dodd, "Political Learning and Political Change: Understanding Development Across Time," in *The Dynamics of American Politics,* ed. Lawrence C. Dodd and Calvin Jillson (Boulder, CO: Westview Press, 1994), 331–364.

120. David Johnston, *The Rhetoric of Leviathan* (Princeton: Princeton University Press, 1986).

121. Harris, *Interpretable,* 118. For a somewhat different analysis of political authority based on a linguistic model, see Hanna Pitkin, "Obligation and Consent—II," *American Political Science Review* 60 (1966): 39, and *Wittgenstein and Justice* (Berkeley: University of California Press, 1972), 193–219.

122. See also Wills, "Wilson's New Meaning," 103.

123. Michael Lienesch has argued that the anti-Federalists perceived the founding primarily as a duty to protect the future rather than as a right to control it (see *New Order,* 148). This characterization can be adopted to describe the Constitution as a whole, partially against the wishes of many Federalists.

124. Note that this conception of the popular sovereign breaks completely from the organic conception emphasized by Paul Kahn. The organic conception, in which we are part of a timeless sovereign body, tends to be materially focused and therefore invites questions of blood relationship to the founders (our "Fathers") and the descriptive representativeness of the founders themselves. Given that conception, the fact that women, for example, could not vote at the founding is of minor importance compared to the even more basic fact that none of *us* voted at the founding. See Kahn, *Legitimacy,* 50–64.

125. Hamilton et al., *Federalist Papers,* No. 2, 38, 37.

126. U.S. Constitution, Preamble, and art. 7.

127. Patrick Henry, in *The Debates in the Several State Conventions on the Adoption of the Federal Constitution,* ed. Jonathan Elliot, 5 vols. (New York: Burt Franklin, 1964), 3:22.

128. Hamilton et al., *Federalist Papers,* No. 2, 38.

129. U.S. Constitution, Amends. 15, 19, 24, and 26. The Thirteenth Amendment may be regarded as extending the boundaries of the popular sovereign, by inviting the slaves into the community through the (at least putative) cessation of a relationship of forceful domination. This characterization depends on whether slavery is regarded as a social but hierarchical institution or as a continuing state of war by one society against another.

130. Those who hope to give the judiciary the role of enforcing the "internal requirements"

of democracy assume a false naturalness in the definition of democracy. The definition of the popular sovereign is not external to sovereignty, but part of sovereignty itself. Yet this suggests that it is not a "neutral" background for the exercise of sovereignty, but an essential, perhaps *the* essential, political task of the sovereign. Perhaps, at some point, the sovereign could effectively write itself out of existence by eliminating the prerequisites of its own deliberations, but the judiciary has no objective criteria for determining that point or for constraining the sovereign's movement along that spectrum. The definition of what is required for free speech, which is basic to the functioning of democracy, is not something "in back of" the sovereign and subject to judicial definition, but it is part of the sovereign self-conscious and one aspect of the sovereign task of self-creation. Democracy may be consistent with much of liberalism, but the priority is with democracy. Cf. Michael Walzer, "Philosophy and Democracy," *Political Theory* 9 (1981): 384; Herzog, "Credentials," 468; Miriam Galston and William A. Galston, "Reason, Consent, and the U.S. Constitution: Bruce Ackerman's *We the People*," *Ethics* 104 (1994): 458; and Michael J. Klarman, "Constitutional Fact/Constitutional Fiction: A Critique of Bruce Ackerman's Theory of Constitutional Moments," *Stanford Law Review* 44 (1992): 794–795. Harris's distinction between the "sovereign people" and the "constitutional people" is useful here. The latter is composed of those given a right to vote on the constitutional text and is defined within the text. The former is logically prior to the text, though active only through the text and therefore can be more inclusive than the constitutional people. The constitutional people exist under the text and are regulated by its rules; the sovereign people are intrinsically unruled. See Harris, *Interpretable*, 202, 74–77. See also Reid, *Revolution*, 3:68, on "supremacy in law" versus "supremacy over law."

131. Since only anarchy would represent true unanimity of will, de Maistre argued that "sovereignty is born the moment when the sovereign begins not to be *the whole people* and that it grows stronger to the degree that it becomes less *the whole people*." Only when there is disagreement among the people is there a need for politics and the use of government force (*Works,* 121 [emphasis in original]).

132. Cf. Robert Axelrod, *The Evolution of Cooperation* (New York: Basic Books, 1984). The sovereign is not just the manifestation of individual cooperation but the representative of a political community.

133. This is not to say that the expression of the sovereign will must be regarded as unique. The popular sovereign always existed and could act again; but in doing so, the sovereign itself was not reconstituted but only its will. Disagreements over past decisions must be passed over as part of the process of forming the sovereign will rather than indicating divisions within the sovereign. See also de Jouvenel, "Rousseau's Theory," 494.

134. This fact is "indicative" of that acceptance but does not constitute that acceptance itself. The meaningful act is not the acquiescence to, but the positive adoption of, constitutional authority.

135. The Federalists' promise to amend the Constitution immediately was instrumental in persuading the anti-Federalists to accept the more limited, ratification model of the state conventions. See also Jack N. Rakove, *Original Meanings* (New York: Vintage, 1996), 94–130.

136. The difficult transition from constitutional politics to normal governmental administration was indicated by the early hesitation in accepting the legitimacy of opposition parties. The shift requires the acceptance of the idea that the president is "our" president as the representative of the constitutional office, but only one party's president as a par-

ticular individual officeholder. The governmental administration not only need not but should not be viewed as or held to the standards of the sovereign. See also Richard Hofstadter, *The Idea of a Party System* (Berkeley: University of California Press, 1969).

137. Rousseau captured the ideal in a different context, contending that "an accuser must convince the accused before the judge. To be treated as a wrongdoer, it is necessary that I be convinced of being one" (*Social Contract,* 138 n.37). The alternative is to convince the judge but not the accused, in which case the will of the state is merely imposed on the accused but possesses no authority other than its capacity to employ force. See Cover, "Violence." As Rousseau recognized, it may not be possible actually to convince the accused. Nonetheless, the accused is brought into the community by being engaged in the dialogue over the content of the law. Moreover, even the dissenting accused should be brought to a point of recognizing the law itself, even if he does not recognize his own divergence from it, that the state is just, even if it is wrong. See also Plamenatz, "Le Forcera D'être Libre," 330–332, and de Jouvenel, "Rousseau's Theory," 489–491.

138. Calvin C. Jillson, *Constitutional Making* (New York: Agathon Press, 1988); Rakove, *Original Meanings,* 35–93.

139. Hamilton et al., *Federalist Papers,* No. 10, 78.

140. See Lutz, *Popular Consent,* 172–173, and 100–110. The number of converts was not large, but the point is illustrative of the nature of the process. Similarly, the relatively expansive right of suffrage employed at the time opened the conventions to conflicting interests and opinions and therefore further indicated that the results would depend on reasoned deliberation and not on forceful imposition. Moreover, the proportion of the society that participated in those elections exceeded the numbers that actually possessed formal suffrage. See also Morgan, *Inventing,* 194.

141. See e.g., de Maistre, *Works,* 120–121; Laski, *Foundations,* 24–27; and Norberto Bobbio, *The Future of Democracy* (Minneapolis: University of Minnesota Press, 1987), 27–29. Bobbio also suggests that the ideal of unitary sovereignty is used by dominant factions to sustain their control over an actual pluralistic society.

142. See, e.g., Webster, *Essays,* 40, 57–58; Holmes, *Passions,* 146–147; and Freeman, "Constitutional Democracy," 353, 356. See also Ludwig Wittgenstein, *Philosophical Investigations* (New York: Macmillan, 1958), § 293. Partially for this reason, Klarman indicates that the sovereign's "precommitment" automatically expires when circumstances or populations change; the sovereign will is stable only within the context of universal stability (see "Fact/Fiction," 796).

143. See, e.g., Freeman, "Original Meaning," 41–42. Similar reasoning has led others, who are less explicit about the process of reasoning, to jettison consent as unnecessary to the determination of constitutional truth; Kahn, *Legitimacy,* 176; Galston and Galston, "Reason," 464–465.

144. See especially Elster, *Ulysses,* 88–102. See also Holmes, *Passions,* 134–177, and Klarman, "Fact/Fiction," 794–796. Holmes adds that precommitments may be necessary to create structuring rules for even a responsible future actor (162–174).

145. See also Arendt, *On Revolution,* 93.

146. On the first strategy, see Kahn, *Legitimacy,* 52–63. On the second, see Madison, *Papers,* 13:19–20; Peterson, "Jefferson," 277–278, 288; and Gardner, "Positivist Foundations." On the third, see Thomas Jefferson, *The Papers of Thomas Jefferson,* ed. Julian Boyd, 27 vols. to date (Princeton: Princeton University Press, 1950–), 15:392–396; Herbert Sloan, " 'The Earth

Belongs in Usufruct to the Living,'" in *Jeffersonian Legacies*, ed. Peter Onuf (Charlottesville: University Press of Virginia, 1993), 281–283, 303; Peterson, "Jefferson," 276–279, 283–286; and Thomas Paine, *The Rights of Man* (New York: Viking Penguin, 1984), 41–45, 66.

147. See also de Jouvenel, *Sovereignty,* 261–262, 276; de Maistre, *Works,* 103, 108, 158; Elster, *Ulysses,* 93–95; Arendt, *On Revolution,* 193–194, 202–204; Holmes, *Passions,* 157–174; Wilson, *Works,* 1:188–191, 305–306; and Peterson, "Jefferson," 276–279, 283–286. The point is not that there are no authorities but that all authority is subject to question and voluntary acceptance. See also Jack Mendelson, "The Habermas-Gadamer Debate," *New German Critique* 18 (1979): 57–64.

148. Gardner suggests that the judiciary could discover some values outside the text that are so universal and deeply held that they too should be regarded as part of the popular will ("Positivist Foundations," 44). His difficulty is in explaining why the judiciary but not elected politicians can see that a given statute is beyond the pale of contemporary political life. A subsidiary problem is that Gardner's tacit consent theory neglects the political aspect of popular sovereignty. The authoritative will emerges through specific debate and a vehicle of expression. It is not simply "in the air" or "in the heads" of isolated individuals. Strangely, Gardner seems cognizant of such concerns in criticizing Ackerman ("Consent," 218 n.117).

149. The contrast between the ratifying and drafting conventions is important in this regard. The product of the Philadelphia Convention, which was relatively isolated from and unresponsive to larger public discussion, could not gain political authority without submitting its work for the approval of the people as a whole.

150. The advantage is only relative, for judges remain both political and part of the federal government. Nonetheless, electoral independence makes the judiciary the branch most capable of serving as a conservator of inherited commitments. See also Hamilton et al., *Federalist Papers,* No. 49, 315–317; No. 78, 467, 471, and Wilson, *Works,* 1:297–300.

151. The celebration of the judicial capacity to reason in a strong sense serves only to replace popular sovereignty with the sovereignty of the judiciary by vesting judges with the creative capacity of constitutional deliberation and decision. The correct interpretive method must be derived from the source of constitutional authority, not annexed to it. Cf. Ronald Dworkin, *A Matter of Principle* (Cambridge: Harvard University Press, 1985), 33–71; Freeman, "Original Meaning," 29–42; and Harris, *Interpretable,* 112.

152. For example, Madison warned that the "legislative department is everywhere extending the sphere of its activity and drawing all power into its impetuous vortex," in part because it is "inspired by a supposed influence over the people with an intrepid confidence in its own strength" (Hamilton et al., *Federalist Papers,* No. 48, 309).

153. This understanding of the judiciary indicates only its possibility, not its reality. The judiciary could also serve to undermine constitutional authority, for example by claiming to represent the sovereign will or by asserting an institutional prerogative and thereby elevating the medium over the message. The authority of judicial pronouncements comes not from a designated power of review but from the correctness of the courts' assessment of the contours of constitutional requirements. The finality of judicial judgment depends on the likelihood of the courts' greater accuracy. Of course, the courts possess their own mechanisms to enforce their will. The point is not that the judiciary is literally without institutional support but only that its traditional and internal base of legitimacy is weak. See also Hamilton et al., *Federalist Papers,* No. 78, 465; Susan Burgess, *Contest for Constitutional Authority* (Lawrence: University Press of Kansas, 1992), 1–27, 109–126; and James

Boyd White, "Judicial Criticism," in *Interpreting Law and Literature,* ed. Sanford Levinson and Steven Mailloux (Evanston, IL: Northwestern University Press, 1988), 393–410.

154. Such an active sovereignty is retained by modern legal positivists, for whom there is always a legislator to make a new rule or issue a decision in the presence of uncertainty, even if that legislator is a judge. See, e.g., H. L. A. Hart, *The Concept of Law* (New York: Oxford University Press, 1961), 70–78, 121–150; Hans Kelsen, *Pure Theory of Law* (Berkeley: University of California Press, 1970), 356; and Schmitt, *Political Theology,* 5, 10–11, 31.

155. Recall that constructions cannot be antagonistic to known constitutional meaning but can operate only within areas of indeterminacy. The question is not one of replacing the popular will but of supplementing it in order to construct determinate meaning.

156. Such consistency may have a normative component, however; it is not merely habit or a sociological concept. See also E. Philip Soper, "Legal Theory and the Obligation of a Judge: The Hart/Dworkin Dispute," *Michigan Law Review* 75 (1977): 479–480. On consent and custom, see Wilson, *Works,* 1:102.

6. THE NATURE AND LIMITS OF ORIGINALIST JURISPRUDENCE

1. For discussions of the rise of New Criticism and the intentional fallacy, see Gerald Graff, *Literature Against Itself* (Chicago: University of Chicago Press, 1979), 129–149; W. K. Wimsatt and Monroe C. Beardsley, "The Intentional Fallacy," *Sewanee Review* 54 (1946): 468; W. K. Wimsatt, "Genesis: A Fallacy Revisited," in *The Disciplines of Criticism,* ed. Peter Demetz et al. (New Haven: Yale University Press, 1968), 193–225; and Monroe C. Beardsley, "Textual Meaning and Authorial Meaning," *Genre* 1 (1968): 169.

2. Oliver Wendell Holmes, *Collected Legal Papers,* ed. Harold J. Laski (Gloucester, MA: Peter Smith, 1952), 203–209.

3. Raoul Berger, " 'Original Intention' in Historical Perspective," *George Washington Law Review* 54 (1986): 296; Robert N. Clinton, "Original Understanding, Legal Realism, and the Interpretation of 'This Constitution,'" *Iowa Law Review* 72 (1987): 1193; and Richard Kay, "Adherence to the Original Intentions in Constitutional Adjudication: Three Objections and Responses," *Northwestern University Law Review* 82 (1988): 233. Cf. H. Jefferson Powell, "The Original Understanding of Original Intent," *Harvard Law Review* 98 (1985): 885.

4. For a cautionary statement, see James Hutson, "The Creation of the Constitution: The Integrity of the Documentary Record," *Texas Law Review* 65 (1986): 1.

5. Richard E. Palmer, *Hermeneutics* (Evanston, IL: Northwestern University Press, 1969), 75–123; and Hans-Georg Gadamer, *Truth and Method* (New York: Continuum, 1975), 153–234.

6. See cites in Gregory Bassham, *Original Intent and the Constitution* (Lanham, MD: Rowman and Littlefield, 1992), 140 n.65, and Michael S. Moore, "The Semantics of Judging," *Southern California Law Review* 54 (1981): 265–266.

7. That the interpretation/construction division does not map onto the interpretation/noninterpretation division, see chapter 1 at n. 9.

8. Thomas Grey, "Do We Have an Unwritten Constitution?" *Stanford Law Review* 27 (1975): 710–714; John Hart Ely, *Democracy and Distrust* (Cambridge: Harvard University Press, 1980), 1; and Michael Perry, *The Constitution, the Courts, and Human Rights* (New Haven: Yale University Press, 1982), 16.

9. Ronald Dworkin, *A Matter of Principle* (Cambridge: Harvard University Press, 1985),

35. But see Lino Graglia, who continues to employ the "noninterpretive" label, in " 'Interpreting' the Constitution: Posner on Bork," *Stanford Law Review* 44 (1992): 1024.

10. However, some interpretive methods are more prone than others to veer off the interpretive path by losing sight of the object to be interpreted, burying the text within the context (see chap. 2).

11. Ely, *Democracy,* 12–13.

12. William F. Harris II, *The Interpretable Constitution* (Baltimore: Johns Hopkins University Press, 1993), 144–158. Although Harris primarily discusses originalists as being in the immanent positivist quadrant of his typology, his division makes clear that they can in fact range across different forms of immanent interpretation. Harris's use of "positivist" in this limited context is somewhat misleading but does not affect the soundness of the division under some kind of label.

13. Robert Bork, like Ely, has run these two arguments together and largely focused on the second; see *The Tempting of America* (New York: Free Press, 1990), 178–185.

14. Charles L. Black Jr., *Structure and Relationship in Constitutional Law* (Baton Rouge: Louisiana State University Press, 1969), 7–8.

15. On the structural component of William Rehnquist's originalism, see Sue Davis, *Justice Rehnquist and the Constitution* (Princeton: Princeton University Press, 1989).

16. I use "conservative" here to refer to the modern American political grouping traditionally known as the conservative movement, not to any sense of judicial conservatism (or traditionalism) or philosophical conservatism (associated with Burke).

17. Richard Epstein, *Takings* (Cambridge: Harvard University Press, 1985); Richard A. Posner, *The Problems of Jurisprudence* (Cambridge: Harvard University Press, 1990), and "Bork and Beethoven," *Stanford Law Review* 42 (1990): 1365; Hadley Arkes, *Beyond the Constitution* (Princeton: Princeton University Press, 1992). Harry Jaffa can also be linked with the natural law tradition; see Harry V. Jaffa et al., *Original Intent and the Framers of the Constitution* (Washington, DC: Regnery Gateway, 1994). For a typology of conservative legal theory, see Michael W. McConnell, "The Counter-Revolution in Legal Thought," *Policy Review* 41 (1987): 18.

18. Roe v. Wade, 410 U.S. 113 (1973); Bork, *Tempting,* 114–116; and Arkes, *Beyond,* 76, 229–231. See also Earl M. Maltz, *Rethinking Constitutional Law* (Lawrence: University Press of Kansas, 1994), 1–14, and Graglia, " 'Interpreting,' " 1022–1023.

19. Judicial restraint is sometimes regarded as adherence to objective interpretive principles; the activist judge simply "makes it up."

20. On an originalist respect for precedent, see Bork, *Tempting,* 155–159; Henry Paul Monaghan, "Stare Decisis and Constitutional Adjudication," *Columbia Law Review* 88 (1988): 723.

21. I take no position on how much of the current law is in fact irreconcilable with that intent, which I think is appropriate in order to evaluate interpretive approaches in a manner that is neutral to policy and partisan disputes. The assumption of critics of originalism is that vast portions of important law are inconsistent with the original text, and it is certainly true that the Court has made little effort to support fully many of its decisions in the original text.

22. The thoughts offered here are given in the context of originalist theory. Therefore, the assumption is that the Court is firmly committed to originalism and that judicial decisions are guided by a sincere effort to apply originalist interpretation. Divisions on the bench over interpretive method would add further complications.

23. Bassham, *Original Intent,* 45; Monaghan, "Stare Decisis," 748–755; Lon Fuller, *The*

Morality of Law (New Haven: Yale University Press, 1969), 218–219; Benjamin N. Cardozo, *The Nature of the Judicial Process* (New Haven: Yale University Press, 1977), 142–150; and Friedrich A. Hayek, *Law, Legislation and Liberty,* 3 vols. (Chicago: University of Chicago Press, 1973–1979), 1:82–90, 115–123.

24. It should be noted that this discussion is consistent with and developed from originalist commitments but is not itself part of originalist theory and is not fully derivable from it. Judicial prudence is necessary to traverse the distance from political error to constitutional theory. An originalist Court would be forced into a form of constitutional construction by the problematic position that it would have inherited. See also Thomas Aquinas, *The Political Ideas of St. Thomas Aquinas,* ed. Dino Bigongiari (New York: Hafner Press, 1953), 78–81.

25. Alexander M. Bickel, *The Least Dangerous Branch* (Indianapolis: Merrill-Bobbitt, 1962), 111–198. Such efforts cannot be taken to extremes, however; see Gerald Gunther, "The Subtle Vices of the 'Passive Virtues'—A Comment on Principle and Expediency in Judicial Review," *Columbia Law Review* 64 (1964): 1.

26. Plessy v. Ferguson, 163 U.S. 537 (1896); Brown v. Board of Education, 347 U.S. 483 (1954). E.g., Missouri ex rel. Gaines v. Canada, 305 U.S. 337 (1938); Sipuel v. University of Oklahoma, 332 U.S. 631 (1948); Shelley v. Kraemer, 334 U.S. 1 (1948); Sweatt v. Painter, 339 U.S. 629 (1950); McLaurin v. Oklahoma State Regents, 339 U.S. 637 (1950); Bolling v. Sharpe, 347 U.S. 497 (1954). See also Richard Kluger, *Simple Justice* (New York: Alfred A. Knopf, 1975), 214–284, and Mark V. Tushnet, *The NAACP's Legal Strategy Against Segregated Education, 1925–1950* (Chapel Hill: University of North Carolina Press, 1987), 70–137.

27. Brown v. Board of Education, 347 U.S. 483 (1954); Brown v. Board of Education, 349 U.S. 294 (1955). See also Randall Kennedy, "The Supreme Court as Teacher: Lessons from the Second Reconstruction," in *The Supreme Court and American Constitutionalism,* ed. Bradford P. Wilson and Ken Masugi (Lanham, MD: Rowman and Littlefield, 1998), 17–25. Cf. Robert Burt, *The Constitution in Conflict* (Cambridge: Harvard University Press, 1992), 271–310. Given the vehemence of feelings on the segregation issue, whether it could have been more gradually dismantled by a more patient and clearer Court is an uncertain historical question, though larger shifts in the South and in the nation at large suggest that it might have been possible. See Gerald Rosenberg, *The Hollow Hope* (Chicago: University of Chicago Press, 1991); Lawrence H. Fuchs, *The American Kaleidoscope* (Hanover, NH: University Press of New England, 1990), 149–173.

28. U.S. v. Lopez, 115 S.Ct. 1624 (1995).

29. Whether *Lopez* goes the way of *Usery* depends on the seriousness of the Court's commitment to reexamining the commerce clause and the adequacy of its interpretive principles. With *Usery,* the Court found itself trapped on the margins of federalism due to an inadequately considered approach to the subject—partially resulting from division on the bench. National League of Cities v. Usery, 426 U.S. 833 (1976); Garcia v. San Antonio Metropolitan Transit Authority, 469 U.S. 528 (1985).

30. For example, Gregory Bassham is generally sympathetic toward originalism but concludes that it would lead to a "constitutional Armageddon" (*Original Intent,* 98). The now classic example is Sen. Edward Kennedy's "Robert Bork's America" speech, quoted at 97. See also Bernard Schwartz, *The New Right and the Constitution* (Boston: Northeastern University Press, 1990).

31. For more extensive discussion of constitutional constructions, see Keith E. Whittington, *Constitutional Construction* (Cambridge: Harvard University Press, 1999).

32. Bassham, *Original Intent,* 86 (emphasis in original).

33. Monaghan, "Stare Decisis," 744.

34. The case of legal tender has been used as an exemplar in this regard; ibid., 744; Bork, *Tempting,* 156.

35. Of course, the Court does have discretion in choosing among a range of available issues and sometimes "signals" its desire to hear certain issues. But discretion over the Court's agenda also suggests that the Court can readily avoid issues. See H. W. Perry, *Deciding to Decide* (Cambridge: Harvard University Press, 1991).

36. This is somewhat overstated, for one difficulty with the courts as a policy-making institution is that the threshold for filing suits is relatively low and thus marginal political movements can gain exaggerated influence through litigation. To some degree, this would require some discretion by the courts not to leap to respond to marginal litigants. Precedent should retain a presumptive authority, even if that authority is contingent only on no further showing of serious inaccuracy. To the extent that challenges become serious (persuasively based on historical evidence, directly requiring a determination of the constitutional issue, fully meeting requirements for standing, and so on), then the courts would be compelled to begin the process of shifting doctrine to the correct position.

37. Bassham, *Original Intent,* 97–98.

38. Even the classic case of school desegregation, the ultimate example in the list of originalist horribles, may have depended far more on a political construction than on judicial action; see Rosenberg, *Hollow Hope.*

39. The current disarray in constitutional theory, and the rise of new theories de-emphasizing judicial supremacy, is partially a reflection of the political and intellectual exhaustion of the Warren Court's adjudication. On the relation of the constitutional theory of the 1970s and 1980s to the Warren Court, see Martin Shapiro, "Fathers and Sons: The Court, The Commentators, and the Search for Values," in *The Burger Court,* ed. Vincent Blasi (New Haven: Yale University Press, 1983), 218–238.

40. See also Mark A. Graber, "Desperately Ducking Slavery: *Dred Scott* and Contemporary Constitutional Theory," *Constitutional Commentary* 14 (1997): 271, and Bruce Ackerman, *We the People* (Cambridge: Harvard University Press, 1991).

41. This is not to imply that courts have not mattered in the nation's social and political history, only that our constitutional practices significantly depend on events that occur outside the judicial arena.

42. Similarly, "Positivists who argue that where there is controversy no duties exist are surely wrong. . . . What we have to look for is not evidence of controversy, but evidence of a practice pertaining to resolving controversy" (Jules L. Coleman, "Legal Duty and Moral Argument," *Social Theory and Practice* 5 [1980]: 404). See also Coleman, "Negative and Positive Positivism," *Journal of Legal Studies* 11 (1982): 151–158; and C. L. Ten, "The Soundest Theory of Law," *Mind* 88 (1979): 530.

43. In coining the phrase, for example, Roscoe Pound pointed to judges reduced "to the purely mechanical task of counting [citations] and of determining the numerical preponderance of authority. Principles were no longer resorted to in order to make rules to fit cases" ("Mechanical Jurisprudence," *Columbia Law Review* 8 [1908]: 607 [footnote omitted]).

44. Frederick Douglass, "The Dred Scott Decision," in *The Life and Writings of Frederick Douglass,* ed. Philip Foner, 5 vols. (New York: International Publishers, 1950–1975), 2:420.

45. On Douglass's change of position, see his "Oath to Support the Constitution," and "Change of Opinion Announced," both in *Life,* 2:115–119 and 2:155–156.

46. Ibid., 2:420. Similarly, in advocating a vision of the Constitution as a "living statute" Edward Corwin asked "why the intention of a law-maker, as distinct from that of the law itself should govern the law's interpretation." The assumption is always that textual intent/meaning can be distinguished from and exists independently of legislative intent. See "Constitution v. Constitutional Theory: The Question of the States v. the Nation," in *Corwin on the Constitution,* ed. Richard Loss, 3 vols. (New York: Cornell University Press, 1987–1988), 2:191. See also Ronald Dworkin, *Freedom's Law* (Cambridge: Harvard University Press, 1996), 287–305.

47. Alternatively, it could all be done immediately in the Congress or by executive order, for the Constitution was seen as providing neither protection nor authorization for slavery. Through either mechanism, the effort was no longer the political one of persuading others to support radical change, but the legal one of enforcing the abolitionist will through the tools of national government power.

48. This tripartite division is borrowed most immediately from Quentin Skinner, "Motives, Intentions and the Interpretation of Texts," in *Meaning and Context,* ed. James Tully (Princeton: Princeton University Press, 1988), 70.

49. See especially Donald Davidson, "A Nice Derangement of Epitaphs," in *Truth and Interpretation,* ed. Ernest LePore (New York: Basil Blackwell, 1986), 433–446.

50. Again, I follow Skinner here; see "Motives," 73. See also Michael Hancher, "Three Kinds of Intention," *Modern Language Notes* 87 (1972): 829.

51. Charles Beard, *An Economic Interpretation of the Constitution* (New York: Free Press, 1986). For critiques, see Forrest McDonald, *We the People* (Chicago: University of Chicago Press, 1956), and Robert E. Brown, *Charles Beard and the Constitution* (Princeton: Princeton University Press, 1956).

52. Skinner, "Motives," 73. "The author for his part need and indeed can do nothing further to realize an active intention; it is realized in the act of intention itself" (Hancher, "Three Kinds," 831 [footnote omitted]).

53. Skinner, "Motives," 76.

54. Powell, "Original," 885.

55. For critiques of the historical thesis, see Charles Lofgren, "The Original Understanding of Original Intent?" *Constitutional Commentary* 5 (1988): 77; Raoul Berger, "The Founders' Views—According to Jefferson Powell," *Texas Law Review* 67 (1989): 1033, and " 'Original Intent' "; Clinton, "Original Understanding"; Kay, "Adherence"; Maltz, *Rethinking* 6:22–26. For a defense, see Paul Finkelman, "The Constitution and the Intentions of the Framers: The Limits of Historical Analysis," *University of Pittsburgh Law Review* 50 (1989): 349, and Leonard W. Levy, *Original Intent and the Framers' Constitution* (New York: Macmillan, 1988), 1–29.

56. Powell, "Original," 895.

57. Chapter 3, n. 66.

58. Bassham also argues that interpretive intentions are not binding, but he appears to do so because of substantive disagreements with specific possible interpretive intentions of the founders (*Original Intent,* 70–71). Of course, the theory of originalism offered here does not allow for the interpreter to select which intentions he would like to follow. Bassham's often admirable discussion of originalism is marred by its ultimate grounding in

an antifoundational pragmatism, which not only leads him to pervert originalism at various points but eventually to abandon it entirely.

59. Richard Kay has suggested that the Ninth and Tenth Amendments serve that purpose as a set of supplementing rules to direct the courts in what to do in the case of indeterminacies. As Bassham has indicated, not every constitutional indeterminacy can be phrased in a form such that those amendments could provide answers. Moreover, that limitation shows that the amendments actually embody a structural substantive intent. They provide specific information clarifying the meaning and application of various other parts of the text, but they do not provide a general directive as to interpretive methodology. See Kay, "Adherence," 255–257, and Bassham, *Original Intent,* 89–90.

60. Raoul Berger, *Congress v. the Supreme Court* (Cambridge: Harvard University Press, 1969). Berger does think that the power of judicial review slipped into the text in Article 3 (198–222). The particulars of any exercised power of judicial review were not clear at the time of the founding, either. See Sylvia Snowiss, *Judicial Review and the Law of the Constitution* (New Haven: Yale University Press, 1990), and Robert Clinton, *Marbury v. Madison and Judicial Review* (Lawrence: University Press of Kansas, 1989).

61. Ronald Dworkin, *Taking Rights Seriously* (Cambridge: Harvard University Press, 1978), 131–149, and *Matter,* 48–49. See also Paul Brest, "The Misconceived Quest for Original Understanding," *Boston University Law Review* 60 (1980): 216–217.

62. It is somewhat misleading to refer to the use of standards to "fill in gaps in meaning," for Dworkin's argument is that there are no gaps in legal meaning. Properly understood, political principles are part of a legal document, and the text is read in terms of those broader principles. See his *Taking Rights,* 1–130; *Matter,* 119–145, and *Law's Empire* (Cambridge: Harvard University Press, 1986), 228–238, 259–260.

63. Dworkin, *Taking Rights,* 134–136. In the initial example, Dworkin stated that in directing his children to be fair "I would not accept that my 'meaning' was limited to these examples" and that he would "want to say that my instructions covered the case [the child] cited, not that I had changed my instructions" by now agreeing with the child's definition of fairness (134).

64. David O. Brink, "Legal Theory, Legal Interpretation, and Judicial Review," *Philosophy and Public Affairs* 17 (1988): 105; Moore, "Semantics," and "A Natural Law Theory of Interpretation," *Southern California Law Review* 58 (1985): 277; and Bassham, *Original Intent,* 75–83.

65. Saul A. Kripke, *Naming and Necessity* (Cambridge: Harvard University Press, 1980); Hilary Putnam, *Mind, Language, Reality* (New York: Cambridge University Press, 1975); Nathan Salmon, *Reference and Essence* (Princeton: Princeton University Press, 1981); R. J. Nelson, *Naming and Reference* (New York: Routledge, 1992); and Michael Devitt and Kim Sterelny, *Language and Reality* (Cambridge: MIT Press, 1987).

66. For descriptivist theories, see John Locke, *An Essay Concerning Human Understanding,* ed. Peter Nidditch (New York: Oxford University Press, 1975), bk. 3; Gottlob Frege, "On Sense and Reference," in *Translations from the Philosophical Writings of Gottlob Frege,* ed. Max Black and Peter Geach (New York: Basil Blackwell, 1980), 56–78; Bertrand Russell, *The Problems of Philosophy* (New York: Oxford University Press, 1959), 54–59; Rudolph Carnap, *Meaning and Necessity* (Chicago: University of Chicago Press, 1956); and John Searle, *Speech Acts* (New York: Cambridge University Press, 1969), 162–174.

67. In practice, the distinction between the two approaches becomes rather murky, primarily depending on individual differences among judges. Because the two approaches

reach similar conclusions by different paths, the paths could conceivably diverge on where to look for evidence of the "best" conceptions under a given concept or the "real essence" of a phrase. Moreover, the semantic approach would fail if either the causal theory of reference or moral realism were incorrect whereas Dworkin's concept/conception distinction could survive the failure of at least the latter.

68. Dworkin, *Taking Rights,* 133–136.

69. Bassham, *Original Intent,* 72–75; Perry, *Constitution,* 70–72; and Stephen Munzer and James Nickel, "Does the Constitution Mean What It Always Meant?" *Columbia Law Review* 77 (1977): 1029. See also chapter 3.

70. Dworkin, *Matter,* 49.

71. Similarly, "The real Constitution does not say 'All trials must be fair.' It contains a series of rules, which the drafters anticipated would produce fair trials" (Frank H. Easterbrook, "Abstraction and Authority," *University of Chicago Law Review* 59 [1992]: 355). Increasing the level of generality for the sake of reaching better results abandons all rules, replacing intended standards with motivating principles.

72. P. F. Strawson, *Logico-Linguistic Papers* (London: Methuen, 1971), 170–190; John Searle, *Intentionality* (New York: Cambridge University Press, 1983), 231–261; Kent Bach, *Thought and Reference* (New York: Oxford, 1987), 4–6, 69–88; and Davidson, "Derangement," 438–443.

73. Kripke, *Naming,* 119, 121.

74. Note that it is no response to argue that I have been thrown back to descriptivism with no way to deal with conflicts over concepts. Presumably, the descriptivist cannot regard a dispute between Newtonians and Einsteinians over the nature of mass as a real dispute, but only as a semantic one, since the two camps have different descriptions of "mass." In my account, the dispute remains real, because each side intends to refer to the same object, even if they describe it differently.

75. Dworkin has recently made a muddle of these distinctions by inventing a category of "semantic originalism." This oxymoron is apparently intended to allow him to gain political mileage from the label "originalism" without actually having to grapple with original meaning. See his "Comment," in Antonin Scalia et al., *A Matter of Interpretation* (Princeton: Princeton University Press, 1997), 119.

76. On the inclusion of morality in positive law, see Coleman, "Legal Duty," 391–392, 404, and "Positive Positivism," 146–152; E. Philip Soper, "Legal Theory and the Obligation of a Judge: The Hart/Dworkin Dispute," *Michigan Law Review* 75 (1977): 512–514. Cf. Stanley C. Brubaker, "Conserving the Constitution," *American Bar Foundation Research Journal* (1987): 279–280.

77. The example is modified from Brink, "Legal Theory," 122–123. Brink's conclusions are the opposite of mine, finding that the "right interpretive results" require reliance on science. The example makes it evident that Brink is either relying on a normative interpretation despite his disavowals or that he is construing the intentions of legislators actually to be something other than their own specific beliefs about waste disposal.

78. In the constitutional context, it is at least plausible that the drafters of the Twenty-fifth Amendment intended "death" to refer to current scientific understandings in order to determine when to trigger presidential succession. Of course, it is possible that an investigation would determine that they did not, and in fact intended death to be defined by contemporary religious standards, for example. See Moore, "Natural Law"; Bassham, *Original Intent,* 82; and Stephen Munzer, "Realistic Limits on Realist Interpretation," *Southern California Law Review* 58 (1985): 468–469.

79. This final example indicates where the semantic theories and Dworkin diverge. Dworkin's concept theory could account for the pornography statute by recognizing that it embodied not just a different conception of toxic but a different concept. The difference between the concepts could be debatable, however, in which case Dworkin would be in just as much trouble.

80. I take it no originalist questions the validity of including specific practices that are directly analogous to practices considered by the founders, such as Richard Kay's electric thumbscrews ("Adherence," 255).

81. Although correct to note the limits of the interpreter's capacity to understand fully the intended meaning of a text, Easterbrook is wrong to assume that "texts do not settle disputes their authors and their contemporary readers could not imagine." The interpreter is not seeking to cross-examine the founders about how they would apply their intentions or what they think of a given case. Although applications may clarify the intended rules, they are only one source of information about such rules and not the definition of the rule itself ("Abstraction," 360–361).

82. It is, of course, possible that no specific level of intent can be reasonably discovered. As in any other case in which the interpreter searches for the intended meaning, the evidence of that meaning (or the meaning itself) may be lacking. At such points the bounds of interpretation have been reached, and government actions must be determined by construction. See also ibid., 360–361, 371–380.

83. This section owes much to discussions with Alex Tabarrok, who cannot be blamed for its conclusions.

84. Jeffrey A. Segal and Harold J. Spaeth, *The Supreme Court and the Attitudinal Model* (New York: Cambridge University Press, 1993), 62, 63.

85. Kenneth Arrow, *Social Choice and Individual Values,* 2d ed. (New Haven: Yale University Press, 1963). The conditions of the model include that people be allowed to vote their preferences freely, choices cannot become losers by gaining support, outcomes may not be imposed externally, a unanimously supported alternative cannot lose to a less supported option, identical preferences must produce the same results such that votes are independent of unrepresented alternatives, and no voter can trump the rest. Further, both individual preferences and social outcomes must be transitive (if A beats B and B beats C, then A must also beat C), there are at least two voters, and there are at least three alternatives. For summaries, see Segal and Spaeth, *Supreme Court,* 62 n.130; William H. Riker, *Liberalism Against Populism* (San Francisco: W. H. Freeman, 1982), 115–136; Dennis Mueller, *Public Choice II* (New York: Cambridge University Press, 1989), 384–399; Peter Ordeshook, *Game Theory and Political Theory* (New York: Cambridge University Press, 1986), 53–96.

86. E.g., Voter 1: A, B, C; Voter 2: B, C, A; Voter 3: C, A, B.

87. See, e.g., Richard D. McKelvey, "General Conditions for Global Intransitivities in Formal Voting Models," *Econometrica* 47 (1979): 1085.

88. See, e.g., Frank Easterbrook, "Ways of Criticizing the Court," *Harvard Law Review* 95 (1982): 815–816. See, generally, Maxwell L. Stearns, ed., *Public Choice and Public Law* (Cincinnati, OH: Anderson Publishing, 1997).

89. Riker concludes, "The unavoidable inference is, therefore, that, so long as a society preserves democratic institutions . . . no meaningful choice can be made" (*Liberalism,* 136). Similarly, Easterbrook has concluded, "Because legislatures have many members, they do not have 'intents' or 'designs,' hidden yet discoverable. Each member may or may not have a design. The body as a whole, however, has only outcomes" ("Statute's Domain," *Univer-*

sity of Chicago Law Review 50 [1983]: 547). See also Kenneth A. Shepsle, "Congress Is a 'They,' Not an 'It': Legislative Intent as an Oxymoron," *International Review of Law and Economics* 12 (1992): 239.

90. It should be noted that "rationality" in this literature is used in a limited sense to refer to adherence to transitivity and the forms of logic. Though it is often obscured by proponents of rational choice, one may be reasonable without being "rational." Moreover, even to the extent that rationality is normatively desirable, it is not certain that it is descriptively accurate of most decision makers. Without that descriptive accuracy, the baneful consequences predicted by the model cannot be extrapolated (though a rather different set of baneful consequences may follow). On the questionable psychological assumptions underlying formal theory, see Shawn Rosenberg, "Rationality, Markets, and Political Analysis: A Social Psychological Critique of Neoclassical Political Economy," in *The Economic Approach to Politics,* ed. Kristen Renwick Monroe (New York: HarperCollins, 1991), 386–404.

91. Kenneth Shepsle, "Prospects for Formal Models of Legislatures," *Legislative Studies Quarterly* 10 (1985): 5, and Gordon Tullock, "Why So Much Stability?" *Public Choice* 37 (1981): 189. For one list of formal responses to the "surprising" presence of stability, see Donald P. Green and Ian Shapiro, *Pathologies of Rational Choice Theory* (New Haven: Yale University Press, 1994): 114–115.

92. Riker, *Liberalism,* 125–128.

93. Kenneth Shepsle, "Institutional Arrangements and Equilibrium in Multidimensional Voting Models," *American Journal of Political Science* 23 (1979): 27, and Kenneth Shepsle and Barry Weingast, "Structure Induced Equilibrium and Legislative Choice," *Public Choice* 37 (1981): 503. For a discussion of SIE models and their limitations, see Keith Krehbiel, "Spatial Models of Legislative Choice," *Legislative Studies Quarterly* 13 (1988): 259.

94. Michael Davis, "Avoiding the Voter's Paradox Democratically," *Theory and Decision* 5 (1974): 295.

95. A complication is that preferences of a political unit can change both endogenously and exogenously, from either a changing of minds or from a changing of members. Formal models can accommodate the latter but largely ignore the former. See also William H. Riker, "Heresthetic and Rhetoric in the Spatial Model," in *Advances in the Spatial Theory of Voting,* ed. James Enelow and Melvin Hinich (New York: Cambridge University Press, 1990), 46–65.

96. Riker, *Liberalism,* 122, 128. Of course, it is possible that debate could further fracture the participants and harden their disagreements instead of acting to homogenize their preferences. In either case, however, recognition of the historicity of political actors reintroduces the interpretive element into democratic institutions. Whether any given discussion makes agreement more or less likely, it does clarify the understandings of the participants and the meaning of any eventual agreement.

97. Likewise, it is not at all clear that the economic model of preferences can be carried over to the political arena. To take Easterbrook's judicial example, it is difficult to imagine that judges seeking to interpret constitutional intentions are (1) incapable of deliberation and renewed interpretation of constitutional meaning, (2) committed to their interpretations as if they were exogenous preferences, or (3) capable of scaling those intentions on a sliding scale. Easterbrook and Posner, though both influenced by formal theory, have expressed doubts as to the validity of its conclusions in this regard; see Daniel A. Farber and Philip P. Frickey, *Law and Public Choice* (Chicago: University of Chicago Press, 1991), 41 n.7 (on general limitations on the application of Arrow's theorem to legislative intent,

see 48–53). On limitations to its application in politics more generally, see Jaan W. White-head, "The Forgotten Limits: Reason and Regulation in Economic Theory," and David Johnston, "Human Agency and Rational Action," both in Monroe, ed., *Economic Approach*, 53–73 and 94–112; Mortimer R. Kadish, "Practice and Paradox: A Comment on Social Choice Theory," *Ethics* 93 (1983): 680; Elaine Mates, "Paradox Lost—Majority Rule Regained," *Ethics* 84 (1973): 48; Rogers M. Smith, "If Politics Matters: Implications for a 'New Institutionalism,'" *Studies in American Political Development* 6 (1992): 1; and Willam N. Nelson, *On Justifying Democracy* (Boston: Routledge and Kegan Paul, 1980), 53–71, 123–124.

98. It is the purposeful creation of cycling situations, not their natural occurrence, that is seen as most threatening by cycle theorists. See Riker, *Liberalism,* 122, and Ordeshook, *Game Theory,* 71–89. The pervasiveness of such manipulation is open to question, how-ever. See, e.g., Kadish, "Practice"; Davis, "Avoiding"; and Green and Shapiro, *Pathologies.*

99. See also Kadish, "Practice," 688–691.

100. Even within the context of social choice situations, however, there remains a need for interpretation. See C. Dyke, "The Question of Interpretation in Economics," *Ratio* 25 (1983): 15. See also Donald N. McCloskey, *The Rhetoric of Economics* (Madison: University of Wis-consin Press, 1985).

101. Indeed, as two recent critics of such models conclude, rational choice theories of pol-itics gain their plausibility precisely in situations in which evidence is unavailable to refute them conclusively. In cases in which evidence to test their results is available, the models have gained little support. See Green and Shapiro, *Pathologies,* 195.

102. Daniel A. Farber, "The Originalism Debate: A Guide for the Perplexed," *Ohio State Law Journal* 49 (1989): 1093.

103. The challenge of social choice theory has led Farber and Frickey to propose a "median voter" model, in which a hypothetical median voter is posited to represent the intentions of the founders (see *Law,* 53–54). The imaginary nature of such a voter is emphasized by our incomplete knowledge of the "intention distribution" of the delegates, which makes discovering the median of an unknown distribution highly suspect. Moreover, such a model works only if intentions are conceptualized as analogous to preferences, being rel-atively discreet, stable, exogenous, ordinal, and so forth. The analogy quickly breaks down, however, especially once intentions about principles and not specific examples are con-sidered.

104. Notice that I am referring to principles that were intended to be in the text. By focus-ing only on a narrow conceptualism, originalists could be overlooking intentions that they would in principle recognize as valid. See also Dworkin, *Freedom's Law,* 77–80.

105. For examples of such a historical method, see Beard, *Economic;* McDonald, *We the People;* and Allan Bogue et al., "Members of the House of Representatives and the Processes of Modernization, 1789–1960," *Journal of American History* 63 (1976): 275.

106. Kay, "Adherence," 248–249. Kay allows for two primary supplementary rules to give further reach to his account. First, assumptions can be made, lacking evidence to the con-trary, that there was a shared intention reflecting general understandings. Second, the Ninth and Tenth Amendments offer "back-up rules" that weight indeterminacy against the fed-eral government (250, 254–256).

107. Bassham, *Original Intent,* 86.

108. Ibid., 87.

109. The evidence must indicate agreement in order to support interpretation. If the evi-

dence demonstrates disagreement, a "larger sphere" of agreement cannot be presumed without further support from the evidence.

110. For typical examples of this argument, see Bassham, *Original Intent,* 100–107; William Brennan, "Address to the Text and Teaching Symposium at Georgetown University," in *The Great Debate* (Washington, DC: Federalist Society, 1986), 11–25; Grey, "Do We Have," 703; Dworkin, *Matter,* 33–57; Brest, "Quest," 224–238; Larry Simon, "The Authority of the Framers of the Constitution: Can Originalist Interpretation Be Justified?" *California Law Review* 73 (1984): 1487; and Paul W. Kahn, *Legitimacy and History* (New Haven: Yale University Press, 1992).

111. See, e.g., William Rehnquist, "The Notion of a Living Constitution," *Texas Law Review* 54 (1976): 693; Bork, *Tempting,* 167–171; and Raoul Berger, *Government by Judiciary* (Cambridge: Harvard University Press, 1977), 373–396.

112. See, e.g., Dworkin, *Taking Rights,* 134–136, and *Matter,* 48–57.

113. See, e.g., Grey, "Do We Have," 705. Dworkin's critique of Grey is sound in the abstract, but it may be less sound in practice. That is, Grey may have been too quick to label some efforts as "non-interpretive," but Dworkin may have been too glib in waving away the problem of distinguishing good faith efforts of interpretation from the simple pursuit of justice. See Dworkin, *Taking Rights,* 134–136.

114. One of the rare exceptions is Chief Justice Charles Evans Hughes's opinion in the Depression-era Home Building and Loan v. Blaisdell, 290 U.S. 443 (1934). In effectively abandoning any plausible interpretation of the contracts clause, Hughes was explicit in his rejection of the proposition that "the great clauses of the Constitution must be confined to the interpretation within which the framers, with the conditions and outlook of their times, would have placed upon them." Despite this bold assertion, Hughes also relied heavily on the "emergency" of the Depression to justify extraordinary measures while reciting Marshall's famous statement that the Constitution was intended to be enduring. Despite the "revolutionary" implications of the Hughes Court's actions, however, subsequent Courts have been unwilling to abandon the commitment to interpretation.

115. James A. Gardner, "The Positivist Foundations of Originalism: An Account and Critique," *Boston University Law Review* 71 (1991): 5. See also John B. Gates and Glenn A. Phelps, "Intentionalism in Constitutional Opinions," *Political Research Quarterly* 49 (1996): 245.

116. Youngstown Sheet and Tube v. Sawyer, 343 U.S. 579 (1952); INS v. Chadha, 462 U.S. 919 (1983); Bowcher v. Synar, 478 U.S. 714 (1986); U.S. Term Limits v. Thornton, 115 S.Ct. 1842 (1995).

117. Cf. Jesse Choper, *Judicial Review and the National Political Process* (Chicago: University of Chicago Press, 1980). It is likely that Choper has not been more influential, however, precisely because he offered a "functionalist" theory of judicial review rather than an interpretive one. Choper's explicit project of abandoning judicial enforcement of clear textual requirements was simply too radical for an enterprise still committed to the goal of interpretation.

118. The Eighteenth Amendment was repealed just fourteen years after its passage. The example of repealing aspects of the inherited text fits uneasily in a living constitutionalism that could readily achieve the same result through judicial interpretation.

119. Similarly, John Stuart Mill argued for a right to divorce on like grounds. The lifetime commitment of the marriage vow was illegitimate in that it sought to bind the unknown future, not of future generations but of the contracting individuals themselves. See Stephen Holmes, *Passions and Constraint* (Chicago: University of Chicago Press, 1995), 143.

120. U.S. Constitution, art. 2, § 1.

121. Mark V. Tushnet, "A Note on the Revival of Textualism in Constitutional Theory," *Southern California Law Review* 58 (1985) 686–687, and Anthony D'Amato, "Aspects of Deconstruction: The 'Easy Case' of the Under-Aged President," *Northwestern University Law Review* 84 (1989): 250.

122. See also Mark V. Tushnet, "The Hardest Question in Constitutional Law," *Minnesota Law Review* 81 (1996): 1.

123. See, e.g., Bassham, *Original Intent*, 101 (footnote omitted). The surprising, and perhaps problematic, addition of James Madison's stealth amendment brings the number passed up to twenty-seven.

124. Texas v. Johnson, 491 U.S. 397 (1989); U.S. v. Eichman, 496 U.S. 310 (1990).

125. See also Donald S. Lutz, "Toward a Theory of Constitutional Amendment," in *Responding to Imperfection*, ed. Sanford Levinson (Princeton: Princeton University Press, 1995).

126. See, e.g., Richard S. Kay, "The Illegality of the Constitution," *Constitutional Commentary* 4 (1987): 57. My claim here is distinct from Bruce Ackerman's point, however. He suggests that the Constitution can be amended outside Article 5, but I merely contend that it could be abandoned outside Article 5 procedures. Thus, he must justify how some constitutional elements can be maintained while others such as Article 5 are severed; how we can stay within the constitutional project while undercutting the basis for that project? If Ackerman could establish that the New Deal was actually a revolutionary moment, in the sense that it replaced the existing constitution with a new one, rather than an evolutionary moment, in which it supplemented the Constitution with unwritten amendments, then he would have a (much different) case. Revolutions are not made in secret, however, although coups d'état sometimes are. See Bruce Ackerman, *We the People* (Cambridge: Harvard University Press, 1991). Cf. Harris, *Interpretable*, 176–208.

127. Paul Kahn has demonstrated this by applying the logic of the objection to a wide variety of theories, concluding that they fall short (*Legitimacy*, 210–223). See also Michael J. Klarman, "Constitutional Fact/Constitutional Fiction: A Critique of Bruce Ackerman's Theory of Constitutional Moments," *Stanford Law Review* 44 (1992): 793–794. Similarly, the Realists' conception of the Constitution as a living document left little room for the exercise of judicial review, and this view was the basis of the New Deal Court's restraint. See, e.g., Karl Llewellyn, "The Constitution as an Institution," *Columbia Law Review* 34 (1934): 7.

128. See, e.g., Whittington, *Construction*; Stephen M. Griffin, *American Constitutionalism* (Princeton: Princeton University Press, 1996); Bruce Ackerman, *We the People*, 2 vols. (Cambridge: Harvard University Press, 1998), vol. 2; and David P. Currie, *The Constitution in Congress* (Chicago: University of Chicago Press, 1997).

129. Dworkin, *Matter*, 119–145.

130. Bassham, *Original Intent*, 87.

131. This requires that an originalist Court call attention to constitutional indeterminacies. By contrast, Bork adopts the dichotomous perspective of judicial supremacists—there are no gray areas for him; actions are always either permitted or prohibited.

132. Many "living constitutionalists" thus denigrate the text as insignificant except as a popular symbol of nationalism and government continuity. The Constitution is transformed from being a source of political authority and constraint on government power to being an instrument for the maintenance of popular quiescence in the face of government action.

133. The judiciary can also relieve government officials of the difficult task of articulating and defending specific requests for power. Franklin Roosevelt focused on altering judicial interpretations of the Constitution in part because the administration could not decide how to gain the power it wanted without giving too much power to future presidents. Making exactly those decisions is, of course, the challenge of written constitutionalism. The judiciary instead gave Roosevelt a constitutional blank check—an outcome that any government official would happily embrace. See, generally, William E. Leuchtenburg, *The Supreme Court Reborn* (New York: Oxford University Press, 1995), 82–162.

134. See also Harris, *Interpretable,* 100, 165.

135. Alexander Hamilton, James Madison, and John Jay, *The Federalist Papers,* ed. Clinton Rossiter (New York: Mentor, 1961), No. 49, 313, 314 (emphasis added).

136. Ibid., 314, 315, 317. See also Madison's letter to Jefferson, responding to the latter's proposal for regularly scheduled redrafting and reratification of constitutions (*Papers of James Madison,* ed. Charles Hobson and Robert Rutland, 21 vols. to date [Charlottesville: University Press of Virginia, 1962–], 13:18–24).

137. For a suggestive discussion of the effort to manage the civil rights movement by drawing it into a discourse of judicial interpretation, see Gerald N. Rosenberg, "Mythmaker, Mythmaker, Make Me a Myth: *Brown* and the Creation of American Ideology," paper presented at annual meeting of the American Political Science Association, New York City, September 1–4, 1994.

Index